WORLD OF MAN

A LIBRARY OF THEORY AND RESEARCH IN THE HUMAN SCIENCES

Editor: R. D. Laing

The Order of Things

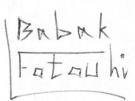

by Michel Foucault

Histoire de la folie à l'âge classique

Madness and Civilization (Tavistock, 1967)

L'Archéologie du savoir

The Archaeology of Knowledge (Tavistock, 1972)

Naissance de la clinique

The Birth of the Clinic (Tavistock, 1973)

also available

ALAN SHERIDAN

Michel Foucault

The Will to Truth

VELASQUEZ: LAS MENINAS
reproduced by courtesy of
the Museo del Prado

The Order of Things

AN ARCHAEOLOGY OF THE HUMAN SCIENCES

MICHEL FOUCAULT

Translated from the French

TAVISTOCK/ROUTLEDGE

LONDON AND NEW YORK

Originally published in French under the title
Les Mots et les choses
by Editions Gallimard

This translation first published in Great Britain in 1970
by Tavistock Publications Limited

First published in paperback in 1974
Reprinted four times
Reprinted 1986

Reprinted 1989
by Routledge
11 New Fetter Lane, London EC4P 4EE
29 West 35th Street, New York, NY 10001

Printed in Great Britain
by J.W. Arrowsmith Ltd., Bristol

ISBN 0-415-04019-1

Contents

CONTENTS

vi

Publisher's Note

A literal translation of the title of the French edition of this work (*Les Mots et les choses*) would have given rise to confusion with two other books that have already appeared under the title *Words and things*. The publisher therefore agreed with the author on the alternative title *The order of things*, which was, in fact, M. Foucault's original preference.

In view of the range of literature referred to in the text, it has not proved feasible in every case to undertake the bibliographical task of tracing English translations of works originating in other languages and locating the passages quoted by M. Foucault. The publisher has accordingly retained the author's references to French works and to French translations of Latin and German works, for example, but has, as far as possible, cited English editions of works originally written in that language.

Foreword to the English edition

This foreword should perhaps be headed 'Directions for Use'. Not because I feel that the reader cannot be trusted – he is, of course, free to make what he will of the book he has been kind enough to read. What right have I, then, to suggest that it should be used in one way rather than another? When I was writing it there were many things that were not clear to me: some of these seemed too obvious, others too obscure. So I said to myself: this is how my ideal reader would have approached my book, if my intentions had been clearer and my project more ready to take form.

1. He would recognize that it was a study of a relatively neglected field. In France at least, the history of science and thought gives pride of place to mathematics, cosmology, and physics – noble sciences, rigorous sciences, sciences of the necessary, all close to philosophy: one can observe in their history the almost uninterrupted emergence of truth and pure reason. The other disciplines, however – those, for example, that concern living beings, languages, or economic facts – are considered too tinged with empirical thought, too exposed to the vagaries of chance or imagery, to age-old traditions and external events, for it to be supposed that their history could be anything other than irregular. At most, they are expected to provide evidence of a state of mind, an intellectual fashion, a mixture of archaism and bold conjecture, of intuition and blindness. But what if empirical knowledge, at a given time and in a given culture, *did* possess a well-defined regularity? If the very possibility of recording facts, of allowing oneself to be convinced by them, of distorting them in traditions or of making purely speculative use of them, if even this was not at the mercy of chance? If errors (and truths), the practice of old beliefs, including not only genuine discoveries, but also the most naïve notions, obeyed, at a given moment, the laws of a certain code of knowledge? If, in

short, the history of non-formal knowledge had itself a system? That was my initial hypothesis – the first risk I took.

2. This book must be read as a comparative, and not a symptomato-logical, study. It was not my intention, on the basis of a particular type of knowledge or body of ideas, to draw up a picture of a period, or to reconstitute the spirit of a century. What I wished to do was to present, side by side, a definite number of elements: the knowledge of living beings, the knowledge of the laws of language, and the knowledge of economic facts, and to relate them to the philosophical discourse that was contemporary with them during a period extending from the seventeenth to the nineteenth century. It was to be not an analysis of Classicism in general, nor a search for a *Weltanschauung*, but a strictly 'regional' study.[1]

But, among other things, this comparative method produces results that are often strikingly different from those to be found in single-discipline studies. (So the reader must not expect to find here a history of biology juxtaposed with a history of linguistics, a history of political economy, and a history of philosophy.) There are shifts of emphasis: the calendar of saints and heroes is somewhat altered (Linnaeus is given more space than Buffon, Destutt de Tracy than Rousseau; the Physiocrats are opposed single-handed by Cantillon). Frontiers are redrawn and things usually far apart are brought closer, and vice versa: instead of relating the biological taxonomies to other knowledge of the living being (the theory of germination, or the physiology of animal movement, or the statics of plants), I have compared them with what might have been said at the same time about linguistic signs, the formation of general ideas, the language of action, the hierarchy of needs, and the exchange of goods.

This had two consequences: I was led to abandon the great divisions that are now familiar to us all. I did not look in the seventeenth and eighteenth centuries for the beginnings of nineteenth-century biology (or philosophy or economics). What I saw was the appearance of figures peculiar to the Classical age: a 'taxonomy' or 'natural history' that was relatively unaffected by the knowledge that then existed in animal or plant physiology; an 'analysis of wealth' that took little account of the assumptions of the 'political arithmetic' that was contemporary with it; and a 'general grammar' that was quite alien to the historical analyses and works of exegesis then being carried out. Epistemological figures, that is, that were not superimposed on the sciences as they were individualized

---

[1] I sometimes use terms like 'thought' or 'Classical science', but they refer practically always to the particular discipline under consideration.

and named in the nineteenth century. Moreover, I saw the emergence, between these different figures, of a network of analogies that transcended the traditional proximities: between the classification of plants and the theory of coinage, between the notion of generic character and the analysis of trade, one finds in the Classical sciences isomorphisms that appear to ignore the extreme diversity of the objects under consideration. The space of knowledge was then arranged in a totally different way from that systematized in the nineteenth century by Comte or Spencer. The second risk I took was in having wished to describe not so much the genesis of our sciences as an epistemological space specific to a particular period.

3. I did not operate, therefore, at the level that is usually that of the historian of science – I should say at the two levels that are usually his. For, on the one hand, the history of science traces the progress of discovery, the formulation of problems, and the clash of controversy; it also analyses theories in their internal economy; in short, it describes the processes and products of the scientific consciousness. But, on the other hand, it tries to restore what eluded that consciousness: the influences that affected it, the implicit philosophies that were subjacent to it, the unformulated thematics, the unseen obstacles; it describes the unconscious of science. This unconscious is always the negative side of science – that which resists it, deflects it, or disturbs it. What I would like to do, however, is to reveal a *positive unconscious* of knowledge: a level that eludes the consciousness of the scientist and yet is part of scientific discourse, instead of disputing its validity and seeking to diminish its scientific nature. What was common to the natural history, the economics, and the grammar of the Classical period was certainly not present to the consciousness of the scientist; or that part of it that was conscious was superficial, limited, and almost fanciful (Adanson, for example, wished to draw up an artificial denomination for plants; Turgot compared coinage with language); but, unknown to themselves, the naturalists, economists, and grammarians employed the same rules to define the objects proper to their own study, to form their concepts, to build their theories. It is these rules of formation, which were never formulated in their own right, but are to be found only in widely differing theories, concepts, and objects of study, that I have tried to reveal, by isolating, as their specific locus, a level that I have called, somewhat arbitrarily perhaps, archaeological. Taking as an example the period covered in this book, I have tried to determine the basis or archaeological system common to a whole series of scientific 'representations'

or 'products' dispersed throughout the natural history, economics, and philosophy of the Classical period.

4. I should like this work to be read as an open site. Many questions are laid out on it that have not yet found answers; and many of the gaps refer either to earlier works or to others that have not yet been completed, or even begun. But I should like to mention three problems.

The problem of change. It has been said that this work denies the very possibility of change. And yet my main concern has been with changes. In fact, two things in particular struck me: the suddenness and thoroughness with which certain sciences were sometimes reorganized; and the fact that at the same time similar changes occurred in apparently very different disciplines. Within a few years (around 1800), the tradition of general grammar was replaced by an essentially historical philology; natural classifications were ordered according to the analyses of comparative anatomy; and a political economy was founded whose main themes were labour and production. Confronted by such a curious combination of phenomena, it occurred to me that these changes should be examined more closely, without being reduced, in the name of continuity, in either abruptness or scope. It seemed to me at the outset that different kinds of change were taking place in scientific discourse – changes that did not occur at the same level, proceed at the same pace, or obey the same laws; the way in which, within a particular science, new propositions were produced, new facts isolated, or new concepts built up (the events that make up the everyday life of a science) did not, in all probability, follow the same model as the appearance of new fields of study (and the frequently corresponding disappearance of old ones); but the appearance of new fields of study must not, in turn, be confused with those overall redistributions that alter not only the general form of a science, but also its relations with other areas of knowledge. It seemed to me, therefore, that all these changes should not be treated at the same level, or be made to culminate at a single point, as is sometimes done, or be attributed to the genius of an individual, or a new collective spirit, or even to the fecundity of a single discovery; that it would be better to respect such differences, and even to try to grasp them in their specificity. In this way I tried to describe the combination of corresponding transformations that characterized the appearance of biology, political economy, philology, a number of human sciences, and a new type of philosophy, at the threshold of the nineteenth century.

The problem of causality. It is not always easy to determine what has caused a specific change in a science. What made such a discovery possible? Why did this new concept appear? Where did this or that theory come from? Questions like these are often highly embarrassing because there are no definite methodological principles on which to base such an analysis. The embarrassment is much greater in the case of those general changes that alter a science as a whole. It is greater still in the case of several corresponding changes. But it probably reaches its highest point in the case of the empirical sciences: for the role of instruments, techniques, institutions, events, ideologies, and interests is very much in evidence; but one does not know how an articulation so complex and so diverse in composition actually operates. It seemed to me that it would not be prudent for the moment to force a solution I felt incapable, I admit, of offering: the traditional explanations – spirit of the time, technological or social changes, influences of various kinds – struck me for the most part as being more magical than effective. In this work, then, I left the problem of causes to one side;[1] I chose instead to confine myself to describing the transformations themselves, thinking that this would be an indispensable step if, one day, a theory of scientific change and epistemological causality was to be constructed.

The problem of the subject. In distinguishing between the epistemological level of knowledge (or scientific consciousness) and the archaeological level of knowledge, I am aware that I am advancing in a direction that is fraught with difficulty. Can one speak of science and its history (and therefore of its conditions of existence, its changes, the errors it has perpetrated, the sudden advances that have sent it off on a new course) without reference to the scientist himself – and I am speaking not merely of the concrete individual represented by a proper name, but of his work and the particular form of his thought? Can a valid history of science be attempted that would retrace from beginning to end the whole spontaneous movement of an anonymous body of knowledge? Is it legitimate, is it even useful, to replace the traditional 'X thought that . . .' by a 'it was known that . . .'? But this is not exactly what I set out to do. I do not wish to deny the validity of intellectual biographies, or the possibility of a history of theories, concepts, or themes. It is simply that I wonder whether such descriptions are themselves enough, whether they do justice to the immense density of scientific discourse, whether there do not exist, outside their customary boundaries, systems of regularities that have a decisive

---

[1] I had approached this question in connection with psychiatry and clinical medicine in two earlier works.

role in the history of the sciences. I should like to know whether the subjects responsible for scientific discourse are not determined in their situation, their function, their perceptive capacity, and their practical possibilities by conditions that dominate and even overwhelm them. In short, I tried to explore scientific discourse not from the point of view of the individuals who are speaking, nor from the point of view of the formal structures of what they are saying, but from the point of view of the rules that come into play in the very existence of such discourse: what conditions did Linnaeus (or Petty, or Arnauld) have to fulfil, not to make his discourse coherent and true in general, but to give it, at the time when it was written and accepted, value and practical application as scientific discourse – or, more exactly, as naturalist, economic, or grammatical discourse?

On this point, too, I am well aware that I have not made much progress. But I should not like the effort I have made in one direction to be taken as a rejection of any other possible approach. Discourse in general, and scientific discourse in particular, is so complex a reality that we not only can, but should, approach it at different levels and with different methods. If there is one approach that I do reject, however, it is that (one might call it, broadly speaking, the phenomenological approach) which gives absolute priority to the observing subject, which attributes a constituent role to an act, which places its own point of view at the origin of all historicity – which, in short, leads to a transcendental consciousness. It seems to me that the historical analysis of scientific discourse should, in the last resort, be subject, not to a theory of the knowing subject, but rather to a theory of discursive practice.

5. This last point is a request to the English-speaking reader. In France, certain half-witted 'commentators' persist in labelling me a 'structuralist'. I have been unable to get it into their tiny minds that I have used none of the methods, concepts, or key terms that characterize structural analysis.

I should be grateful if a more serious public would free me from a connection that certainly does me honour, but that I have not deserved. There may well be certain similarities between the works of the structuralists and my own work. It would hardly behove me, of all people, to claim that my discourse is independent of conditions and rules of which I am very largely unaware, and which determine other work that is being done today. But it is only too easy to avoid the trouble of analysing such work by giving it an admittedly impressive-sounding, but inaccurate, label.

Preface

This book first arose out of a passage in Borges, out of the laughter that shattered, as I read the passage, all the familiar landmarks of my thought – *our* thought, the thought that bears the stamp of our age and our geography – breaking up all the ordered surfaces and all the planes with which we are accustomed to tame the wild profusion of existing things, and continuing long afterwards to disturb and threaten with collapse our age-old distinction between the Same and the Other. This passage quotes a 'certain Chinese encyclopaedia' in which it is written that 'animals are divided into: (a) belonging to the Emperor, (b) embalmed, (c) tame, (d) sucking pigs, (e) sirens, (f) fabulous, (g) stray dogs, (h) included in the present classification, (i) frenzied, (j) innumerable, (k) drawn with a very fine camelhair brush, (l) *et cetera*, (m) having just broken the water pitcher, (n) that from a long way off look like flies'. In the wonderment of this taxonomy, the thing we apprehend in one great leap, the thing that, by means of the fable, is demonstrated as the exotic charm of another system of thought, is the limitation of our own, the stark impossibility of thinking *that*.

But what is it impossible to think, and what kind of impossibility are we faced with here? Each of these strange categories can be assigned a precise meaning and a demonstrable content; some of them do certainly involve fantastic entities – fabulous animals or sirens – but, precisely because it puts them into categories of their own, the Chinese encyclopaedia localizes their powers of contagion; it distinguishes carefully between the very real animals (those that are frenzied or have just broken the water pitcher) and those that reside solely in the realm of imagination. The possibility of dangerous mixtures has been exorcized, heraldry and fable have been relegated to their own exalted peaks: no inconceivable amphibious maidens, no clawed wings, no disgusting, squamous epidermis, none of those polymorphous and demoniacal faces, no creatures breathing fire. The quality of monstrosity here does not affect any real body, nor does it produce modifications of any kind in the bestiary of the imagination; it does not lurk in the depths of any strange power. It would not even be present at all in this classification had it not insinuated itself into the empty space, the interstitial blanks *separating* all these entities from one another. It is not the 'fabulous' animals that are impossible, since they are designated as such, but the narrowness of the distance separating them from (and juxtaposing them to) the stray dogs, or the animals that from a long way off look like flies. What transgresses the boundaries of all imagination, of all possible thought, is simply that alphabetical series (a, b, c, d) which links each of those categories to all the others.

Moreover, it is not simply the oddity of unusual juxtapositions that we are faced with here. We are all familiar with the disconcerting effect of the proximity of extremes, or, quite simply, with the sudden vicinity of things that have no relation to each other; the mere act of enumeration that heaps them all together has a power of enchantment all its own: 'I am no longer hungry,' Eusthenes said. 'Until the morrow, safe from my saliva all the following shall be: Aspics, Acalephs, Acanthocephalates, Amoebocytes, Ammonites, Axolotls, Amblystomas, Aphislions, Anacondas, Ascarids, Amphisbaenas, Angleworms, Amphipods, Anaerobes, Annelids, Anthozoans. . . .' But all these worms and snakes, all these creatures redolent of decay and slime are slithering, like the syllables which designate them, in Eusthenes' saliva: that is where they all have their *common locus*, like the umbrella and the sewing-machine on the operating table; startling though their propinquity may be, it is nevertheless warranted by that *and*, by that *in*, by that *on* whose solidity provides proof of the possibility of juxtaposition. It was certainly improbable that arachnids, ammonites, and annelids should one day mingle on Eusthenes' tongue, but, after all, that welcoming and voracious mouth certainly provided them with a feasible lodging, a roof under which to coexist.

The monstrous quality that runs through Borges's enumeration consists, on the contrary, in the fact that the common ground on which such meetings are possible has itself been destroyed. What is impossible is not the propinquity of the things listed, but the very site on which their propinquity would be possible. The animals '(i) frenzied, (j) innumerable, (k) drawn with a very fine camelhair brush' – where could they ever meet, except in the immaterial sound of the voice pronouncing their enumeration, or on the page transcribing it? Where else could they be juxtaposed except in the non-place of language? Yet, though language can spread them before us, it can do so only in an unthinkable space. The central category of animals 'included in the present classification', with its explicit reference to paradoxes we are familiar with, is indication enough that we shall never succeed in defining a stable relation of contained to container between each of these categories and that which includes them all: if all the animals divided up here can be placed without exception in one of the divisions of this list, then aren't all the other divisions to be found in that one division too? And then again, in what space would that single, inclusive division have *its* existence? Absurdity destroys the *and* of the enumeration by making impossible the *in* where the things enumerated would be divided up. Borges adds no figure to the atlas of the impossible; nowhere does he strike the spark of poetic confrontation; he simply dispenses with the least obvious, but most compelling, of necessities; he does away with the *site*, the mute ground upon which it is possible for entities to be juxtaposed. A vanishing trick that is masked or, rather, laughably indicated by our alphabetical order, which is to be taken as the clue (the only visible one) to the enumerations of a Chinese encyclopaedia. . . . What has been removed, in short, is the famous 'operating table'; and rendering to Roussel[1] a small part of what is still his due, I use that word 'table' in two superimposed senses: the nickel-plated, rubbery table swathed in white, glittering beneath a glass sun devouring all shadow – the table where, for an instant, perhaps forever, the umbrella encounters the sewing-machine; and also a table, a *tabula*, that enables thought to operate upon the entities of our world, to put them in order, to divide them into classes, to group them according to names that designate their similarities and their differences – the table upon which, since the beginning of time, language has intersected space.

That passage from Borges kept me laughing a long time, though not without a certain uneasiness that I found hard to shake off. Perhaps because there arose in its wake the suspicion that there is a worse kind of disorder than that of the *incongruous*, the linking together of things that are inappropriate; I mean the disorder in which fragments of a large number of possible orders glitter separately in the dimension, without law or geometry, of the *heteroclite*; and that word should be taken in its most literal, etymological sense: in such a state, things are 'laid', 'placed', 'arranged' in sites so very different from one another that it is impossible

---

[1] Raymond Roussel, the French novelist. Cf. Michel Foucault's *Raymond Roussel* (Paris, 1963). [Translator's note.]

to find a place of residence for them, to define a *common locus* beneath them all. *Utopias* afford consolation: although they have no real locality there is nevertheless a fantastic, untroubled region in which they are able to unfold; they open up cities with vast avenues, superbly planted gardens, countries where life is easy, even though the road to them is chimerical. *Heterotopias* are disturbing, probably because they secretly undermine language, because they make it impossible to name this *and* that, because they shatter or tangle common names, because they destroy 'syntax' in advance, and not only the syntax with which we construct sentences but also that less apparent syntax which causes words and things (next to and also opposite one another) to 'hold together'. This is why utopias permit fables and discourse: they run with the very grain of language and are part of the fundamental dimension of the *fabula*; heterotopias (such as those to be found so often in Borges) desiccate speech, stop words in their tracks, contest the very possibility of grammar at its source; they dissolve our myths and sterilize the lyricism of our sentences.

It appears that certain aphasiacs, when shown various differently coloured skeins of wool on a table top, are consistently unable to arrange them into any coherent pattern; as though that simple rectangle were unable to serve in their case as a homogeneous and neutral space in which things could be placed so as to display at the same time the continuous order of their identities or differences as well as the semantic field of their denomination. Within this simple space in which things are normally arranged and given names, the aphasiac will create a multiplicity of tiny, fragmented regions in which nameless resemblances agglutinate things into unconnected islets; in one corner, they will place the lightest-coloured skeins, in another the red ones, somewhere else those that are softest in texture, in yet another place the longest, or those that have a tinge of purple or those that have been wound up into a ball. But no sooner have they been adumbrated than all these groupings dissolve again, for the field of identity that sustains them, however limited it may be, is still too wide not to be unstable; and so the sick mind continues to infinity, creating groups then dispersing them again, heaping up diverse similarities, destroying those that seem clearest, splitting up things that are identical, superimposing different criteria, frenziedly beginning all over again, becoming more and more disturbed, and teetering finally on the brink of anxiety.

The uneasiness that makes us laugh when we read Borges is certainly related to the profound distress of those whose language has been destroyed: loss of what is 'common' to place and name. Atopia, aphasia. Yet our text from Borges proceeds in another direction; the mythical homeland Borges assigns to that distortion of classification that prevents us from applying it, to that picture that lacks all spatial coherence, is a precise region whose name alone constitutes for the West a vast reservoir of utopias. In our dreamworld, is not China precisely this privileged *site* of *space*? In our traditional imagery, the Chinese culture is the most meticulous, the most rigidly ordered, the one most deaf to temporal events, most attached to the pure delineation of space; we think of it as a civilization of dikes and dams beneath the eternal face of the sky; we see it, spread and frozen, over the entire surface of a continent surrounded by walls. Even its writing does not reproduce the fugitive flight of the voice in horizontal lines; it erects the motionless and still-recognizeable images of things themselves in vertical columns. So much so that the Chinese encyclopaedia quoted by Borges, and the taxonomy it proposes, lead to a kind of thought without space, to words and categories that lack all life and place, but are rooted in a ceremonial space, overburdened with complex figures, with tangled paths, strange places, secret passages, and unexpected communications. There would appear to be, then, at the other extremity of the earth we inhabit, a culture entirely devoted to the ordering of space, but one that does not distribute the multiplicity of existing things into any of the categories that make it possible for us to name, speak, and think.

When we establish a considered classification, when we say that a cat and a dog resemble each other less than two greyhounds do, even if both are tame or embalmed, even if both are frenzied, even if both have just broken the water pitcher, what is the ground on which we are able to establish the validity of this classification with complete certainty? On what 'table', according to what grid of identities, similitudes, analogies, have we become accustomed to sort out so many different and similar things? What is this coherence – which, as is immediately apparent, is neither determined by an *a priori* and necessary concatenation, nor imposed on us by immediately perceptible contents? For it is not a question of linking consequences, but of grouping and isolating, of analysing, of matching and pigeon-holing concrete contents; there is nothing more tentative, nothing more empirical (superficially, at least) than the process of establishing an order among things; nothing that demands a sharper eye or a surer, better-articulated language; nothing that more insistently requires that one allow oneself to be carried along by the proliferation of qualities and forms. And yet an eye not consciously prepared might well group together certain similar figures and distinguish between others on the basis of such and such a difference: in fact, there is no similitude and no distinction, even for the wholly untrained perception, that is not the result of a precise operation and of the application of a preliminary criterion. A 'system of elements' – a definition of the segments by which the resemblances and differences can be shown, the types of variation by which those segments can be affected, and, lastly, the threshold above which there is a difference and below which there is a similitude – is indispensable for the establishment of even the simplest form of order. Order is, at one and the same time, that which is given in things as their inner law, the hidden network that determines the way they confront one another, and also that which has no existence except in the grid created by a glance, an examination, a language; and it is only in the blank spaces of this grid that order manifests itself in depth as though already there, waiting in silence for the moment of its expression.

The fundamental codes of a culture – those governing its language, its schemas of perception, its exchanges, its techniques, its values, the hierarchy of its practices – establish for every man, from the very first, the empirical orders with which he will be dealing and within which he will be at home. At the other extremity of thought, there are the scientific theories or the philosophical interpretations which explain why order exists in general, what universal law it obeys, what principle can account for it, and why this particular order has been established and not some other. But between these two regions, so distant from one another, lies a domain which, even though its role is mainly an intermediary one, is nonetheless fundamental: it is more confused, more obscure, and probably less easy to analyse. It is here that a culture, imperceptibly deviating from the empirical orders prescribed for it by its primary codes, instituting an initial separation from them, causes them to lose their original transparency, relinquishes its immediate and invisible powers, frees itself sufficiently to discover that these orders are perhaps not the only possible ones or the best ones; this culture then finds itself faced with the stark fact that there exists, below the level of its spontaneous orders, things that are in themselves capable of being ordered, that belong to a certain unspoken order; the fact, in short, that order *exists*. As though emancipating itself to some extent from its linguistic, perceptual, and practical grids, the culture superimposed on them another kind of grid which neutralized them, which by this superimposition both revealed and excluded them at the same time, so that the culture, by this very process, came face to face with order in its primary state. It is on the basis of this newly perceived order that the codes of language, perception, and practice are criticized and rendered partially invalid. It is on the basis of this order, taken as a firm foundation, that general theories as to the ordering of things, and the interpretation that such an ordering involves, will be constructed. Thus, between the already 'encoded' eye and reflexive knowledge there is a middle region which liberates order itself: it is here that it appears, according to the culture and the age in question, continuous and graduated or discontinuous and piecemeal, linked to space or constituted anew at each instant by the driving force of time, related to a series of variables or defined by separate systems of coherences, composed of resemblances which are either successive or corresponding, organized around increasing differences, etc. This middle region, then, in so far as it makes manifest the modes of being of order, can be posited as the most fundamental of all: anterior to words, perceptions, and gestures, which are then taken to be more or less exact, more or less happy, expressions of it (which is why this experience of order in its pure primary state always plays a critical role); more solid, more archaic, less dubious, always more 'true' than the theories that attempt to give those expressions explicit form, exhaustive application, or philosophical foundation. Thus, in every culture, between the use of what one might call the ordering codes and reflections upon order itself, there is the pure experience of order and of its modes of being.

The present study is an attempt to analyse that experience. I am concerned to show its developments, since the sixteenth century, in the mainstream of a culture such as ours: in what way, as one traces – against the current, as it were – language as it has been spoken, natural creatures as they have been perceived and grouped together, and exchanges as they have been practised; in what way, then, our culture has made manifest the existence of order, and how, to the modalities of that order, the exchanges owed their laws, the living beings their constants, the words their sequence and their representative value; what modalities of order have been recognized, posited, linked with space and time, in order to create the positive basis of knowledge as we find it employed in grammar and philology, in natural history and biology, in the study of wealth and political economy. Quite obviously, such an analysis does not belong to the history of ideas or of science: it is rather an inquiry whose aim is to rediscover on what basis knowledge and theory became possible; within what space of order knowledge was constituted; on the basis of what historical *a priori*, and in the element of what positivity, ideas could appear, sciences be established, experience be reflected in philosophies, rationalities be formed, only, perhaps, to dissolve and vanish soon afterwards. I am not concerned, therefore, to describe the progress of knowledge towards an objectivity in which today's science can finally be recognized; what I am attempting to bring to light is the epistemological field, the *episteme* in which knowledge, envisaged apart from all criteria having reference to its rational value or to its objective forms, grounds its positivity and thereby manifests a history which is not that of its growing perfection, but rather that of its conditions of possibility; in this account, what should appear are those configurations within the *space* of knowledge which have given rise to the diverse forms of empirical science. Such an enterprise is not so much a history, in the traditional meaning of that word, as an 'archaeology'.[1]

Now, this archaeological inquiry has revealed two great discontinuities in the *episteme* of Western culture: the first inaugurates the Classical age (roughly half-way through the seventeenth century) and the second, at the beginning of the nineteenth century, marks the beginning of the modern age. The order on the basis of which we think today does not have the same mode of being as that of the Classical thinkers. Despite the impression we may have of an almost uninterrupted development of the European *ratio* from the Renaissance to our own day, despite our possible belief that the classifications of Linnaeus, modified to a greater or lesser degree, can still lay claim to some sort of validity, that Condillac's theory of value can be recognized to some extent in nineteenth-century marginalism, that Keynes was well aware of the affinities between his own analyses and those of Cantillon, that the language of *general grammar* (as exemplified in the authors of Port-Royal or in Bauzée) is not so very far removed from our own – all this quasi-continuity on the level of ideas and themes is doubtless only a surface appearance; on the archaeological level, we see that the system of positivities was transformed in a wholesale fashion at the end of the eighteenth and beginning of the nineteenth century. Not that reason made any progress: it was simply that the mode of being of things, and of the order that divided them up before presenting them to the understanding, was profoundly altered. If the natural history of Tournefort, Linnaeus, and Buffon can be related to anything

[1] The problems of method raised by such an 'archaeology' will be examined in a later work.

at all other than itself, it is not to biology, to Cuvier's comparative anatomy, or to Darwin's theory of evolution, but to Bauzée's general grammar, to the analysis of money and wealth as found in the works of Law, or Véron de Fortbonnais, or Turgot. Perhaps knowledge succeeds in engendering knowledge, ideas in transforming themselves and actively modifying one another (but how? – historians have not yet enlightened us on this point); one thing, in any case, is certain: archaeology, addressing itself to the general space of knowledge, to its configurations, and to the mode of being of the things that appear in it, defines systems of simultaneity, as well as the series of mutations necessary and sufficient to circumscribe the threshold of a new positivity.

In this way, analysis has been able to show the coherence that existed, throughout the Classical age, between the theory of representation and the theories of language, of the natural orders, and of wealth and value. It is this configuration that, from the nineteenth century onward, changes entirely; the theory of representation disappears as the universal foundation of all possible orders; language as the spontaneous *tabula*, the primary grid of things, as an indispensable link between representation and things, is eclipsed in its turn; a profound historicity penetrates into the heart of things, isolates and defines them in their own coherence, imposes upon them the forms of order implied by the continuity of time; the analysis of exchange and money gives way to the study of production, that of the organism takes precedence over the search for taxonomic characteristics, and, above all, language loses its privileged position and becomes, in its turn, a historical form coherent with the density of its own past. But as things become increasingly reflexive, seeking the principle of their intelligibility only in their own development, and abandoning the space of representation, man enters in his turn, and for the first time, the field of Western knowledge. Strangely enough, man – the study of whom is supposed by the naïve to be the oldest investigation since Socrates – is probably no more than a kind of rift in the order of things, or, in any case, a configuration whose outlines are determined by the new position he has so recently taken up in the field of knowledge. Whence all the chimeras of the new humanisms, all the facile solutions of an 'anthropology' understood as a universal reflection on man, half-empirical, half-philosophical. It is comforting, however, and a source of profound relief to think that man is only a recent invention, a figure not yet two centuries old, a new wrinkle in our knowledge, and that he will disappear again as soon as that knowledge has discovered a new form.

It is evident that the present study is, in a sense, an echo of my undertaking to write a history of madness in the Classical age; it has the same articulations in time, taking the end of the Renaissance as its starting-point, then encountering, at the beginning of the nineteenth century, just as my history of madness did, the threshold of a modernity that we have not yet left behind. But whereas in the history of madness I was investigating the way in which a culture can determine in a massive, general form the difference that limits it, I am concerned here with observing how a culture experiences the propinquity of things, how it establishes the *tabula* of their relationships and the order by which they must be considered. I am concerned, in short, with a history of resemblance: on what conditions was Classical thought able to reflect relations of similarity or equivalence between things, relations that would provide a foundation and a justification for their words, their classifications, their systems of exchange? What historical *a priori* provided the starting-point from which it was possible to define the great checkerboard of distinct identities established against the confused, undefined, faceless, and, as it were, indifferent background of differences? The history of madness would be the history of the Other – of that which, for a given culture, is at once interior and foreign, therefore to be excluded (so as to exorcize the interior danger) but by being shut away (in order to reduce its otherness); whereas the history of the order imposed on things would be the history of the Same – of that which, for a given culture, is both dispersed and related, therefore to be distinguished by kinds and to be collected together into identities.

And if one considers that disease is at one and the same time disorder – the existence of a perilous otherness within the human body, at the very heart of life – and a natural phenomenon with its own constants, resemblances, and types, one can see what scope there would be for an archaeology of the medical point of view. From the limit-experience of the Other to the constituent forms of medical knowledge, and from the latter to the order of things and the conceptions of the Same, what is available to archaeological analysis is the whole of Classical knowledge, or rather the threshold that separates us from Classical thought and constitutes our modernity. It was upon this threshold that the strange figure of knowledge called man first appeared and revealed a space proper to the human sciences. In attempting to uncover the deepest strata of Western culture, I am restoring to our silent and apparently immobile soil its rifts, its instability, its flaws; and it is the same ground that is once more stirring under our feet.

PART I

CHAPTER I

Las Meninas

I

The painter is standing a little back from his canvas[1]. He is glancing at his model; perhaps he is considering whether to add some finishing touch, though it is also possible that the first stroke has not yet been made. The arm holding the brush is bent to the left, towards the palette; it is motionless, for an instant, between canvas and paints. The skilled hand is suspended in mid-air, arrested in rapt attention on the painter's gaze; and the gaze, in return, waits upon the arrested gesture. Between the fine point of the brush and the steely gaze, the scene is about to yield up its volume.

But not without a subtle system of feints. By standing back a little, the painter has placed himself to one side of the painting on which he is working. That is, for the spectator at present observing him he is to the right of his canvas, while the latter, the canvas, takes up the whole of the extreme left. And the canvas has its back turned to that spectator: he can see nothing of it but the reverse side, together with the huge frame on which it is stretched. The painter, on the other hand, is perfectly visible in his full height; or at any rate, he is not masked by the tall canvas which may soon absorb him, when, taking a step towards it again, he returns to his task; he has no doubt just appeared, at this very instant, before the eyes of the spectator, emerging from what is virtually a sort of vast cage projected backwards by the surface he is painting. Now he can be seen, caught in a moment of stillness, at the neutral centre of this oscillation. His dark torso and bright face are half-way between the visible and the invisible: emerging from that canvas beyond our view, he moves into our gaze; but when, in a moment, he makes a step to the right, removing himself from our gaze, he will be standing exactly in front of the canvas he is painting; he will enter that region where his painting, neglected for an instant, will, for him, become visible once more, free of shadow and

3

free of reticence. As though the painter could not at the same time be seen on the picture where he is represented and also see that upon which he is representing something. He rules at the threshold of those two incompatible visibilities.

The painter is looking, his face turned slightly and his head leaning towards one shoulder. He is staring at a point to which, even though it is invisible, we, the spectators, can easily assign an object, since it is we, ourselves, who are that point: our bodies, our faces, our eyes. The spectacle he is observing is thus doubly invisible: first, because it is not represented within the space of the painting, and, second, because it is situated precisely in that blind point, in that essential hiding-place into which our gaze disappears from ourselves at the moment of our actual looking. And yet, how could we fail to see that invisibility, there in front of our eyes, since it has its own perceptible equivalent, its sealed-in figure, in the painting itself? We could, in effect, guess what it is the painter is looking at if it were possible for us to glance for a moment at the canvas he is working on; but all we can see of that canvas is its texture, the horizontal and vertical bars of the stretcher, and the obliquely rising foot of the easel. The tall, monotonous rectangle occupying the whole left portion of the real picture, and representing the back of the canvas within the picture, reconstitutes in the form of a surface the invisibility in depth of what the artist is observing: that space in which we are, and which we are. From the eyes of the painter to what he is observing there runs a compelling line that we, the onlookers, have no power of evading: it runs through the real picture and emerges from its surface to join the place from which we see the painter observing us; this dotted line reaches out to us ineluctably, and links us to the representation of the picture.

In appearance, this locus is a simple one; a matter of pure reciprocity: we are looking at a picture in which the painter is in turn looking out at us. A mere confrontation, eyes catching one another's glance, direct looks superimposing themselves upon one another as they cross. And yet this slender line of reciprocal visibility embraces a whole complex network of uncertainties, exchanges, and feints. The painter is turning his eyes towards us only in so far as we happen to occupy the same position as his subject. We, the spectators, are an additional factor. Though greeted by that gaze, we are also dismissed by it, replaced by that which was always there before we were: the model itself. But, inversely, the painter's gaze, addressed to the void confronting him outside the picture, accepts as many models as there are spectators; in this precise but neutral place, the observer and the observed take part in a ceaseless exchange. No gaze is stable, or rather, in the neutral furrow of the gaze piercing at a right angle through the canvas, subject and object, the spectator and the model, reverse their roles to infinity. And here the great canvas with its back to us on the extreme left of the picture exercises its second function: stubbornly invisible, it prevents the relation of these gazes from ever being discoverable or definitely established. The opaque fixity that it establishes on one side renders forever unstable the play of metamorphoses established in the centre between spectator and model. Because we can see only that reverse side, we do not know who we are, or what we are doing. Seen or seeing? The painter is observing a place which, from moment to moment, never ceases to change its content, its form, its face, its identity. But the attentive immobility of his eyes refers us back to another direction which they have often followed already, and which soon, there can be no doubt, they will take again: that of the motionless canvas upon which is being traced, has already been traced perhaps, for a long time and forever, a portrait that will never again be erased. So that the painter's sovereign gaze commands a virtual triangle whose outline defines this picture of a picture: at the top – the only visible corner – the painter's eyes; at one of the base angles, the invisible place occupied by the model; at the other base angle, the figure probably sketched out on the invisible surface of the canvas.

As soon as they place the spectator in the field of their gaze, the painter's eyes seize hold of him, force him to enter the picture, assign him a place at once privileged and inescapable, levy their luminous and visible tribute from him, and project it upon the inaccessible surface of the canvas within the picture. He sees his invisibility made visible to the painter and transposed into an image forever invisible to himself. A shock that is augmented and made more inevitable still by a marginal trap. At the extreme right, the picture is lit by a window represented in very sharp perspective; so sharp that we can see scarcely more than the embrasure; so that the flood of light streaming through it bathes at the same time, and with equal generosity, two neighbouring spaces, overlapping but irreducible: the surface of the painting, together with the volume it represents (which is to say, the painter's studio, or the salon in which his easel is now set up), and, in front of that surface, the real volume occupied by the spectator (or again, the unreal site of the model). And as it passes through the room from right to left, this vast flood of golden light carries both the spectator towards the painter and the model towards the canvas; it is this light too, which, washing over the painter, makes him visible to the spectator and turns into golden lines, in the model's eyes, the frame of that enigmatic canvas on which his image, once transported there, is to be imprisoned. This extreme, partial, scarcely indicated window frees a whole flow of daylight which serves as the common locus of the representation. It balances the invisible canvas on the other side of the picture: just as that canvas, by turning its back to the spectators, folds itself in against the picture representing it, and forms, by the superimposition of its reverse and visible side upon the surface of the picture depicting it, the ground, inaccessible to us, on which there shimmers the Image *par excellence*, so does the window, a pure aperture, establish a space as manifest as the other is hidden; as much the common ground of painter, figures, models, and spectators, as the other is solitary (for no one is looking at it, not even the painter). From the right, there streams in through an invisible window the pure volume of a light that renders all representation visible; to the left extends the surface that conceals, on the other side of its all too visible woven texture, the representation it bears. The light, by flooding the scene (I mean the room as well as the canvas, the room represented on the canvas, and the room in which the canvas stands), envelops the figures and the spectators and carries them with it, under the painter's gaze, towards the place where his brush will represent them. But that place is concealed from us. We are observing ourselves being observed by the painter, and made visible to his eyes by the same light that enables us to see him. And just as we are about to apprehend ourselves, transcribed by his hand as though in a mirror, we find that we can in fact apprehend nothing of that mirror but its lustreless back. The other side of a psyche.

Now, as it happens, exactly opposite the spectators – ourselves – on the wall forming the far end of the room, Velázquez has represented a series of pictures; and we see that among all those hanging canvases there is one that shines with particular brightness. Its frame is wider and darker than those of the others; yet there is a fine white line around its inner edge diffusing over its whole surface a light whose source is not easy to determine; for it comes from nowhere, unless it be from a space within itself. In this strange light, two silhouettes are apparent, while above them, and a little behind them, is a heavy purple curtain. The other pictures reveal little more than a few paler patches buried in a darkness without depth. This particular one, on the other hand, opens onto a perspective of space in which recognizable forms recede from us in a light that belongs only to itself. Among all these elements intended to provide representations, while impeding them, hiding them, concealing them because of their position or their distance from us, this is the only one that fulfils its function in all honesty and enables us to see what it is supposed to show. Despite its distance from us, despite the shadows all around it. But it isn't a picture: it is a mirror. It offers us at last that enchantment of the double that until now has been denied us, not only by the distant paintings but also by the light in the foreground with its ironic canvas.

Of all the representations represented in the picture this is the only one visible; but no one is looking at it. Upright beside his canvas, his attention entirely taken up by his model, the painter is unable to see this looking-glass shining so softly behind him. The other figures in the picture are also, for the most part, turned to face what must be taking place in front – towards the bright invisibility bordering the canvas, towards that balcony of light where their eyes can gaze at those who are gazing back at them, and not towards that dark recess which marks the far end of the room in which they are represented. There are, it is true, some heads turned away from us in profile: but not one of them is turned far enough to see, at the back of the room, that solitary mirror, that tiny glowing rectangle which is nothing other than visibility, yet without any gaze able to grasp it, to render it actual, and to enjoy the suddenly ripe fruit of the spectacle it offers.

It must be admitted that this indifference is equalled only by the mirror's own. It is reflecting nothing, in fact, of all that is there in the same space as itself: neither the painter with his back to it, nor the figures in the centre of the room. It is not the visible it reflects, in those bright depths. In Dutch painting it was traditional for mirrors to play a duplicating role: they repeated the original contents of the picture, only inside an unreal, modified, contracted, concave space. One saw in them the same things as one saw in the first instance in the painting, but decomposed and re-composed according to a different law. Here, the mirror is saying nothing that has already been said before. Yet its position is more or less completely central: its upper edge is exactly on an imaginary line running half-way between the top and the bottom of the painting, it hangs right in the middle of the far wall (or at least in the middle of the portion we can see); it ought, therefore, to be governed by the same lines of perspective as the picture itself; we might well expect the same studio, the same painter, the same canvas to be arranged within it according to an identical space; it could be the perfect duplication.

In fact, it shows us nothing of what is represented in the picture itself. Its motionless gaze extends out in front of the picture, into that necessarily invisible region which forms its exterior face, to apprehend the figures arranged in that space. Instead of surrounding visible objects, this mirror cuts straight through the whole field of the representation, ignoring all it might apprehend within that field, and restores visibility to that which resides outside all view. But the invisibility that it overcomes in this way is not the invisibility of what is hidden: it does not make its way around any obstacle, it is not distorting any perspective, it is addressing itself to what is invisible both because of the picture's structure and because of its existence as painting. What it is reflecting is that which all the figures within the painting are looking at so fixedly, or at least those who are looking straight ahead; it is therefore what the spectator would be able to see if the painting extended further forward, if its bottom edge were brought lower until it included the figures the painter is using as models. But it is also, since the picture does stop there, displaying only the painter and his studio, what is exterior to the picture, in so far as it is a picture – in other words, a rectangular fragment of lines and colours intended to represent something to the eyes of any possible spectator. At the far end of the room, ignored by all, the unexpected mirror holds in its glow the figures that the painter is looking at (the painter in his represented, objective reality, the reality of the painter at his work); but also the figures that are looking at the painter (in that material reality which the lines and the colours have laid out upon the canvas). These two groups of figures are both equally inaccessible, but in different ways: the first because of an effect of composition peculiar to the painting; the second because of the law that presides over the very existence of all pictures in general. Here, the action of representation consists in bringing one of these two forms of invisibility into the place of the other, in an unstable superimposition – and in rendering them both, at the same moment, at the other extremity of the picture – at that pole which is the very height of its representation: that of a reflected depth in the far recess of the painting's depth. The mirror provides a metathesis of visibility that affects both the space represented in the picture and its nature as representation; it allows us to see, in the centre of the canvas, what in the painting is of necessity doubly invisible.

A strangely literal, though inverted, application of the advice given, so it is said, to his pupil by the old Pachero when the former was working in his studio in Seville: 'The image should stand out from the frame.'

II

But perhaps it is time to give a name at last to that image which appears in the depths of the mirror, and which the painter is contemplating in front of the picture. Perhaps it would be better, once and for all, to determine the identities of all the figures presented or indicated here, so as to avoid embroiling ourselves forever in those vague, rather abstract designations, so constantly prone to misunderstanding and duplication, 'the painter', 'the characters', 'the models', 'the spectators', 'the images'. Rather than pursue to infinity a language inevitably inadequate to the visible fact, it would be better to say that Velázquez composed a picture; that in this picture he represented himself, in his studio or in a room of the Escurial, in the act of painting two figures whom the Infanta Margarita has come there to watch, together with an entourage of duennas, maids of honour, courtiers, and dwarfs; that we can attribute names to this group of people with great precision: tradition recognizes that here we have Doña Maria Agustina Sarmiente, over there Nieto, in the foreground Nicolaso Pertusato, an Italian jester. We could then add that the two personages serving as models to the painter are not visible, at least directly; but that we can see them in a mirror; and that they are, without any doubt, King Philip IV and his wife, Mariana.

These proper names would form useful landmarks and avoid ambiguous designations; they would tell us in any case what the painter is looking at, and the majority of the characters in the picture along with him. But the relation of language to painting is an infinite relation. It is not that words are imperfect, or that, when confronted by the visible, they prove insuperably inadequate. Neither can be reduced to the other's terms: it is in vain that we say what we see; what we see never resides in what we say. And it is in vain that we attempt to show, by the use of images, metaphors, or similes, what we are saying; the space where they achieve their splendour is not that deployed by our eyes but that defined by the sequential elements of syntax. And the proper name, in this particular context, is merely an artifice: it gives us a finger to point with, in other words, to pass surreptitiously from the space where one speaks to the space where one looks; in other words, to fold one over the other as though they were equivalents. But if one wishes to keep the relation of language to vision open, if one wishes to treat their incompatibility as a starting-point for speech instead of as an obstacle to be avoided, so as to stay as close as possible to both, then one must erase those proper names and preserve the infinity of the task. It is perhaps through the medium of this grey, anonymous language, always over-meticulous and repetitive because too broad, that the painting may, little by little, release its illuminations.

We must therefore pretend not to know who is to be reflected in the depths of that mirror, and interrogate that reflection in its own terms.

First, it is the reverse of the great canvas represented on the left. The reverse, or rather the right side, since it displays in full face what the canvas, by its position, is hiding from us. Furthermore, it is both in opposition to the window and a reinforcement of it. Like the window, it provides a ground which is common to the painting and to what lies outside it. But the window operates by the continuous movement of an effusion which, flowing from right to left, unites the attentive figures, the painter, and the canvas, with the spectacle they are observing; whereas the mirror, on the other hand, by means of a violent, instantaneous movement, a movement of pure surprise, leaps out from the picture in order to reach that which is observed yet invisible in front of it, and then, at the far end of its fictitious depth, to render it visible yet indifferent to every gaze. The compelling tracer line, joining the reflection to that which it is reflecting, cuts perpendicularly through the lateral flood of light. Lastly – and this is the mirror's third function – it stands adjacent to a doorway which forms an opening, like the mirror itself, in the far wall of the room. This doorway too forms a bright and sharply defined rectangle whose soft light does not shine through into the room. It would be nothing but a gilded panel if it were not recessed out from the room by means of one leaf of a carved door, the curve of a curtain, and the shadows of several steps. Beyond the steps, a corridor begins; but instead of losing itself in obscurity, it is dissipated in a yellow dazzle where the light, without coming in, whirls around on itself in dynamic repose. Against this background, at once near and limitless, a man stands out in full-length silhouette; he is seen in profile; with one hand he is holding back the weight of a curtain; his feet are placed on different steps; one knee is bent. He may be about to enter the room; or he may be merely observing what is going on inside it, content to surprise those within without being seen himself. Like the mirror, his eyes are directed towards the other side of the scene; nor is anyone paying any more attention to him than to the mirror. We do not know where he has come from: it could be that by following uncertain corridors he has just made his way around the outside of the room in which these characters are collected and the painter is at work;

perhaps he too, a short while ago, was there in the forefront of the scene, in the invisible region still being contemplated by all those eyes in the picture. Like the images perceived in the looking-glass, it is possible that he too is an emissary from that evident yet hidden space. Even so, there is a difference: he is there in flesh and blood; he has appeared from the outside, on the threshold of the area represented; he is indubitable – not a probable reflection but an irruption. The mirror, by making visible, beyond even the walls of the studio itself, what is happening in front of the picture, creates, in its sagittal dimension, an oscillation between the interior and the exterior. One foot only on the lower step, his body entirely in profile, the ambiguous visitor is coming in and going out at the same time, like a pendulum caught at the bottom of its swing. He repeats on the spot, but in the dark reality of his body, the instantaneous movement of those images flashing across the room, plunging into the mirror, being reflected there, and springing out from it again like visible, new, and identical species. Pale, minuscule, those silhouetted figures in the mirror are challenged by the tall, solid stature of the man appearing in the doorway.

But we must move down again from the back of the picture towards the front of the stage; we must leave that periphery whose volute we have just been following. Starting from the painter's gaze, which constitutes an off-centre centre to the left, we perceive first of all the back of the canvas, then the paintings hung on the wall, with the mirror in their centre, then the open doorway, then more pictures, of which, because of the sharpness of the perspective, we can see no more than the edges of the frames, and finally, at the extreme right, the window, or rather the groove in the wall from which the light is pouring. This spiral shell presents us with the entire cycle of representation: the gaze, the palette and brush, the canvas innocent of signs (these are the material tools of representation), the paintings, the reflections, the real man (the completed representation, but as it were freed from its illusory or truthful contents, which are juxtaposed to it); then the representation dissolves again: we can see only the frames, and the light that is flooding the pictures from outside, but that they, in return, must reconstitute in their own kind, as though it were coming from elsewhere, passing through their dark wooden frames. And we do, in fact, see this light on the painting, apparently welling out from the crack of the frame; and from there it moves over to touch the brow, the cheekbones, the eyes, the gaze of the painter, who is holding a palette in one hand and in the other a fine brush . . . And so the spiral is closed, or rather, by means of that light, is opened.

This opening is not, like the one in the back wall, made by pulling back a door; it is the whole breadth of the picture itself, and the looks that pass across it are not those of a distant visitor. The frieze that occupies the foreground and the middle ground of the picture represents – if we include the painter – eight characters. Five of these, their heads more or less bent, turned or inclined, are looking straight out at right angles to the surface of the picture. The centre of the group is occupied by the little Infanta, with her flared pink and grey dress. The princess is turning her head towards the right side of the picture, while her torso and the big panniers of her dress slant away slightly towards the left; but her gaze is directed absolutely straight towards the spectator standing in front of the painting. A vertical line dividing the canvas into two equal halves would pass between the child's eyes. Her face is a third of the total height of the picture above the lower frame. So that here, beyond all question, resides the principal theme of the composition; this is the very object of this painting. As though to prove this and to emphasize it even more, Velázquez has made use of a traditional visual device: beside the principal figure he has placed a secondary one, kneeling and looking in towards the central one. Like a donor in prayer, like an angel greeting the Virgin, a maid of honour on her knees is stretching out her hands towards the princess. Her face stands out in perfect profile against the background. It is at the same height as that of the child. This attendant is looking at the princess and only at the princess. A little to the right, there stands another maid of honour, also turned towards the Infanta, leaning slightly over her, but with her eyes clearly directed towards the front, towards the same spot already being gazed at by the painter and the princess. Lastly, two other groups made up of two figures each: one of these groups is further away; the other, made up of the two dwarfs, is right in the foreground. One character in each of these pairs is looking straight out, the other to the left or the right. Because of their positions and their size, these two groups correspond and themselves form a pair: behind, the courtiers (the woman, to the left, looks to the right); in front, the dwarfs (the boy, who is at the extreme right, looks in towards the centre of the picture). This group of characters, arranged in this manner, can be taken to constitute, according to the way one looks at the picture and the centre of reference chosen, two different figures. The first would be a large X: the top left-hand point of this X would be the painter's eyes; the top right-hand one, the male courtier's eyes; at the bottom left-hand corner there is the corner of the canvas represented with its back towards us (or, more exactly, the foot of the easel); at the bottom right-hand corner, the dwarf (his foot on the dog's back). Where these two lines intersect, at the centre of the X, are the eyes of the Infanta. The second figure would be more that of a vast curve, its two ends determined by the painter on the left and the male courtier on the right – both these extremities occurring high up in the picture and set back from its surface; the centre of the curve, much nearer to us, would coincide with the princess's face and the look her maid of honour is directing towards her. This curve describes a shallow hollow across the centre of the picture which at once contains and sets off the position of the mirror at the back.

There are thus two centres around which the picture may be organized, according to whether the fluttering attention of the spectator decides to settle in this place or in that. The princess is standing upright in the centre of a St Andrew's cross, which is revolving around her with its eddies of courtiers, maids of honour, animals, and fools. But this pivoting movement is frozen. Frozen by a spectacle that would be absolutely invisible if those same characters, suddenly motionless, were not offering us, as though in the hollow of a goblet, the possibility of seeing in the depths of a mirror the unforeseen double of what they are observing. In depth, it is the princess who is superimposed on the mirror; vertically, it is the reflection that is superimposed on the face. But, because of the perspective, they are very close to one another. Moreover, from each of them there springs an ineluctable line: the line issuing from the mirror crosses the whole of the depth represented (and even more, since the mirror forms a hole in the back wall and brings a further space into being behind it); the other line is shorter: it comes from the child's eyes and crosses only the foreground. These two sagittal lines converge at a very sharp angle, and the point where they meet, springing out from the painted surface, occurs in front of the picture, more or less exactly at the spot from which we are observing it. It is an uncertain point because we cannot see it; yet it is an inevitable and perfectly defined point too, since it is determined by those two dominating figures and confirmed further by other, adjacent dotted lines which also have their origin inside the picture and emerge from it in a similar fashion.

What is there, then, we ask at last, in that place which is completely inaccessible because it is exterior to the picture, yet is prescribed by all the lines of its composition? What is the spectacle, what are the faces that are reflected first of all in the depths of the Infanta's eyes, then in the courtiers' and the painter's, and finally in the distant glow of the mirror? But the

13

question immediately becomes a double one: the face reflected in the mirror is also the face that is contemplating it; what all the figures in the picture are looking at are the two figures to whose eyes they too present a scene to be observed. The entire picture is looking out at a scene for which it is itself a scene. A condition of pure reciprocity manifested by the observing and observed mirror, the two stages of which are uncoupled at the two lower corners of the picture: on the left the canvas with its back to us, by means of which the exterior point is made into pure spectacle; to the right the dog lying on the floor, the only element in the picture that is neither looking at anything nor moving, because it is not intended, with its deep reliefs and the light playing on its silky hair, to be anything but an object to be seen.

Our first glance at the painting told us what it is that creates this spectacle-as-observation. It is the two sovereigns. One can sense their presence already in the respectful gaze of the figures in the picture, in the astonishment of the child and the dwarfs. We recognize them, at the far end of the picture, in the two tiny silhouettes gleaming out from the looking-glass. In the midst of all those attentive faces, all those richly dressed bodies, they are the palest, the most unreal, the most compromised of all the painting's images: a movement, a little light, would be sufficient to eclipse them. Of all these figures represented before us, they are also the most ignored, since no one is paying the slightest attention to that reflection which has slipped into the room behind them all, silently occupying its unsuspected space; in so far as they are visible, they are the frailest and the most distant form of all reality. Inversely, in so far as they stand outside the picture and are therefore withdrawn from it in an essential invisibility, they provide the centre around which the entire representation is ordered: it is they who are being faced, it is towards them that everyone is turned, it is to their eyes that the princess is being presented in her holiday clothes; from the canvas with its back to us to the Infanta, and from the Infanta to the dwarf playing on the extreme right, there runs a curve (or again, the lower fork of the X opens) that orders the whole arrangement of the picture to their gaze and thus makes apparent the true centre of the composition, to which the Infanta's gaze and the image in the mirror are both finally subject.

In the realm of the anecdote, this centre is symbolically sovereign, since it is occupied by King Philip IV and his wife. But it is so above all because of the triple function it fulfils in relation to the picture. For in it there occurs an exact superimposition of the model's gaze as it is being painted, of the spectator's as he contemplates the painting, and of the painter's as he is composing his picture (not the one represented, but the one in front of us which we are discussing). These three 'observing' functions come together in a point exterior to the picture: that is, an ideal point in relation to what is represented, but a perfectly real one too, since it is also the starting-point that makes the representation possible. Within that reality itself, it cannot not be invisible. And yet, that reality is pro-jected within the picture – projected and diffracted in three forms which correspond to the three functions of that ideal and real point. They are: on the left, the painter with his palette in his hand (a self-portrait of Velázquez); to the right, the visitor, one foot on the step, ready to enter the room; he is taking in the scene from the back, but he can see the royal couple, who are the spectacle itself, from the front; and lastly, in the centre, the reflection of the king and the queen, richly dressed, motionless, in the attitude of patient models.

A reflection that shows us quite simply, and in shadow, what all those in the foreground are looking at. It restores, as if by magic, what is lack-ing in every gaze: in the painter's, the model, which his represented double is duplicating over there in the picture; in the king's, his portrait, which is being finished off on that slope of the canvas that he cannot perceive from where he stands; in that of the spectator, the real centre of the scene, whose place he himself has taken as though by usurpation. But perhaps this generosity on the part of the mirror is feigned; perhaps it is hiding as much as and even more than it reveals. That space where the king and his wife hold sway belongs equally well to the artist and to the spectator: in the depths of the mirror there could also appear – there ought to appear – the anonymous face of the passer-by and that of Velázquez. For the function of that reflection is to draw into the interior of the picture what is intimately foreign to it: the gaze which has organized it and the gaze for which it is displayed. But because they are present within the picture, to the right and to the left, the artist and the visitor cannot be given a place in the mirror: just as the king appears in the depths of the looking-glass precisely because he does not belong to the picture.

In the great volute that runs around the perimeter of the studio, from the gaze of the painter, with his motionless hand and palette, right round to the finished paintings, representation came into being, reached completion, only to dissolve once more into the light; the cycle was complete. The lines that run through the depth of the picture, on the other hand, are not complete; they all lack a segment of their trajectories. This gap is caused by the absence of the king – an absence that is an artifice on the part of the painter. But this artifice both conceals and indicates another vacancy which is, on the contrary, immediate: that of the painter and the spectator when they are looking at or composing the picture. It may be that, in this picture, as in all the representations of which it is, as it were, the manifest essence, the profound invisibility of what one sees is inseparable from the invisibility of the person seeing – despite all mirrors, reflections, imitations, and portraits. Around the scene are arranged all the signs and successive forms of representation; but the double relation of the representation to its model and to its sovereign, to its author as well as to the person to whom it is being offered, this relation is necessarily interrupted. It can never be present without some residuum, even in a representation that offers itself as a spectacle. In the depth that traverses the picture, hollowing it into a fictitious recess and projecting it forward in front of itself, it is not possible for the pure felicity of the image ever to present in a full light both the master who is representing and the sovereign who is being represented.

Perhaps there exists, in this painting by Velàzquez, the representation as it were, of Classical representation, and the definition of the space it opens up to us. And, indeed, representation undertakes to represent itself here in all its elements, with its images, the eyes to which it is offered, the faces it makes visible, the gestures that call it into being. But there, in the midst of this dispersion which it is simultaneously grouping together and spreading out before us, indicated compellingly from every side, is an essential void: the necessary disappearance of that which is its foundation – of the person it resembles and the person in whose eyes it is only a resemblance. This very subject – which is the same – has been elided. And representation, freed finally from the relation that was impeding it, can offer itself as representation in its pure form.

NOTES

[1] See frontispiece.

CHAPTER 2

The Prose of the World

I THE FOUR SIMILITUDES

Up to the end of the sixteenth century, resemblance played a constructive role in the knowledge of Western culture. It was resemblance that largely guided exegesis and the interpretation of texts; it was resemblance that organized the play of symbols, made possible knowledge of things visible and invisible, and controlled the art of representing them. The universe was folded in upon itself: the earth echoing the sky, faces seeing themselves reflected in the stars, and plants holding within their stems the secrets that were of use to man. Painting imitated space. And representation – whether in the service of pleasure or of knowledge – was posited as a form of repetition: the theatre of life or the mirror of nature, that was the claim made by all language, its manner of declaring its existence and of formulating its right of speech.

We must pause here for a while, at this moment in time when resemblance was about to relinquish its relation with knowledge and disappear, in part at least, from the sphere of cognition. How, at the end of the sixteenth century, and even in the early seventeenth century, was similitude conceived? How did it organize the figures of knowledge? And if the things that resembled one another were indeed infinite in number, can one, at least, establish the forms according to which they might resemble one another?

The semantic web of resemblance in the sixteenth century is extremely rich: *Amicitia, Aequalitas* (*contractus, consensus, matrimonium, societas, pax, et similia*), *Consonantia, Concertus, Continuum, Paritas, Proportio, Similitudo, Conjunctio, Copula*[1]. And there are a great many other notions that intersect, overlap, reinforce, or limit one another on the surface of thought. It is enough for the moment to indicate the principal figures that determine the knowledge of resemblance with their articulations. There are four of these that are, beyond doubt, essential.

First of all, *convenientia*. This word really denotes the adjacency of places more strongly than it does similitude. Those things are 'convenient' which come sufficiently close to one another to be in juxtaposition; their edges touch, their fringes intermingle, the extremity of the one also denotes the beginning of the other. In this way, movement, influences, passions, and properties too, are communicated. So that in this hinge between two things a resemblance appears. A resemblance that becomes double as soon as one attempts to unravel it: a resemblance of the place, the site upon which nature has placed the two things, and thus a similitude of properties; for in this natural container, the world, adjacency is not an exterior relation between things, but the sign of a relationship, obscure though it may be. And then, from this contact, by exchange, there arise new resemblances; a common regimen becomes necessary; upon the similitude that was the hidden reason for their propinquity is superimposed a resemblance that is the visible effect of that proximity. Body and soul, for example, are doubly 'convenient': the soul had to be made dense, heavy, and terrestrial for God to place it in the very heart of matter. But through this propinquity, the soul receives the movements of the body and assimilates itself to that body, while 'the body is altered and corrupted by the passions of the soul' [2]. In the vast syntax of the world, the different beings adjust themselves to one another; the plant communicates with the animal, the earth with the sea, man with everything around him. Resemblance imposes adjacencies that in their turn guarantee further resemblances. Place and similitude become entangled: we see mosses growing on the outsides of shells, plants in the antlers of stags, a sort of grass on the faces of men; and the strange zoophyte, by mingling together the properties that make it similar to the plants as well as to the animals, also juxtaposes them[3]. All so many signs of 'convenience'.

Convenientia is a resemblance connected with space in the form of a graduated scale of proximity. It is of the same order as conjunction and adjustment. This is why it pertains less to the things themselves than to the world in which they exist. The world is simply the universal 'convenience' of things; there are the same number of fishes in the water as there are animals, or objects produced by nature or man, on the land (are there not fishes called *Episcopus*, others called *Catena*, and others called *Priapus*?); the same number of beings in the water and on the surface of the earth as there are in the sky, the inhabitants of the former corresponding with those of the latter; and lastly, there are the same number of beings in the whole of creation as may be found eminently contained in God himself, 'the Sower of Existence, of Power, of Knowledge and of Love'[4]. Thus, by this linking of resemblance with space, this 'convenience' that brings like things together and makes adjacent things similar, the world is linked together like a chain. At each point of contact there begins and ends a link that resembles the one before it and the one after it; and from circle to circle, these similitudes continue, holding the extremes apart (God and matter), yet bringing them together in such a way that the will of the Almighty may penetrate into the most unawakened corners. It is this immense, taut, and vibrating chain, this rope of 'convenience', that Porta evokes in a passage from his *Magie naturelle*:

As with respect to its vegetation the plant stands convenient to the brute beast, so through feeling does the brutish animal to man, who is conformable to the rest of the stars by his intelligence; these links proceed so strictly that they appear as a rope stretched from the first cause as far as the lowest and smallest of things, by a reciprocal and continuous connection; in such wise that the superior virtue, spreading its beams, reaches so far that if we touch one extremity of that cord it will make tremble and move all the rest[5].

The second form of similitude is *aemulatio*: a sort of 'convenience' that has been freed from the law of place and is able to function, without motion, from a distance. Rather as though the spatial collusion of *convenientia* had been broken, so that the links of the chain, no longer connected, reproduced their circles at a distance from one another in accordance with a resemblance that needs no contact. There is something in emulation of the reflection and the mirror: it is the means whereby things scattered through the universe can answer one another. The human face, from afar, emulates the sky, and just as man's intellect is an imperfect reflection of God's wisdom, so his two eyes, with their limited brightness, are a reflection of the vast illumination spread across the sky by sun and moon; the mouth is Venus, since it gives passage to kisses and words of love; the nose provides an image in miniature of Jove's sceptre and Mercury's staff[6]. The relation of emulation enables things to imitate one another from one end of the universe to the other without connection or proximity: by duplicating itself in a mirror the world abolishes the distance proper to it; in this way it overcomes the place alloted to each thing. But which of these reflections coursing through space are the original images? Which is the reality and which the projection? It is often not possible to say, for emulation is a sort of natural twinship existing in

19

things; it arises from a fold in being, the two sides of which stand immediately opposite to one another. Paracelsus compares this fundamental duplication of the world to the image of two twins 'who resemble one another completely, without its being possible for anyone to say which of them brought its similitude to the other'[7].

However, emulation does not leave the two reflected figures it has confronted in a merely inert state of opposition. One may be weaker, and therefore receptive to the stronger influence of the other, which is thus reflected in his passive mirror. Are not the stars, for example, dominant over the plants of the earth, of which they are the unchanged model, the unalterable form, and over which they have been secretly empowered to pour the whole dynasty of their influences? The dark earth is the mirror of the star-sown sky, but the two rivals are neither of equal value nor of equal dignity in that tournament. The bright colours of the flowers reproduce, without violence, the pure form of the sky. As Crollius says:

> The stars are the matrix of all the plants and every star in the sky is only the spiritual prefiguration of a plant, such that it represents that plant, and just as each herb or plant is a terrestrial star looking up at the sky, so also each star is a celestial plant in spiritual form, which differs from the terrestrial plants in matter alone . . . , the celestial plants and herbs are turned towards the earth and look directly down upon the plants they have procreated, imbuing them with some particular virtue[8].

But the lists may remain open, and the untroubled mirror reflect only the image of 'two wrathful soldiers'. Similitude then becomes the combat of one form against another – or rather of one and the same form separated from itself by the weight of matter or distance in space. Man as Paracelsus describes him is, like the firmament, 'constellated with stars', but he is not bound to it like 'the thief to his galley-oar, the murderer to the wheel, the fish to the fisherman, the quarry to the huntsman'. It pertains to the firmament of man to be 'free and powerful', to 'bow to no order', and 'not to be ruled by any other created beings'. His inner sky may remain autonomous and depend only upon itself, but on condition that by means of his wisdom, which is also knowledge, he comes to resemble the order of the world, takes it back into himself and thus recreates in his inner firmament the sway of that other firmament in which he sees the glitter of the visible stars. If he does this, then the wisdom of the mirror will in turn be reflected back to envelop the world in which it has been placed; its great ring will spin out into the depths of the heavens, and beyond; man will discover that he contains 'the stars within himself . . . , and that he is thus the bearer of the firmament with all its influences' [9].

Emulation is posited in the first place in the form of a mere reflection, furtive and distant; it traverses the spaces of the universe in silence. But the distance it crosses is not annulled by the subtle metaphor of emulation; it remains open to the eye. And in this duel, the two confronting figures seize upon one another. Like envelops like, which in turn surrounds the other, perhaps to be enveloped once more in a duplication which can continue *ad infinitum*. The links of emulation, unlike the elements of *convenientia*, do not form a chain but rather a series of concentric circles reflecting and rivalling one another.

The third form of similitude is *analogy*. An old concept already familiar to Greek science and medieval thought, but one whose use has probably become different now. In this analogy, *convenientia* and *aemulatio* are superimposed. Like the latter, it makes possible the marvellous confrontation of resemblances across space; but it also speaks, like the former, of adjacencies, of bonds and joints. Its power is immense, for the similitudes of which it treats are not the visible, substantial ones between things themselves; they need only be the more subtle resemblances of relations. Disencumbered thus, it can extend, from a single given point, to an endless number of relationships. For example, the relation of the stars to the sky in which they shine may also be found: between plants and the earth, between living beings and the globe they inhabit, between minerals such as diamonds and the rocks in which they are buried, between sense organs and the face they animate, between skin moles and the body of which they are the secret marks. An analogy may also be turned around upon itself without thereby rendering itself open to dispute. The old analogy of plant to animal (the vegetable is an animal living head down, its mouth – or roots – buried in the earth), is neither criticized nor disposed of by Cesalpino; on the contrary, he gives it added force, he multiplies it by itself when he makes the discovery that a plant is an upright animal, whose nutritive principles rise from the base up to the summit, channelled along a stem that stretches upwards like a body and is topped by a head – spreading flowers and leaves: a relation that inverts but does not contradict the initial analogy, since it places 'the root in the lower part of the plant and the stem in the upper part, for the venous network in animals also begins in the lower part of the belly, and the principal vein rises up to the heart and head' [10].

This reversibility and this polyvalency endow analogy with a universal field of application. Through it, all the figures in the whole universe can be drawn together. There does exist, however, in this space, furrowed in every direction, one particularly privileged point: it is saturated with analogies (all analogies can find one of their necessary terms there), and as they pass through it, their relations may be inverted without losing any of their force. This point is man: he stands in proportion to the heavens, just as he does to animals and plants, and as he does also to the earth, to metals, to stalactites or storms. Upright between the surfaces of the universe, he stands in relation to the firmament (his face is to his body what the face of heaven is to the ether; his pulse beats in his veins as the stars circle the sky according to their own fixed paths; the seven orifices in his head are to his face what the seven planets are to the sky); but he is also the fulcrum upon which all these relations turn, so that we find them again, their similarity unimpaired, in the analogy of the human animal to the earth it inhabits: his flesh is a glebe, his bones are rocks, his veins great rivers, his bladder is the sea, and his seven principal organs are the metals hidden in the shafts of mines[11]. Man's body is always the possible half of a universal atlas. It is well known how Pierre Belon drew, and drew in the greatest detail, the first comparative illustration of the human skeleton and that of birds: in it, we see

> the pinion called the appendix which is in proportion to the wing and in the same place as the thumb on the hand; the extremity of the pinion which is like the fingers in us . . . ; the bone given as legs to the bird corresponding to our heel; just as we have four toes on our feet, so the birds have four fingers of which the one behind is proportionate to the big toe in us[12].

So much precision is not, however, comparative anatomy except to an eye armed with nineteenth-century knowledge. It is merely that the grid through which we permit the figures of resemblance to enter our knowledge happens to coincide at this point (and at almost no other) with that which sixteenth-century learning had laid over things.

In fact, Belon's description has no connection with anything but the positivity which, in his day, made it possible. It is neither more rational nor more scientific than an observation such as Aldrovandi's comparison of man's baser parts to the fouler parts of the world, to Hell, to the darkness of Hell, to the damned souls who are like the excrement of the Universe[13]; it belongs to the same analogical cosmography as the comparison, classic in Crollius's time, between apoplexy and tempests: the storm begins when the air becomes heavy and agitated, the apoplectic attack at the moment when our thoughts become heavy and disturbed; then the clouds pile up, the belly swells, the thunder explodes and the bladder bursts; the lightning flashes and the eyes glitter with a terrible brightness, the rain falls, the mouth foams, the thunderbolt is unleashed and the spirits burst open breaches in the skin; but then the sky becomes clear again, and in the sick man reason regains ascendancy[14]. The space occupied by analogies is really a space of radiation. Man is surrounded by it on every side; but, inversely, he transmits these resemblances back into the world from which he receives them. He is the great fulcrum of proportions – the centre upon which relations are concentrated and from which they are once again reflected.

Lastly, the fourth form of resemblance is provided by the play of *sympathies*. And here, no path has been determined in advance, no distance laid down, no links prescribed. Sympathy plays through the depths of the universe in a free state. It can traverse the vastest spaces in an instant: it falls like a thunderbolt from the distant planet upon the man ruled by that planet; on the other hand, it can be brought into being by a simple contact – as with those 'mourning roses that have been used at obsequies' which, simply from their former adjacency with death, will render all persons who smell them 'sad and moribund'[15]. But such is its power that sympathy is not content to spring from a single contact and speed through space; it excites the things of the world to movement and can draw even the most distant of them together. It is a principle of mobility: it attracts what is heavy to the heaviness of the earth, what is light up towards the weightless ether; it drives the root towards the water, and it makes the great yellow disk of the sunflower turn to follow the curving path of the sun. Moreover, by drawing things towards one another in an exterior and visible movement, it also gives rise to a hidden interior movement – a displacement of qualities that take over from one another in a series of relays: fire, because it is warm and light, rises up into the air, towards which its flames untiringly strive; but in doing so it loses its dryness (which made it akin to the earth) and so acquires humidity (which links it to water and air); it disappears therefore into light vapour, into blue smoke, into clouds: it has become air. Sympathy is an instance of the *Same* so strong and so insistent that it will not rest content to be merely one of the forms of likeness; it has the dangerous power of *assimilating*, of rendering things identical to one another, of mingling them, of causing their individuality to disappear – and thus of rendering them foreign to what they were before. Sympathy transforms. It alters, but in the direction of identity, so that if its power were not counterbalanced it would reduce the world to a point, to a homogeneous mass, to the featureless form of the Same: all its parts would hold together and communicate with one another without a break, with no distance between them, like those metal chains held suspended by sympathy to the attraction of a single magnet[16].

This is why sympathy is compensated for by its twin, antipathy. Antipathy maintains the isolation of things and prevents their assimilation; it encloses every species within its impenetrable difference and its propensity to continue being what it is:

> It is fairly widely known that the plants have hatreds between themselves . . . it is said that the olive and the vine hate the cabbage; the cucumber flies from the olive . . . Since they grow by means of the sun's warmth and the earth's humour, it is inevitable that any thick and opaque tree should be pernicious to the others, and also the tree that has several roots[17].

And so to infinity, through all time, the world's beings will hate one another and preserve their ferocious appetites in opposition to all sympathy.

> The rat of India is pernicious to the crocodile, since Nature has created them enemies; in such wise that when that violent reptile takes his pleasure in the sun, the rat lays an ambush for it of mortal subtlety; perceiving that the crocodile, lying unaware for delight, is sleeping with its jaws agape, it makes its way through them and slips down the wide throat into the crocodile's belly, gnawing through the entrails of which, it emerges at last from the slain beast's bowel.

But the rat's enemies are lying in wait for it in their turn: for it lives in discord with the spider, and 'battling with the aspic it oft so dies'. Through this play of antipathy, which disperses them, yet draws them with equal force into mutual combat, makes them into murderers and then exposes them to death in their turn, things and animals and all the forms of the world remain what they are.

The identity of things, the fact that they can resemble others and be drawn to them, though without being swallowed up or losing their singularity – this is what is assured by the constant counterbalancing of

sympathy and antipathy. It explains how things grow, develop, intermingle, disappear, die, yet endlessly find themselves again; in short, how
there can be space (which is nevertheless not without landmarks or repetitions, not without havens of similitude) and time (which nevertheless
allows the same forms, the same species, the same elements to reappear
indefinitely).

> Though yet of themselves the four bodies (water, air, fire, earth) be
> simple and possessed of their distinct qualities, yet forasmuch as the
> Creator has ordained that the elementary bodies shall be composed of
> mingled elements, therefore are their harmonies and discordancies
> remarkable, as we may know from their qualities. The element of fire
> is hot and dry; it has therefore an antipathy to those of water, which is
> cold and damp. Hot air is humid, cold earth is dry, which is an antipathy.
> That they may be brought into harmony, air has been placed between
> fire and water, water between earth and air. Inasmuch as the air is hot,
> it marches well with fire and its humidity goes well with that of water.
> The humidity of water is heated by the heat of the air and brings relief
> to the cold dryness of the earth[18].

Because of the movement and the dispersion created by its laws, the
sovereignty of the sympathy–antipathy pair gives rise to all the forms of
resemblance. The first three similitudes are thus all resumed and explained
by it. The whole volume of the world, all the adjacencies of 'convenience',
all the echoes of emulation, all the linkages of analogy, are supported,
maintained, and doubled by this space governed by sympathy and
antipathy, which are ceaselessly drawing things together and holding
them apart. By means of this interplay, the world remains identical; resemblances continue to be what they are, and to resemble one another.
The same remains the same, riveted onto itself.

II SIGNATURES

And yet the system is not closed. One aperture remains: and through it
the whole interplay of resemblances would be in danger of escaping
from itself, or of remaining hidden in darkness, if there were not a further
form of similitude to close the circle – to render it at once perfect and
manifest.

Convenientia, aemulatio, analogy, and *sympathy* tell us how the world
must fold in upon itself, duplicate itself, reflect itself, or form a chain with

itself so that things can resemble one another. They tell us what the paths of similitude are and the directions they take; but not where it is, how one sees it, or by what mark it may be recognized. Now there is a possibility that we might make our way through all this marvellous teeming abundance of resemblances without even suspecting that it has long been prepared by the order of the world, for our greater benefit. In order that we may know that aconite will cure our eye disease, or that ground walnut mixed with spirits of wine will ease a headache, there must of course be some mark that will make us aware of these things: otherwise, the secret would remain indefinitely dormant. Would we ever know that there is a relation of twinship or rivalry between a man and his planet, if there were no sign upon his body or among the wrinkles on his face that he is an emulator of Mars or akin to Saturn? These buried similitudes must be indicated on the surface of things; there must be visible marks for the invisible analogies. Is not any resemblance, after all, both the most obvious and the most hidden of things? Because it is not made up of juxtaposed fragments, some identical and others different, it is all of a piece, a similitude that can be seen and yet not seen. It would thus lack any criterion if it did not have within it – or above it or beside it – a decisive element to transform its uncertain glimmer into bright certainty.

There are no resemblances without signatures. The world of similarity can only be a world of signs. Paracelsus says:

It is not God's will that what he creates for man's benefit and what he has given us should remain hidden . . . And even though he has hidden certain things, he has allowed nothing to remain without exterior and visible signs in the form of special marks – just as a man who has buried a hoard of treasure marks the spot that he may find it again[19].

A knowledge of similitudes is founded upon the unearthing and decipherment of these signatures. It is useless to go no further than the skin or bark of plants if you wish to know their nature; you must go straight to their marks – 'to the shadow and image of God that they bear or to their internal virtue, which has been given to them by heaven as a natural dowry, . . . a virtue, I say, that is to be recognized rather by its signature'[20]. The system of signatures reverses the relation of the visible to the invisible. Resemblance was the invisible form of that which, from the depths of the world, made things visible; but in order that this form may be brought out into the light in its turn there must be a visible figure that will draw it out from its profound invisibility. This is why

26

the face of the world is covered with blazons, with characters, with ciphers and obscure words – with 'hieroglyphics', as Turner called them. And the space inhabited by immediate resemblances becomes like a vast open book; it bristles with written signs; every page is seen to be filled with strange figures that intertwine and in some places repeat themselves. All that remains is to decipher them: 'Is it not true that all herbs, plants, trees and other things issuing from the bowels of the earth are so many magic books and signs?'[21] The great untroubled mirror in whose depths things gazed at themselves and reflected their own images back to one another is, in reality, filled with the murmur of words. The mute reflections all have corresponding words which indicate them. And by the grace of one final form of resemblance, which envelops all the others and encloses them within a single circle, the world may be compared to a man with the power of speech:

> Just as the secret movements of his understanding are manifested by his voice, so it would seem that the herbs speak to the curious physician through their signatures, discovering to him . . . their inner virtues hidden beneath nature's veil of silence[22].

But we must pause a little here to examine this language itself. To examine the signs of which it is made up and the way in which these signs refer back to what they indicate.

There exists a sympathy between aconite and our eyes. This unexpected affinity would remain in obscurity if there were not some signature on the plant, some mark, some word, as it were, telling us that it is good for diseases of the eye. This sign is easily legible in its seeds: they are tiny dark globes set in white skinlike coverings whose appearance is much like that of eyelids covering an eye[23]. It is the same with the affinity of the walnut and the human head: what cures 'wounds of the pericranium' is the thick green rind covering the bones – the shell – of the fruit; but internal head ailments may be prevented by use of the nut itself 'which is exactly like the brain in appearance'[24]. The sign of affinity, and what renders it visible, is quite simply analogy; the cipher of sympathy resides in the proportion.

But what signature can the proportion itself bear in order to make itself recognizable? How is one to know that the lines of a hand or the furrows on a brow are tracing on a man's body the tendencies, accidents, or obstacles present in the whole vast fabric of his life? How indeed, if not because we know that sympathy creates communication between our bodies and the heavens, and transmits the movement of the planets to the affairs of men. And if not, too, because the shortness of a line reflects the simple image of a short life, the intersection of two furrows an obstacle in one's path, the upward direction of a wrinkle a man's rise to success. Breadth is a sign of wealth and importance; continuity denotes good fortune, discontinuity ill fortune[25]. The great analogy between body and destiny has its sign in the whole system of mirrors and attractions. It is sympathies and emulations that indicate analogies.

Emulation may be recognized by analogy: the eyes are stars because they spread light over our faces just as stars light up the darkness, and because blind people exist in the world like clairvoyants in the darkest of nights. It can also be recognized through *convenientia*: we have known, ever since the Greeks, that the strongest and bravest animals have large and well-developed extremities to their limbs, as though their strength had communicated itself to the most distant parts of their bodies. In the same way, man's face and hands must resemble the soul to which they are joined. The recognition of the most visible similitudes occurs, therefore, against a background of the discovery that things in general are 'convenient' among themselves. And if one then considers that conveniency is not always defined by actual localization, but that many beings separated in space are also 'convenient' (as with a disease and its remedy, man and his stars, or a plant and the soil it needs), then again a sign of their conveniency is essential. And what other sign is there that two things are linked to one another unless it is that they have a mutual attraction for each other, as do the sun and the sunflower, or water and a cucumber shoot, that there is an affinity and, as it were, a sympathy between them?

And so the circle is closed. Though it is apparent what a complicated system of duplications was necessary to achieve this. Resemblances require a signature, for none of them would ever become observable were it not legibly marked. But what are these signs? How, amid all the aspects of the world and so many interlacing forms, does one recognize that one is faced at any given moment with a character that should give one pause because it indicates a secret and essential resemblance? What form constitutes a sign and endows it with its particular value as a sign? – Resemblance does. It signifies exactly in so far as it resembles what it is indicating (that is, a similitude). But what it indicates is not the homology; for its distinct existence as a signature would then be indistinguishable from the face of which it is the sign; it is *another* resemblance, an adjacent similitude, one of another type which enables us to recognize the first, and which is revealed in its turn by a third. Every resemblance receives a signature; but this signature is no more than an intermediate form of the same resemblance. As a result, the totality of these marks, sliding over the great circle of similitudes, forms a second circle which would be an exact duplication of the first, point by point, were it not for that tiny degree of displacement which causes the sign of sympathy to reside in an analogy, that of analogy in emulation, that of emulation in convenience, which in turn requires the mark of sympathy for its recognition. The signature and what it denotes are of exactly the same nature; it is merely that they obey a different law of distribution; the pattern from which they are cut is the same.

The form making a sign and the form being signalized are resemblances, but they do not overlap. And it is in this respect that resemblance in sixteenth-century knowledge is without doubt the most universal thing there is: at the same time that which is most clearly visible, yet something that one must nevertheless search for, since it is also the most hidden; what determines the form of knowledge (for knowledge can only follow the paths of similitude), and what guarantees its wealth of content (for the moment one lifts aside the signs and looks at what they indicate, one allows Resemblance itself to emerge into the light of day and shine with its own inner light).

Let us call the totality of the learning and skills that enable one to make the signs speak and to discover their meaning, hermeneutics; let us call the totality of the learning and skills that enable one to distinguish the location of the signs, to define what constitutes them as signs, and to know how and by what laws they are linked, semiology: the sixteenth century superimposed hermeneutics and semiology in the form of similitude. To search for a meaning is to bring to light a resemblance. To search for the law governing signs is to discover the things that are alike. The grammar of beings is an exegesis of these things. And what the language they speak has to tell us is quite simply what the syntax is that binds them together. The nature of things, their coexistence, the way in which they are linked together and communicate is nothing other than their resemblance. And that resemblance is visible only in the network of signs that crosses the world from one end to the other. 'Nature' is trapped in the thin layer that holds semiology and hermeneutics one above the other; it is neither mysterious nor veiled, it offers itself to our cognition, which it sometimes leads astray, only in so far as this superimposition

29

necessarily includes a slight degree of non-coincidence between the resemblances. As a result, the grid is less easy to see through; its transparency is clouded over from the very first. A dark space appears which must be made progressively clearer. That space is where 'nature' resides, and it is what one must attempt to know. Everything would be manifest and immediately knowable if the hermeneutics of resemblance and the semiology of signatures coincided without the slightest parallax. But because the similitudes that form the graphics of the world are one 'cog' out of alignment with those that form its discourse, knowledge and the infinite labour it involves find here the space that is proper to them: it is their task to weave their way across this distance, pursuing an endless zigzag course from resemblance to what resembles it.

III THE LIMITS OF THE WORLD

Such, sketched in its most general aspects, is the sixteenth-century *episteme*. This configuration carries with it a certain number of consequences.

First and foremost, the plethoric yet absolutely poverty-stricken character of this knowledge. Plethoric because it is limitless. Resemblance never remains stable within itself; it can be fixed only if it refers back to another similitude, which then, in turn, refers to others; each resemblance, therefore, has value only from the accumulation of all the others, and the whole world must be explored if even the slightest of analogies is to be justified and finally take on the appearance of certainty. It is therefore a knowledge that can, and must, proceed by the infinite accumulation of confirmations all dependent on one another. And for this reason, from its very foundations, this knowledge will be a thing of sand. The only possible form of link between the elements of this knowledge is addition. Hence those immense columns of compilation, hence their monotony. By positing resemblance as the link between signs and what they indicate (thus making resemblance both a third force and a sole power, since it resides in both the mark and the content in identical fashion), sixteenth-century knowledge condemned itself to never knowing anything but the same thing, and to knowing that thing only at the unattainable end of an endless journey.

And it is here that we find that only too well-known category, the microcosm, coming into play. This ancient notion was no doubt revived, during the Middle Ages and at the beginning of the Renaissance, by a certain neo-Platonist tradition. But by the sixteenth century it had come to play a fundamental role in the field of knowledge. It hardly matters whether it was or was not, as was once claimed, a world view or *Weltanschauung*. The fact is that it had one, or rather two, precise functions in the epistemological configuration of this period. As a *category of thought*, it applies the interplay of duplicated resemblances to all the realms of nature; it provides all investigation with an assurance that everything will find its mirror and its macrocosmic justification on another and larger scale; it affirms, inversely, that the visible order of the highest spheres will be found reflected in the darkest depths of the earth. But, understood as a *general configuration* of nature, it poses real and, as it were, tangible limits to the indefatigable to-and-fro of similitudes relieving one another. It indicates that there exists a greater world, and that its perimeter defines the limit of all created things; that at the far extremity of this great world there exists a privileged creation which reproduces, within its restricted dimensions, the immense order of the heavens, the stars, the mountains, rivers, and storms; and that it is between the effective limits of this constituent analogy that the interplay of resemblances takes place. By this very fact, however immense the distance from microcosm to macrocosm may be, it cannot be infinite; the beings that reside within it may be extremely numerous, but in the end they can be counted; and, consequently, the similitudes that, through the action of the signs they require, always rest one upon another, can cease their endless flight. They have a perfectly closed domain to support and buttress them. Nature, like the interplay of signs and resemblances, is closed in upon itself in conformity with the duplicated form of the cosmos.

We must therefore be careful not to invert the relations here. There is no doubt that the idea of the microcosm was, as we say, 'important' in the sixteenth century; it would probably have been one of the most frequently mentioned terms in the results of any poll taken at the time. But we are not concerned here with a study of opinions, which could be undertaken only by a statistical analysis of contemporary records. If, on the other hand, one investigates sixteenth-century knowledge at its archaeological level – that is, at the level of what made it possible – then the relations of macrocosm and microcosm appear as a mere surface effect. It was not because people believed in such relations that they set about trying to hunt down all the analogies in the world. But there was a necessity lying at the heart of their knowledge: they had to find an adjustment between the infinite richness of a resemblance introduced as a third term between signs and their meaning, and the monotony that imposed the same pattern of resemblance upon the sign and what it signified. In an *episteme* in which signs and similitudes were wrapped around one another in an endless spiral, it was essential that the relation of microcosm to macrocosm should be conceived as both the guarantee of that knowledge and the limit of its expansion.

It was this same necessity that obliged knowledge to accept magic and erudition on the same level. To us, it seems that sixteenth-century learning was made up of an unstable mixture of rational knowledge, notions derived from magical practices, and a whole cultural heritage whose power and authority had been vastly increased by the rediscovery of Greek and Roman authors. Perceived thus, the learning of that period appears structurally weak: a common ground where fidelity to the Ancients, a taste for the supernatural, and an already awakened awareness of that sovereign rationality in which we recognize ourselves, confronted one another in equal freedom. And this tripartite period would consequently be reflected in the mirror of each work and each divided mind occurring within it. . . . In fact, it is not from an insufficiency of structure that sixteenth-century knowledge suffers. On the contrary, we have already seen how very meticulous the configurations are that define its space. It is this very rigour that makes the relation of magic to erudition inevitable – they are not selected contents but required forms. The world is covered with signs that must be deciphered, and those signs, which reveal resemblances and affinities, are themselves no more than forms of similitude. To know must therefore be to interpret: to find a way from the visible mark to that which is being said by it and which, without that mark, would lie like unspoken speech, dormant within things.

> But we men discover all that is hidden in the mountains by signs and outward correspondences; and it is thus that we find out all the properties of herbs and all that is in stones. There is nothing in the depths of the seas, nothing in the heights of the firmament that man is not capable of discovering. There is no mountain so vast that it can hide from the gaze of man what is within it; it is revealed to him by corresponding signs[26].

Divination is not a rival form of knowledge; it is part of the main body of knowledge itself. Moreover, these signs that must be interpreted indicate what is hidden only in so far as they resemble it; and it is not possible to act upon those marks without at the same time operating upon

32

that which is secretly indicated by them. This is why the plants that re-present the head, or the eyes, or the heart, or the liver, will possess an efficacity in regard to that organ; this is why the animals themselves will react to the marks that designate them. Paracelsus asks:

Tell me, then, why snakes in Helvetia, Algoria, Swedland understand the Greek words Osy, Osya, Osy . . . In what academies did they learn them, so that scarcely have they heard the word than they immediately turn tail in order not to hear it again? Scarcely do they hear the word when, notwithstanding their nature and their spirit, they remain im-mobile and poison no one with their venomous wounds.

And let no one say that this is merely the effect of the sound made by the words when pronounced: 'If you write these words alone on vellum, parchment or paper at a favourable time, then place them in front of the serpent, it will stay no less motionless than if you had pronounced them aloud.' The project of elucidating the 'Natural Magics', which occupies an important place at the end of the sixteenth century and survives into the middle of the seventeenth, is not a vestigial phenomenon in the European consciousness; it was revived – as Campanella expressly tells us[27] – and for contemporary reasons: because the fundamental con-figuration of knowledge consisted of the reciprocal cross-reference of signs and similitudes. The form of magic was inherent in this way of knowing.

And by the same token, so was erudition: for, in the treasure handed down to us by Antiquity, the value of language lay in the fact that it was the sign of things. There is no difference between the visible marks that God has stamped upon the surface of the earth, so that we may know its inner secrets, and the legible words that the Scriptures, or the sages of Antiquity, have set down in the books preserved for us by tradition. The relation to these texts is of the same nature as the relation to things: in both cases there are signs that must be discovered. But God, in order to exercise our wisdom, merely sowed nature with forms for us to decipher (and it is in this sense that knowledge should be *divinatio*), whereas the Ancients have already provided us with interpretations, which we need do no more than gather together. Or which we would need only to gather together, were it not for the necessity of learning their language, reading their texts, and understanding what they have said. The heritage of Antiquity, like nature itself, is a vast space requiring interpretation; in both cases there are signs to be discovered and then, little by little, made to speak. In other words, *divinatio* and *eruditio* are both part of the same hermeneutics; but this develops, following similar forms, on two different levels: one moves from the mute sign to the thing itself (and makes nature speak); the other moves from the unmoving graphism to clear speech (it restores sleeping languages to life). But just as natural signs are linked to what they indicate by the profound relation of resemblance, so the discourse of the Ancients is in the image of what it expresses; if it has the value of a precious sign, that is because, from the depth of its being, and by means of the light that has never ceased to shine through it since its origin, it is adjusted to things themselves, it forms a mirror for them and emulates them; it is to eternal truth what signs are to the secrets of nature (it is the mark whereby the word may be deciphered); and it possesses an ageless affinity with the things that it unveils. It is useless therefore to demand its title to authority; it is a treasury of signs linked by similitude to that which they are empowered to denote. The only difference is that we are dealing with a treasure-hoard of the second degree, one that refers to the notations of nature, which in their turn indicate obscurely the pure gold of things themselves. The truth of all these marks – whether they are woven into nature itself or whether they exist in lines on parchments and in libraries – is everywhere the same: coeval with the institution of God.

There is no difference between marks and words in the sense that there is between observation and accepted authority, or between verifiable fact and tradition. The process is everywhere the same: that of the sign and its likeness, and this is why nature and the word can intertwine with one another to infinity, forming, for those who can read it, one vast single text.

IV THE WRITING OF THINGS

In the sixteenth century, real language is not a totality of independent signs, a uniform and unbroken entity in which things could be reflected one by one, as in a mirror, and so express their particular truths. It is rather an opaque, mysterious thing, closed in upon itself, a fragmented mass, its enigma renewed in every interval, which combines here and there with the forms of the world and becomes interwoven with them: so much so that all these elements, taken together, form a network of marks in which each of them may play, and does in fact play, in relation to all the others, the role of content or of sign, that of secret or of indicator.

In its raw, historical sixteenth-century being, language is not an arbitrary system; it has been set down in the world and forms a part of it, both because things themselves hide and manifest their own enigma like a language and because words offer themselves to men as things to be deciphered. The great metaphor of the book that one opens, that one pores over and reads in order to know nature, is merely the reverse and visible side of another transference, and a much deeper one, which forces language to reside in the world, among the plants, the herbs, the stones, and the animals.

Language partakes in the world-wide dissemination of similitudes and signatures. It must, therefore, be studied itself as a thing in nature. Like animals, plants, or stars, its elements have their laws of affinity and convenience, their necessary analogies. Ramus divided his grammar into two parts. The first was devoted to etymology, which means that one looked in it to discover, not the original meanings of words, but the intrinsic 'properties' of letters, syllables, and, finally, whole words. The second part dealt with syntax: its purpose was to teach 'the building of words together by means of their properties', and it consisted 'almost entirely in the convenience and mutual communion of properties, as of the noun with the noun or with the verb, of the adverb with all the words to which it is adjoined, of the conjunction in the order of things conjoined'[28]. Language is not what it is because it has a meaning; its representative content, which was to have such importance for grammarians of the seventeenth and eighteenth centuries that it provided them with the guiding thread of their analyses, has no role to play here. Words group syllables together, and syllables letters, because there are virtues placed in individual letters that draw them towards each other or keep them apart, exactly as the marks found in nature also repel or attract one another. The study of grammar in the sixteenth century is based upon the same epistemological arrangement as the science of nature or the esoteric disciplines. The only differences are that there is only one nature and there are several languages; and that in the esoteric field the properties of words, syllables, and letters are discovered by another discourse which always remains secret, whereas in grammar it is the words and phrases of everyday life that themselves express their properties. Language stands halfway between the visible forms of nature and the secret conveniences of esoteric discourse. It is a fragmented nature, divided against itself and deprived of its original transparency by admixture; it is a secret that carries within itself, though near the surface, the decipherable signs of what it is trying to say. It is at the same time a buried revelation and a revelation that is gradually being restored to ever greater clarity.

In its original form, when it was given to men by God himself, language was an absolutely certain and transparent sign for things, because it resembled them. The names of things were lodged in the things they designated, just as strength is written in the body of the lion, regality in the eye of the eagle, just as the influence of the planets is marked upon the brows of men: by the form of similitude. This transparency was destroyed at Babel as a punishment for men. Languages became separated and incompatible with one another only in so far as they had previously lost this original resemblance to the things that had been the prime reason for the existence of language. All the languages known to us are now spoken only against the background of this lost similitude, and in the space that it left vacant. There is only one language that retains a memory of that similitude, because it derives in direct descent from that first vocabulary which is now forgotten; because God did not wish men to forget the punishment inflicted at Babel; because this language had to be used in order to recount God's ancient Alliance with his people; and lastly, because it was in this language that God addressed himself to those who listened to him. Hebrew therefore contains, as if in the form of fragments, the marks of that original name-giving. And those words pronounced by Adam as he imposed them upon the various animals have endured, in part at least, and still carry with them in their density, like an embedded fragment of silent knowledge, the unchanging properties of beings:

> Thus the stork, so greatly lauded for its charity towards its father and its mother, is called in Hebrew *Chasida*, which is to say, meek, charitable, endowed with pity . . . The horse is named *Sus*, thought to be from the verb *Hasas*, unless that verb is rather derived from the noun, and it signifies to rise up, for among all four-footed animals the horse is most proud and brave, as Job depicts it in Chapter 39[29].

But these are no more than fragmentary monuments; all other languages have lost these radical similitudes, which have been preserved in Hebrew only in order to show that it was once the common language of God, Adam, and the animals of the newly created earth.

But though language no longer bears an immediate resemblance to the things it names, this does not mean that it is separate from the world; it still continues, in another form, to be the locus of revelations and to be included in the area where truth is both manifested and expressed. True, it is no longer nature in its primal visibility, but neither is it a mysterious instrument with powers known only to a few privileged persons. It is rather the figuration of a world redeeming itself, lending its ear at last to the true word. This is why it was God's wish that Latin, the language of his Church, should spread over the whole of the terrestrial globe. And it is also why all the languages of the world, as it became possible to know them through this conquest, make up together the image of the truth. Their interlacing and the space in which they are deployed free the sign of the redeemed world, just as the arrangement of the first names bore a likeness to the things that God had given to Adam for his use. Claude Duret points out that the Hebrews, the Canaans, the Samaritans, the Chaldeans, the Syrians, the Egyptians, the Carthaginians, the Phoenicians, the Arabs, the Saracens, the Turks, the Moors, the Persians, and the Tartars all write from right to left, following 'the course and daily movement of the first heaven, which is most perfect, according to the opinion of the great Aristotle, tending towards unity'; the Greeks, the Georgians, the Maronites, the Serbians, the Jacobites, the Copts, the Poznanians, and of course the Romans and all Europeans write from left to right, following 'the course and movement of the second heaven, home of the seven planets'; the Indians, Cathayans, Chinese, and Japanese write from top to bottom, in conformity with the 'order of nature, which has given men heads at the tops of their bodies and feet at the bottom'; 'in opposition to the aforementioned', the Mexicans write either from bottom to top or else in 'spiral lines, such as those made by the sun in its annual journey through the Zodiac'. And thus 'by these five diverse sorts of writing the secrets and mysteries of the world's frame and the form of the cross, the unity of the heaven's rotundity and that of the earth, are properly denoted and expressed'[30]. The relation of languages to the world is one of analogy rather than of signification; or rather, their value as signs and their duplicating function are superimposed; they speak the heaven and the earth of which they are the image; they reproduce in their most material architecture the cross whose coming they announce – that coming which establishes its existence in its own turn through the Scriptures and the Word. Language possesses a symbolic function; but since the disaster at Babel we must no longer seek for it – with rare exceptions[31] – in the words themselves but rather in the very existence of language, in its total relation to the totality of the world, in the intersecting of its space with the loci and forms of the cosmos.

Hence the form of the encyclopaedic project as it appears at the end of the sixteenth century or in the first years of the seventeenth: not to reflect what one knows in the neutral element of language – the use of the alphabet as an arbitrary but efficacious encyclopaedic order does not appear until the second half of the seventeenth century[32] – but to reconstitute the very order of the universe by the way in which words are linked together and arranged in space. It is this project that we find in Grégoire's *Syntaxeon artis mirabilis* (1610), and in Alstedius's *Encyclopaedia* (1630); or again in the *Tableau de tous les arts libéraux* by Christophe de Savigny, who contrives to spatialize acquired knowledge both in accordance with the cosmic, unchanging, and perfect form of the circle and in accordance with the sublunary, perishable, multiple, and divided form of the tree; it is also to be found in the work of La Croix du Maine, who envisages a space that would be at once an Encyclopaedia and a Library, and would permit the arrangement of written texts according to the forms of adjacency, kinship, analogy, and subordination prescribed by the world itself[33]. But in any case, such an interweaving of language and things, in a space common to both, presupposes an absolute privilege on the part of writing.

This privilege dominated the entire Renaissance, and was no doubt one of the great events in Western culture. Printing, the arrival in Europe of Oriental manuscripts, the appearance of a literature no longer created for the voice or performance and therefore not governed by them, the precedence given to the interpretation of religious texts over the tradition and magisterium of the Church – all these things bear witness, without its being possible to indicate causes and effects, to the fundamental place accorded in the West to Writing. Henceforth, it is the primal nature of language to be written. The sounds made by voices provide no more than a transitory and precarious translation of it. What God introduced into the world was written words; Adam, when he imposed their first names upon the animals, did no more than read those visible and silent marks; the Law was entrusted to the Tables, not to men's memories; and it is in a book that the true Word must be found again. Vigenère and Duret[34] both said – and in almost identical terms – that the written had always preceded the spoken, certainly in nature, and perhaps even in the knowledge of men. For it was very possible that before Babel, before the Flood, there had already existed a form of writing composed of the marks of nature itself, with the result that its characters would have had the power to act upon things directly, to attract them or repel them, to represent their properties, their virtues, and their secrets. A primitively natural writing, of which certain forms of esoteric knowledge, and the cabala first and foremost, may perhaps have preserved the scattered memory and were now attempting to retrieve its long-dormant powers. Esoterism in the sixteenth century is a phenomenon of the written word, not the spoken word. At all events, the latter is stripped of all its powers; it is merely the female part of language, Vigenère and Duret tell us, just as its intellect is passive; Writing, on the other hand, is the active intellect, the 'male principle' of language. It alone harbours the truth.

This primacy of the written word explains the twin presence of two forms which, despite their apparent antagonism, are indissociable in sixteenth-century knowledge. The first of these is a non-distinction between what is seen and what is read, between observation and relation, which results in the constitution of a single, unbroken surface in which observation and language intersect to infinity. And the second, the inverse of the first, is an immediate dissociation of all language, duplicated, without any assignable term, by the constant reiteration of commentary.

Later, Buffon was to express astonishment at finding in the work of a naturalist like Aldrovandi such an inextricable mixture of exact descriptions, reported quotations, fables without commentary, remarks dealing indifferently with an animal's anatomy, its use in heraldry, its habitat, its mythological values, or the uses to which it could be put in medicine or magic. And indeed, when one goes back to take a look at the *Historia serpentum et draconum*, one finds the chapter 'On the serpent in general' arranged under the following headings: equivocation (which means the various meanings of the word *serpent*), synonyms and etymologies, differences, form and description, anatomy, nature and habits, temperament, coitus and generation, voice, movements, places, diet, physiognomy, antipathy, sympathy, modes of capture, death and wounds caused by the serpent, modes and signs of poisoning, remedies, epithets, denominations, prodigies and presages, monsters, mythology, gods to which it is dedicated, fables, allegories and mysteries, hieroglyphics, emblems and symbols, proverbs, coinage, miracles, riddles, devices, heraldic signs, historical facts, dreams, simulacra and statues, use in human diet, use in medicine, miscellaneous uses. Whereupon Buffon comments: 'Let it be judged after that what proportion of natural history is to be found in such a hotch-potch of writing. There is no description here, only legend.' And indeed, for Aldrovandi and his contemporaries, it was all *legenda* – things to be read. But the reason for this was not that they preferred the authority of men to the precision of an unprejudiced eye, but that nature,

in itself, is an unbroken tissue of words and signs, of accounts and characters, of discourse and forms. When one is faced with the task of writing an
animal's *history*, it is useless and impossible to choose between the profes-
sion of naturalist and that of compiler: one has to collect together into
one and the same form of knowledge all that has been *seen* and *heard*,
all that has been *recounted*, either by nature or by men, by the language
of the world, by tradition, or by the poets. To know an animal or a plant,
or any terrestrial thing whatever, is to gather together the whole dense
layer of signs with which it or they may have been covered; it is to rediscover also all the constellations of forms from which they derive their
value as heraldic signs. Aldrovandi was neither a better nor a worse observer
than Buffon; he was neither more credulous than he, nor less attached to
the faithfulness of the observing eye or to the rationality of things. His
observation was simply not linked to things in accordance with the same
system or by the same arrangement of the *episteme*. For Aldrovandi was
meticulously contemplating a nature which was, from top to bottom,
written.

Knowledge therefore consisted in relating one form of language to
another form of language; in restoring the great, unbroken plain of words
and things; in making everything speak. That is, in bringing into being,
at a level above that of all marks, the secondary discourse of commentary.
The function proper to knowledge is not seeing or demonstrating; it is
interpreting. Scriptural commentary, commentaries on Ancient authors,
commentaries on the accounts of travellers, commentaries on legends
and fables: none of these forms of discourse is required to justify its claim
to be expressing a truth before it is interpreted; all that is required of it is
the possibility of talking about it. Language contains its own inner principle of proliferation. 'There is more work in interpreting interpretations
than in interpreting things; and more books about books than on any
other subject; we do nothing but write glosses on one another'[35].
These words are not a statement of the bankruptcy of a culture buried
beneath its own monuments; they are a definition of the inevitable relation that language maintained with itself in the sixteenth century. This
relation enabled language to accumulate to infinity, since it never ceased
to develop, to revise itself, and to lay its successive forms one over
another. Perhaps for the first time in Western culture, we find revealed
the absolutely open dimension of a language no longer able to halt itself,
because, never being enclosed in a definitive statement, it can express its
truth only in some future discourse and is wholly intent on what it will

have said; but even this future discourse itself does not have the power to halt the progression, and what it says is enclosed within it like a promise, a bequest to yet another discourse. . . . The task of commentary can never, by definition, be completed. And yet commentary is directed entirely towards the enigmatic, murmured element of the language being commented on: it calls into being, below the existing discourse, another discourse that is more fundamental and, as it were, 'more primal', which it sets itself the task of restoring. There can be no commentary unless, below the language one is reading and deciphering, there runs the sovereignty of an original Text. And it is this text which, by providing a foundation for the commentary, offers its ultimate revelation as the promised reward of commentary. The necessary proliferation of the exegesis is therefore measured, ideally limited, and yet ceaselessly animated, by this silent dominion. The language of the sixteenth century – understood not as an episode in the history of any one tongue, but as a global cultural experience – found itself caught, no doubt, between these interacting elements, in the interstice occurring between the primal Text and the infinity of Interpretation. One speaks upon the basis of a writing that is part of the fabric of the world; one speaks about it to infinity, and each of its signs becomes in turn written matter for further discourse; but each of these stages of discourse is addressed to that primal written word whose return it simultaneously promises and postpones.

It will be seen that the experience of language belongs to the same archaeological network as the knowledge of things and nature. To know those things was to bring to light the system of resemblances that made them close to and dependent upon one another; but one could discover the similitudes between them only in so far as there existed, on their surface, a totality of signs forming the text of an unequivocal message. But then, these signs themselves were no more than a play of resemblances, and they referred back to the infinite and necessarily uncompleted task of knowing what is similar. In the same way, though the analogy is inverted, language sets itself the task of restoring an absolutely primal discourse, but it can express that discourse only by trying to approximate to it, by attempting to say things about it that are similar to it, thereby bringing into existence the infinity of adjacent and similar fidelities of interpretation. The commentary resembles endlessly that which it is commenting upon and which it can never express; just as the knowledge of nature constantly finds new signs for resemblance because resemblance cannot be known in itself, even though the signs can never be anything but similitudes. And just as this infinite play within nature finds its link, its form, and its limitation in the relation of the microcosm to the macrocosm, so does the infinite task of commentary derive its strength from the promise of an effectively written text which interpretation will one day reveal in its entirety.

V THE BEING OF LANGUAGE

Ever since the Stoics, the system of signs in the Western world had been a ternary one, for it was recognized as containing the significant, the signified, and the 'conjuncture' (the τύγχανον). From the seventeenth century, on the other hand, the arrangement of signs was to become binary, since it was to be defined, with Port-Royal, as the connection of a significant and a signified. At the Renaissance, the organization is different, and much more complex: it is ternary, since it requires the formal domain of marks, the content indicated by them, and the similitudes that link the marks to the things designated by them; but since resemblance is the form of the signs as well as their content, the three distinct elements of this articulation are resolved into a single form.

This arrangement, together with the interplay it authorizes, is found also, though inverted, in the experience of language. In fact, language exists first of all, in its raw and primitive being, in the simple, material form of writing, a stigma upon things, a mark imprinted across the world which is a part of its most ineffaceable forms. In a sense, this layer of language is unique and absolute. But it also gives rise to two other forms of discourse which provide it with a frame: above it, there is commentary, which recasts the given signs to serve a new purpose, and below it, the text, whose primacy is presupposed by commentary to exist hidden beneath the marks visible to all. Hence there are three levels of language, all based upon the single being of the written word. It is this complex interaction of elements that was to disappear with the end of the Renaissance. And in two ways: because the forms oscillating endlessly between one and three terms were to be fixed in a binary form which would render them stable; and because language, instead of existing as the material writing of things, was to find its area of being restricted to the general organization of representative signs.

This new arrangement brought about the appearance of a new problem, unknown until then: in the sixteenth century, one asked oneself how it was possible to know that a sign did in fact designate what it signified;

from the seventeenth century, one began to ask how a sign could be linked to what it signified. A question to which the Classical period was to reply by the analysis of representation; and to which modern thought was to reply by the analysis of meaning and signification. But given the fact itself, language was never to be anything more than a particular case of representation (for the Classics) or of signification (for us). The profound kinship of language with the world was thus dissolved. The primacy of the written word went into abeyance. And that uniform layer, in which the *seen* and the *read*, the visible and the expressible, were endlessly interwoven, vanished too. Things and words were to be separated from one another. The eye was thenceforth destined to see and only to see, the ear to hear and only to hear. Discourse was still to have the task of speaking that which is, but it was no longer to be anything more than what it said.

This involved an immense reorganization of culture, a reorganization of which the Classical age was the first and perhaps the most important stage, since it was responsible for the new arrangement in which we are still caught – since it is the Classical age that separates us from a culture in which the signification of signs did not exist, because it was reabsorbed into the sovereignty of the Like; but in which their enigmatic, monotonous, stubborn, and primitive being shone in an endless dispersion.

There is nothing now, either in our knowledge or in our reflection, that still recalls even the memory of that being. Nothing, except perhaps literature – and even then in a fashion more allusive and diagonal than direct. It may be said in a sense that 'literature', as it was constituted and so designated on the threshold of the modern age, manifests, at a time when it was least expected, the reappearance, of the living being of language. In the seventeenth and eighteenth centuries, the peculiar existence and ancient solidity of language as a thing inscribed in the fabric of the world were dissolved in the functioning of representation; all language had value only as discourse. The art of language was a way of 'making a sign' – of simultaneously signifying something and arranging signs around that thing; an art of naming, therefore, and then, by means of a reduplication both demonstrative and decorative, of capturing that name, of enclosing and concealing it, of designating it in turn by other names that were the deferred presence of the first name, its secondary sign, its figuration, its rhetorical panoply. And yet, throughout the nineteenth century, and right up to our own day – from Hölderlin to Mallarmé and on to Antonin Artaud – literature achieved autonomous existence, and

43

separated itself from all other language with a deep scission, only by forming a sort of 'counter-discourse', and by finding its way back from the representative or signifying function of language to this raw being that had been forgotten since the sixteenth century.

It is possible to believe that one has attained the very essence of literature when one is no longer interrogating it at the level of what it says but only in its significant form: in doing so, one is limiting one's view of language to its Classical status. In the modern age, literature is that which compensates for (and not that which confirms) the signifying function of language. Through literature, the being of language shines once more on the frontiers of Western culture – and at its centre – for it is what has been most foreign to that culture since the sixteenth century; but it has also, since this same century, been at the very centre of what Western culture has overlain. This is why literature is appearing more and more as that which must be thought; but equally, and for the same reason, as that which can never, in any circumstance, be thought in accordance with a theory of signification. Whether one analyses it from the point of view of what is signified (of what it is trying to say, of its 'ideas', of what it promises, or of what it commits one to) or from the point of view of that which signifies (with the help of paradigms borrowed from linguistics or psychoanalysis) matters little: all that is merely incidental. In both cases one would be searching for it outside the ground in which, as regards our culture, it has never ceased for the past century and a half to come into being and to imprint itself. Such modes of decipherment belong to a Classical situation of language – the situation that predominated during the seventeenth century, when the organization of signs became binary, and when signification was reflected in the form of the representation; for at that time literature really was composed of a signifying element and a signified content, so that it was proper to analyse it accordingly. But from the nineteenth century, literature began to bring language back to light once more in its own being: though not as it had still appeared at the end of the Renaissance. For now we no longer have that primary, that absolutely initial, word upon which the infinite movement of discourse was founded and by which it was limited; henceforth, language was to grow with no point of departure, no end, and no promise. It is the traversal of this futile yet fundamental space that the text of literature traces from day to day.

NOTES

[1] P. Grégoire, *Syntaxeon artis mirabilis* (Cologne, 1610, p. 28).

[2] G. Porta, *La Physionomie humaine* (Fr. trans. 1655, p. 1).

[3] U. Aldrovandi, *Monstrorum historia* (Bononiae, 1647, p. 663).

[4] T. Campanella, *Realis philosophia* (Frankfurt, 1623, p. 98).

[5] G. Porta, *Magie naturelle* (Fr. trans. Rouen, 1650, p. 22).

[6] Aldrovandi, *Monstrorum historia*, p. 3.

[7] Paracelsus, *Liber Paramirum* (trans. Grillot de Givry, Paris, 1913, p. 3).

[8] O. Crollius, *Traité des signatures* (Fr. trans. Lyon, 1624, p. 18).

[9] Paracelsus, loc. cit.

[10] Cesalpino, *De plantis libri*, XVI (1583).

[11] Crollius, *Traité des signatures*, p. 88.

[12] P. Belon, *Histoire de la nature des oiseaux* (Paris, 1555, p. 37).

[13] Aldrovandi, *Monstrorum historia*, p. 4.

[14] Crollius, *Traité des signatures*, p. 87.

[15] Porta, *Magie naturelle*, p. 72.

[16] Ibid.

[17] J. Cardan, *De la subtilité* (Fr. trans. Paris, 1656, p. 154).

[18] S.G.S. *Annotations au Grand Miroir du Monde de Duchesne*, p. 498.

[19] Paracelsus, *Die 9 Bücher der Natura Rerum* (*Works*, ed. Suhdorff, vol. IX, p. 393).

[20] Crollius, *Traité des signatures*, p. 4.

[21] Ibid., p. 6.

[22] Ibid., p. 6.

[23] Ibid., p. 33.

[24] Ibid., pp. 33-4.

[25] J. Cardan, *Métoposcopie* (1658 edn., pp. iii–viii).

[26] Paracelsus, *Archidoxis magica* (Fr. trans. 1909, pp. 21-3).

[27] T. Campanella, *De sensu rerum et magia* (Frankfurt, 1620).

[28] P. Ramus, *Grammaire* (Paris, 1572, p. 3 and pp. 125-6).

[29] Claude Duret, *Trésor de l'histoire des langues* (Cologne, 1613, p. 40).

[30] Duret, loc. cit.

[31] In *Mithridates*, J. M. Gesner cites onomatopeias of course, but only as exceptions to a rule (2nd edn., Tiguri, 1610, pp. 3-4).

[32] Except with regard to languages, since the alphabet is the raw material of language. Cf. Chapter II of Gesner's *Mithridates*. The first alphabetical encyclopaedia is L. Moréri's *Grand Dictionnaire historique* of 1674.

[33] La Croix du Maine, *Les cents Buffets pour dresser une bibliothèque parfaite* (1583).

[34] Blaise de Vigenère, *Traité des chiffres* (Paris, 1537, pp. 1 and 2); C. Duret, *Trésor de l'histoire des langues*, pp. 19 and 20.

[35] Montaigne, *Essais* (1580-8, livre III, chap. XIII).

CHAPTER 3

Representing

I DON QUIXOTE

With all their twists and turns, Don Quixote's adventures form the boundary: they mark the end of the old interplay between resemblance and signs and contain the beginnings of new relations. Don Quixote is not a man given to extravagance, but rather a diligent pilgrim breaking his journey before all the marks of similitude. He is the hero of the Same. He never manages to escape from the familiar plain stretching out on all sides of the Analogue, any more than he does from his own small province. He travels endlessly over that plain, without ever crossing the clearly defined frontiers of difference, or reaching the heart of identity. Moreover, he is himself like a sign, a long, thin graphism, a letter that has just escaped from the open pages of a book. His whole being is nothing but language, text, printed pages, stories that have already been written down. He is made up of interwoven words; he is writing itself, wandering through the world among the resemblances of things. Yet not entirely so: for in his reality as an impoverished hidalgo he can become a knight only by listening from afar to the age-old epic that gives its form to Law. The book is not so much his existence as his duty. He is constantly obliged to consult it in order to know what to do or say, and what signs he should give himself and others in order to show that he really is of the same nature as the text from which he springs. The chivalric romances have provided once and for all a written prescription for his adventures. And every episode, every decision, every exploit will be yet another sign that Don Quixote is a true likeness of all the signs that he has traced from his book. But the fact that he wishes to be like them means that he must put them to the test, that the (legible) signs no longer resemble (visible) people. All those written texts, all those extravagant romances are, quite literally, unparalleled: no one in the world ever did

46

resemble them; their timeless language remains suspended, unfulfilled by any similitude; they could all be burned in their entirety and the form of the world would not be changed. If he is to resemble the texts of which he is the witness, the representation, the real analogue, Don Quixote must also furnish proof and provide the indubitable sign that they are telling the truth, that they really are the language of the world. It is incumbent upon him to fulfil the promise of the books. It is his task to recreate the epic, though by a reverse process: the epic recounted (or claimed to re-count) real exploits, offering them to our memory; Don Quixote, on the other hand, must endow with reality the signs-without-content of the narrative. His adventures will be a deciphering of the world: a diligent search over the entire surface of the earth for the forms that will prove that what the books say is true. Each exploit must be a proof: it consists, not in a real triumph – which is why victory is not really important – but in an attempt to transform reality into a sign. Into a sign that the signs of language really are in conformity with things themselves. Don Quixote reads the world in order to prove his books. And the only proofs he gives himself are the glittering reflections of resemblances.

His whole journey is a quest for similitudes: the slightest analogies are pressed into service as dormant signs that must be reawakened and made to speak once more. Flocks, serving girls, and inns become once more the language of books to the imperceptible degree to which they resemble castles, ladies, and armies – a perpetually untenable resemblance which transforms the sought-for proof into derision and leaves the words of the books forever hollow. But non-similitude itself has its model, and one that it imitates in the most servile way: it is to be found in the trans-formations performed by magicians. So all the indices of non-resemblance, all the signs that prove that the written texts are not telling the truth, resemble the action of sorcery, which introduces difference into the in-dubitable existence of similitude by means of deceit. And since this magic has been foreseen and described in the books, the illusory difference that it introduces can never be anything but an enchanted similitude, and, there-fore, yet another sign that the signs in the books really do resemble the truth.

Don Quixote is a negative of the Renaissance world; writing has ceased to be the prose of the world; resemblances and signs have dissolved their former alliance; similitudes have become deceptive and verge upon the visionary or madness; things still remain stubbornly within their ironic identity: they are no longer anything but what they are; words wander

THE ORDER OF THINGS

off on their own, without content, without resemblance to fill their emptiness; they are no longer the marks of things; they lie sleeping between the pages of books and covered in dust. Magic, which permitted the decipherment of the world by revealing the secret resemblances beneath its signs, is no longer of any use except as an explanation, in terms of madness, of why analogies are always proved false. The erudition that once read nature and books alike as parts of a single text has been relegated to the same category as its own chimeras: lodged in the yellowed pages of books, the signs of language no longer have any value apart from the slender fiction which they represent. The written word and things no longer resemble one another. And between them, Don Quixote wanders off on his own.

Yet language has not become entirely impotent. It now possesses new powers, and powers peculiar to it alone. In the second part of the novel, Don Quixote meets characters who have read the first part of his story and recognize him, the real man, as the hero of the book. Cervantes's text turns back upon itself, thrusts itself back into its own density, and becomes the object of its own narrative. The first part of the hero's adventures plays in the second part the role originally assumed by the chivalric romances. Don Quixote must remain faithful to the book that he has now become in reality; he must protect it from errors, from counterfeits, from apocryphal sequels; he must fill in the details that have been left out; he must preserve its truth. But Don Quixote himself has not read this book, and does not have to read it, since he is the book in flesh and blood. Having first read so many books that he became a sign, a sign wandering through a world that did not recognize him, he has now, despite himself and without his knowledge, become a book that contains his truth, that records exactly all that he has done and said and seen and thought, and that at last makes him recognizable, so closely does he resemble all those signs whose ineffaceable imprint he has left behind him. Between the first and second parts of the novel, in the narrow gap between those two volumes, and by their power alone, Don Quixote has achieved his reality – a reality he owes to language alone, and which resides entirely inside the words. Don Quixote's truth is not in the relation of the words to the world but in that slender and constant relation woven between themselves by verbal signs. The hollow fiction of epic exploits has become the representative power of language. Words have swallowed up their own nature as signs.

Don Quixote is the first modern work of literature, because in it we see the cruel reason of identities and differences make endless sport of signs and similitudes; because in it language breaks off its old kinship with things and enters into that lonely sovereignty from which it will reappear, in its separated state, only as literature; because it marks the point where resemblance enters an age which is, from the point of view of resemblance, one of madness and imagination. Once similitude and signs are sundered from each other, two experiences can be established and two characters appear face to face. The madman, understood not as one who is sick but as an established and maintained deviant, as an indispensable cultural function, has become, in Western experience, the man of primitive re-semblances. This character, as he is depicted in the novels or plays of the Baroque age, and as he was gradually institutionalized right up to the advent of nineteenth-century psychiatry, is the man who is *alienated* in *analogy*. He is the disordered player of the Same and the Other. He takes things for what they are not, and people one for another; he cuts his friends and recognizes complete strangers; he thinks he is unmasking when, in fact, he is putting on a mask. He inverts all values and all proportions, because he is constantly under the impression that he is deciphering signs: for him, the crown makes the king. In the cultural perception of the madman that prevailed up to the end of the eighteenth century, he is Different only in so far as he is unaware of Difference; he sees nothing but resemblances and signs of resemblance everywhere; for him all signs resemble one another, and all resemblances have the value of signs. At the other end of the cultural area, but brought close by sym-metry, the poet is he who, beneath the named, constantly expected differences, rediscovers the buried kinships between things, their scattered resemblances. Beneath the established signs, and in spite of them, he hears another, deeper, discourse, which recalls the time when words glittered in the universal resemblance of things; in the language of the poet, the Sovereignty of the Same, so difficult to express, eclipses, the distinction existing between signs.

This accounts, no doubt, for the confrontation of poetry and madness in modern Western culture. But it is no longer the old Platonic theme of inspired madness. It is the mark of a new experience of language and things. At the fringes of a knowledge that separates beings, signs, and similitudes, and as though to limit its power, the madman fulfils the function of *homosemanticism*: he groups all signs together and leads them with a resemblance that never ceases to proliferate. The poet fulfils the opposite function: his is the *allegorical* role; beneath the language of

49

signs and beneath the interplay of their precisely delineated distinctions, he strains his ears to catch that 'other language', the language, without words or discourse, of resemblance. The poet brings similitude to the signs that speak it, whereas the madman loads all signs with a resemblance that ultimately erases them. They share, then, on the outer edge of our culture and at the point nearest to its essential divisions, that 'frontier' situation – a marginal position and a profoundly archaic silhouette – where their words unceasingly renew the power of their strangeness and the strength of their contestation. Between them there has opened up a field of knowledge in which, because of an essential rupture in the Western world, what has become important is no longer resemblances but identities and differences.

II ORDER

Establishing discontinuities is not an easy task even for history in general. And it is certainly even less so for the history of thought. We may wish to draw a dividing-line; but any limit we set may perhaps be no more than an arbitrary division made in a constantly mobile whole. We may wish to mark off a period; but have we the right to establish symmetrical breaks at two points in time in order to give an appearance of continuity and unity to the system we place between them? Where, in that case, would the cause of its existence lie? Or that of its subsequent disappearance and fall? What rule could it be obeying by both its existence and its disappearance? If it contains a principle of coherence within itself, whence could come the foreign element capable of rebutting it? How can a thought melt away before anything other than itself? Generally speaking, what does it mean, no longer being able to think a certain thought? Or to introduce a new thought?

Discontinuity – the fact that within the space of a few years a culture sometimes ceases to think as it had been thinking up till then and begins to think other things in a new way – probably begins with an erosion from outside, from that space which is, for thought, on the other side, but in which it has never ceased to think from the very beginning. Ultimately, the problem that presents itself is that of the relations between thought and culture: how is it that thought has a place in the space of the world, that it has its origin there, and that it never ceases, in this place or that, to begin anew? But perhaps it is not yet time to pose this problem; perhaps we should wait until the archaeology of thought has been established more firmly, until it is better able to gauge what it is capable of describing directly and positively, until it has defined the particular systems and internal connections it has to deal with, before attempting to encompass thought and to investigate how it contrives to escape itself. For the moment, then, let it suffice that we accept these discontinuities in the simultaneously manifest and obscure empirical order wherever they posit themselves.

At the beginning of the seventeenth century, during the period that has been termed, rightly or wrongly, the Baroque, thought ceases to move in the element of resemblance. Similitude is no longer the form of knowledge but rather the occasion of error, the danger to which one exposes oneself when one does not examine the obscure region of confusions. 'It is a frequent habit,' says Descartes, in the first lines of his *Regulae*, 'when we discover several resemblances between two things, to attribute to both equally, even on points in which they are in reality different, that which we have recognized to be true of only one of them'[1]. The age of resemblance is drawing to a close. It is leaving nothing behind it but games. Games whose powers of enchantment grow out of the new kinship between resemblance and illusion; the chimeras of similitude loom up on all sides, but they are recognized as chimeras; it is the privileged age of *trompe-l'œil* painting, of the comic illusion, of the play that duplicates itself by representing another play, of the *quid pro quo*, of dreams and visions; it is the age of the deceiving senses; it is the age in which the poetic dimension of language is defined by metaphor, simile, and allegory. And it was also in the nature of things that the knowledge of the sixteenth century should leave behind it the distorted memory of a muddled and disordered body of learning in which all the things in the world could be linked indiscriminately to men's experiences, traditions, or credulities. From then on, the noble, rigorous, and restrictive figures of similitude were to be forgotten. And the signs that designated them were to be thought of as the fantasies and charms of a knowledge that had not yet attained the age of reason.

We already find a critique of resemblance in Bacon – an empirical critique that concerns, not the relations of order and equality between things, but the types of mind and the forms of illusion to which they might be subject. We are dealing with a doctrine of the *quid pro quo*. Bacon does not dissipate similitudes by means of evidence and its attendant rules. He shows them, shimmering before our eyes, vanishing as one draws near, then re-forming again a moment later, a little further off. They are *idols*.

The *idols of the den* and the *idols of the theatre* make us believe that things resemble what we have learned and the theories we have formed for ourselves; other idols make us believe that things are linked by resemblances between themselves.

> The human Intellect, from its peculiar nature, easily supposes a greater order and equality in things than it actually finds; and, while there are many things in Nature unique, and quite irregular, still it feigns parallels, correspondents, and relations that have no existence. Hence that fiction, 'that among the heavenly bodies all motion takes place by perfect circles'.

Such are the *idols of the tribe*, spontaneous fictions of the mind; to which are added – as effects and sometimes as causes – the confusions of language: one and the same name being applied indifferently to things that are not of the same nature. These are the *idols of the market*[2]. Only prudence on the part of the mind can dissipate them, if it abjures its natural haste and levity in order to become 'penetrating' and ultimately perceive the differences inherent in nature.

The Cartesian critique of resemblance is of another type. It is no longer sixteenth-century thought becoming troubled as it contemplates itself and beginning to jettison its most familiar forms; it is Classical thought excluding resemblance as the fundamental experience and primary form of knowledge, denouncing it as a confused mixture that must be analysed in terms of identity, difference, measurement, and order. Though Descartes rejects resemblance, he does so not by excluding the act of comparison from rational thought, nor even by seeking to limit it, but on the contrary by universalizing it and thereby giving it its purest form. Indeed, it is by means of comparison that we discover 'form, extent, movement and other such things' – that is to say, simple natures – in all subjects in which they may be present. And, moreover, in a deduction of the type 'all of A is B, all of B is C, therefore all of A is C', it is clear that the mind 'makes a comparison between the term sought and the term given, to wit A and C, with relation to the knowledge that both are B'. In consequence, if one makes an exception of the intuition one may have of a single thing, one can say that all knowledge 'is obtained by the comparison of two or more things with each other'[3]. But in fact, there can be no true knowledge except by intuition, that is, by a singular act of pure and attentive intelligence, and by deduction, which links the observed evidence together. How then can comparison, which is required for the acquisition of almost all knowledge and which, by definition, is neither an isolated observation nor a deduction, stand as an authority for a true thought? 'Almost all the labour accomplished by human reason consists without doubt in rendering this operation possible'[4].

There exist two forms of comparison, and only two: the comparison of measurement and that of order. One can measure sizes or multiplicities, in other words continuous sizes or discontinuous sizes; but in both cases the use of measurement presupposes that, unlike calculation, which proceeds from elements towards a totality, one considers the whole first and then divides it up into parts. This division results in a number of units, of which some are merely conventional or 'borrowed' (in the case of continuous size) and others (in the case of multiplicities or discontinuous sizes) are the units of arithmetic. The comparison of two sizes or two multiplicities requires, in any case, that they both be analysed according to a common unit; so that comparison effected according to measurement is reducible, in every case, to the arithmetical relations of equality and inequality. Measurement enables us to analyse like things according to the calculable form of identity and difference[5].

Order, on the other hand, is established without reference to an exterior unit: 'I can recognize, in effect, what the order is that exists between A and B without considering anything apart from those two outer terms'; one cannot know the order of things 'in their isolated nature', but by discovering that which is the simplest, then that which is the next simplest, one can progress inevitably to the most complex things of all. Whereas comparison by measurement requires a division to begin from, then the application of a common unit, here, comparison and order are one and the same thing: comparison by means of order is a simple act which enables us to pass from one term to another, then to a third, etc., by means of an 'absolutely uninterrupted'[6] movement. In this way we establish series in which the first term is a nature that we may intuit independently of any other nature; and in which the other terms are established according to increasing differences.

Such, then, are the two types of comparison: the one analyses into units in order to establish relations of equality and inequality; the other establishes elements, the simplest that can be found, and arranges differences according to the smallest possible degrees. Now, it is possible to use the measurement of sizes and multiplicities in establishing an order; arithmetical values can always be arranged according to a series; a multiplicity of units can therefore 'be arranged according to an order such that the difficulty, which previously lay in the knowing of measurement, comes finally to depend solely on the consideration of order'[7]. And it is precisely in this that the method and its 'progress' consist: the reduction of all measurement (all determination by equality and inequality) to a serial arrangement which, beginning from the simplest, will show up all differences as degrees of complexity. After being analysed according to a given unit and the relations of equality or inequality, the like is analysed according to its evident identity and differences: *differences* that can be thought in the order of *inferences*. However, this order or generalized form of comparison can be established only according to its position in the body of our acquired knowledge; the absolute character we recognize in what is simple concerns not the being of things but rather the manner in which they can be known. A thing can be absolute according to one relation yet relative according to others[8]; order can be at once necessary and natural (in relation to thought) and arbitrary (in relation to things), since, according to the way in which we consider it, the same thing may be placed at differing points in our order.

All this was of the greatest consequence to Western thought. Resemblance, which had for long been the fundamental category of knowledge – both the form and the content of what we know – became dissociated in an analysis based on terms of identity and difference; moreover, whether indirectly by the intermediary of measurement, or directly and, as it were, on the same footing, comparison became a function of order; and, lastly, comparison ceased to fulfil the function of revealing how the world is ordered, since it was now accomplished according to the order laid down by thought, progressing naturally from the simple to the complex. As a result, the entire *episteme* of Western culture found its fundamental arrangements modified. And, in particular, the empirical domain which sixteenth-century man saw as a complex of kinships, resemblances, and affinities, and in which language and things were endlessly interwoven – this whole vast field was to take on a new configuration. This new configuration may, I suppose, be called 'rationalism'; one might say, if one's mind is filled with ready-made concepts, that the seventeenth century marks the disappearance of the old superstitious or magical beliefs and the entry of nature, at long last, into the scientific order. But what we must grasp and attempt to reconstitute are the modifications that affected knowledge itself, at that archaic level which makes possible both knowledge itself and the mode of being of what is to be known.

These modifications may be summed up as follows. First, the substitution of analysis for the hierarchy of analogies: in the sixteenth century, the fundamental supposition was that of a total system of correspondence (earth and sky, planets and faces, microcosm and macrocosm), and each particular similitude was then lodged within this overall relation. From now on, every resemblance must be subjected to proof by comparison, that is, it will not be accepted until its identity and the series of its differences have been discovered by means of measurement with a common unit, or, more radically, by its position in an order. Furthermore, the interplay of similitudes was hitherto infinite: it was always possible to discover new ones, and the only limitation came from the fundamental ordering of things, from the finitude of a world held firmly between the macrocosm and the microcosm. A complete enumeration will now be possible: whether in the form of an exhaustive census of all the elements constituting the envisaged whole, or in the form of a categorical arrangement that will articulate the field of study in its totality, or in the form of an analysis of a certain number of points, in sufficient number, taken along the whole length of a series. Comparison, then, can attain to perfect certainty: the old system of similitudes, never complete and always open to fresh possibilities, could, it is true, through successive confirmations, achieve steadily increasing probability; but it was never certain. Complete enumeration, and the possibility of assigning at each point the necessary connection with the next, permit an absolutely certain knowledge of identities and differences: 'Enumeration alone, whatever the question to which we are applying ourselves, will permit us always to deliver a true and certain judgement upon it'[9]. The activity of the mind – and this is the fourth point – will therefore no longer consist in *drawing things together*, in setting out on a quest for everything that might reveal some sort of kinship, attraction, or secretly shared nature within them, but, on the contrary, in *discriminating*, that is, in establishing their identities, then the inevitability of the connections with all the successive degrees of a series. In this sense, discrimination imposes upon comparison the primary and fundamental investigation of difference: providing oneself by intuition with a distinct representation of things, and apprehending clearly the inevitable connection between one element in a series and that which immediately follows it. Lastly, a final consequence, since to know is to discriminate, history and science will become separated from one another. On the one hand there will be erudition, the perusal of written works, the interplay of their authors' opinions; this interplay may well, in some cases, possess an indicative value, not so much because of the agreement it produces as because of the disagreement: 'When the question at issue is a difficult one, it is more probable that there were few rather than many to discover the truth about it.' Over against this history, and lacking any common unit of measurement with it, are the confident judgements we are able to make by means of intuitions and their serial connection. These and these alone are what constitute science, and even if we had 'read all the arguments of Plato and Aristotle, . . . what we would have learned would not be sciences, it appears, but history' [10]. This being so, the written word ceases to be included among the signs and forms of truth; language is no longer one of the figurations of the world, or a signature stamped upon things since the beginning of time. The manifestation and sign of truth are to be found in evident and distinct perception. It is the task of words to translate that truth if they can; but they no longer have the right to be considered a mark of it. Language has withdrawn from the midst of beings themselves and has entered a period of transparency and neutrality.

This is a general phenomenon in seventeenth-century culture – a more general one than the particular fortunes of Cartesianism.

We must, in fact, distinguish between three things. On the one hand, there was the mechanism that, for what was really a fairly short period (not quite the last fifty years of the seventeenth century), offered a theoretical model to certain fields of knowledge such as medicine or physiology. There was also an attempt, rather diverse in the forms it took, to mathematicize empirical knowledge; though constant and continuous in the case of astronomy and part of physics, it was only sporadic in other fields – sometimes actually attempted (as with Condorcet), sometimes suggested as a universal ideal and a horizon for research (as with Condillac or Destutt), and sometimes, too, rejected even as a possibility (by Buffon, for example). But neither this endeavour nor the attempts of mechanism should be confused with the relation that all Classical knowledge, in its most general form, maintains with the *mathesis*, understood as a universal science of measurement and order. Under cover of the empty and obscurely incantatory phrases 'Cartesian influence' or 'Newtonian model', our historians of ideas are in the habit of confusing these three things and defining Classical rationalism as the tendency to make nature mechanical and calculable. Others are slightly more perceptive, and go to a great deal of trouble to discover beneath this rationalism a play of 'contrary forces': the forces of nature and life refusing to let themselves be reduced either to algebra or to dynamics, and thus preserving, in the depths of Classicism itself, the natural resources of the non-rationalizable. These two forms of analysis are equally inadequate; for the fundamental element of the Classical *episteme* is neither the success or failure of mechanism, nor the right to mathematicize or the impossibility of mathematicizing nature, but rather a link with the mathesis which, until the end of the eighteenth century, remains constant and unaltered. This link has two essential characteristics. The first is that relations between beings are indeed to be conceived in the form of order and measurement, but with this fundamental imbalance, that it is always possible to reduce problems of measurement to problems of order. So that the relation of all knowledge to the mathesis is posited as the possibility of establishing an ordered succession between things, even non-measurable ones. In this sense, *analysis* was very quickly to acquire the value of a universal method; and the Leibnizian project of establishing a mathematics of qualitative orders is situated at the very heart of Classical thought; its gravitational centre. But, on the other hand, this relation to the mathesis as a general science of order does not signify that knowledge is absorbed into mathematics, or that the latter becomes the foundation for all possible knowledge; on the contrary, in correlation with the quest for a mathesis, we perceive the appearance of a certain number of empirical fields now being formed and defined for the very first time. In none of these fields, or almost none, is it possible to find any trace of mechanism or mathematicization; and yet they all rely for their foundation upon a possible science of order. Although they were all dependent upon *analysis* in general, their particular instrument was not the *algebraic method* but the *system of signs*. So there first appeared general grammar, natural history, and the analysis of wealth, all sciences of order in the domain of words, beings, and needs; and none of these empirical studies, new in the Classical period and co-extensive with it in duration (their chronological frontiers are marked by Lancelot and Bopp, Ray and Cuvier, Petty and Ricardo, the first group writing around 1660 and the second around 1800–10), could have been founded without the relation that the entire *episteme* of Western culture maintained at that time with a universal science of order.

This relation to *Order* is as essential to the Classical age as the relation to *Interpretation* was to the Renaissance. And just as interpretation in the sixteenth century, with its superimposition of a semiology upon a hermeneutics, was essentially a knowledge based upon similitude, so the ordering of things by means of signs constitutes all empirical forms of knowledge as knowledge based upon identity and difference. The simultaneously endless and closed, full and tautological world of resemblance now finds itself dissociated and, as it were, split down the middle: on the one side, we shall find the signs that have become tools of analysis, marks of identity and difference, principles whereby things can be reduced to order, keys for a taxonomy; and, on the other, the empirical and murmuring resemblance of things, that unreacting similitude that lies beneath thought and furnishes the infinite raw material for divisions and distributions. On the one hand, the general theory of signs, divisions, and classifications; on the other, the problem of immediate resemblances, of the spontaneous movement of the imagination, of nature's repetitions. And between the two, the new forms of knowledge that occupy the area opened up by this new split.

III   THE REPRESENTATION OF THE SIGN

What is a sign in the Classical age? For what was altered in the first half of the seventeenth century, and for a long time to come – perhaps right up to our own day – was the entire organization of signs, the conditions under which they exercise their strange function; it is this, among so many other things one knows or sees, that causes them to emerge suddenly as signs; it is their very being. On the threshold of the Classical age, the sign ceases to be a form of the world; and it ceases to be bound to what it marks by the solid and secret bonds of resemblance or affinity.

Classical thought defines it according to three variables[11]. First, the certainty of the relation: a sign may be so constant that one can be sure of its accuracy (in the sense that breathing denotes life), but it may also be simply probable (in the sense that pallor probably denotes pregnancy). Second, the type of relation: a sign may belong to the whole that it denotes (in the sense that a healthy appearance is part of the health it denotes) or be separate from it (in the sense that the figures of the Old Testament are distant signs of the Incarnation and Redemption). Third, the origin of the relation: a sign may be natural (in the sense that a reflection in a mirror denotes that which it reflects) or conventional (in the sense that a word may signify an idea to a given group of men). None of these forms of relation necessarily implies resemblance; even the natural sign does not require that: a cry is a spontaneous sign of fear, but not analogous to it; or again, as Berkeley puts it, visual sensations are signs of touch established in us by God, yet they do not resemble it in any way[12].

These three variables replace resemblance in defining the sign's efficacity in the domains of empirical knowledge.

1. The sign, since it is always either certain or probable, should find its area of being within knowledge. In the sixteenth century, signs were thought to have been placed upon things so that men might be able to uncover their secrets, their nature or their virtues; but this discovery was merely the ultimate purpose of signs, the justification of their presence; it was a possible way of using them, and no doubt the best; but they did not need to be known in order to exist: even if they remained silent, even if no one were to perceive them, they were just as much *there*. It was not knowledge that gave them their signifying function, but the very language of things. From the seventeenth century onward, the whole domain of the sign is divided between the certain and the probable: that is to say, there can no longer be an unknown sign, a mute mark. This is not because men are in possession of all the possible signs, but because there can be no sign until there exists a *known* possibility of substitution between two *known* elements. The sign does not wait in silence for the coming of a man capable of recognizing it: it can be constituted only by an act of knowing.

It is here that knowledge breaks off its old kinship with *divinatio*. The latter always presupposed signs anterior to it: so that knowledge always resided entirely in the opening up of a discovered, affirmed, or secretly transmitted, sign. Its task was to uncover a language which God had previously distributed across the face of the earth; it is in this sense that it was the divination of an essential implication, and that the object of its divination was *divine*. From now on, however, it is within knowledge itself that the sign is to perform its signifying function; it is from knowledge that it will borrow its certainty or its probability. And though God still employs signs to speak to us through nature, he is making use of our knowledge, and of the relations that are set up between our impressions, in order to establish in our minds a relation of signification. Such is the role of feeling in Malebranche or of sensation in Berkeley; in natural judgement, in feeling, in visual impressions, and in the perception of the third dimension, what we are dealing with are hasty and confused, but pressing, inevitable, and obligatory kinds of knowledge serving as signs for discursive kinds of knowledge which we humans, because we are not pure intelligences, no longer have the time or the permission to attain to ourselves and by the unaided strength of our own minds. In Malebranche and Berkeley, the sign arranged by God is the cunning and thoughtful superimposition of two kinds of knowledge. There is no longer any *divinatio* involved – no insertion of knowledge in the enigmatic, open, and sacred area of signs – but a brief and concentrated kind of knowledge: the contraction of a long sequence of judgements into the rapidly assimilated form of the sign. And it will also be seen how, by a reversal of direction, knowledge, having enclosed the signs within its own space, is now able to accommodate probability: between one impression and another the relation will be that of sign to signified, in other words, a relation which, like that of succession, will progress from the weakest probability towards the greatest certainty.

> The connection of ideas does not imply the relation of *cause* and *effect*, but only of a mark or *sign* with the thing *signified*. The *fire* which I see is not the cause of the pain I suffer upon my approaching it, but the mark that forewarns me of it[13].

The knowledge that divined, *at random*, signs that were absolute and older than itself has been replaced by a network of signs built up step by step in accordance with a knowledge of what is probable. Hume has become possible.

2. The second variable of the sign: the form of its relation with what it signifies. By means of the interplay of conveniency, emulation, and above all sympathy, similitude was able in the sixteenth century to triumph over space and time; for it was within the power of the sign to draw things together and unite them. With the advent of Classical thought, on the other hand, the sign becomes characterized by its essential dispersion. The circular world of converging signs is replaced by an infinite progression. Within this space, the sign can have one of two positions: either it can be claimed, as an element, to be part of that which it serves to designate; or else it is really and actually separated from what it serves to designate. The truth is, however, that this alternative is not a radical one, since the sign, in order to function, must be simultaneously an insertion in that which it signifies and also distinct from it. For the sign to be, in effect, what it is, it must be presented as an object of knowledge at the same time as that which it signifies. As Condillac points out, a sound could never become the verbal sign of something for a child unless the child had heard it at least once at the moment of perceiving the object[14]. But if one element of a perception is to become a sign for it, it is not enough merely for that element to be part of the perception; it must be differentiated *qua* element and be distinguished from the total impression

with which it is confusedly linked; consequently, that total impression itself must have been divided up, and attention must have been directed towards one of the intermingled regions composing it, in order to isolate one of them. The constitution of the sign is thus inseparable from analysis. Indeed, it is the result of it, since without analysis the sign could not become apparent. But it is also the instrument of analysis, since once defined and isolated it can be applied to further impressions; and in relation to them it plays the role of a grid, as it were. Because the mind analyses, the sign appears. Because the mind has signs at its disposal, analysis never ceases. It is understandable why, from Condillac to Destutt de Tracy and Gerando, the general theory of signs and the definition of the power of analysis of thought were so exactly superimposed to form a single and unbroken theory of knowledge.

When the *Logique de Port-Royal* states that a sign can be inherent in what it designates or separate from it, it is demonstrating that the sign, in the Classical age, is charged no longer with the task of keeping the world close to itself and inherent in its own forms, but, on the contrary, with that of spreading it out, of juxtaposing it over an indefinitely open surface, and of taking up from that point the endless deployment of the substitutes in which we conceive of it. And it is by this means that it is offered simultaneously to analysis and to combination, and can be ordered from beginning to end. The sign in Classical thought does not erase distances or abolish time: on the contrary, it enables one to unfold them and to traverse them step by step. It is the sign that enables things to become distinct, to preserve themselves within their own identities, to dissociate themselves or bind themselves together. Western reason is entering the age of judgement.

3. There remains a third variable: the one that can assume the two values of nature and of convention. It had long been known – and well before Plato's *Cratylus* – that signs can be either given by nature or established by man. Nor was the sixteenth century ignorant of this fact, since it recognized human languages to be instituted signs. But the artificial signs owed their power only to their fidelity to natural signs. These latter, even at a remove, were the foundation of all others. From the seventeenth century, the values allotted to nature and convention in this field are inverted: if natural, a sign is no more than an element selected from the world of things and constituted as a sign by our knowledge. It is therefore strictly limited, rigid, inconvenient, and impossible for the mind to master. When, on the other hand, one establishes a

conventional sign, it is always possible (and indeed necessary) to choose it in such a way that it will be simple, easy to remember, applicable to an indefinite number of elements, susceptible of subdivision within itself and of combination with other signs; the man-made sign is the sign at the peak of its activity. It is the man-made sign that draws the dividing-line between man and animal; that transforms imagination into voluntary memory, spontaneous attention into reflection, and instinct into rational knowledge[15]. It is also what Itard found lacking in the 'wild man of Aveyron'[16]. Natural signs are merely rudimentary sketches for these conventional signs, the vague and distant design that can be realized only by the establishment of arbitrariness.

But this arbitrariness is measured by its function; and has its rules very exactly defined by that function. An arbitrary system of signs must permit the analysis of things into their simplest elements; it must be capable of decomposing them into their very origins; but it must also demonstrate how combinations of those elements are possible, and permit the ideal genesis of the complexity of things. 'Arbitrary' stands in opposition to 'natural' only if one is attempting to designate the manner in which signs have been established. But this arbitrariness is also the grid of analysis and the combinative space through which nature is to posit itself as that which it is – at the level of primal impressions and in all the possible forms of their combination. In its perfect state, the system of signs is that simple, absolutely transparent language which is capable of naming what is elementary; it is also that complex of operations which defines all possible conjunctions. To our eyes, this search for origins and this calculus of combinations appear incompatible, and we are only too ready to interpret them as an ambiguity in seventeenth- and eighteenth-century thought. The same is true of the interaction between the system and nature. In fact, there is no contradiction at all for thought at that time. More precisely, there exists a single, necessary arrangement running through the whole of the Classical *episteme*: the association of a universal calculus and a search for the elementary within a system that is artificial and is, for that very reason, able to make nature visible from its primary elements right to the simultaneity of all their possible combinations. In the Classical age, to make use of signs is not, as it was in preceding centuries, to attempt to rediscover beneath them the primitive text of a discourse sustained, and retained, forever; it is an attempt to discover the arbitrary language that will authorize the deployment of nature within its space, the final terms of its analysis and the laws of its composition. It is no longer the task of knowledge to dig out the ancient Word from the unknown places where it may be hidden; its job now is to fabricate a language, and to fabricate it well – so that, as an instrument of analysis and combination, it will really be the language of calculation.

It is now possible to define the instruments laid down for the use of Classical thought by the sign system. It was this system that introduced into knowledge probability, analysis, and combination, and the justified arbitrariness of the system. It was the sign system that gave rise simultaneously to the search for origins and to calculability; to the constitution of tables that would fix the possible compositions, and to the restitution of a genesis on the basis of the simplest elements; it was the sign system that linked all knowledge to a language, and sought to replace all languages with a system of artificial symbols and operations of a logical nature. At the level of the history of opinions, all this would appear, no doubt, as a tangled network of influences in which the individual parts played by Hobbes, Berkeley, Leibniz, Condillac, and the 'Idéologues' would be revealed. But if we question Classical thought at the level of what, archaeologically, made it possible, we perceive that the dissociation of the sign and resemblance in the early seventeenth century caused these new forms – probability, analysis, combination, and universal language system – to emerge, not as successive themes engendering one another or driving one another out, but as a single network of necessities. And it was this network that made possible the individuals we term Hobbes, Berkeley, Hume, or Condillac.

IV DUPLICATED REPRESENTATION

However, the property of signs most fundamental to the Classical *episteme* has not yet been mentioned. Indeed, the very fact that the sign can be more or less probable, more or less distant from what it signifies, that it can be either natural or arbitrary, without its nature or its value as a sign being affected – all this shows clearly enough that the relation of the sign to its content is not guaranteed by the order of things in themselves. The relation of the sign to the signified now resides in a space in which there is no longer any intermediary figure to connect them: what connects them is a bond established, inside knowledge, between the *idea of one thing* and the *idea of another*. The *Logique de Port-Royal* states this as follows: 'The sign encloses two ideas, one of the thing representing, the other of the thing represented; and its nature consists in exciting the first by means of the second'[17]. This dual theory of the sign is in unequi-vocal opposition to the more complex organization of the Renaissance; at that time, the theory of the sign implied three quite distinct elements: that which was marked, that which did the marking, and that which made it possible to see in the first the mark of the second; and this last element was, of course, resemblance: the sign provided a mark exactly in so far as it was 'almost the same thing' as that which it designated. It is this unitary and triple system that disappears at the same time as 'thought by resemblance', and is replaced by a strictly binary organization.

But there is one condition that must be fulfilled if the sign is indeed to be this pure duality. In its simple state as an idea, or an image, or a per-ception, associated with or substituted for another, the signifying element is not a sign. It can become a sign only on condition that it manifests, in addition, the relation that links it to what it signifies. It must represent; but that representation, in turn, must also be represented within it. This is a condition indispensable to the binary organization of the sign, and one that the *Logique de Port-Royal* sets forth even before telling us what a sign is: 'When one looks at a certain object only in so far as it represents another, the idea one has of it is the idea of a sign, and that first object is called a sign'[18]. The signifying idea becomes double, since superim-posed upon the idea that is replacing another there is also the idea of its representative power. This appears to give us three terms: the idea signi-fied, the idea signifying, and, within this second term, the idea of its role as representation. What we are faced with here is not, however, a surrep-titious return to a ternary system, but rather an inevitable displacement within the two-term figure, which moves backward in relation to itself and comes to reside entirely within the signifying element. In fact, the signifying element has no content, no function, and no determination other than what it represents: it is entirely ordered upon and transparent to it. But this content is indicated only in a representation that posits itself as such, and that which is signified resides, without residuum and without opacity, within the representation of the sign. It is characteristic that the first example of a sign given by the *Logique de Port-Royal* is not the word, nor the cry, nor the symbol, but the spatial and graphic representation – the drawing as map or picture. This is because the pic-ture has no other content in fact than that which it represents, and yet that content is made visible only because it is represented by a representa-tion. The binary arrangement of the sign, as it appears in the seventeenth century, replaces an organization which, in different modes, had been ternary ever since the time of the Stoics, and even since the first Greek grammarians; and this new binary arrangement presupposes that the sign is a duplicated representation doubled over upon itself. An idea can be the sign of another, not only because a bond of representation can be established between them, but also because this representation can always be represented within the idea that is representing. Or again, because representation in its peculiar essence is always perpendicular to itself: it is at the same time *indication* and *appearance*; a relation to an object and a manifestation of itself. From the Classical age, the sign is the *representativity* of the representation in so far as it is *representable*.

This has very considerable consequences. First, the importance of signs in Classical thought. Before, they were means of knowing and the keys to knowledge; now, they are co-extensive with representation, that is, with thought as a whole; they reside within it but they run through its entire extent. Whenever one representation is linked to another and represents that link within itself, there is a sign: the abstract idea signifies the concrete perception from which it has been formed (Condillac); the general idea is no more than a particular idea serving as a sign for other particular ideas (Berkeley); imaginings are signs of the perceptions from which they arose (Hume, Condillac); sensations are signs of one another (Berkeley, Condillac); and, finally, it is possible that sensations may themselves be (as in Berkeley) signs of what God wishes to tell us, which would make them, as it were, signs for a complex of signs. Analysis of representation and the theory of signs interpenetrate one another absolutely; and when the day came, at the end of the eighteenth century, for Ideology to raise the question of whether the idea or the sign should be accorded primacy, when Destutt could reproach Gerando for having created a theory of signs before defining the idea[19], this meant that their immediate link was already becoming confused, and that idea and sign would soon cease to be perfectly transparent to one another.

A second consequence: this universal extension of the sign within the field of representation precludes even the possibility of a theory of signification. For to ask ourselves questions about what signification is presupposes that it is a determinate form in our consciousness. But if phenomena are posited only in a representation that, in itself and because of its own representability, is wholly a sign, then signification cannot constitute a problem. Moreover, it is not even visible. All representations are interconnected as signs; all together, they form, as it were, an immense network; each one posits itself in its transparency as the sign of what it represents; and yet – or rather, by this very fact – no specific activity of consciousness can ever constitute a signification. No doubt it is because Classical thought about representation excludes any analysis of signification that we today, who conceive of signs only upon the basis of such an analysis, have so much trouble, despite the evidence, in recognizing that Classical philosophy, from Malebranche to Ideology, was through and through a philosophy of the sign.

No meaning exterior or anterior to the sign; no implicit presence of a previous discourse that must be reconstituted in order to reveal the autochthonous meaning of things. Nor, on the other hand, any act constitutive of signification or any genesis interior to consciousness. This is because there is no intermediary element, no opacity intervening between the sign and its content. Signs, therefore, have no other laws than those that may govern their contents: any analysis of signs is at the same time, and without need for further inquiry, the decipherment of what they are trying to say. Inversely, the discovery of what is signified is nothing more than a reflection upon the signs that indicate it. As in the sixteenth century, 'semiology' and 'hermeneutics' are superimposed – but in a different form. In the Classical age they no longer meet and join in the third element of resemblance; their connection lies in that power proper to representation of representing itself. There will therefore be no theory of signs separate and differing from an analysis of meaning. Yet the system does grant a certain privilege to the former over the latter; since it does not accord that which is signified a nature different from that accorded to the sign, meaning cannot be anything more than the totality of the signs arranged in their progression; it will be given in the complete *table* of signs. But, on the other hand, the complete network of signs is linked together and articulated according to patterns proper to meaning. The table of the signs will be the *image* of the things. Though the meaning itself is entirely on the side of the sign, its functioning is entirely on the side of that which is signified. This is why the analysis of language, from Lancelot to Destutt de Tracy, is conducted on the basis of an abstract theory of verbal signs and in the form of a general grammar: but it always takes the meaning of words as its guiding thread; it is also why natural history manifests itself as an analysis of the characters of living beings, and why, nevertheless, the taxonomies used, artificial though they may be, are always intended to unite with the natural order, or at least to dissociate it as little as possible; it is also why the analysis of wealth is conducted on the basis of money and exchange, but value is always based upon need. In the Classical age, the pure science of signs has value as the direct discourse of that which is signified.

Finally, a third consequence, which probably extends up to our own time: the binary theory of the sign, the theory upon which the whole general science of the sign has been founded since the seventeenth century, is linked according to a fundamental relation with a general theory of representation. If the sign is the pure and simple connection between what signifies and what is signified (a connection that may be arbitrary or not, voluntary or imposed, individual or collective), then the relation can be established only within the general element of representation: the signifying element and the signified element are linked only in so far as they are (or have been or can be) represented, and in so far as the one actually represents the other. It was therefore necessary that the Classical theory of the sign should provide itself with an 'ideology' to serve as its foundation and philosophical justification, that is, a general analysis of all forms of representation, from elementary sensation to the abstract and complex idea. It was also necessary that Saussure, rediscovering the project of a general semiology, should have given the sign a definition that could seem 'psychologistic' (the linking of a concept and an image): this is because he was in fact rediscovering the Classical condition for conceiving of the binary nature of the sign.

V   THE IMAGINATION OF RESEMBLANCE

So signs are now set free from that teeming world throughout which the Renaissance had distributed them. They are lodged henceforth within the confines of representation, in the interstices of ideas, in that narrow space in which they interact with themselves in a perpetual state of decomposition and recomposition. As for similitude, it is now a spent force, outside the realm of knowledge. It is merely empiricism in its most unrefined form; like Hobbes, one can no longer 'regard it as being a part of philosophy', unless it has first been erased in its inexact form of resemblance and transformed by knowledge into a relationship of equality or order. And yet similitude is still an indispensable border of knowledge. For no equality or relation of order can be established between two things unless their resemblance has at least occasioned their comparison. Hume placed the relation of identity among those 'philosophical' relations that presuppose reflection; whereas, for him, resemblance belonged to natural relations, to those that constrain our minds by means of an inevitable but 'calm force'.

> Let the philosopher pride himself on his precision as much as he will . . .
> I nevertheless dare defy him to make a single step in his progress without
> the aid of resemblance. Throw but one glance upon the metaphysical
> aspect of the sciences, even the least abstract of them, and then tell
> me whether the general inductions that are derived from particular
> facts, or rather the kinds themselves, the species and all abstract notions,
> can be formed otherwise than by means of resemblance[20].

At the border of knowledge, similitude is that barely sketched form, that rudimentary relation which knowledge must overlay to its full extent, but which continues, indefinitely, to reside below knowledge in the manner of a mute and ineffaceable necessity.

As in the sixteenth century, resemblance and sign respond inevitably to one another, but in a new way. Whereas similitude once required a mark in order for its secret to be uncovered, it is now the undifferentiated, shifting, unstable base upon which knowledge can establish its relations, its measurements, and its identities. This results in a double reversal: first, because it is the sign – and with it the whole of discursive knowledge – that requires a basis of similitude, and, second, because it is no longer a question of making a previous content manifest to knowledge but of providing a content that will be able to offer a ground upon which forms of knowledge can be applied. Whereas in the sixteenth century resemblance was the fundamental relation of being to itself, and the hinge of the whole world, in the Classical age it is the simplest form in which what is to be known, and what is furthest from knowledge itself, appears. It is through resemblance that representation can be known, that is, compared with other representations that may be similar to it, analysed into elements (elements common to it and other representations), combined with those representations that may present partial identities, and finally laid out into an ordered table. Similitude in Classical philosophy (that is, in a philosophy of analysis) plays a role parallel to that which will be played by diversity in critical thought and the philosophies of judgement.

In this limiting and conditional position (that without which and beyond which one cannot know), resemblance is situated on the side of imagination, or, more exactly, it can be manifested only by virtue of imagination, and imagination, in turn, can be exercised only with the aid of resemblance. And, in effect, if we suppose in the uninterrupted chain of representation certain impressions, the very simplest that can be, without the slightest degree of resemblance between them, then there would be no possibility whatever of the second recalling the first, causing it to reappear, and thus authorizing its representation in the imagination; those impressions would succeed one another in the most total differentiation – so total that it could not even be perceived, since no representation would be able to immobilize itself in one place, reanimate a former one, and juxtapose itself to it so as to give rise to a comparison; even that tiny overlap of identity necessary for all differentiation would not be provided. Perpetual change would pass before us without guidelines and in perpetual monotony. If representation did not possess the obscure power of making a past impression present once more, then no impression would ever appear as either similar to or dissimilar from a previous one. This power of recall implies at least the possibility of causing two impressions to appear as quasi-likenesses (as neighbours or contemporaries, existing in almost the same way) when one of those impressions only is present, while the other has ceased, perhaps a long time ago, to exist. Without imagination, there would be no resemblance between things.

The double requisite is patent. There must be, in the things represented, the insistent murmur of resemblance; there must be, in the representation, the perpetual possibility of imaginative recall. And neither of these requisites can dispense with the other, which completes and confronts it. Hence the two directions of analysis followed throughout the Classical age, consistently drawing closer and closer together until finally, in the second half of the eighteenth century, they were able to express their common truth in Ideology. On the one hand, we find the analysis that provides an account of the inversion of the series of representations to form a non-actual but simultaneous table of comparisons: the analysis of impressions, of reminiscence, of imagination, of memory, of all that involuntary background which is, as it were, the mechanics of the image in time. And, on the other hand, there is the analysis that gives an account of the resemblance between things – of their resemblance before their reduction to order, their decomposition into identical and different elements, the tabular redistribution of their unordered similitudes. Why is it, then, that things are given in an overlapping mixture, in an interpenetrating jumble in which their essential order is confused, yet still visible enough to show through in the form of resemblances, vague similitudes, and allusive opportunities for a memory on the alert? The first series of problems corresponds roughly with the *analytic of imagination*,

69

as a positive power to transform the linear time of representation into a simultaneous space containing virtual elements; the second corresponds roughly with the *analysis of nature*, including the lacunae, the disorders that confuse the tabulation of beings and scatter it into a series of representations that vaguely, and from a distance, resemble one another.

Now, these two opposing stages (the first the negative one of the disorder in nature and in our impressions, the other the positive one of the power to reconstitute order out of those impressions) are united in the idea of a 'genesis'. And this in two possible ways. Either the negative stage (that of disorder and vague resemblance) is attributed to the imagination itself, which then exercises a double function: if it is able to restore order solely by duplicating representation, it is able to do so only in so far as it would prevent us from perceiving directly, and in their analytic truth, the identities and differences of things. The power of imagination is only the inverse, the other side, of its defect. It exists within man, at the suture of body and soul. It is there that Descartes, Malebranche, and Spinoza analysed it, both as the locus of error and as the power of attaining to truth, even mathematical truth; they recognized in it the stigma of finitude, whether as the sign of a fall outside the area of intelligibility or as the mark of a limited nature. Alternatively, the positive stage of imagination can be attributed to shifting resemblances and the vague murmur of similitudes. It is the disorder of nature due to its own history, to its catastrophes, or perhaps merely to its jumbled plurality, which is no longer capable of providing representation with anything but things that resemble one another. So that representation, perpetually bound to contents so very close to one another, repeats itself, recalls itself, duplicates itself quite naturally, causes almost identical impressions to arise again and again, and engenders imagination. It was in just this proliferation of a nature that is multiple, yet obscurely and irrationally re-created, in the enigmatic fact of a nature that prior to all order resembles itself, that Condillac and Hume sought for the link between resemblance and imagination. Their solutions were strictly contradictory, but they were both answers to the same problem. It is in any case understandable that the second type of analysis should have so easily been deployed in the mythical form of the first man (Rousseau), or that of the awakening consciousness (Condillac), or that of the stranger suddenly thrust into the world (Hume): this genesis functioned exactly instead of and in place of *Genesis* itself.

One further remark. Though the notions of nature and human nature have a certain importance in the Classical age, this is not because the hidden and inexhaustibly rich source of power which we call nature had suddenly been discovered as a field for empirical inquiry; nor is it because a tiny, singular, and complex subregion called human nature had been isolated within this vast field of nature. In fact, these two concepts function in such a way as to guarantee the kinship, the reciprocal bond, between imagination and resemblance. It is true that imagination is apparently only one of the properties of human nature, and resemblance one of the effects of nature; but if we follow the archaeological network that provides Classical thought with its laws, we see quite clearly that human nature resides in that narrow overlap of representation which permits it to represent itself to itself (all human nature is there: just enough outside representation for it to present itself again, in the blank space that separates the presence of representation and the 're-' of its repetition); and that nature is nothing but the impalpable confusion within representation that makes the resemblance there perceptible before the order of the identities is yet visible. Nature and human nature, within the general configuration of the *episteme*, permit the reconciliation of resemblance and imagination that provides a foundation for, and makes possible, all the empirical sciences of order.

In the sixteenth century, resemblance was linked to a system of signs; and it was the interpretation of those signs that opened up the field of concrete knowledge. From the seventeenth century, resemblance was pushed out to the boundaries of knowledge, towards the humblest and basest of its frontiers. There, it links up with imagination, with doubtful repetitions, with misty analogies. And instead of opening up the way to a science of interpretation, it implies a genesis that leads from those unrefined forms of the Same to the great tables of knowledge developed according to the forms of identity, of difference, and of order. The project of a science of order, with a foundation such as it had in the seventeenth century, carried the implication that it had to be paralleled by an accompanying genesis of consciousness, as indeed it was, effectively and uninterruptedly, from Locke to the 'Idéologues'.

VI MATHESIS AND 'TAXINOMIA'

The project of a general science of order; a theory of signs analysing representation; the arrangement of identities and differences into ordered tables: these constituted an area of empiricity in the Classical age that had not existed until the end of the Renaissance and that was destined to disappear early in the nineteenth century. It is so difficult for us to reinstate now, and so thickly overlaid by the system of positivities to which our own knowledge belongs, that it has for long passed unperceived. It is distorted and masked by the use of categories and patterns that are our own. An attempt is apparently being made to reconstitute what the 'sciences of life', of 'nature' or 'man', were, in the seventeenth and eighteenth centuries, while it is quite simply forgotten that man and life and nature are none of them domains that present themselves to the curiosity of knowledge spontaneously and passively.

What makes the totality of the Classical *episteme* possible is primarily the relation to a knowledge of order. When dealing with the ordering of simple natures, one has recourse to a mathesis, of which the universal method is algebra. When dealing with the ordering of complex natures (representations in general, as they are given in experience), one has to constitute a *taxinomia*, and to do that one has to establish a system of signs. These signs are to the order of composite natures what algebra is to the order of simple natures. But in so far as empirical representations must be analysable into simple natures, it is clear that the *taxinomia* relates wholly to the mathesis; on the other hand, since the perception of proofs is only one particular case of representation in general, one can equally well say that mathesis is only one particular case of *taxinomia*. Similarly, the signs established by thought itself constitute, as it were, an algebra of complex representations; and algebra, inversely, is a method of providing simple natures with signs and of operating upon those signs. We therefore have the arrangement shown below:

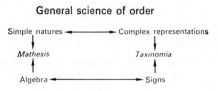

General science of order

Simple natures ⟷ Complex representations

Mathesis   Taxinomia

Algebra ⟷ Signs

But that is not all. *Taxinomia* also implies a certain continuum of things (a non-discontinuity, a plenitude of being) and a certain power of the imagination that renders apparent what is not, but makes possible, by this very fact, the revelation of that continuity. The possibility of a science of empirical orders requires, therefore, an analysis of knowledge – an analysis that must show how the hidden (and as it were confused) continuity of being can be reconstituted by means of the temporal connection provided by discontinuous representations. Hence the necessity, constantly manifested throughout the Classical age, of questioning the origin of knowledge. In fact, these empirical analyses are not in opposition to the project of a universal mathesis, in the sense that scepticism is to rationalism; they were already included in the requisites of a knowledge that is no longer posited as experience of the Same but as the establishment of Order. Thus, at the two extremities of the Classical *episteme*, we have a *mathesis* as the science of calculable order and a *genesis* as the analysis of the constitution of orders on the basis of empirical series. On the one hand, we have a utilization of the symbols of possible operations upon identities and differences; on the other, we have an analysis of the marks progressively imprinted in the mind by the resemblances between things and the retrospective action of imagination. Between the *mathesis* and the *genesis* there extends the region of signs – of signs that span the whole domain of empirical representation, but never extend beyond it. Hedged in by calculus and genesis, we have the area of the *table*. This kind of knowledge involves the allotting of a sign to all that our representation can present us with: perceptions, thoughts, desires; these signs must have a value as characters, that is, they must articulate the representation as a whole into distinct subregions, all separated from one another by assignable characteristics; in this way they authorize the establishment of a simultaneous system according to which the representations express their proximity and their distance, their adjacency and their separateness – and therefore the network, which, outside chronology, makes patent their kinship and reinstates their relations of order within a permanent area. In this manner the table of identities and differences may be drawn up.

It is in this area the we encounter *natural history* – the science of the characters that articulate the continuity and the tangle of nature. It is also in this area that we encounter the *theory of money* and the *theory of value* – the science of the signs that authorize exchange and permit the establishment of equivalences between men's needs or desires. Lastly, it is also in this region that we find *general grammar* – the science of the signs by means of which men group together their individual perceptions and pattern the continuous flow of their thoughts. Despite their differences, these three domains existed in the Classical age only in so far as the fundamental area of the ordered table was established between the calculation of equalities and the genesis of representations.

It is patent that these three notions – *mathesis, taxinomia, genesis* – designate not so much separate domains as a solid grid of kinships that defines the general configuration of knowledge in the Classical age. *Taxinomia* is not in opposition to mathesis: it resides within it and is distinguished from it; for it too is a science of order – a qualitative mathesis. But understood in the strict sense mathesis is a science of equalities, and therefore of attributions and judgements; it is the science of *truth*. *Taxinomia*, on the other hand, treats of identities and differences; it is the science of articulations and classifications; it is the knowledge of *beings*. In the same way, genesis is contained within *taxinomia*, or at least finds in it its primary possibility. But *taxinomia* establishes the table of visible differences; genesis presupposes a progressive series; the first treats of signs in their spatial simultaneity, as a syntax; the second divides them up into an analogon of time, as a chronology. In relation to mathesis, *taxinomia* functions as an ontology confronted by an apophantics; confronted by genesis, it functions as a semiology confronted by history. It defines, then, the general law of beings, and at the same time the conditions under which it is possible to know them. Hence the fact that the theory of signs in the Classical period was able to support simultaneously both a science with a dogmatic approach, which purported to be a knowledge of nature itself, and a philosophy of representation, which, in the course of time, became more and more nominalist and more and more sceptical. Hence, too, the fact that such an arrangement has disappeared so completely that later ages have lost even the memory of its existence; this is because after the Kantian critique, and all that occurred in Western culture at the end of the eighteenth century, a new type of division was established: on the one hand mathesis was regrouped so as to constitute an apophantics and an ontology, and it is in this form that it has dominated the formal disciplines right up to our day; on the other hand, history and semiology (the latter absorbed, moreover, by the former) united to form those interpretative disciplines whose power has extended from Schleiermacher to Nietzsche and Freud.

In any case, the Classical *episteme* can be defined in its most general arrangement in terms of the articulated system of a *mathesis*, a *taxinomia*, and a *genetic analysis*. The sciences always carry within themselves the project, however remote it may be, of an exhaustive ordering of the world; they are always directed, too, towards the discovery of simple elements and their progressive combination; and at their centre they form a table on which knowledge is displayed in a system contemporary with itself.

The centre of knowledge, in the seventeenth and eighteenth centuries, is the *table*. As for the great controversies that occupied men's minds, these are accommodated quite naturally in the folds of this organization.

It is quite possible to write a history of thought in the Classical period using these controversies as starting-points or themes. But one would then be writing only a history of opinions, that is, of the choices operated according to individuals, environments, social groups; and a whole method of inquiry is thereby implied. If one wishes to undertake an archaeological analysis of knowledge itself, it is not these celebrated controversies that ought to be used as the guidelines and articulation of such a project. One must reconstitute the general system of thought whose network, in its positivity, renders an interplay of simultaneous and apparently contradictory opinions possible. It is this network that defines the conditions that make a controversy or problem possible, and that bears the historicity of knowledge. If the Western world did battle with itself in order to know whether life was nothing but movement or whether nature was sufficiently well ordered to prove the existence of God, it was not because a problem had been opened up; it was because, after dispersing the undefined circle of signs and resemblances, and before organizing the series of causality and history, the *episteme* of Western culture had opened up an area to form a table over which it wandered endlessly, from the calculable forms of order to the analysis of the most complex representations. And we see the marks of this movement on the historical surface of the themes, controversies, problems, and preferences of opinion. Acquired learning spanned from one end to the other a 'space of knowledge' which had suddenly appeared in the seventeenth century and which was not to be closed again until a hundred and fifty years later.

We must now undertake the analysis of this tabulated space, in those subregions in which it is visible in its clearest form, that is, in the theories of language, classification, and money.

It may be objected that the mere fact of attempting to analyse general grammar, natural history, and economics simultaneously and *en bloc* – by relating them to a general theory of signs and representation – presupposes a question that could originate only in our own century. It is true that the Classical age was no more able than any other culture to circumscribe or name its own general system of knowledge. But that system was in fact sufficiently constricting to cause the visible forms of knowledge to trace their kinships upon it themselves, as though methods, concepts, types of analysis, acquired experiences, minds, and finally men themselves, had all been displaced at the behest of a fundamental network defining the implicit but inevitable unity of knowledge. History has provided us with innumerable examples of these displacements. The connecting paths between the theories of knowledge, of signs, and of grammar were trodden so many times: Port-Royal produced its *Grammaire* as a complement and natural sequel to its *Logique*, the former being connected to the latter by a common analysis of signs; Condillac, Destutt de Tracy, and Gerando articulated one upon the other the decomposition of knowledge into its conditions or 'elements', and the reflection upon those signs of which language forms only the most visible application and use. There is also a well-trodden connection between the analysis of representation and signs and the analysis of wealth: Quesnay the physiocrat wrote the article on 'Évidence' for the *Encyclopédie*; Condillac and Destutt included in their theory of knowledge and language that of trade and economics, which for them possessed political and also moral value; it is well known that Turgot wrote the article on 'Étymologie' for the *Encyclopédie* and the first systematic parallel between money and words; that Adam Smith, in addition to his great work on economics, wrote a treatise on the origin of languages. There is a connecting path between the theory of natural classifications and theories of language: Adanson did not merely attempt to create, in the botanical field, a nomenclature that was both artificial and coherent; he aimed at (and in part carried out) a whole reorganization of writing in terms of the phonetic data of language; Rousseau left among his posthumous works some rudiments of botany and a treatise on the origin of languages.

Such, traced out, as it were, in dotted lines, was the great grid of empirical knowledge: that of non-quantitative orders. And perhaps the deferred but insistent unity of a *Taxinomia universalis* appeared in all clarity in the work of Linnaeus, when he conceived the project of discovering in all the concrete domains of nature or society the same distributions and the same order[21]. The limit of knowledge would be the perfect transparency of representations to the signs by which they are ordered.

NOTES

[1] Descartes, *Œuvres philosophiques* (Paris, 1963 edn., t. I, p. 77).
[2] F. Bacon, *Novum Organum* (1620, book I, xlv and lix).
[3] Descartes, *Regulae*, XIV, p. 168.
[4] Ibid., XIV, p. 168.
[5] Ibid., XIV, p. 182.

[6] Ibid., VI, p. 102; VII, p. 109.

[7] Ibid., XIV, p. 182.

[8] Ibid., VI, p. 103.

[9] Ibid., VII, p. 110.

[10] Ibid., III, p. 86.

[11] *Logique de Port-Royal*, Ière partie, chap. IV.

[12] G. Berkeley, *An essay towards a new theory of vision* (1709, CXLVII).

[13] G. Berkeley, *A treatise concerning the principles of human knowledge* (1710, LXV).

[14] Condillac, *Essai sur l'origine des connaissances humaines* (Œuvres, Paris, 1798, t. I, pp. 188–208).

[15] Ibid., p. 75.

[16] J. Itard, *Rapport sur les nouveaux développements de Victor de l'Aveyron* (1806); reprinted in L. Malson, *Les Enfants sauvages* (Paris, 1964).

[17] *Logique de Port-Royal*, Ière partie, chap. IV.

[18] Ibid.

[19] Destutt de Tracy, *Eléments d'Idéologie* (Paris, year XI, t. II, p. 1).

[20] Merian, *Réflexions philosophiques sur la ressemblance* (1767, pp. 3 and 4).

[21] Linnaeus, *Philosophie botanique*, sections 155 and 256.

CHAPTER 4

Speaking

I CRITICISM AND COMMENTARY

The existence of language in the Classical age is both pre-eminent and unobtrusive.

Pre-eminent, because words have been allotted the task and the power of 'representing thought'. But representing in this case does not mean translating, giving a visible version of, fabricating a material double that will be able, on the external surface of the body, to reproduce thought in its exactitude. Representing must be understood in the strict sense: language represents thought as thought represents itself. To constitute language or give it life from within, there is no essential and primitive act of signification, but only, at the heart of representation, the power that it possesses to represent itself, that is, to analyse itself by juxtaposing itself to itself, part by part, under the eye of reflection, and to delegate itself in the form of a substitute that will be an extension of it. In the Classical age, nothing is given that is not given to representation; but, by that very fact, no sign ever appears, no word is spoken, no proposition is ever directed at any content except by the action of a representation that stands back from itself, that duplicates and reflects itself in another representation that is its equivalent. Representations are not rooted in a world that gives them meaning; they open of themselves on to a space that is their own, whose internal network gives rise to meaning. And language exists in the gap that representation creates for itself. Words do not, then, form a thin film that duplicates thought on the outside; they recall thought, they indicate it, but inwards first of all, among all those representations that represent other representations. The language of the Classical age is much closer to the thought it is charged with expressing than is generally supposed; but it is not parallel to it; it is caught in the grid of thought, woven into the very fabric it is unrolling. It is not an exterior effect of thought, but thought itself.

And, because of this, it makes itself invisible, or almost so. In any case, it has become so transparent to representation that its very existence ceases to be a problem. The Renaissance came to a halt before the brute fact that language existed: in the density of the world, a graphism mingling with things or flowing beneath them; marks made upon manuscripts or the pages of books. And all these insistent marks summoned up a secondary language – that of commentary, exegesis, erudition – in order to stir the language that lay dormant within them and to make it speak at last; the existence of language preceded, as if by a mute stubbornness, what one could read in it and the words that gave it sound. From the seventeenth century, it is this massive and intriguing existence of language that is eliminated. It no longer appears hidden in the enigma of the mark; it has not yet appeared in the theory of signification. From an extreme point of view, one might say that language in the Classical era does not exist. But that it functions: its whole existence is located in its representative role, is limited precisely to that role and finally exhausts it. Language has no other locus, no other value, than in representation; in the hollow it has been able to form.

In this way, Classical language discovers a certain relation with itself which had hitherto been neither possible nor conceivable. In relation to itself, the language of the sixteenth century was in a position of perpetual commentary; but this commentary can take place only if there is language – language that silently pre-exists within the discourse by which one tries to make that language speak; there can be no commentary without the absolute precondition of the text; and, inversely, if the world is a network of marks and words, how else is one to speak of them but in the form of commentary? From the Classical age, language is deployed within representation and in that duplication of itself which hollows itself out. Henceforth, the primary Text is effaced, and with it, the entire, inexhaustible foundation of the words whose mute being was inscribed in things; all that remains is representation, unfolding in the verbal signs that manifest it, and hence becoming *discourse*. For the enigma of a speech which a second language must interpret is substituted the essential discursivity of representation: the open possibility, as yet neutral and undifferentiating, but which it will be the task of discourse to fulfil and to determine. When this discourse becomes in turn an object of language, it is not questioned as if it were saying something without actually saying it, as if it were a language enclosed upon itself; one no longer attempts to uncover the great enigmatic statement that lies hidden beneath its signs; one asks how it functions: what representations it designates, what elements it cuts out and removes, how it analyses and composes, what play of substitutions enables it to accomplish its role of representation. *Commentary* has yielded to *criticism*.

This new relation that language establishes with itself is neither a simple nor a unilateral one. Criticism would appear to contrast with commentary in the same way as the analysis of a visible form with the discovery of a hidden content. But since this form is that of representation, criticism can analyse language only in terms of truth, precision, appropriateness, or expressive value. Hence the combined role of criticism and ambiguity – the former never succeeding in freeing itself from the latter. Criticism questions language as if language was a pure function, a totality of mechanisms, a great autonomous play of signs; but, at the same time, it cannot fail to question it as to its truth or falsehood, its transparency or opacity, and therefore as to exactly how what it says is present in the words by which it represents it. It is on the basis of this double, fundamental necessity that the opposition between content and form gradually emerged and finally assumed the importance we know it to have. But no doubt this opposition was consolidated only at a relatively late date, when, in the nineteenth century, the critical relation had itself been weakened. In the Classical period, criticism was applied, without dissociation and, as it were, *en bloc*, to the representative role of language. It then assumed four forms, which, though distinct, were interdependent and articulated upon each other. It was deployed first, in the reflexive order, as a critique of *words*: the impossibility of constructing a science or a philosophy with the received vocabulary; a denunciation in general terms which confused what was distinct in representation with the abstract terms which separated what should remain united; the need to build up the vocabulary of a perfectly analytic language. It was also expressed in the grammatical order as an analysis of the representative *values* of syntax, word order, and sentence construction. Is a language in a higher state of perfection when it has declensions or a system of prepositions? Is it preferable for the word order to be free or strictly determined? What system of tenses best expresses relations of sequence? Criticism also examines the forms of *rhetoric*: the analysis of *figures*, that is, the types of discourse, with the expressive value of each, the analysis of *tropes*, that is, the different relations that words may have with the same representative content (designation by a part or the whole, the essential or the accessory, the event or the circumstance, the thing itself or its analogues). Lastly, faced with existing and already written language, criticism sets out to define its *relation* with what it represents; hence the importance assumed, since the seventeenth century, by critical methods in the exegesis of religious texts; it was no longer a question, in fact, of repeating what had already been said in them, but of defining through what figures and images, by following what order, to what expressive ends, and in order to declare what truth, God or the Prophets had given a discourse the particular form in which it was communicated to us.

Such is the diversity of the critical dimension that is necessarily established when language questions itself on the basis of its function. Since the Classical age, commentary and criticism have been in profound opposition. By speaking of language in terms of representations and truth, criticism judges it and profanes it. Now as language in the irruption of its being, and questioning it as to its secret, commentary halts before the precipice of the original text, and assumes the impossible and endless task of repeating its own birth within itself: it sacralizes language. These two ways by which language establishes a relation with itself were now to enter into a rivalry from which we have not yet emerged – and which may even be sharpening as time passes. This is because since Mallarmé, literature, the privileged object of criticism, has drawn closer and closer to the very being of language, and requires therefore a secondary language which is no longer in the form of criticism, but of commentary. And in fact every critical language since the nineteenth century has become imbued with exegesis, just as the exegeses of the Classical period were imbued with critical methods. However, until the connection between language and representation is broken, or at least transcended, in our culture, all secondary languages will be imprisoned within the alternative of criticism or commentary. And in their indecision they will proliferate *ad infinitum*.

II GENERAL GRAMMAR

Once the existence of language has been eliminated, all that remains is its function in representation: its nature and its virtues as *discourse*. For discourse is merely representation itself represented by verbal signs. But what, then, is the particularity of these signs, and this strange power that enables them, better than any others, to signalize representation, to analyse it, and to recombine it? What is the peculiar property possessed by language and not by any other system of signs?

At first sight, it is possible to define words according to their arbitrariness or their collective character. At its primary root, language is made up, as Hobbes says, of a system of notations that individuals first chose for themselves; by means of these marks they are able to recall representations, link them together, dissociate them, and operate upon them. It is these notations that by covenant or violence were imposed upon the collectivity; but the meaning of the words does not pertain, in any case, to anything but each individual's representation, and even though it may be accepted by everyone it has no other existence than in the thought of individuals taken separately: 'That then which words are the marks of,' says Locke, 'are the ideas of the speaker: nor can any one apply them as marks, immediately, to anything else but the ideas that he himself hath'[1]. What distinguishes language from all other signs and enables it to play a decisive role in representation is, therefore, not so much that it is individual or collective, natural or arbitrary, but that it analyses representation according to a necessarily successive order: the sounds, in fact, can be articulated only one by one; language cannot represent thought, instantly, in its totality; it is bound to arrange it, part by part, in a linear order. Now, such an order is foreign to representation. It is true that thoughts succeed one another in time, but each one forms a unity, whether one agrees with Condillac[2] that all the elements of a representation are given in an instant and that only reflection is able to unroll them one by one, or whether one agrees with Destutt de Tracy[3] that they succeed one another with a rapidity so great that it is not practically possible to observe or to retain their order. It is these representations, pressed in on one another in this way, that must be sorted out into linear propositions: to my gaze, 'the brightness is within the rose'; in my discourse, I cannot avoid it coming either before or after it[4]. If the mind had the power to express ideas 'as it perceives them', there can be no doubt that 'it would express them all at the same time'[5]. But that is precisely what is not possible, for, though 'thought is a simple operation', 'its expression is a successive operation'[6]. It is here that the peculiar property of language resides, that which distinguishes it both from representation (of which, in its turn, it is nevertheless the representation) and from signs (to which it belongs without any other particular privilege). It does not stand in opposition to thought as the exterior does to the interior, or expression to reflection; it does not stand in opposition to all the other signs – gestures, mime, translation, paintings, emblems[7] – as the arbitrary to the natural or the collective to the singular. But it does stand in relation to all

82

that as the successive to the contemporaneous. It is to thought and to signs what algebra is to geometry: it replaces the simultaneous comparison of parts (or magnitudes) with an order whose degrees must be traversed one after the other. It is in this strict sense that language is an *analysis* of thought: not a simple patterning, but a profound establishment of order in space.

It is here that we find that new epistemological domain that the Classical age called 'general grammar'. It would be nonsense to see this purely and simply as the application of a logic to the theory of language. But it would be equally nonsensical to attempt to interpret it as a sort of pre-figuration of a linguistics. *General grammar is the study of verbal order in its relation to the simultaneity that it is its task to represent.* Its proper object is therefore neither thought nor any individual language, but *discourse*, understood as a sequence of verbal signs. This sequence is artificial in relation to the simultaneity of representations, and in so far as this is so language must be in opposition to thought, as what is reflected upon is to what is immediate. And yet the sequence is not the same in all languages: some of them place the action in the middle of the sentence; others at the end; some name the principal object of the representation first, others the accessory circumstances; as the *Encyclopédie* points out, what renders foreign languages opaque to one another, and so difficult to translate, is not so much the differences between the words as the incompatibility of their sequences[8]. In relation to the evident, necessary, universal order introduced into representation by science, and by algebra in particular, language is spontaneous and un-thought-out; it is, as it were, natural. It is equally, according to the point of view from which one looks at it, an already analysed representation and a reflection in the primitive state. In fact, it is the concrete link between representation and reflection. It is not so much the instrument of men's intercommunication as the path by which, necessarily, representation communicates with reflection. This is why *general grammar* assumed so much importance for philosophy during the eighteenth century: it was, at one and the same time, the spontaneous form of science – a kind of logic not controlled by the mind[9] – and the first reflective decomposition of thought: one of the most primitive breaks with the immediate. It constituted, as it were, a philosophy in-herent in the mind – metaphysics, Adam Smith pointed out, was an essential ingredient in the formation of even the least of adjectives[10] – and one that any philosophy had to work through if it was to rediscover, among so many diverse choices, the necessary and evident order of representation. Language is the original form of all reflection, the primary theme of any critique. It is this ambiguous thing, as broad as knowledge, yet always interior to representation, that *general grammar* takes as its object.

But a certain number of consequences must at once be drawn here.

1. The first is that it is easy to see how the sciences of language are divided up in the Classical period: on the one hand, rhetoric, which deals with *figures* and *tropes*, that is, with the manner in which language is spatialized in verbal signs; on the other, grammar, which deals with articulation and order, that is, with the manner in which the analysis of representation is arranged in accordance with a sequential series. Rhetoric defines the spatiality of representation as it comes into being with language; grammar defines in the case of each individual language the order that distributes that spatiality in time. This is why, as we shall see, grammar presupposes languages, even the most primitive and spontaneous ones, to be rhetorical in nature.

2. On the other hand, grammar, as reflection upon language in general, expresses the relation maintained by the latter with universality. This relation can take two forms, according to whether one takes into consideration the possibility of a *universal language* or that of a *universal discourse*. In the Classical period, what was denoted by the term universal language was not the primitive, pure, and unimpaired speech that would be able, if it were rediscovered beyond the punishment of oblivion, to restore the understanding that reigned before Babel. It refers to a tongue that would have the ability to provide every representation, and every element of every representation, with the sign by which it could be marked in a univocal manner; it would also be capable of indicating in what manner the elements in a representation are composed and how they are linked to one another; and since it would possess the necessary instruments with which to indicate all the possible relationships between the various segments of representation, this language would also, by that very fact, be able to accommodate itself to all possible orders. At once characteristic and combinative, the universal language does not re-establish the order of days gone by: it invents signs, a syntax, and a grammar, in which all conceivable order must find its place. As for universal discourse, that too is by no means the unique text that preserves in the cipher of its secret the key to unlock all knowledge; it is rather the possibility of defining the natural and necessary progress of the mind from the simplest representations to the most refined analyses or the most complex combinations: this discourse is knowledge arranged in accordance with the unique

order laid down for it by its origin. It traverses the whole field of knowledge, though as it were in a subterranean manner, in order to reveal, on the basis of representation, the possibility of that knowledge, to reveal its origin, and its natural, linear, and universal link. This common denominator, this foundation underlying all knowledge, this origin expressed in a continuous discourse is Ideology, a language that duplicates the spontaneous thread of knowledge along the whole of its length:

> Man, by his nature, always tends towards the nearest and most pressing result. He thinks first of his needs, then of his pleasures. He occupies himself with agriculture, with medicine, with war, with practical politics, then with poetry and the arts, before turning his thoughts to philosophy; and when he turns back upon himself and begins to reflect, he prescribes rules for his judgement, which is logic, for his discourse, which is grammar, for his desires, which is ethics. He then believes himself to have reached the summit of theory. . .;

but he perceives that all these operations have 'a common source' and that 'this sole centre of all truths is the knowledge of his intellectual faculties' [11].

The universal characteristic and ideology stand in the same opposition to one another as do the universality of language in general (which arranges all possible orders in the simultaneity of a single fundamental table) and the universality of an exhaustive discourse (which reconstitutes the single genesis, common to the whole sequence of all possible branches of knowledge). But their aim and their common possibility reside in a power that the Classical age attributes to language: that of providing adequate signs for all representations, whatever they may be, and of establishing possible links between them. In so far as language can represent all representations it is with good reason the element of the universal. There must exist within it at least the possibility of a language that will gather into itself, between its words, the totality of the world, and, inversely, the world, as the totality of what is representable, must be able to become, in its totality, an Encyclopaedia. And Charles Bonnet's great dream merges at this point with what language is in its connection and kinship with representation:

> I delight in envisaging the innumerable multitude of Worlds as so many books which, when collected together, compose the immense Library of the Universe or the true Universal Encyclopaedia. I conceive that the marvellous gradation that exists between these different

worlds facilitates in superior intelligences, to whom it has been given to traverse or rather to read them, the acquisition of truths of every kind, which it encompasses, and instils in their understanding that order and that concatenation which are its principal beauty. But these celestial Encyclopaedists do not all possess the Encyclopaedia of the Universe to the same degree; some possess only a few branches of it, others possess a greater number, others grasp even more still; but all have eternity in which to increase and perfect their learning and develop all their faculties[12].

Against this background of an absolute Encyclopaedia, human beings constitute intermediary forms of a composite and limited universality: alphabetical encyclopaedias, which accommodate the greatest possible quantity of learning in the arbitrary order provided by letters; pasigraphies, which make it possible to transcribe all the languages of the world by means of a single system of figures[13]; polyvalent lexicons, which establish synonymies between a greater or lesser number of languages; and, finally, rational encyclopaedias, which claim to 'exhibit as far as is possible the order and concatenation of human learning' by examining 'their genealogy and their filiation, the causes that must have given rise to them and the characteristics that distinguish them'[14]. Whatever the partial character of these projects, whatever the empirical circumstances of such undertakings, the foundation of their possibility in the Classical *episteme* is that, though language had been entirely reduced to its function within representation, representation, on the other hand, had no relation with the universal except through the intermediary of language.

3. Knowledge and language are rigorously interwoven. They share, in representation, the same origin and the same functional principle; they support one another, complement one another, and criticize one another incessantly. In their most general form, both knowing and speaking consist first of all in the simultaneous analysis of representation, in the discrimination of its elements, in the establishing of the relations that combine those elements, and the possible sequences according to which they can be unfolded. It is in one and the same movement that the mind speaks and knows: 'It is by the same processes that one learns to speak and that one discovers either the principles of the world's system or those of the human mind's operations, that is, all that is sublime in our knowledge'[15]. But language is knowledge only in an unreflecting form; it imposes itself on individuals from the outside, guiding them, willy nilly, towards notions

that may be concrete or abstract, exact or with little foundation. Knowledge, on the other hand, is like a language whose every word has been examined and every relation verified. To know is to speak correctly, and as the steady progress of the mind dictates; to speak is to know as far as one is able, and in accordance with the model imposed by those whose birth one shares. The sciences are well-made languages, just as languages are sciences lying fallow. All languages must therefore be renewed; in other words, explained and judged according to that analytic order which none of them now follows exactly; and readjusted if necessary so that the chain of knowledge may be made visible in all its clarity, without any shadows or lacunae. It is thus part of the very nature of grammar to be prescriptive, not by any means because it is an attempt to impose the norms of a beautiful language obedient to the rules of taste, but because it refers the radical possibility of speech to the ordering system of representation. Destutt de Tracy once observed that the best treatises on logic, in the eighteenth century, were written by grammarians: this is because the prescriptions of grammar at that time were of an analytic and not an aesthetic order.

And this link between language and knowledge opens up a whole historical field that had not existed in previous periods. Something like a history of knowledge becomes possible; because, if language is a spontaneous science, obscure to itself and unpractised, this also means, in return, that it will be brought nearer to perfection by knowledge, which cannot lodge itself in the words it needs without leaving its imprint in them, and, as it were, the empty mould of its content. Languages, though imperfect knowledge themselves, are the faithful memory of the progress of knowledge towards perfection. They lead into error, but they record what has been learned. In their chaotic order, they give rise to false ideas; but true ideas leave in them the indelible mark of an order that chance on its own could never have created. What civilizations and peoples leave us as the monuments of their thought is not so much their texts as their vocabularies, their syntaxes, the sounds of their languages rather than the words they spoke; not so much their discourse as the element that made it possible, the discursivity of their language.

The language of a people gives us its vocabulary, and its vocabulary is a sufficiently faithful and authoritative record of all the knowledge of that people; simply by comparing the different states of a nation's vocabulary at different times one could form an idea of its progress.

Every science has its name, every notion within a science has its name too, everything known in nature is designated, as is everything invented in the arts, as well as phenomena, manual tasks, and tools[16].

Hence the possibility of writing a history of freedom and slavery based upon languages[17], or even a history of opinions, prejudices, superstitions, and beliefs of all kinds, since what is written on these subjects is always of less value as evidence than are the words themselves[18]. Hence, too, the project of creating an encyclopaedia 'of the sciences and arts', which would not follow the connecting links of knowledge itself but would be accommodated in the form of the language, within the space opened up in words themselves; for that is where future ages would have to look to find what we have known or thought, since words, in their roughly hewn state, are distributed along that mid-way line that marks the adjacency of science to perception and of reflection to images. It is in them that what we imagine becomes what we know, and, on the other hand, that what we know becomes what we represent to ourselves every day. The old relation to the *text*, which was the Renaissance definition of erudition, has now been transformed: it has become, in the Classical age, the relation to the pure element of the *language*.

Thus we see glowing into life the luminous element in which language and learning, correct discourse and knowledge, universal language and analysis of thought, the history of mankind and the sciences of language freely communicate. Even when it was intended for publication, the knowledge of the Renaissance was arranged within an enclosed space. The 'Academy' was a closed circle which projected the essentially secret form of knowledge onto the surface of social configurations. For the primary task of that knowledge was to draw speech from mute signs: it had to recognize their forms, interpret them, and retranscribe them by means of other graphic signs which then had to be deciphered in their turn; so that even the discovery of the secret did not escape this array of obstacles, which had rendered it at once so difficult and yet so precious. In the Classical age, knowing and speaking are interwoven in the same fabric; in the case of both knowledge and language, it is a question of providing representation with the signs by means of which it can unfold itself in obedience to a necessary and visible order. Even when stated, knowledge in the sixteenth century was still a secret, albeit a shared one. Even when hidden, knowledge in the seventeenth and eighteenth centuries is discourse with a veil drawn over it. This is because it is of the very

nature of science to enter into the system of verbal communications[19],
and of the very nature of language to be knowledge from its very first
word. Speaking, enlightening, and knowing are, in the strict sense of
the term, *of the same order*. The interest shown by the Classical age in
science, the publicity accorded to its controversies, its extremely exoteric
character, its opening up to the uninitiated, Fontenelle's popularization
of astronomy, Voltaire reading Newton, all this is doubtless nothing
more than a sociological phenomenon. It did not provoke the slightest
alteration in the history of thought, or modify the development of knowledge one jot. It explains nothing, except of course on the doxographic
level where it should be situated; but its condition of possibility is nevertheless there, in that reciprocal kinship between knowledge and language.
The nineteenth century was to dissolve that link, and to leave behind it,
in confrontation, a knowledge closed in upon itself and a pure language
that had become, in nature and function, enigmatic – something that has
been called, since that time, *Literature*. Between the two, the intermediary
languages – descendants of, or outcasts from, both knowledge and language – were to proliferate to infinity.

4. Because it had become analysis and order, language entered into
relations with time unprecedented hitherto. The sixteenth century accepted that languages succeeded one another in history and were capable
of engendering one another. The oldest were the mother languages. The
most archaic of all, since it was the tongue of the Eternal when he addressed himself to men, was Hebrew, and Hebrew was thought to have
given rise to Syriac and Arabic; then came Greek, from which both Coptic
and Egyptian were derived; Latin was the common ancestor of Italian,
Spanish, and French; lastly, 'Teutonic' had given rise to German, English,
and Flemish[20]. In the seventeenth century, the relation of language to
time is inverted: it is no longer time that allots languages their places,
one by one, in world history; it is languages that unfold representations
and words in a sequence of which they themselves define the laws. It is
by means of this internal order, and the positions it allots to its words,
that each language defines its specificity, and no longer by means of its
place in a historical series. For language, time is its interior mode of analysis, not its place of birth. Hence the paucity of interest shown by the
Classical age in chronological filiation, to the point of denying, contrary
to all the 'evidence' – our evidence, that is – the kinship of Italian or
French with Latin[21]. The kinds of series that existed in the sixteenth
century, and were to reappear in the nineteenth, were replaced by

typologies, typologies of order. There is the group of languages that places the subject being dealt with first; next the action undertaken or undergone by that subject; and last the object upon which it is exercised: as witness, French, English, Spanish. Opposed to these is the group of languages that places 'sometimes the action, sometimes the object, sometimes the modification or circumstance first': for example Latin, or 'Slavonian', in which the function of words is indicated, not by their positions, but by their inflections. Finally, there is the third group made up of mixed languages (such as Greek or Teutonic), 'which have something of both the other groups, possessing an article as well as cases'[22]. But it must be understood that it is not the presence or absence of inflections that defines the possible or necessary order of the words in each language. It is order as analysis and a sequential alignment of representations that constitutes the preliminary form and prescribes the use of declensions or articles. Those languages that follow the order 'of imagination and interest' do not determine any constant position for words: they are obliged to emphasize them by means of inflections (these are the 'transpositive' languages). If, on the other hand, they follow the uniform order of reflection, they need only indicate the number and gender of substantives by means of an article; position in the analytic ordering of the sentence has a functional value in itself: these are the 'analogical' languages[23]. Languages are related to and distinguished from one another according to a table of possible types of word order. The table shows them all simultaneously, but suggests which were the most ancient languages; it may be admitted, in fact, that the most spontaneous order (that of images and passions) must have preceded the most considered (that of logic); external dating is determined by the internal forms of analysis and order. Time has become interior to language.

The history of the various languages is no longer anything more than a question of erosion or accident, introduction, meetings, and the mingling of various elements; it has no law, no progress, no necessity proper to it. How, for instance, was the Greek language formed?

> It was Phoenician merchants, adventurers from Phrygia, from Macedonia and Illyria, Galatians, Scythians, and bands of exiles or fugitives who loaded the first stratum of the Greek language with so many kinds of innumerable particles and so many dialects[24].

French is made up of Latin and Gothic nouns, Gallic constructions, Arabic articles and numerals, words borrowed from the English and the

Italians – as journeys, wars, or trade agreements dictated[25]. This is because languages evolve in accordance with the effects of migrations, victories and defeats, fashions, and commerce; but not under the impulsion of any historicity possessed by the languages themselves. They do not obey any internal principle of development; they simply unfold representations and their elements in a linear sequence. If there does exist a time for languages that is positive, then it must not be looked for outside them, in the sphere of history, but in the ordering of their words, in the form left by discourse.

It is now possible to circumscribe the epistemological field of *general grammar*, which appeared during the second half of the seventeenth century and faded away again during the last years of the following century. General grammar is not at all the same as comparative grammar: the comparisons it makes between different languages are not its object; they are merely employed as a method. This is because its generality does not consist in the discovery of peculiarly grammatical laws, common to all linguistic domains, which could then be used to display the structure of any possible language in an ideal and constricting unity; if it is indeed general, then it is so to the extent that it attempts to make visible, below the level of grammatical rules, but at the same level as their foundation, the representative function of discourse – whether it be the vertical function, which designates what is represented, or the horizontal function, which links what is represented to the same mode as thought. Since it makes language visible as a representation that is the articulation of another representation, it is indisputably 'general'; what it treats of is the interior duplication existing within representation. But since that articulation can be accomplished in many different ways, there must be, paradoxically, various general grammars: French, English, Latin, German, etc.[26]. General grammar does not attempt to define the laws of all languages, but to examine each particular language, in turn, as a mode of the articulation of thought upon itself. In every language, taken in isolation, representation provides itself with 'characters'. General grammar is intended to define the system of identities and differences that these spontaneous characters presuppose and employ. It must establish the *taxonomy* of each language. In other words, the basis, in each of them, for the possibility of discourse.

Hence the two directions that it necessarily takes. Since discourse links its parts together in the same way as representation does its elements, general grammar must study the representative function of words in relation to each other; which presupposes in the first place an analysis of the links that connect words together (theory of the proposition and in particular of the verb), then an analysis of the various types of words and of the way in which they pattern the representation and are distinguished from each other (theory of articulation). However, since discourse is not simply a representative whole, but a duplicated representation that denotes another representation – the one that it is in fact representing – general grammar must also study the way in which words designate what they say, first of all in their primitive value (theory of origins and of the root), then in their permanent capacity for displacement, extension, and reorganization (theory of rhetoric and of derivation).

III THE THEORY OF THE VERB

The proposition is to language what representation is to thought, at once its most general and most elementary form, since as soon as it is broken down we no longer encounter the discourse but only its elements, in the form of so much scattered raw material. Below the proposition we do indeed find words, but it is not in them that language is created. It is true that in the beginning man emitted only simple cries, but these did not begin to be language until they contained – if only within their monosyllable – a relation that was of the order of a proposition. The yell of the primitive man in a struggle becomes a true word only when it is no longer the lateral expression of his pain, and when it has validity as a judgement or as a statement of the type 'I am choking'[27]. What constitutes a word as a word and raises it above the level of cries and noises is the proposition concealed within it. If the wild man of Aveyron did not attain to speech, it was because words remained for him merely the vocal marks of things and of the impressions that those things made upon his mind; they had acquired no propositional value. He could, it is true, pronounce the word 'milk' when a bowl of milk was put in front of him; but that was merely 'the confused expression of that alimentary liquid, of the vessel containing it, and of the desire produced by it'[28]; the word never became a sign representing the thing, for at no point did he ever wish to say that the milk was hot, or ready, or expected. It is in fact the proposition that detaches the vocal sign from its immediate expressive values and establishes its supreme linguistic possibility. For Classical thought, language begins not with expression, but with discourse. When one says 'no', one is not translating one's refusal into a mere cry; one is contracting into the form of a single word 'an entire proposition: . . . I do not feel that, or I do not believe that'[29].

'Let us go directly to the proposition, the essential object of grammar'[30]. In the proposition, all the functions of language are led back to the three elements that alone are indispensable to the formation of a proposition: the subject, the predicate, and the link between them. Even then, the subject and predicate are of the same nature, since the proposition affirms that the one is identical to or akin to the other; it is therefore possible for them, under certain conditions, to exchange functions. The only difference, though it is a decisive one, is that manifested by the irreducibility of the verb: as Hobbes[31] says:

> In every proposition three things are to be considered, *viz.* the two names, which are the *subject* and the *predicate*, and their *copulation*; both which names raise in our mind the thought of one and the same thing; but the copulation makes us think of the cause for which those names were imposed on that thing.

The verb is the indispensable condition for all discourse; and wherever it does not exist, at least by implication, it is not possible to say that there is language. All nominal propositions conceal the invisible presence of a verb, and Adam Smith[32] thinks that, in its primitive form, language was composed only of impersonal verbs (such as 'it is raining' or 'it is thundering'), and that all the other parts of discourse became detached from this original verbal core as so many derived and secondary details. The threshold of language lies at the point where the verb first appears. This verb must therefore be treated as a composite entity, at the same time a word among other words, subjected to the same rules of case and agreement as other words, and yet set apart from all other words, in a region which is not that of the spoken, but rather that from which one speaks. It is on the fringe of discourse, at the connection between what is said and what is saying itself, exactly at that point where signs are in the process of becoming language.

It is this function that we must now examine – by stripping the verb of all that has constantly overlaid and obscured it. We must not stop, as Aristotle did, at the fact that the verb signifies tenses (there are many other words, adverbs, adjectives, nouns, that can carry temporal significations). Nor must we stop, as Scaliger did, at the fact that it expresses actions or passions, whereas nouns denote things – and permanent things (for there is precisely the very noun 'action' to be considered). Nor must we attach importance, as Buxtorf did, to the different persons of the verb, for these can also be designated by certain pronouns. What we must do before all else is to reveal, in all clarity, the essential function of the verb: the verb *affirms*, it indicates 'that the discourse in which this word is employed is the discourse of a man who does not merely conceive of nouns, but judges them'[33]. A proposition exists – and discourse too – when we affirm the existence of an attributive link between two things, when we say that this *is* that[34]. The entire species of the verb may be reduced to the single verb that signifies *to be*. All the others secretly make use of this unique function, but they have hidden it beneath a layer of determinations: attributes have been added to it, and instead of saying 'I am singing', we say 'I sing'[35]; indications of time have been added, and instead of saying 'before now I am singing', we say 'I sang'; lastly, certain languages have integrated the subject itself into their verbs, and thus we find the Romans saying, not *ego vivit*, but *vivo*. All of this is merely accretion and sedimentation around and over a very slight yet essential verbal function, 'there is only the verb *to be* . . . that has remained in this state of simplicity'[36]. The entire essence of language is concentrated in that singular word. Without it, everything would have remained silent, and though men, like certain animals, would have been able to make use of their voices well enough, yet not one of those cries hurled through the jungle would ever have proved to be the first link in the great chain of language.

In the Classical period, language in its raw state – that mass of signs impressed upon the world in order to exercise our powers of inter-rogation – vanished from sight, but language itself entered into new rela-tions with being, ones more difficult to grasp, since it is by means of a word that language expresses being and is united to it; it affirms being from within itself; and yet it could not exist as language if that word, on its own, were not, in advance, sustaining all possibility of discourse. With-out a way of designating being, there would be no language at all; but without language, there would be no verb *to be*, which is only one part of language. This simple word is the representation of being in language; but it is equally the representative being of language – that which, by enabling language to affirm what it says, renders it susceptible of truth or error. In this respect it is different from all the signs that may or may not be consistent with, faithful to, or well adapted to, what they designate, but that are never true or false. Language is, wholly and entirely, *dis-course*; and it is so by virtue of this singular power of a word to leap across the system of signs towards the being of that which is signified.

But from where does this power derive? And what is this meaning, which, by overflowing the words containing it, forms the basis of the proposition? The grammarians of *Port-Royal* said that the meaning of the verb *to be* was affirmation – which indicated well enough in what region of language its absolute privilege lay, but not at all in what it consisted. We must not imagine that the verb *to be* contains the idea of affirmation, for the word *affirmation* itself, and also the word *yes*, contain it equally well[37]; what the verb *to be* provides is rather the affirmation of the idea. But is the affirmation of an idea also the expression of its existence? This is in fact what Bauzée thinks, and he also takes it to be one reason why variations of time have been concentrated into the form of the verb: for the essence of things does not change, it is only their existence that appears and disappears, it is only their existence that has a past and a future[38]. To which Condillac can observe in reply that if existence can be withdrawn from things, this must mean that it is no more than an attribute, and that the verb can affirm death as well as existence. The only thing that the verb affirms is the coexistence of two representations: for example, those of a tree and greenness, or of man and existence or death; this is why the tenses of verbs do not indicate the time when things existed in the absolute, but a relative system of anteriority or simultaneity between different things[39]. Coexistence is not, in fact, an attribute of the thing itself; it is no more than a form of the representation: to say that the greenness and the tree coexist is to say that they are linked together in all, or most of, the impressions I receive.

So that the essential function of the verb *to be* is to relate all language to the representation that it designates. The being towards which it spills over its signs is neither more nor less than the being of thought. Comparing language to a picture, one late-eighteenth-century grammarian defines nouns as forms, adjectives as colours, and the verb as the canvas itself, upon which the colours are visible. An invisible canvas, entirely overlaid by the brightness and design of the words, but one that provides language with the site on which to display its painting. What the verb designates, then, is the representative character of language, the fact that it has its place in thought, and that the only word capable of crossing the frontier of signs and providing them with a foundation in truth never attains to anything other than representation itself. So that the function of the verb is found to be identified with the mode of existence of language, which it traverses throughout its length: to speak is at the same time to represent by means of signs and to give signs a synthetic form governed

95

by the verb. As Destutt says, the verb is attribution, the sustaining power, and the form of all attributes:

> The verb *to be* is found in all propositions, because we cannot say that a thing *is* in such and such a way without at the same time saying that it is . . . But this word *is* which is in all propositions is always a part of the attribute [predicate] in those propositions, it is always the beginning and the basis of the attribute, it is the general and common attribute[40].

It will be seen how the function of the verb, once it had reached this point of generality, had no other course but to become dissociated, as soon as the unitary domain of general grammar itself disappeared. When the dimension of the purely grammatical was opened up, the proposition was to become no more than a syntactical unit. The verb was merely to figure in it along with all the other words, with its own system of agreement, inflections, and cases. And at the other extreme, the power of manifestation of language was to reappear in an autonomous question, more archaic than grammar. And throughout the nineteenth century, language was to be examined in its enigmatic nature as *verb*: in that region where it is nearest to being, most capable of naming it, of transmitting or giving effulgence to its fundamental meaning, of rendering it absolutely manifest. From Hegel to Mallarmé, this astonishment in the face of the relations of being and language was to counterbalance the reintroduction of the verb into the homogeneous order of grammatical functions.

IV ARTICULATION

The verb *to be*, a mixture of attribution and affirmation, the junction of discourse with the primary and radical possibility of speech, defines the first constant of the proposition, and also the most fundamental. Beside it, on either side, are elements: parts of discourse or 'oration'. These sites are still neutral, and determined solely by the slender, almost imperceptible, yet central figure designating being; they function, on either side of this 'judicator' as the thing to be judged – the *judicandum* – and the thing judged – the *judicatum*[41]. How can this pure design of the proposition be transformed into distinct sentences? How can discourse express the whole content of a representation?

Because it is made up of words that *name*, part by part, what is given to representation.

The word designates, that is, in its very nature it is a noun or name. A proper noun, since it is directed always towards a particular representation, and towards no other. So, in contrast to the uniformity of the verb, which is never more than the universal expression of attribution, nouns proliferate in endless differentiation. There ought to be as many of them as there are things to name. But each name would then be so strongly attached to the single representation it designated that one could never formulate even the slightest attribution; and language would fall back to a lower level:

> If we had no other substantives but proper nouns, it would be necessary to create an infinite multiplicity of them. These words, whose great number would overburden our memories, would produce no order in the objects of our learning, nor, consequently, in our ideas, and all our discourse would be in the greatest state of confusion[42].

Nouns cannot function in a sentence and permit attribution unless one of the two (the attribute at least) designates some element common to several representations. The generality of the noun is as necessary to the parts of discourse as is the designation of being to the form of the proposition.

This generality may be acquired in two ways. Either by a horizontal articulation, grouping together individuals that have certain identities in common and separating those that are different; such an articulation then forms a sequential generalization of groups growing gradually larger and larger (and less and less numerous); it may also subdivide them almost to infinity by means of fresh distinctions, and thus return to the proper noun from which it began[43]; the entire order of the resulting coordinations and subordinations is covered by a grid of language, and each one of these points will be found upon it together with its name: from the individual to the species, then from the species to the genus and on to the class, language is articulated precisely upon the dimension of increasing generalities; this taxonomic function is manifested in language by the substantives: we say an animal, a quadruped, a dog, a spaniel[44]. Or else by a vertical articulation, linked to the first, for each is indispensable to the other; this second articulation distinguishes the things that subsist by themselves from those – modifications, features, accidents, or characteristics – that one can never meet in an independent state: deep down, substances; on the surface, qualities; this division – this metaphysic, as Adam Smith called it – is manifested in discourse by the presence of adjectives, which designate everything in representation that cannot subsist by itself. The primary articulation of language (if we leave aside the verb *to be*, which is as much a condition of discourse as it is a part of it) is thus aligned along two orthogonal axes: one proceeding from the individual unit to the general; the other proceeding from the substance to the quality. At their point of intersection stands the common noun; at one extremity the proper noun, at the other the adjective.

But these two types of representation can distinguish words from one another only to precisely that degree to which representation is analysed according to this same model. As the authors of *Port-Royal* put it: words 'that signify things are called substantival nouns, such as *earth*, *sun*. Those that signify manners, while at the same time indicating the subject with which the manners agree, are called adjectival nouns, such as *good*, *just*, *round*' [45]. However, there does exist a certain amount of play between the articulation of language and that of representation. When we speak of 'whiteness', we are certainly designating a quality, but we are designating it by means of a substantive; when we speak of 'humans' we are employing an adjective to designate individuals that subsist by themselves. This displacement is not an indication that language obeys other laws than those of representation, but, on the contrary, that it has relations, with itself and in its own density, that are identical with those of representation. For is it not, in fact, a duplicated kind of representation, and thus able to combine with the elements of its representation another representation distinct from the first, even though the only function and meaning of the second representation is the representation of the first? If discourse seizes upon the adjective designating a modification and gives it within the sentence the value of the very *substance* of the proposition, then that adjective becomes substantival; the noun, on the other hand, which behaves within the sentence like an accident, becomes adjectival, even though it is designating substances, as hitherto.

> Because substance is that which subsists of itself, the term substantive has been given to all those words that subsist by themselves in discourse, even though they may signify accidents. And, on the other hand, the term adjective has been given to those words that signify substances when, in their manner of signifying, they must be joined in discourse to other nouns [46].

The relations between the elements of the proposition are identical with those of representation; but this identity is not carefully arranged point by point, so that every substance is designated by a substantive and every accident by an adjective. The identity here is total and a matter of nature: the proposition *is* a representation; it is articulated according to the same modes as representation; but it possesses the power to articulate the representation it transforms into discourse in more than one way. It is, in itself, a representation providing the articulation for another, with a possibility of displacement that constitutes at the same time the freedom of discourse and the differences between languages.

Such is the first stratum of articulation – the most superficial or in any case the most apparent. Once this has been established, everything can become discourse; but in the form of a still rather undifferentiated language: we still have nothing but the monotony of the verb *to be* and its attributive function to link our nouns together. Now, the elements of representation are articulated according to a whole network of complex relations (succession, subordination, consequence) that must be brought over into language if it is to become truly representative. Hence all the words, syllables, even letters, which, circulating among the nouns and the verbs, are given the task of designating those ideas that in *Port-Royal* were termed 'accessory' [47]; there must be prepositions and conjunctions; there must be syntactical signs indicating the relations of identity or agreement, and those of dependence or case[48]: marks of plurality and gender, declension endings; and, finally, there must be words relating common nouns to the individuals they designate – the articles or demonstratives that Lemercier called 'concretizers' or 'disabstractors' [49]. Such a scattering of words constitutes an articulation inferior to the unity of the name (whether substantival or adjectival) as required by the naked form of the proposition: none of them possesses in its own right, and in an isolated state, a fixed and determinate representative content; they cannot cover an idea – even an accessory one – until they have been linked together with other words; whereas nouns and verbs are 'absolute significants', these words, on the other hand, have no power of signification except in a relative mode. It is true that they are addressed to representation; they exist only in so far as the latter, in the process of analysing itself, makes the interior network of these relationships visible; but they themselves have value only through the grammatical whole of which they are a part. They establish a new articulation in language, one of a composite nature, at once representative and grammatical, though without either of these two orders being able to fit exactly over the other.

At this stage, then, the sentence is peopled with syntactical elements cut out according to much more delicate patterns than the broad figures of the proposition. This new and more complicated patterning presents general grammar with a necessary choice: either to pursue its analysis at a lower level than nominal unity, and to bring into prominence, before signification, the insignificant elements of which it is constructed, or to reduce that nominal unity by means of a regressive process, to recognize its existence within more restricted units, and to find its efficacity as representation below the level of whole words, in particles, in syllables, and even in single letters themselves. These possibilities are presented – indeed, they are prescribed – as soon as the theory of languages takes as its object discourse and the analysis of its representative values. They define the *point of heresy* that splits all eighteenth-century grammar.

Shall we suppose, Harris asks, that all signification is, like the body, divisible into an infinity of other significations, themselves divisible to infinity? That would be an absurdity; we must therefore necessarily admit that there are significant sounds of which no part can possess signification of itself[50]. Signification disappears as soon as the representative values of words are dissociated or suspended: instead, there appear, in their independence, raw materials that are not articulated upon thought and whose links cannot be reduced to those of discourse. There is a 'mechanics' proper to agreements, to cases, to inflections, to syllables, and to sounds, and no representative value can provide us with an account of that mechanics. Language must be treated like a mechanical construction susceptible of gradual improvement[51]: in its simplest form, the sentence is composed only of a subject, a verb, and a predicate; and every addition of meaning requires a fresh and entire proposition; in the same way, the most rudimentary machines presuppose principles of movement that differ for each of their organs. But as they are perfected, so they subordinate all their organs to one and the same principle, of which the organs are then only the intermediaries, the means of transformation, the points of application; similarly, as languages perfect themselves, they transmit the sense of a proposition by means of grammatical organs that do not in themselves possess any representative value, but perform the tasks of making it more specific, of linking its elements together, of indicating its actual determinations. In a single continuous sentence it is possible to indicate relations of time, of consequence, of possession, and of localization, all of which certainly enter into the subject-verb-predicate series, but cannot be pinned down by so broad a distinction. Hence the importance accorded since Bauzée[52] to the theories of the complement, of subordination. Hence, too, the growing role of syntax; at the time of Port-Royal, syntax was identified with the construction and ordering of words, and thus with the interior development of the proposition[53]; with Sicard it became independent: it is syntax 'that determines the proper form of each word'[54]. These were the preliminary sketches for the grammatical autonomy to be defined later, at the very end of the century, by Sylvestre de Saci, when he became the first – together with Sicard – to distinguish between the logical analysis of the proposition and the grammatical analysis of the sentence[55].

It is understandable why analyses of this kind should have remained in suspense as long as discourse remained the object of grammar; as soon as a stratum of articulation was reached where representative values crumbled away, there was a movement from the other side of grammar, where grammar no longer had any power, into the domain of usage and history – syntax, in the eighteenth century, was thought of as the locus of the arbitrary in which the habits of each people were deployed according to whim[56].

In any case, such analyses could not, in the eighteenth century, be anything more than abstract possibilities; not prefigurations of what was to be philology, but the non-privileged branch of a choice. Opposite, and with the same point of heresy as its starting-point, we see developing a reflection, which, for us and the science of language we have constructed since the nineteenth century, is void of all value, but which at that time enabled all analysis of verbal signs to be retained within discourse itself. And which, by means of this exact overlaying, came to be included in the positive figures of knowledge. There was a search for the obscure nominal function that was thought to be invested and concealed in those words, in those syllables, in those inflections, in those letters that the over-generalized analysis of the proposition was allowing to pass through its net. Because, after all, as the authors of *Port-Royal* pointed out, all connective particles must have a certain content, since they represent the manner in which objects are linked together, and in which they are connected in our representations[57]. May one not suppose that they have been names like all the others? But that instead of substituting themselves for objects they have taken the place of those gestures by which men indicated them or simulated their connections and their succession[58]? It is these words that have either gradually lost their own particular meaning (which was not always visible, in any case, since it was linked to the gestures, the body, and the situation of the speaker) or incorporated themselves into other words, in which they found a stable support, and to which they gave in return a whole system of modifications[59]. So that all words, of whatever kind, are dormant names: verbs have joined adjectival names to the verb to be; conjunctions and prepositions are the names of gestures now frozen into immobility; declensions and conjugations are no more than names that have been absorbed. Words, now, can open up and restore their freedom of flight to all the names that have been lodged within them. As Le Bel said, stating it as a fundamental principle of analysis, 'there is no group of which the parts have not existed separately before being grouped together'[60]; this enabled him to reduce all words to syllabic elements in which the old forgotten names at last made their reappearance – the only vocables that possessed the possibility of existing side by side with the verb to be: *Romulus*, for example[61], comes from *Roma* and *moliri* (to build); and *Roma* comes from *ro*, which denoted strength (*robur*) and *ma*, which denoted magnitude (*magnus*). In the same way, Thiébault discovers three latent significations in *abandonner*: *a*, which 'presents the idea of the tendency or destination of one thing towards another'; *ban*, which 'gives the idea of the totality of the social body', and *do*, which indicates 'the act whereby one relinquishes something'[62].

And if one is forced to descend below the level of individual syllables to the very letters of the words, one can still find the values of a rudimentary form of nomination. A task to which, to his greater – though even more perishable – glory, Court de Gébelin really applied himself: 'the labial contact, the easiest to bring into play, the gentlest, the most gracious, served to designate the first beings man comes to know, those who surround him and to whom he owes everything' (papa, mama). On the other hand, 'the teeth are as firm as the lips are mobile and flexible; the intonations that proceed from them are strong, sonorous, noisy . . .' It is by means of dental contact that one expresses the ideas that lie behind such verbs as *tonner* (to thunder), *retentir* (to resound), *étonner* (to astonish); it is by this means too that one denotes *tambours* (drums), *timbales* (timpani), and *trompettes* (trumpets). Vowels, too, in isolation, are able to unfold the secret of the age-old names that usage has buried within them: A for possession (*avoir*, to have), E for existence, I for *puissance* (power), O for *étonnement* (astonishment, eyes opened wide), U for *humidité* (humidity) and therefore for *humeur* (mood)[63]. And perhaps, in the very oldest stratum of our history, consonants and vowels, differentiated only as two still vague groups, formed as it were the two sole names upon which human speech is ultimately articulated: the singing vowels speaking our passions; the rough consonants our needs[64]. It is still possible to distinguish the rocky tongues of the North – a forest of gutturals, of hunger and cold – from the Southern tongues that are all vowels, born of early morning encounters between shepherds when 'the first fires of love were bursting from the pure crystal of the springs'.

Throughout its density, even down to the most archaic of those sounds that first rescued it from its state as pure cry, language preserves its representative function; in each one of its articulations, from the depths of time, it has always *named*. It is nothing in itself but an immense rustling of denominations that are overlying one another, contracting into one another, hiding one another, and yet preserving themselves in existence in order to permit the analysis or the composition of the most complex representations. Within sentences, in that very depth where signification seems to be relying upon the mute support of insignificant syllables, there is always a dormant nomination, a form that holds imprisoned within its vocal walls the reflection of an invisible and yet indelible representation. For nineteenth-century philology, such analyses remained, in the literal sense of the word, 'a dead letter'. But not so for a whole way of experiencing language – at first esoteric and mystic at the time of Saint-Marc, Reveroni, Fabre d'Olivet, Oegger, then literary when the enigma of the word re-emerged in all its density of being, with Mallarmé, Roussel, Leiris, or Ponge. The idea that, when we destroy words, what is left is neither mere noise nor arbitrary, pure elements, but other words, which, when pulverized in turn, will set free still other words – this idea is at once the negative of all the modern science of languages and the myth in which we now transcribe the most obscure and the most real powers of language. It is probably because it is arbitrary, and because one can define the condition upon which it attains its power of signification, that language can become the object of a science. But it is because it has never ceased to speak within itself, because it is penetrated as far as we can reach within it by inexhaustible values, that we can speak within it in that endless murmur in which literature is born. But in the Classical period the relation was not at all the same; the two figures fitted over each other exactly: in order that language could be entirely comprised within the general form of the proposition, each word, down to the least of its molecules, had to be a meticulous form of nomination.

V DESIGNATION

And yet, the theory of 'generalized nomination' reveals at the extremity of language a certain relation to things that is of an entirely different nature from that of the propositional form. If, fundamentally, the function of language is to name, that is, to raise up a representation or point it out, as though with a finger, then it is indication and not judgement. It is linked to things by a mark, a notation, an associated figure, a gesture of designation: nothing that could be reduced to a relation of predication. The principle of primal nomination, of the origin of words, is balanced by the formal primacy of judgement. As though, on either side of language, unfolded in all its articulations, there lay its being, in its verbal role as attribution, and its origin, in its role as primary designation. The latter permits the substitution of a sign for that which is indicated, the former makes possible the linking of one content to another. And thus we encounter once again, in their opposition yet also in their affinity, the two functions of connection and substitution that have been allotted to the sign in general with its power of analysing representation.

To bring the origin of language back into the light of day means also to rediscover the primitive moment in which it was pure designation. And one ought, by this means, to provide at the same time an explanation for its arbitrariness (since that which designates can be as different from that which it indicates as a gesture from the object towards which it is directed), and for its profound relation with that which it names (since a particular syllable or word has always been chosen to designate a particular thing). The first of these requirements is fulfilled by the analysis of the language of action, the second by the study of roots. But these two things are not in opposition to one another in the same way as, in the *Cratylus*, are explanation in terms of 'nature' and explanation in terms of 'law'; on the contrary, they are absolutely indispensable to one another, since the first gives an account of the substitution of the sign for the thing designated and the second justifies the permanent power of designation possessed by that sign.

The language of action is spoken by the body; and yet, it is not something given from the very first. All that nature permits is that man, in the various situations in which he finds himself, should be able to make gestures; his face is agitated by movements; he emits inarticulate cries – in other words, cries that are 'coined neither by the tongue nor by the lips' [65]. All this is not yet either language or even sign, but the effect and consequence of our animality. This manifest agitation nevertheless has the virtue of being universal, since it depends solely upon the conformation of our organs. Hence the possibility for man to observe that it is identical in himself and his companions. He is therefore able to associate the cry he hears from another's mouth, the grimace he sees upon that other's face, with the same representations that have, on several occasions, accompanied his own cries and movements. He is able to accept this mimesis as the mark and substitute of the other's thought. As a sign. Comprehension is beginning. He can also, in return, employ this mimesis that has become a sign in order to excite in his companions the idea that he himself is experiencing, the sensations, the needs, the difficulties that are ordinarily associated with certain gestures and certain sounds: a cry expressly directed in another's presence and towards an object, a pure interjection[66]. With this concerted use of the sign (which is already expression), something like a language is in the process of being born.

It is evident, from these analyses common to Condillac and Destutt, that the language of action does indeed link language to nature by means of a genesis – but in order to detach it from nature rather than to give it roots there, to emphasize its indelible difference from the cry and to provide a basis for that which constitutes its artifice. As long as it is a simple extension of the body, action has no power to speak: it is not language. It becomes language, but only at the end of definite and complex operations: the notation of an analogy of relations (the other's cry is to what he is experiencing – that which is unknown – what my cry is to my appetite or my fear); inversion of time and voluntary use of the sign before the representation it designates (before experiencing a sensation of hunger strong enough to make me cry out, I emit the cry that is associated with it); lastly, the purpose of arousing in the other the representation corresponding to the cry or gesture (but with this particularity, that, by emitting a cry, I do not arouse, and do not intend to arouse, the sensation of hunger, but the representation of the relation between this sign and my own desire to eat). Language is possible only upon the basis of this entanglement. It rests not upon a natural movement of comprehension or expression, but upon the reversible and analysable relations of signs and representations. Language does not come into being when representation is exteriorized, but only when, in a concerted fashion, it detaches a sign from itself and causes itself to be represented by that sign. It is not, therefore, because he functions as a speaking subject, or from within a language already made, that man discovers, all around him, signs that might be taken as so many mute words to be deciphered and rendered audible again; it is because representation provides itself with signs that words can come into being, and with them a whole language that is no more than the ulterior organization of vocal signs. Despite its name, the 'language of action' calls into existence the irreducible network of signs that separates language from action.

And in this way it bases its artifice in nature. For the elements of which this language of action is composed (sounds, gestures, grimaces) are suggested successively by nature, and yet they have no identity of content – for the most part – with what they designate, but above all relations of simultaneity or succession. The cry does not resemble fear, nor the outstretched hand the sensation of hunger. Once they have become concerted, these signs will remain without 'fantasy and without caprice'[67], since they have been established once and for all by nature; but they will not express the nature of what they designate, for they are in no way its image. And from this starting-point men will be able to establish a language of convention: they now have at their disposal enough signs as marks for things to enable them to invent further signs that will analyse and combine the primary ones. In his *Discours sur l'origine de l'inégalité*[68], Rousseau made the point that no language can have an agreement between men as its basis, since such an agreement presupposes that some established, recognized, and practised language already exists; we would therefore have to imagine it as having been received by men, not built by them. In fact, the language of action confirms this necessity and renders this hypothesis futile. Man receives from nature the material to make signs, and those signs serve him first of all as a means of reaching agreement with other men as to the choice of those that shall be retained, the values that they shall be recognized as possessing, and the rules for employing them; after that, they serve him as a means of forming new signs on the model of the primary ones. The first form of agreement consists in selecting the vocal signs (which are easier to recognize from a distance and the only ones that can be used when it is dark), the second in composing, in order to designate representations still left without signs, sounds close to those indicating neighbouring representations. It is in this way that language, properly speaking, is constituted, by a series of analogies that are a lateral extension of the language of action or at least of its vocal element: language resembles this vocal element, and 'it is this resemblance that facilitates the understanding of it. We term it analogy ... You observe that analogy, which gives us law, does not permit us to choose signs at random or arbitrarily.'[69]

The genesis of language in the language of action entirely avoids the alternatives of natural imitation and arbitrary convention. In that which is natural – in the signs that arise spontaneously through the medium of our bodies – there is no resemblance; and where there is employment of resemblances it is after a voluntary agreement has been reached between men. Nature juxtaposes the differences and binds them together by force; reflection discovers the resemblances, and analyses and develops them. The first phase makes artifice possible, but with material imposed upon all men in identical fashion; the second excludes arbitrary choice but opens up channels for analysis that will not be exactly superimposable in the case of all men and all peoples. The law of nature is constituted by the difference between words and things – the vertical division between language and that lying beneath it which it is the task of language to designate; the rule prescribed by conventions is the resemblance that exists between words, the great horizontal network that forms words from other words and propagates them *ad infinitum*.

It now becomes comprehensible why the theory of roots in no way contradicts the analysis of the language of action, but is to be found within it. Roots are those rudimentary words that are to be found, always identical, in a great number of languages – perhaps in all; they have been imposed upon language by nature in the form of involuntary cries spontaneously employed by the language of action. It was there that men sought them out in order to give them a place in their conventional languages. And if all peoples, in all climates, chose these same elementary sounds from among the raw material of the language of action, that is because they discerned in them, though in a secondary and reflective manner, a resemblance with the object they designated, or the possibility of applying it to an analogous object. The resemblance of the root to what it names assumes its value as a verbal sign only through the agency of the convention that brought men together and regulated their language of action so as to create a language. In this way, from within representation, signs are united with the very nature of what they designate, and the primitive treasury of vocables is imposed, in identical fashion, on all languages.

Roots may be formed in several ways. By onomatopoeia, of course, which is not a spontaneous expression, but the deliberate articulation of a sign that is also a resemblance: 'to make the same sound with one's voice as the object that one wishes to name'[70]. By employing a resemblance experienced in one's sensations: 'the impression made by the colour red, which is vivid, rapid, harsh to the eye, will be very well rendered by the sound R, which makes an analogous impression upon the ear'[71]. By imposing movements upon the organs of the voice analogous to those one wishes to signify: 'so that the sound resulting from the form and natural movement of the organ when placed in this state becomes the name of the object'; the throat rasps to designate the rubbing of one body against another, it hollows itself inside to indicate a concave surface[72]. Finally, by employing the sounds an organ naturally produces to designate that organ: the glottal stop determined the name of the throat in which it occurs, and the dentals (*d* and *t*) are used to designate the teeth[73]. Using these conventional articulations of resemblance, every language is able to provide itself with its pack of primitive roots. The pack is a small one, since the roots are almost all monosyllabic and exist only in very small numbers – two hundred for Hebrew, according to Bergier's estimate[74]; and even smaller when one remembers that (because of the relations of resemblance that they establish) they are common to almost all of our languages: de Brosses thinks that all of them together, from all the dialects of Europe and the Orient, would not fill 'a single sheet of writing paper'. But it is on the basis of them that each language develops its own particularity: 'their development is prodigious. Just as one elm seed produces a great tree, which by growing new shoots from each root produces in the end an entire forest'[75].

Language can now reveal its genealogy, the genealogy that de Brosses attempted to display in a dimension of continuous filiation that he called the 'Universal Archaeologist'[76]. At the top of this space, one would write the roots – very few in number – employed in all European and Oriental languages; below each root one could place the more complicated words derived from it, but taking care to place first those that are nearest to the roots, and to follow them in a sequence sufficiently tight for there to be as small a distance as possible between each word in the series. In this way one would be able to constitute a number of perfect and exhaustive series, of absolutely continuous chains in which the breaks, if there were any, would indicate the place of a word, a dialect, or a language no longer in existence[77]. Once this vast, seamless expanse had been constituted, one would have a two-dimensional space that one could cross either on abscissae or on ordinates: vertically, one would have the complete filiation of each root; horizontally, one would have the words employed in any given language; the further away one moved from the primitive roots, the more complicated – and no doubt more recent –

would the languages defined by any transversal line become, but, at the same time, the more subtle and efficacious would the words be as instruments for the analysis of representations. And thus superimposed, the historical space and the grid of thought would be exactly coincidental.

This quest for the roots of language may well appear to be a return to the historical hypothesis and to the theory of mother-languages that Classicism seemed, for a time, to have suspended. In reality, an analysis of its roots does not replace language in a history that is, as it were, the environment into which it was born and in which it developed. Rather, it makes history a journey, accomplished in successive stages, across the simultaneous patterning of representation and words. In the Classical period, language is not a fragment of history authorizing at any given moment a definite mode of thought and reflection; it is an area of analysis upon which time and human knowledge pursue their journey. And the fact that language does not become – or become once again – through the agency of the root theory a historical entity is proved quite easily by the way in which etymologies were sought for in the eighteenth century. The guiding thread used for such investigations was not the material transformations undergone by the word, but the constancy of its significations.

This search had two aspects: definition of the root, and isolation of the inflectional endings and prefixes. To define the root was to discover an etymology. It was an art with codified rules[78]; one had to strip the word of all the subsequent traces that might have been left upon it by combinations and inflections; arrive at a monosyllabic element; follow that element through the entire past of the language, through all the ancient 'charts and glossaries'; then follow it back into other and more primitive languages. And it must also be accepted that at any point along this backward journey the monosyllable may change: all the vowels may replace one another in the history of a root, for the vowels are the voice itself, which knows no discontinuity or rupture; the consonants, on the other hand, are modified according to certain privileged channels: gutturals, linguals, palatals, dentals, labials, and nasals all make up families of homophonous consonants within which changes of pronunciation are made for preference, though without any obligation[79]. The only indelible constant guaranteeing the continuity of the root throughout its history is the unity of meaning: the representative area that persists indefinitely. This is because 'nothing perhaps can limit inductions and everything can serve as a basis for them, from total resemblance to the very slightest of resemblances': the meaning of words is 'the surest source of enlightenment we can consult'[80].

VI DERIVATION

How is it that words, which in their primary essence are names and designations, and which are articulated just as representation itself is analysed, can move irresistibly away from their original signification and acquire either a broader or more limited adjacent meaning? How can they change not only their forms but their field of application? How can they acquire new sounds, and also new contents, to such an extent that various languages, equipped in the first place with a number of probably identical roots, have formed different sounds, to say nothing of words whose meanings are lost to us?

The modifications of form obey no rule, are more or less endless, and never stable. All their causes are external: ease of pronunciation, fashions, habits, climate – cold weather encourages 'unvoiced labials', hot weather 'guttural aspirates'[81]. The alterations of meaning, on the other hand – since they are so limited as to justify an etymological science, which, if not absolutely exact, is at least 'probable'[82] – do obey fixed principles. These principles, which foment the internal history of languages, are all of a spatial order. Some concern the visible resemblance or adjacency between things; others concern the area in which language and the form it uses to preserve itself coexist. Figures and writing.

We know of two broad types of writing: that which retraces the meaning of words, and that which analyses and reconstitutes their sounds. Between these two there is a strict dividing-line, whether one accepts that the second took over from the first among certain peoples as the result of a veritable 'stroke of genius'[83], or whether one accepts – so different are they from one another – that they both appeared more or less simultaneously, the first among graphically oriented peoples, the second among song-oriented peoples[84]. To represent the meaning of words graphically is originally to make an exact drawing of the thing to be designated. In fact, it is scarcely writing at all – at the very most a pictorial reproduction with the aid of which one can scarcely transcribe anything more than the most concrete form of narrative. According to Warburton, the Mexicans scarcely knew of any other method[85]. True writing began when the attempt was made to represent, no longer the thing itself, but one of its constituent elements, or one of the circumstances that habitually attend it, or again some other thing that it resembles. These three methods produced three techniques: the curiological writing of the Egyptians – the crudest of the three – which employs 'the principal circumstance of a subject in lieu of the whole' (a bow for a battle, a ladder for a siege); then the 'tropal' hieroglyphics – somewhat more perfected – which employ some notable circumstance (since God is all-powerful he knows everything and sees all that men do: he is therefore represented by an eye); finally, symbolic writing, which makes use of more or less concealed resemblances (the rising sun is expressed by the head of a crocodile whose round eyes are just level with the surface of the water) [86]. We can recognize here the three great figures of rhetoric: synecdoche, metonymy, catachresis. And it is by following the nervure laid down by these figures that those languages paralleled with a symbolic form of writing will be able to evolve. They become endowed, little by little, with poetic powers; their primary nominations become the starting-points for long metaphors; these metaphors become progressively more complicated, and are soon so far from their points of origin that it is difficult to recall them. This is how superstitions arise whereby people believe that the sun is a crocodile, or that God is a great eye keeping watch on the world; it is also how esoteric forms of knowledge arise among those (the priests) who pass on the metaphors to their successors from generation to generation; and it is how allegorical discourse (so frequent in the most ancient literatures) comes into being, as well as the illusion that knowledge consists in understanding resemblances.

But the history of a language endowed with a figurative writing soon comes to a halt. For it is hardly possible to achieve much progress in such a language. Its signs do not multiply with the meticulous analysis of representations but with the most distant analogies; so that it is the imagination of the peoples using them that is encouraged rather than their powers of reflection, their credulity rather than science. Moreover, knowledge necessitates two kinds of apprenticeship: first in words (as with all languages), then with written signs that have no bearing upon the pronunciation of the words; a human life-span is not too long for this double education; and if one has had, in addition, the leisure to make some discovery, one has no signs at one's disposal to hand it on. Inversely, since it bears no intrinsic relation to the word it represents, a transmitted sign always remains dubious: from one age to the next one can never be sure that the same sound resides in the same figure. Innovations are therefore impossible, and traditions compromised. With the result that the only

III

concern of the learned is to maintain 'a superstitious respect' for the learning handed down by their ancestors and for the institutions preserving that heritage: 'they feel that any change in manners will bring change in the language, and that any change in the language will confound and annul all their knowledge'[87]. When a people possesses nothing but a figurative form of writing, its politics must exclude history, or at least all history other than pure and simple conservation. It is here, according to Volney[88], in this relation of space to language, that the essential difference between East and West is situated. As though the spatial arrangement of the language prescribed the law of time; as though their particular language did not come to men via history, but that, inversely, their only means of access to history was via their system of signs. It is in this nexus of representation, words, and space (the words representing the space of the representation, and in turn representing themselves in time) that the destiny of peoples is silently formed.

With alphabetic writing, in fact, the history of men is entirely changed. They transcribe in space, not their ideas but sounds, and from those sounds they extract the common elements in order to form a small number of unique signs whose combination will enable them to form all possible syllables and words. Whereas symbolic writing, in attempting to spatialize representations themselves, obeys the confused law of similitudes, and causes language to slip out of the forms of reflective thought, alphabetical writing, by abandoning the attempt to draw the representation, transposes into its analysis of sounds the rules that are valid for reason itself. So that it does not matter that letters do not represent ideas, since they can be combined together in the same way as ideas, and ideas can be linked together and disjoined just like the letters of the alphabet[89]. The disruption of the exact parallelism between representation and graphic signs makes it possible to bring language, even written language, as a totality, into the general domain of analysis, thus allowing the progress of writing and that of thought to provide each other with mutual support[90]. The same graphic signs can break down all new words, and hand on each new discovery, as soon as it is made, without fear of its being forgotten; the same alphabet can be used to transcribe different languages, and thus to convey the ideas of one people to another. Since it is very easy to learn this alphabet, because of its very small number of elements, everyone is able to devote to reflection and to the analysis of ideas the time that the hieroglyphic peoples wasted in learning how to write. And so it is within language itself, exactly in that fold of words where analysis and space meet, that the first but endless possibility of progress arises. In its root, progress, as defined in the eighteenth century, is not a movement within history, but the result of a fundamental relation between space and language:

> The arbitrary signs of language and writing provide men with the means of ensuring the possession of their ideas and of communicating them to others in the manner of an inheritance, constantly augmented with the new discoveries of each age; and the human race, considered from its origin, appears to the eyes of the philosopher as an immense whole that itself possesses, like every individual, its childhood and its progress[91].

Language gives the perpetual disruption of time the continuity of space, and it is to the degree that it analyses, articulates, and patterns representation that it has the power to link our knowledge of things together across the dimension of time. With the advent of language, the chaotic monotony of space is fragmented, while at the same time the diversity of temporal successions is unified.

There remains one last problem, however. For though writing is indeed the buttress and ever-watchful guardian of these progressively more refined analyses, it is neither their principle nor even their initial movement. This latter is a slipping movement common to attention, to signs, and to words. In any representation, the mind can attach itself, and attach a verbal sign, to one element of that representation, to a circumstance attending it, to some other, absent, thing that is similar to it and is recalled to memory on account of it[92]. There is no doubt that this is how language developed and gradually drifted away from primary designations. Originally, everything had a name – a proper or peculiar name. Then the name became attached to a single element of the thing, and became applicable to all the other individual things that also contained that element: it is no longer a particular oak that is called *tree*, but anything that includes at least a trunk and branches. The name also became attached to a conspicuous circumstance: *night* came to designate, not the end of this particular day, but the period of darkness separating all sunsets from all dawns. Finally, it attached itself to analogies: everything was called a *leaf* that was as thin and flexible as the leaf of a tree[93]. The progressive analysis and more advanced articulation of language, which enable us to give a single name to several things, were developed along the lines of these three fundamental figures so well known to rhetoric: synecdoche, metonymy, and catachresis (or metaphor, if the analogy is less immediately perceptible). For these things are not the effect of a refinement of style; on the contrary, they reveal the mobility peculiar to all language whenever it is spontaneous: 'La Halle produces more figures of speech in one market day than our academic assemblies do in a week'[94]. It is very probable that this mobility was even greater in the beginnings of language than it is now: today, the analysis is so detailed, the grid so fine, the relations of coordination and subordination are so firmly established, that words scarcely have any opportunity to move from their places. But at the beginning of human history, when words were few, when representations were still confused and not well analysed, when the passions both modified them and provided them with a basis, words had greater mobility. One might even say that words were figurative before being proper: in other words, that they had scarcely attained their status as particular names before they were being scattered over representations by the force of spontaneous rhetoric. As Rousseau says, we probably talked about giants before designating men[95]. Boats were originally designated by their sails, and the soul, the 'psyche', was initially given the figurative form of the moth[96].

So that at the base of spoken language, as with writing, what we discover is the rhetorical dimension of words: that freedom of the sign to alight, according to the analysis of representation, upon some internal element, upon some adjacent point, upon some analogous figure. And if languages possess the diversity we observe in them; if from the starting-point of their primitive designations, which were doubtless common to them all owing to the universality of human nature, they have not ceased to develop according to the dictates of differing forms; if they have all had their own history, fashions, customs, and periods of oblivion; this is because words have their *locus*, not in *time*, but in a *space* in which they are able to find their original site, change their positions, turn back upon themselves, and slowly unfold a whole developing curve: a *tropological* space. And in this way one returns once more to what had served as a starting-point for reflection upon language. Language was of all signs the one having the property of being sequential: not because it was itself part of a chronology, but because it drew out into sequential sounds the simultaneity of representation. But this succession, which analyses discontinuous elements and brings them into view one after the other, traverses the space offered by representation to the mind's eye. So that language merely arranges into a linear order the scattered fragments represented. The proposition unfolds and makes audible the figure that rhetoric makes visible. Without this tropological space, language would not be formed of all those common names that make it possible to establish a predicative relation. And without this analysis of the words, the figures would have remained mute and momentary; and since they would have been perceived only in the incandescence of the instant, they would have fallen forthwith into a darkness in which there is not even any time.

From the theory of the proposition to that of derivation, all Classical reflection upon language – all that was called 'general grammar' – is merely a detailed commentary upon the simple phrase: 'language analyses'. It was upon this point, in the seventeenth century, that the whole Western experience of language foundered – the experience that had always led men to believe, until then, that *language spoke*.

VII THE QUADRILATERAL OF LANGUAGE

A few concluding remarks. The four theories – of the proposition, of articulation, of designation, and of derivation – form, as it were, the segments of a quadrilateral. They confront each other in pairs and reinforce each other in pairs. Articulation gives content to the pure and still empty verbal form of the proposition; it fills that form, yet is in opposition to it, as a nomination that differentiates things is in opposition to the predication that links them together. The theory of designation reveals the point of attachment of all the nominal forms cut out by articulation; but they are in opposition to articulation, just as the instantaneous, gestural, perpendicular designation is in opposition to patterns based on generalities. The theory of derivation indicates the continuous movement of words from their source of origin, but the slipping that occurs on the surface of representation is in opposition to the single stable bond that links one root to one representation. Finally, derivation leads back to the proposition, since without it all designation would remain folded in on itself and could never acquire the generality that alone can authorize a predicating link; yet derivation is created by means of a spatial figure, whereas the proposition unfolds in obedience to a sequential and linear order.

It should be noted that there also exist diagonal relations, as it were, between the opposing corners of this rectangle. First of all, between articulation and derivation: if the existence of an articulated language is possible, with words in juxtaposition, interlocking, or arranging themselves in relation to one another, then it is so only in so far as the words of that language – starting from their original values and from the simple act of designation that was their basis – have never ceased to move further and further away, by a process of derivation, thus acquiring a variable extension; hence an axis that cuts across the whole quadrilateral of language; and it is along this line that the state of a language is marked off: its articulative capacities are determined by the distance it has moved along the line of derivation; such a reading defines both its historical posture and its power of discrimination. The other diagonal runs from the proposition back to the origin, that is, from the affirmation at the heart of every act of judgement to the designation implied by any act of nomination; it is along this axis that the relation of words to what they represent is established: here it becomes apparent that words never speak anything other than the being of representation, but that they always name something represented. The first diagonal marks the progress of a language from the point of view of its specification; the second the endless interleaving of language and representation – the duplicating process which is the reason why the verbal sign is always representing a representation. On this latter line, the word functions as a substitute (with its power to represent); on the former, as an element (with its power to make combinations and break them down).

At the point where these two diagonals intersect, at the centre of the quandrilateral, where the duplicating process of representation is revealed as analysis, where the substitute has the power of distribution, and where, in consequence, there resides the possibility and the principle of a general taxonomy of representation, there is the *name*. To name is at the same time to give the verbal representation of a representation, and to place it in a general table. The entire Classical theory of language is organized around this central and privileged entity. All the various functions of language intersect within it, since it is by nomination that representations are enabled to enter as figures into a proposition. It is therefore also through nomination that discourse is articulated upon knowledge. Only the judgement, of course, can be true or false. But if all names were exact, if the analysis upon which they are based had been perfectly thought out, if the language in question had been 'well made', there would be no difficulty in pronouncing true judgements, and error, should it occur, would be as easy to uncover and as evident as in a calculation in algebra. But the imperfection of analysis, and all the slight shifts caused by derivation, have caused names to be attached to analyses, abstractions, and combinations that are in fact illegitimate. There would be no disadvantage in this (any more than in giving names to fabulous monsters) if words did not posit themselves as being representations of representations: with the result that we cannot think of a word – however abstract, general, and empty it may be – without affirming the possibility of what it represents. This is why, in the middle of the quadrilateral of language, the name appears both as the point upon which all the structures of a language converge (for the name is its most secret, most closely guarded figure, the pure internal result of all its conventions, rules, and history), and as the point from which all language in general can enter into a relation with the truth according to which it will be judged.

This is the nexus of the entire Classical experience of language: the reversible character of grammatical analysis, which is at one and the same time science and prescription, a study of words and a rule for constructing them, employing them, and remoulding them into their representative function; the fundamental nominalism of philosophy from Hobbes to Ideology, a nominalism that is inseparable from a critique of language and from all that mistrust with regard to general and abstract words that we find in Malebranche, Berkeley, Condillac, and Hume; the great utopia of a perfectly transparent language in which things themselves could be named without any penumbra of confusion, either by a totally arbitrary but precisely thought-out system (artificial language), or by a language so natural that it would translate thought like a face expressing a passion (it was this language of immediate sign that Rousseau dreamed of in the first of his *Dialogues*). One might say that it is the Name that organizes all Classical discourse; to speak or to write is not to say things or to express oneself, it is not a matter of playing with language, it is to make one's way towards the sovereign act of nomination, to move, through language, towards the place where things and words are conjoined in their common essence, and which makes it possible to give them a name. But once that name has been spoken, all the language that has led up to it, or that has been crossed in order to reach it, is reabsorbed into it and disappears. So that Classical discourse, in its profound essence, tends always towards this boundary; but, in surviving it, pushes the boundary further away. It continues on its way in the perpetually maintained suspension of the Name. This is why, in its very possibility, it is linked with rhetoric, that is, with all the space that surrounds the name, causes it to oscillate around what it represents, and reveals the elements, or the adjacency, or the analogies of what it names. The figures through which discourse passes act as a deterrent to the name, which then arrives at the last moment to fulfil and abolish them. The name is the *end* of discourse. And possibly all Classical literature resides in this space, in this striving to reach a name that remains always formidable because it exhausts, and thereby kills, the possibility of speech. It is this striving movement that carried the experience of language onwards from the restrained confession of *La Princesse de Clèves* to the immediate violence of *Juliette*. In the latter, nomination is at last posited in its starkest nudity, and the rhetorical figures, which until then had been holding it in suspense, collapse and become the endless figures of desire – and the same names, constantly repeated, exhaust themselves in their effort to cross those figures, without ever being able to reach their end.

All Classical literature resides in the movement that proceeds from the figure of the name to the name itself, passing from the task of naming the same thing yet again by means of new figures (which is preciosity) to that of finding words that will at last name accurately that which has never been named before or that which has remained dormant in the enveloping folds of words too far removed from it: of this latter kind are those secrets of the soul, those impressions born at the frontier of things and the body for which the language of the *Cinquième Rêverie* made itself spontaneously transparent. Later, Romanticism was to believe that it had broken with the previous age because it had learned to name things by their name. In fact all Classicism tended towards this end: Hugo was the fulfilment of Voiture's promise. But, by this very fact, the name ceases to be the reward of language; it becomes instead its enigmatic raw material. The only moment – an intolerable one, for long buried in secrecy – at which the name was at the same time the fulfilment and the substance of language, its promise and its raw material, was when, with Sade, it was traversed throughout its whole expanse by desire, of which it was at once the place of occurrence, the satisfaction, and the perpetual recurrence. Hence the fact that Sade's works play the role of an incessant primordial murmur in our culture. With this violence of the name being uttered at last for its own sake, language emerges in all its brute being as a thing; the other 'parts of oration' assume in turn their autonomy, escaping from the sovereignty of the name, and ceasing to form around it an accessory circle of ornaments. And since there is no longer any particular beauty in 'retaining' language around the frontiers of the name, in making it show what it does not say, the result will be a non-discursive discourse whose role will be to manifest language in its brute being. This proper being of language is what the nineteenth century was to call the Word (*le Verbe*), as opposed to the Classical 'verb', whose function is to pin language, discreetly but continuously, to the being of representation. And the discourse that contains this being and frees it for its own sake is literature.

Around the privileged position occupied by the name in the Classical period, the theoretical segments (proposition, articulation, designation, and derivation) constitute the frontiers of what the experience of language was at that time. Our step-by-step analysis of these segments was not undertaken in order to provide a history of grammatical conceptions in the seventeenth and eighteenth centuries, or to establish the general out-line of what men might have thought about language at that time. The intention was to determine in what conditions language could become the object of a period's knowledge, and between what limits this epistemo-logical domain developed. Not to calculate the common denominator of men's opinions, but to define what made it possible for opinions about language – whatever the opinions may have been – to exist at all. This is why our rectangle defines a periphery rather than provides an interior figure, and it shows how language intertwines with what is exterior and indispensable to it. We have seen that language existed only by virtue of the proposition: without at least the implicit presence of the verb *to be*, and of the predicative relation for which it provides authority, it would not be language that we were dealing with at all, but a collection of signs like any others. The propositional form posits as a condition of language the affirmation of a relation of identity or difference: we can speak only in so far as this relation is possible. But the other three theoretical segments enclose a quite different requirement: if it is to be possible to derive words from their first source, if an original kinship is to be already in existence between a root and its signification, if there is to be an articulated pattern-ing of representations, there must be a murmur of analogies rising from things, perceptible even in the most immediate experience; there must be resemblances that posit themselves from the very start. If everything were absolute diversity, thought would be doomed to singularity, and like Condillac's statue before it began to remember and make comparisons, it would be doomed also to absolute dispersion and absolute monotony. Neither memory nor imagination, nor, therefore, reflection, would be possible. And it would be impossible to compare things with each other, to define their identical characteristics, and to establish a common name for them. There would be no language. If language exists, it is because below the level of identities and differences there is the foundation provided by continuities, resemblances, repetitions, and natural criss-crossings. Resemblance, excluded from knowledge since the early seventeenth century, still constitutes the outer edge of language: the ring surrounding the domain of that which can be analysed, reduced to order, and known. Discourse dissipates the murmur, but without it it could not speak.

It is now possible to grasp how solid and tightly knit the unity of language is in the Classical experience. It is this unity that, through the play of an articulated designation, enables resemblance to enter the propositional relation, that is, a system of identities and differences as based upon the verb *to be* and manifested by the network of *names*. The fundamental task of Classical 'discourse' is *to ascribe a name to things, and in that name to name their being*. For two centuries, Western discourse was the locus of ontology. When it named the being of all representation in general, it was philosophy: theory of knowledge and analysis of ideas. When it ascribed to each thing represented the name that was fitted to it, and laid out the grid of a well-made language across the whole field of representation, then it was science – nomenclature and taxonomy.

NOTES

[1] John Locke, *An essay concerning human understanding* (1690, book III, chap. II, section 2).

[2] Condillac, *Grammaire* (*Œuvres*, t. V, pp. 39–40).

[3] Destutt de Tracy, *Éléments d'Idéologie*, t. I.

[4] U. Domergue, *Grammaire générale analytique* (Paris, year VII, t. I, pp. 10–11).

[5] Condillac, *Grammaire* (*Œuvres*, t. V, p. 336).

[6] Abbé Sicard, *Éléments de grammaire générale* (3rd edn., Paris, 1808, t. II, p. 113).

[7] Destutt de Tracy, *Éléments d'Idéologie*, t. I, pp. 261–6.

[8] *Encyclopédie*, article on 'Langue'.

[9] Condillac, *Grammaire* (*Œuvres*, t. V, pp. 4–5 and 67–73).

[10] Adam Smith, *Considerations concerning the formation of languages*.

[11] Destutt de Tracy, *Éléments d'Idéologie*, préface, t. I, p. 2.

[12] C. Bonnet, *Contemplation de la nature* (*Œuvres complètes*, t. IV, p. 136 note).

[13] Destutt de Tracy, *Mèmoires de l'Academie des Sciences morales et politiques*, t. III, p. 535.

[14] D'Alembert, *Discours préliminaire de 'l'Encyclopédie'*.

[15] Destutt de Tracy, *Éléments d'Idéologie*, t. I, p. 24.

[16] Diderot, article on 'Encyclopédie' in the *Encyclopédie*, t. V, p. 637.

[17] Rousseau, *Essai sur l'origine des langues* (*Œuvres*, Paris, 1826 edn., t. XIII, pp. 220-1).

[18] Cf. Michaelis, *De l'influence des opinions sur le langage* (1759, Fr. trans. Paris, 1762): we know that the Greeks identified both fame and public opinion by the word δοχα; and that the Teutons believed in the fertilizing virtues of storms from their expression *das liebe Gewitter* (pp. 24 and 40).

[19] It is thought (cf., for instance, W. Warburton, *The divine legation of Moses* (1737-41, book IV, sections II–VI)) that the knowledge of the Ancients, and, above all, that of the Egyptians, was not first of all secret then subsequently made public, but that, having first been constructed communally, it was later confiscated, masked, and travestied by the priests. Esoterism, far from being the first form of knowledge, is only a perversion of it.

[20] E. Guichard, *Harmonie étymologique* (1606). Cf. other classifications of the same type in Scaliger, *Diatribe de Europaeorum linguis*, or Wilkins, *An essay towards real character* (London, 1668, p. 3 *et seq.*).

[21] Le Blan, *Théorie nouvelle de la parole* (Paris, 1750), according to which Latin bequeathed nothing to Italian, Spanish, or French other than 'the heritage of a few words'.

[22] Abbé Girard, *Les Vrais Principes de la langue française* (Paris, 1747, t. I, pp. 22-5).

[23] On this problem and the discussions it has raised, cf. Bauzée, *Grammaire générale* (Paris, 1767); Abbé Batteux, *Nouvel examen du préjugé de l'inversion* (Paris, 1767); and Abbé d'Olivet, *Remarques sur la langue française* (Paris, 1771).

[24] Abbé Pluche, *La Mécanique des langues* (reissued 1811, p. 26).

[25] Ibid., p. 23.

[26] Cf. for example, Buffier, *Grammaire française* (Paris, new edn., 1723). This is why, at the end of the eighteenth century, the expression 'philosophical grammar' came to be preferred to that of 'general grammar', which 'would be that of all languages'; D. Thiébault, *Grammaire philosophique* (Paris, 1802, t. I, pp. 6 and 7).

[27] Destutt de Tracy, *Éléments d'Idéologie*, t. II, p. 87.

[28] J. Itard, *Rapport sur les nouveaux développements de Victor de l'Aveyron*, 1964 edn., p. 209.

[29] Destutt de Tracy, *Éléments d'Idéologie*, t. II, p. 60.

[30] U. Domergue, *Grammaire générale analytique*, p. 34.

[31] Hobbes, *Logic*, chap. III, section 3.

[32] Adam Smith, *Considerations concerning the formation of languages*.

[33] *Logique de Port-Royal*, pp. 106-7.

[34] Condillac, *Grammaire*, p. 115.

[35] In the French this phrase reads: '. . . au lieu de dire "je suis chantant", on dit "je chante" '. The significance of the author's remark is lost on the English reader since he can indeed say 'I am singing' whereas the Frenchman cannot say 'je suis chantant'. This form, often known as the 'progressive', is not to be found in French, or in most other languages. [Translator's note.]

[36] *Logique de Port-Royal*, p. 107. Cf. Condillac, *Grammaire*, pp. 132-4. In his *L'Origine des connaissances*, the history of the verb is analysed in a somewhat different fashion, but not its function. D. Thiébault, *Grammaire philosophique*, t. I, p. 216.

[37] Cf. *Logique de Port-Royal*, p. 107, and Abbé Girard, *Les Vrais Principes de la langue française*, p. 56.

[38] Bauzée, *Grammaire générale*, I, p. 426 et seq.

[39] Condillac, *Grammaire*, pp. 185-6.

[40] Destutt de Tracy, *Éléments d'Idéologie*, t. II, p. 64.

[41] U. Domergue, *Grammaire générale analytique*, p. 11.

[42] Condillac, *Grammaire*, p. 152.

[43] Ibid., p. 155.

[44] Ibid., p. 153. Cf. also A. Smith, *Considerations concerning the formation of languages*, pp. 408-10.

[45] *Logique de Port-Royal*, p. 101.

[46] Ibid., pp. 59-60.

[47] Ibid., p. 101.

[48] Duclos, *Commentaire à la 'Grammaire de Port-Royal'* (Paris, 1754, p. 213).

[49] J.-B. Lemercier. *Lettre sur la possibilité de faire de la grammaire un Art-Science* (Paris, 1806, pp. 63-5).

[50] James Harris, *Hermes*.

[51] A. Smith, *Considerations concerning the formation of languages*, pp. 430-1.

[52] Bauzée (*Grammaire générale*) was the first to employ the term 'complement'.

[53] *Logique de Port-Royal*, p. 117 et seq.

[54] Abbé Sicard, *Éléments de grammaire générale*, t. II, p. 2.

[55] Sylvestre de Saci, *Principes de grammaire générale* (1799). Cf. also U. Domergue, *Grammaire générale analytique*, pp. 29-30.

[56] Cf., for example, Abbé Girard, *Les Vrais Principes de la langue française*, pp. 82-3.

[57] *Logique de Port-Royal*, p. 59.

[58] Batteux, *Nouvel examen du préjugé de l'inversion*, pp. 23-4.

[59] Ibid., pp. 24-8.

[60] Le Bel, *Anatomie de la langue latine* (Paris, 1764, p. 24).

[61] Ibid., p. 8.

[62] D. Thiébault, *Grammaire philosophique*, pp. 172-3.

[63] Court de Gébelin, *Histoire naturelle de la parole* (1816 edn., pp. 98-104).

[64] Rousseau, *Essai sur l'origine des langues* (*Œuvres*, 1826 edn., t. XIII, pp. 144–51 and 188–92).

[65] Condillac, *Grammaire*, p. 8.

[66] All the parts of discourse are, therefore, merely the fragments, broken down and recombined, of that initial interjection (Destutt de Tracy, *Éléments d'Idéologie*, t. II, p. 75).

[67] Condillac, *Grammaire*, p. 10.

[68] Rousseau, *Discours sur l'origine de l'inégalité* (cf. Condillac, *Grammaire*, p. 27, note 1).

[69] Condillac, *Grammaire*, pp. 11–12.

[70] De Brosses, *Traité de la formation mécanique des langues* (Paris, 1765, t. I, p. 9).

[71] Abbé Copineau, *Essai synthétique sur l'origine et la formation des langues* (Paris, 1774, pp. 34–5).

[72] De Brosses, *Traité de la formation mécanique des langues*, t. I, pp. 16–18.

[73] Ibid., t. I, p. 14.

[74] Bergier, *Les Éléments primitifs des langues* (Paris, 1764, pp. 7–8).

[75] De Brosses, *Traité de la formation mécanique des langues*, t. I, p. 18.

[76] Ibid., t. II, pp. 490–9.

[77] Ibid., t. I, préface, p. l.

[78] Cf., especially, Turgot's article on 'Étymologie' in the *Encyclopédie*.

[79] These, together with a few accessory variants, are the only laws of phonetic variation recognized by de Brosses (*Traité de la formation mécanique des langues*, pp. 108–23), Bergier (*Éléments primitifs des langues*, pp. 45–62), Court de Gébelin (*Histoire naturelle de la parole*, pp. 59–64), and Turgot ('Étymologie' in the *Encyclopédie*).

[80] Turgot, article 'Étymologie' in the *Encyclopédie*. Cf. de Brosses, op. cit., p. 420.

[81] De Brosses, *Traité de la formation mécanique des langues*, t. I, pp. 66–7.

[82] Turgot, article 'Étymologie' in the *Encyclopédie*.

[83] Duclos, *Remarques sur la grammaire générale*, pp. 43–4.

[84] Destutt de Tracy, *Éléments d'Idéologie*, II, pp. 307–12.

[85] Warburton, *The divine legation of Moses*.

[86] Warbuton, op. cit.

[87] Destutt de Tracy, *Éléments d'Idéologie*, t. II, pp. 284–300.

[88] Volney, *Les Ruines* (Paris, 1791, chap. XIV).

[89] Condillac, *Grammaire*, chap. 2.

[90] Adam Smith, *Considerations concerning the formation of languages*.

[91] Turgot, *Tableau des progrès successifs de l'esprit humain* (1750; *Œuvres*, ed. Schelle, p. 215).

[92] Condillac, *Essai sur l'origine des connaissances humaines* (*Œuvres*, t. I, pp. 75–87).

[93] Du Marsais, *Traité des tropes* (1811 edn., pp. 150–1).

[94] Ibid., p. 2.

[95] Rousseau, *Essai sur l'origine des langues*, pp. 152–3.

[96] De Brosses, *Traité de la prononciation mécanique*, p. 267.

CHAPTER 5

Classifying

I WHAT THE HISTORIANS SAY

Histories of ideas or of the sciences – by which is meant here an average cross-section of them – credit the seventeenth century, and especially the eighteenth, with a new curiosity: the curiosity that caused them, if not to discover the sciences of life, at least to give them a hitherto unsuspected scope and precision. A certain number of causes and several essential manifestations are traditionally attributed to this phenomenon.

On the side of origins or motives, we place the new privileges accorded to observation: the powers attributed to it since Bacon and the technical improvements introduced in it by the invention of the microscope. Alongside these is set the then recently attained prestige of the physical sciences, which provided a model of rationality; since it had proved possible, by means of experimentation and theory, to analyse the laws of movement or those governing the reflection of light beams, was it not normal to seek, by means of experiments, observations, or calculations, the laws that might govern the more complex but adjacent realm of living beings? Cartesian mechanism, which subsequently proved an obstacle, was used at first, the historians tell us, as a sort of instrument of transference, and led, rather in spite of itself, from mechanical rationality to the discovery of that other rationality which is that of the living being. Still on the side of causes, and in a somewhat pell-mell fashion, the historians of ideas place a variety of new interests: the economic attitude towards agriculture – the Physiocrats' beliefs were evidence of this, but so too were the first efforts to create an agronomy; then, half-way between husbandry and theory, a curiosity with regard to exotic plants and animals, which attempts were made to acclimatize, and of which the great voyages of inquiry or exploration – that of Tournefort to the Middle East, for example, or that of Adanson to Senegal – brought back descriptions, engravings, and specimens; and then, above all, the ethical valorization of nature, together with the whole of that movement, ambiguous in its principle, by means of which – whether one was an aristocrat or a bourgeois – one 'invested' money and feeling into a land that earlier periods had for so long left fallow. Rousseau, at the heart of the eighteenth century, was a student of botany.

In their list of manifestations, the historians then include the varied forms that were taken by these new sciences of life, and the 'spirit', as they put it, that directed them. Apparently, under the influence of Descartes, they were mechanistic to begin with, and continued to be so to the end of the seventeenth century; then the first efforts of an infant chemistry made its imprint upon them, but throughout the eighteenth century the vitalist themes are thought to have attained or returned to their privileged status, finally coalescing to form a unitary doctrine – that 'vitalism' which in slightly differing forms was professed by Bordeu and Barthez in Montpellier, by Blumenbach in Germany, and by Diderot then Bichat in Paris. Under these different theoretical regimens, questions were asked that were almost always the same but were given each time a different solution: the possibility of classifying living beings – some, like Linnaeus, holding that all of nature can be accommodated within a taxonomy, others, like Buffon, holding that it is too rich and various to be fitted within so rigid a framework; the generative process, with the more mechanistically minded in favour of preformation, and others believing in the specific development of germs; analysis of functions (circulation after Harvey, sensation, motivity, and, towards the end of the century, respiration).

After examining these problems and the discussions they give rise to, it is simple enough for the historians to reconstruct the great controversies that are said to have divided men's opinions and passions, as well as their reasoning. By these means they believe that they can discover the traces of a major conflict between a theology that sees the providence of God and the simplicity, mystery, and foresight of his ways residing beneath each form and in all its movements, and a science that is already attempting to define the autonomy of nature. They also recognize the contradiction between a science still too attached to the old pre-eminence of astronomy, mechanics, and optics, and another science that already suspects all the irreducible and specific contents there may be in the realms of life. Lastly, the historians see the emergence, as though before their very eyes, of an opposition between those who believe in the immobility of nature – in the manner of Tournefort, and above all Linnaeus – and those who, with Bonnet, Benoît de Maillet, and Diderot, already have a presentiment of life's creative powers, of its inexhaustible power of transformation, of its plasticity, and of that movement by means of which it envelops all its productions, ourselves included, in a time of which no one is master. Long before Darwin and long before Lamarck, the great debate on evolution would appear to have been opened by the *Telliamed*, the *Palingénésie* and the *Rêve de d'Alembert*. Mechanism and theology, supporting one another or ceaselessly conflicting with one another, tended to keep the Classical age as close as possible to its origin – on the side of Descartes and Malebranche; whereas, opposite them, irreligion and a whole confused intuition of life, conflicting in turn (as in Bonnet) or acting as accomplices (as with Diderot), are said to be drawing it towards its imminent future – towards the nineteenth century, which is supposed to have provided the still obscure and fettered endeavours of the eighteenth with their positive and rational fulfilment in a science of life which did not need to sacrifice rationality in order to preserve in the very quick of its consciousness the specificity of living things, and that somewhat subterranean warmth which circulates between them – the object of our knowledge – and us, who are here to know them.

It would be pointless to go back over the presuppositions inherent in such a method. Let it suffice here to point out its consequences: the difficulty of apprehending the network that is able to link together such diverse investigations as attempts to establish a taxonomy and microscopic observations; the necessity of recording as observed facts the conflicts between those who were fixists and those who were not, or between the experimentalists and the partisans of the system; the obligation to divide knowledge into two interwoven fabrics when in fact they were alien to one another – the first being defined by what was known already and from elsewhere (the Aristotelian or scholastic inheritance, the weight of Cartesianism, the prestige of Newton), the second by what still remained to be known (evolution, the specificity of life, the notion of organism); and above all the application of categories that are strictly anachronistic in relation to this knowledge. Obviously, the most important of all these refers to life. Historians want to write histories of biology in the eighteenth century; but they do not realize that biology did not exist then, and that the pattern of knowledge that has been familiar to us for a hundred and fifty years is not valid for a previous period. And that, if biology was unknown, there was a very simple reason for it: that life itself did not exist. All that existed was living beings, which were viewed through a grid of knowledge constituted by *natural history*.

II NATURAL HISTORY

How was the Classical age able to define this realm of 'natural history', the proofs and even the unity of which now appear to us so distant, and as though already blurred? What is this field in which nature appeared sufficiently close to itself for the individual beings it contained to be classified, and yet so far removed from itself that they had to be so by the medium of analysis and reflection?

One has the impression – and it is often expressed – that the history of nature must have appeared as Cartesian mechanism ebbed. When it had at last become clear that it was impossible to fit the entire world into the laws of rectilinear movement, when the complexity of the vegetable and animal kingdoms had sufficiently resisted the simple forms of extended substance, then it became necessary for nature to manifest itself in all its strange richness; and the meticulous observation of living beings was thus born upon the empty strand from which Cartesianism had just withdrawn. Unfortunately, things do not happen as simply as that. It is quite possible – though it would be a matter requiring careful scrutiny – that one science can arise out of another; but no science can be generated by the absence of another, or from another's failure, or even from some obstacle another has encountered. In fact, the possibility of natural history, with Ray, Jonston, Christophorus Knauth, is contemporaneous with Cartesianism itself, and not with its failure. Mechanism from Descartes to d'Alembert and natural history from Tournefort to Daubenton were authorized by the same *episteme*.

For natural history to appear, it was not necessary for nature to become denser and more obscure, to multiply its mechanisms to the point of acquiring the opaque weight of a history that can only be retraced and described, without any possibility of measuring it, calculating it, or explaining it; it was necessary – and this is entirely the opposite – for History to become Natural. In the sixteenth century, and right up to the middle of the seventeenth, all that existed was histories: Belon had written a *History of the nature of birds*; Duret, an *Admirable history of plants*; Aldrovandi, a *History of serpents and dragons*. In 1657, Jonston published a *Natural history of quadrupeds*. This date of birth is not, of course, absolutely definitive[1]; it is there only to symbolize a landmark, and to indicate, from afar, the apparent enigma of an event. This event is the sudden separation, in the realm of *Historia*, of two orders of knowledge henceforward to be considered different. Until the time of Aldrovandi, History was the inextricable and completely unitary fabric of all that was visible of things and of the signs that had been discovered or lodged in them: to write the history of a plant or an animal was as much a matter of describing its elements or organs as of describing the resemblances that could be found in it, the virtues that it was thought to possess, the legends and stories with which it had been involved, its place in heraldry, the medicaments that were concocted from its substance, the foods it provided, what the ancients recorded of it, and what travellers might have said of it. The history of a living being was that being itself, within the whole semantic network that connected it to the world. The division, so evident to us, between what we see, what others have observed and handed down, and what others imagine or naïvely believe, the great tripartition, apparently so simple and so immediate, into *Observation*, *Document*, and *Fable*, did not exist. And this was not because science was hesitating between a rational vocation and the vast weight of naïve tradition, but for the much more precise and much more constraining reason that signs were then part of things themselves, whereas in the seventeenth century they become modes of representation.

When Jonston wrote his *Natural history of quadrupeds*, did he know any more about them than Aldrovandi did, a half-century earlier? Not a great deal more, the historians assure us. But that is not the question. Or, if we must pose it in these terms, then we must reply that Jonston knew a great deal less than Aldrovandi. The latter, in the case of each animal he examined, offered the reader, and on the same level, a description of its anatomy and of the methods of capturing it; its allegorical uses and mode of generation; its habitat and legendary mansions; its food and the best ways of cooking its flesh. Jonston subdivides his chapter on the horse under twelve headings: name, anatomical parts, habitat, ages, generation, voice, movements, sympathy and antipathy, uses, medicinal uses[2]. None of this was omitted by Aldrovandi, and he gives us a great deal more besides. The essential difference lies in what is *missing* in Jonston. The whole of animal semantics has disappeared, like a dead and useless limb. The words that had been interwoven in the very being of the beast have been unravelled and removed: and the living being, in its anatomy, its form, its habits, its birth and death, appears as though stripped naked. Natural history finds its locus in the gap that is now opened up between things and words – a silent gap, pure of all verbal sedimentation, and yet articulated according to the elements of representation, those same elements that can now without let or hindrance be named. Things touch against the banks of discourse because they appear in the hollow space of representation. It is not therefore at the moment when one gives up calculation that one finally begins to observe. We must not see the constitution of natural history, with the empirical climate in which it develops, as an experiment forcing entry, willy-nilly, into a knowledge that was keeping watch on the truth of nature elsewhere; natural history – and this is why it appeared at precisely this moment – is the space opened up in representation by an analysis which is anticipating the possibility of naming; it is the possibility of *seeing* what one will be able to *say*, but what one could not say subsequently, or see at a distance, if things and words, distinct from one another, did not, from the very first, communicate in a representation. The descriptive order proposed for natural history by Linnaeus, long after Jonston, is very characteristic. According to this order, every chapter dealing with a given animal should follow the following plan: name, theory, kind, species, attributes, use, and, to conclude, *Litteraria*. All the language deposited upon things by time is pushed back into the very last category, like a sort of supplement in which discourse is allowed to recount itself and record discoveries, traditions, beliefs, and poetical figures. Before this language of language, it is the thing itself that appears, in its own characters, but within the reality that has been patterned from the very outset by the name. The constitution of a natural science in the classical age is not the effect, either direct or indirect, of the transference of a rationality formed elsewhere (for geometrical or mechanical purposes). It is a separate formation, one that has its own archaeology, even though it is linked (though in a correlative and simultaneous mode) to the general theory of signs and to the project for a universal mathesis.

Thus the old word 'history' changes its value, and perhaps rediscovers one of its archaic significations. In any case, though it is true that the historian, for the Greeks, was indeed the individual who *sees* and who recounts from the starting-point of his sight, it has not always been so in our culture. Indeed, it was at a relatively late date, on the threshold of the Classical age, that he assumed – or resumed – this role. Until the mid-seventeenth century, the historian's task was to establish the great compilation of documents and signs – of everything, throughout the world, that might form a mark, as it were. It was the historian's responsibility to restore to language all the words that had been buried. His existence was defined not so much by what he saw as by what he retold, by a secondary speech which pronounced afresh so many words that had been muffled. The Classical age gives history a quite different meaning: that of undertaking a meticulous examination of things themselves for the first time, and then of transcribing what it has gathered in smooth, neutralized, and faithful words. It is understandable that the first form of history constituted in this period of 'purification' should have been the history of nature. For its construction requires only words applied, without intermediary, to things themselves. The documents of this new history are not other words, texts or records, but unencumbered spaces in which things are juxtaposed: herbariums, collections, gardens; the locus of this history is a non-temporal rectangle in which, stripped of all commentary, of all enveloping language, creatures present themselves one beside another, their surfaces visible, grouped according to their common features, and thus already virtually analysed, and bearers of nothing but their own individual names. It is often said that the establishment of botanical gardens and zoological collections expressed a new curiosity about exotic plants and animals. In fact, these had already claimed men's interest for a long while. What had changed was the space in which it was possible to see them and from which it was possible to describe them. To the Renaissance, the strangeness of animals was a spectacle: it was featured in fairs, in tournaments, in fictitious or real combats, in reconstitutions of legends in which the bestiary displayed its ageless fables. The natural history room and the garden, as created in the Classical period, replace the circular procession of the 'show' with the arrangement of things in a 'table'. What came surreptitiously into being between the age of the theatre and that of the catalogue was not the desire for knowledge, but a new way of connecting things both to the eye and to discourse. A new way of making history.

We also know what methodological importance these 'natural' allocations assumed, at the end of the eighteenth century, in the classification of words, languages, roots, documents, records – in short, in the constitution of a whole environment of history (in the now familiar sense of the word) in which the nineteenth century was to rediscover, after this pure tabulation of things, the renewed possibility of talking about words. And of talking about them, not in the style of commentary, but in a mode that was to be considered as positive, as objective, as that of natural history.

131

The ever more complete preservation of what was written, the establishment of archives, then of filing systems for them, the reorganization of libraries, the drawing up of catalogues, indexes, and inventories, all these things represent, at the end of the Classical age, not so much a new sensitivity to time, to its past, to the density of history, as a way of introducing into the language already imprinted on things, and into the traces it has left, an order of the same type as that which was being established between living creatures. And it is in this classified time, in this squared and spatialized development, that the historians of the nineteenth century were to undertake the creation of a history that could at last be 'true' – in other words, liberated from Classical rationality, from its ordering and theodicy: a history restored to the irruptive violence of time.

III STRUCTURE

Thus arranged and understood, natural history has as a condition of its possibility the common affinity of things and language with representation; but it exists as a task only in so far as things and language happen to be separate. It must therefore reduce this distance between them so as to bring language as close as possible to the observing gaze, and the things observed as close as possible to words. Natural history is nothing more than the nomination of the visible. Hence its apparent simplicity, and that air of naïveté it has from a distance, so simple does it appear and so obviously imposed by things themselves. One has the impression that with Tournefort, with Linnaeus or Buffon, someone has at last taken on the task of stating something that had been visible from the beginning of time, but had remained mute before a sort of invincible distraction of men's eyes. In fact, it was not an age-old inattentiveness being suddenly dissipated, but a new field of visibility being constituted in all its density.

Natural history did not become possible because men looked harder and more closely. One might say, strictly speaking, that the Classical age used its ingenuity, if not to see as little as possible, at least to restrict deliberately the area of its experience. Observation, from the seventeenth century onward, is a perceptible knowledge furnished with a series of systematically negative conditions. Hearsay is excluded, that goes without saying; but so are taste and smell, because their lack of certainty and their variability render impossible any analysis into distinct elements that could be universally acceptable. The sense of touch is very narrowly limited to the designation of a few fairly evident distinctions (such as that between smooth and rough); which leaves sight with an almost exclusive privilege, being the sense by which we perceive extent and establish proof, and, in consequence, the means to an analysis *partes extra partes* acceptable to everyone: the blind man in the eighteenth century can perfectly well be a geometrician, but he cannot be a naturalist[3]. And, even then, everything that presents itself to our gaze is not utilizable: colours especially can scarcely serve as a foundation for useful comparisons. The area of visibility in which observation is able to assume its powers is thus only what is left after these exclusions: a visibility freed from all other sensory burdens and restricted, moreover, to black and white. This area, much more than the receptivity and attention at last being granted to things themselves, defines natural history's condition of possibility, and the appearance of its screened objects: lines, surfaces, forms, reliefs.

It may perhaps be claimed that the use of the microscope compensates for these restrictions; and that though sensory experience was being restricted in the direction of its more doubtful frontiers, it was nevertheless being extended towards the new objects of a technically controlled form of observation. In fact, it was the same complex of negative conditions that limited the realm of experience and made the use of optical instruments possible. To attempt to improve one's power of observation by looking through a lens, one must renounce the attempt to achieve knowledge by means of the other senses or from hearsay. A change of scale in the visual sphere must have more value than the correlations between the various kinds of evidence that may be provided by one's impressions, one's reading, or learned compilations. Though indefinite confinement of the visible within its own extent is made more easily perceptible to the eye by a microscope, it is nevertheless not freed from it. And the best proof of this is probably that optical instruments were used above all as a means of resolving problems of generation. In other words, as a means of discovering how the forms, arrangements, and characteristic proportions of individual adults, and of their species, could be handed on down the centuries while preserving their strictly defined identity. The microscope was called upon not to go beyond the frontiers of the fundamental domain of visibility, but to resolve one of the problems it posed: the maintenance of specific visible forms from generation to generation. The use of the microscope was based upon a non-instrumental relation between things and the human eye – a relation that defines natural history. It was Linnaeus, after all, who said that *Naturalia* – as opposed to *Coelestia* and *Elementa* – were intended to be transmitted directly to the senses[4]. And Tournefort thought that, in order to gain a knowledge of plants, 'rather than scrutinize each of their variations with a religious scruple', it was better to analyse them 'as they fall beneath the gaze'[5].

To observe, then, is to be content with seeing – with seeing a few things systematically. With seeing what, in the rather confused wealth of representation, can be analysed, recognized by all, and thus given a name that everyone will be able to understand: 'All obscure similitudes,' said Linnaeus, 'are introduced only to the shame of art'[6]. Displayed in themselves, emptied of all resemblances, cleansed even of their colours, visual representations will now at last be able to provide natural history with what constitutes its proper object, with precisely what it will convey in the well-made language it intends to construct. This object is the extension of which all natural beings are constituted – an extension that may be affected by four variables. And by four variables only: the form of the elements, the quantity of those elements, the manner in which they are distributed in space in relation to each other, and the relative magnitude of each element. As Linnaeus said, in a passage of capital importance, 'every note should be a product of number, of form, of proportion, of situation'[7]. For example, when one studies the reproductive organs of a plant, it is sufficient, but indispensable, to enumerate the stamens and pistil (or to record their absence, according to the case), to define the form they assume, according to what geometrical figure they are distributed in the flower (circle, hexagon, triangle), and what their size is in relation to the other organs. These four variables, which can be applied in the same way to the five parts of the plant – roots, stem, leaves, flowers, fruits – specify the extension available to representation well enough for us to articulate it into a description acceptable to everyone: confronted with the same individual entity, everyone will be able to give the same description; and, inversely, given such a description everyone will be able to recognize the individual entities that correspond to it. In this fundamental articulation of the visible, the first confrontation of language and things can now be established in a manner that excludes all uncertainty.

Each visibly distinct part of a plant or an animal is thus describable in so far as four series of values are applicable to it. These four values affecting, and determining, any given element or organ are what botanists term its *structure*. 'By the structure of a plant's parts we mean the composition and arrangement of the pieces that make up its body.'[8] Structure also makes possible the description of what one sees, and this in two ways which are neither contradictory nor mutually exclusive. Number and magnitude can always be assigned by means of a count or a measure; they can therefore be expressed in quantitative terms. Forms and arrangements, on the other hand, must be described by other methods: either by identification with geometrical figures, or by analogies that must all be 'of the utmost clarity'[9]. In this way it becomes possible to describe certain fairly complex forms on the basis of their very visible resemblance to the human body, which serves as a sort of reservoir for models of visibility, and acts as a spontaneous link between what one can see and what one can say[10].

By limiting and filtering the visible, structure enables it to be transcribed into language. It permits the visibility of the animal or plant to pass over in its entirety into the discourse that receives it. And ultimately, perhaps, it may manage to reconstitute itself in visible form by means of words, as with the botanical calligrams dreamed of by Linnaeus[11]. His wish was that the order of the description, its division into paragraphs, and even its typographical modules, should reproduce the form of the plant itself. That the printed text, in its variables of form, arrangement, and quantity, should have a vegetable structure. 'It is beautiful to follow nature: to pass from the Root to the Stems, to the Petioles, to the Leaves, to the Peduncles, to the Flowers.' The description would have to be divided into the same number of paragraphs as there are parts in the plant, everything concerning its principal parts being printed in large type, and the analysis of the 'parts of parts' being conveyed in small type. One would then add what one knew of the plant from other sources in the same way as an artist completes his sketch by introducing the interplay of light and shade: 'the Adumbration would exactly contain the whole history of the plant, such as its names, its structure, its external assemblage, its nature, its use.' The plant is thus engraved in the material of the language into which it has been transposed, and recomposes its pure form before the reader's very eyes. The book becomes the herbarium of living structures. And let no one reply that this is merely the reverie of a systematizer and does not represent the whole of natural history. Buffon was a constant adversary of Linnaeus, yet the same structure exists in his work and plays the same role: 'The method of examination will be directed towards form, magnitude, the different parts, their number, their position, and the very substance of the thing'[12]. Buffon and Linnaeus employ the same grid; their gaze occupies the same surface of contact upon things;

135

there are the same black squares left to accommodate the invisible; the same open and distinct spaces to accommodate words.

By means of structure, what representation provides in a confused and simultaneous form is analysed and thereby rendered suitable to the linear unwinding of language. In effect, description is to the object one looks at what the proposition is to the representation it expresses: its arrangement in a series, elements succeeding elements. But it will be remembered that language in its empirical form implied a theory of the proposition and a theory of articulation. In itself, the proposition remained empty; and the ability of articulation to give form to authentic discourse was conditional upon its being linked together by the patent or secret function of the verb *to be*. Natural history is a science, that is, a language, but a securely based and well-constructed one: its propositional unfolding is indisputably an articulation; the arrangement of its elements into a linear series patterns representation according to an evident and universal mode. Whereas one and the same representation can give rise to a considerable number of propositions, since the names that embody it articulate it according to different modes, one and the same animal, or one and the same plant, will be described in the same way, in so far as their structure governs their passage from representation into language. The theory of *structure*, which runs right through natural history in the Classical age, superimposes the roles played in language by the *proposition* and *articulation* in such a way that they perform one and the same function.

And it is by this means that structure links the possibility of a natural history to the mathesis. In fact, it reduces the whole area of the visible to a system of variables all of whose values can be designated, if not by a quantity, at least by a perfectly clear and always finite description. It is therefore possible to establish the system of identities and the order of differences existing between natural entities. Adanson was of the opinion that one day it would be possible to treat botany as a rigorously mathematical science, and that it would prove permissible to pose botanical problems in the same way as one does algebraic or geometrical ones: 'find the most obvious point that establishes the line of separation or discussion between the scabious family and the honeysuckle family'; or again, find a known genus of plants (whether natural or artificial is unimportant) that stands exactly half-way between Dog's-bane and Borage[13]. By virtue of structure, the great proliferation of beings occupying the surface of the globe is able to enter both into the sequence of a descriptive language and into the field of a mathesis that would also be a general science of order. And this constituent relation, complex as it is, is established within the apparent simplicity of a *description of the visible*.

All this is of great importance for the definition of natural history in terms of its object. The latter is provided by surfaces and lines, not by functions or invisible tissues. The plant and the animal are seen not so much in their organic unity as by the visible patterning of their organs. They are paws and hoofs, flowers and fruits, before being respiratory systems or internal liquids. Natural history traverses an area of visible, simultaneous, concomitant variables, without any internal relation of subordination or organization. In the seventeenth and eighteenth centuries anatomy lost the leading role that it had played during the Renaissance and that it was to resume in Cuvier's day; it was not that curiosity had diminished in the meantime, or that knowledge had regressed, but rather that the fundamental arrangement of the visible and the expressible no longer passed through the thickness of the body. Hence the epistemological precedence enjoyed by botany: the area common to words and things constituted a much more accommodating, a much less 'black' grid for plants than for animals; in so far as there are a great many constituent organs visible in a plant that are not so in animals, taxonomic knowledge based upon immediately perceptible variables was richer and more coherent in the botanical order than in the zoological. We must therefore reverse what is usually said on this subject: it is not because there was a great interest in botany during the seventeenth and eighteenth centuries that so much investigation was undertaken into methods of classification. But because it was possible to know and to say only within a taxonomic area of visibility, the knowledge of plants was bound to prove more extensive than that of animals.

At the institutional level, the inevitable correlatives of this patterning were botanical gardens and natural history collections. And their importance, for Classical culture, does not lie essentially in what they make it possible to see, but in what they hide and in what, by this process of obliteration, they allow to emerge: they screen off anatomy and function, they conceal the organism, in order to raise up before the eyes of those who await the truth the visible relief of forms, with their elements, their mode of distribution, and their measurements. They are books furnished with structures, the space in which characteristics combine, and in which classifications are physically displayed. One day, towards the end of the eighteenth century, Cuvier was to topple the glass jars of the Museum, smash them open and dissect all the forms of animal visibility that the

Classical age had preserved in them. This iconoclastic gesture, which Lamarck could never bring himself to make, does not reveal a new curiosity directed towards a secret that no one had the interest or courage to uncover, or the possibility of uncovering, before. It is rather, and much more seriously, a mutation in the natural dimension of Western culture: the end of *history* in the sense in which it was understood by Tournefort, Linnaeus, Buffon, and Adanson – and in the sense in which it was understood by Boissier de Sauvages also, when he opposed *historical* knowledge of the visible to *philosophical* knowledge of the invisible, of what is hidden and of causes[14]. And it was also to be the beginning of what, by substituting anatomy for classification, organism for structure, internal subordination for visible character, the series for tabulation, was to make possible the precipitation into the old flat world of animals and plants, engraved in black on white, a whole profound mass of time to which men were to give the renewed name of *history*.

IV CHARACTER

Structure is that designation of the visible which, by means of a kind of pre-linguistic sifting, enables it to be transcribed into language. But the description thus obtained is nothing more than a sort of proper noun: it leaves each being its strict individuality and expresses neither the table to which it belongs, nor the area surrounding it, nor the site it occupies. It is designation pure and simple. And for natural history to become language, the description must become a 'common noun'. It has been seen how, in spontaneous language, the primary designations, which concerned only individual representations, after having originated in the language of action and the resultant primitive roots, had little by little, through the momentum of derivation, acquired more general values. But natural history is a well-constructed language: it should not accept the constraint imposed by derivation and its forms; it should not lend credit to any etymology[15]. It should unite in one and the same operation what everyday language keeps separate: not only must it designate all natural entities very precisely, but it must also situate them within the system of identities and differences that unites them to and distinguishes them from all the others. Natural history must provide, simultaneously, a certain *designation* and a controlled *derivation*. And just as the theory of structure superimposed articulation and the proposition so that they became one and the same, so the theory of *character* must identify the values that designate and the area in which they are derived. Tournefort says:

> To know plants is to know with precision the names that have been given to them in relation to the structure of some of their parts . . . The idea of the character that essentially distinguishes plants from one another ought invariably to be one with the name of each plant[16].

Establishing character is at the same time easy and difficult. Easy, because natural history does not have to establish a system of names based upon representations that are difficult to analyse, but only to derive it from a language that has already been unfolded in the process of description. The process of naming will be based, not upon what one sees, but upon elements that have already been introduced into discourse by structure. It is a matter of constructing a secondary language based upon that primary, but certain and universal, language. But a major difficulty appears immediately. In order to establish the identities and differences existing between all natural entities, it would be necessary to take into account every feature that might have been listed in a given description. Such an endless task would push the advent of natural history back into an inaccessible never-never land, unless there existed techniques that would avoid this difficulty and limit the labour of making so many comparisons. It is possible, *a priori*, to state that these techniques are of two types. Either that of making total comparisons, but only within empirically constituted groups in which the number of resemblances is manifestly so high that the enumeration of the differences will not take long to complete; and in this way, step by step, the establishment of all identities and distinctions can be guaranteed. Or that of selecting a finite and relatively limited group of characteristics, whose variations and constants may be studied in any individual entity that presents itself. This last procedure was termed the System, the first the Method. They are usually contrasted, in the same way as Linnaeus is contrasted with Buffon, Adanson, or Antoine-Laurent de Jussieu – or as a rigid and simple conception of nature is contrasted with the detailed and immediate perception of its relations, or as the idea of a motionless nature is contrasted with that of a teeming continuity of beings all communicating with one another, mingling with one another, and perhaps being transformed into one another. . . . And yet the essential does not lie in this conflict between the great intuitions of nature. It lies rather in the network of necessity which at this point rendered the choice between two ways of constituting natural history as a language both possible and indispensable. The rest is merely a logical and inevitable consequence.

From the elements that the *System* juxtaposes in great detail by means of description, it selects a particular few. These define the privileged and, in fact, exclusive structure in relation to which identities or differences as a whole are to be examined. Any difference not related to one of these elements will be considered irrelevant. If, like Linnaeus, one selects as the characteristic elements 'all the different parts related to fructification'[17], then a difference of leaf or stem or root or petiole must be systematically ignored. Similarly, any identity not occurring in one of these selected elements will have no value in the definition of the character. On the other hand, when these elements are similar in two individuals they receive a common denomination. The structure selected to be the locus of pertinent identities and differences is what is termed the *character*. According to Linnaeus, the character should be composed of 'the most careful description of the fructification of the first species. All the other species of the genus are compared with the first, all discordant notes being eliminated; finally, after this process, the character emerges'[18].

The system is arbitrary in its basis, since it deliberately ignores all differences and all identities not related to the selected structure. But there is no law that says that it will not be possible to arrive one day, through a use of this technique, at the discovery of a natural system – one in which all the differences in the character would correspond to differences of the same value in the plant's general structure; and in which, inversely, all the individuals or all the species grouped together under a common character would in fact have the same relation of resemblance in all and each of their parts. But one cannot find the way to this natural system unless one has first established with certainty an artificial system, at least in certain of the vegetable or animal domains. This is why Linnaeus does not seek to establish a natural system immediately, 'before a complete knowledge has been attained of everything that is relevant'[19] to his system. It is true that the natural method constitutes 'the first and last wish of botanists', and that all its 'fragments should be searched for with the greatest care'[20], as Linnaeus himself searches for them in his *Classes Plantarum*; but until this natural method appears in its certain and finished form, 'artificial systems are absolutely necessary'[21].

Moreover, the system is relative: it is able to function according to a desired degree of precision. If the selected character is composed of a large structure, having a large number of variables, then as soon as one passes from one individual to another, even if it is immediately adjacent, the differences will appear at once: the character in this case is very close to pure description[22]. If, on the other hand, the selected structure is limited in extent, and its variables few, then the differences will be rare and the individuals grouped in compact masses. The character is chosen according to the degree of detail required in the classification. In order to establish genera, Tournefort chose the combination of flower and fruit as his character. Not, as with Cesalpino, because these were the most useful parts of the plant, but because they permitted a numerically satisfying combinability: the elements that would be taken from the other three parts (roots, stems, and leaves) were, in effect, either too numerous if treated together or too few if taken separately[23]. Linnaeus calculated that the thirty-eight organs of reproduction, each comprising the four variables of number, form, situation, and proportion, would produce 5,776 configurations, or sufficient to define the genera[24]. If one wishes to obtain groups more numerous than genera, then one must make use of more limited characters ('factitious characters agreed upon between botanists'), as, for example, the stamens alone, or the pistil alone. In this way one would be able to distinguish classes or orders[25].

In this way, a grid can be laid out over the entire vegetable or animal kingdom. Each group can be given a name. With the result that any species, without having to be described, can be designated with the greatest accuracy by means of the names of the different groups in which it is included. Its complete name will cross the entire network of characters that one has established, right up to the largest classifications of all. But for convenience, as Linnaeus points out, part of this name should remain 'silent' (one does not name the class and order), while the other part should be 'sounded' (one must name the genus, the species, and the variety[26]. The plant thus recognized in its essential character and designated upon that basis will express at the same time that which accurately designates it and the relation linking it to those plants that resemble it and belong to the same genus (and thus to the same family and the same order). It will have been given at the same time its proper name and the whole series of common names (manifest or hidden) in which it resides. 'The generic name is, as it were, the official currency of our botanical republic'[27]. Natural history will have accomplished its fundamental task, which is that of 'arrangement and designation'[28].

The *Method* is another technique for resolving the same problem. Instead of selecting, from the totality described, the elements – whether few or numerous – that are to be used as characters, the method consists in deducing them stage by stage. Deduction is to be taken here in the sense of subtraction. One begins – as Adanson did in his examination of the plants of Senegal[29] – with a species either arbitrarily chosen or encountered by chance. One describes it in its entirety, leaving out none of its parts and determining all the values that the variables have derived from it. This process is repeated with the next species, also given by the arbitrary nature of representation; the description should be as total as in the first instance, but with the one difference that nothing that has been mentioned in the first description should be repeated in the second. Only the differences are listed. And similarly with the third species in relation to the first two, and so on indefinitely. So that, at the very end, all the different features of all the plants have been listed once, but never more than once. And by arranging the later and progressively more sparse descriptions around the earlier ones, we shall be able to perceive, through the original chaos, the emergence of the general table of relations. The character that distinguishes each species or each genus is the only feature picked out from the background of tacit identities. Indeed, such a technique would probably be the most reliable, only the number of existing species is so great that it would be impossible to deal with them all. Nevertheless, the examination of such species as we do meet with reveals the existence of great 'families', of very broad groups in which the species and the genera have a considerable number of identities. So considerable, indeed, that they signalize themselves by a very large number of characteristics, even to the least analytic eye; the resemblance between all the species of Ranunculus, or between all the species of Aconite, is immediately apparent to the senses. At this point, in order to prevent the task becoming infinite, one is obliged to reverse the process. One admits the existence of the great families that are manifestly recognizable, and whose general features have been defined, as it were blindfold, by the first descriptions of them. These are the common features that we now establish in a positive way; then, whenever we meet with a genus or species that is manifestly contained by them, it will suffice to indicate what difference distinguishes it from the others that serve it as a sort of natural entourage. A knowledge of each species can be acquired easily upon the basis of this general characterization: 'We shall divide each of the three kingdoms into several families which will group together all those beings that are strikingly related, and we shall review all the general and particular characters of the beings contained within those families'; in this way we shall be assured of relating all these beings to their natural families; and thus, beginning with the ferret and the wolf, the dog and the bear, we shall come to know sufficient about the lion, the tiger, and the hyena, which are animals of the same family[30].

It is immediately apparent in what way the method and the system are opposed. There can be only one method; but one can invent and apply a considerable number of systems: Adanson alone set out sixty-five[31]. The system is arbitrary throughout its development, but once the system of variables – the character – has been defined at the outset, it is no longer possible to modify it, to add or subtract even one element. The method is imposed from without, by the total resemblances that relate things together; it immediately transcribes perception into discourse; it remains, in its point of departure, very close to description; but it is always possible to apply to the general character it has defined empirically such modifications as may be imposed: a feature one had thought essential to a whole group of plants or animals may very well prove to be no more than a particularity of a few of them, if one discovers others that, without possessing that feature, belong quite obviously to the same family; the method must always be ready to rectify itself. As Adanson says, the system is like 'the trial and error method in mathematics': it is the result of a decision, but it must be absolutely coherent; the method, on the other hand, is

a given arrangement of objects or facts grouped together according to certain given conventions or resemblances, which one expresses by a general notion applicable to all those objects, without, however, regarding that fundamental notion or principle as absolute or invariable, or as so general that it cannot suffer any exception . . . The method differs from the system only in the idea that the author attaches to his principles, regarding them as variables in the method and as absolutes in the system[32].

Moreover, the system can recognize only relations of coordination between animal or vegetable structures. Since the character is selected, not on account of its functional importance but on account of its combinative efficacity, there is no proof that in the internal hierarchy of any individual plant such and such a form of pistil or arrangement of stamens necessarily entails such and such a structure: if the germ of the Adoxa is placed between the calyx and the corolla, or if, in the arum, the stamens are arranged between the pistils, these are nothing more or less than 'singular structures'[33]; their slight importance is a product of their rarity alone, whereas the equal division of calyx and corolla derives its value only from its frequency[34]. The method, on the other hand, because it proceeds from identities and differences of the most general kind to those that are less so, is capable of bringing out vertical relations of subordination. It enables us, in fact, to see which characters are important enough never to be negated within a given family. In relation to the system, the reversal is very important: the most essential characters make it possible to distinguish the largest and most visibly distinct families, whereas, for Tournefort or Linnaeus, the essential character defined the genus; and it was sufficient for the naturalists' 'agreement' to select a factitious character that would distinguish between classes or orders. In the method, general organization and its internal dependencies are more important than the lateral application of a constant apparatus of variables.

Despite these differences, both system and method rest upon the same epistemological base. It can be defined briefly by saying that, in Classical terms, a knowledge of empirical individuals can be acquired only from the continuous, ordered, and universal tabulation of all possible differences. In the sixteenth century, the identity of plants or animals was assured by the positive mark (sometimes hidden, often visible) which they all bore: what distinguished the various species of birds, for instance, was not the differences that existed *between* them but the fact that this one hunted its food at night, that another lived on the water, that yet another fed on living flesh[35]. Every being bore a mark, and the species was measured by the extent of a common emblem. So that each species identified itself by itself, expressed its individuality independently of all the others: it would have been perfectly possible for all those others not to exist, since the criteria of definition would not thereby have been modified for those that remained visible. But, from the seventeenth century, there can no longer be any signs except in the analysis of representations according to identities and differences. That is, all designation must be accomplished by means of a certain relation to all other possible designations. To know what properly appertains to one individual is to have before one the classification – or the possibility of classifying – all others. Identity and what marks it are defined by the differences that remain. An animal or a plant is not what is indicated – or betrayed – by the stigma that is to be found imprinted upon it; it is what the others are not; it exists in itself only in so far as it is bounded by what is distinguishable from it. Method and system are simply two ways of defining identities by means of the general grid of differences. Later on, beginning with Cuvier, the identity of species was to be determined in the same way by a set of differences, but the differences were in this case to emerge from the background of the great organic unities possessing their own internal systems of dependencies (skeleton, respiration, circulation); the invertebrates were to be defined, not only by their lack of vertebrae, but also by a certain mode of respiration, by the existence of a type of circulation, and by a whole organic cohesiveness outlining a positive unity. The internal laws of the organism were to replace differential characters as the object of the natural sciences. Classification, as a fundamental and constituent problem of natural history, took up its position historically, and in a necessary fashion, between a theory of the *mark* and a theory of the *organism*.

V CONTINUITY AND CATASTROPHE

At the heart of this well-constructed language that natural history has become, one problem remains. It is possible after all that the transformation of structure into character may never be possible, and that the common noun may never be able to emerge from the proper noun. Who can guarantee that the descriptions, once made, are not going to display elements that vary so much from one individual to the next, or from one species to the next, that any attempt to use them as the basis for a common noun would be doomed in advance? Who can be certain that each structure is not strictly isolated from every other structure, and that it will not function as an individual mark? In order that the simplest character can become apparent, it is essential that at least one element in the structure examined first should be repeated in another. For the general order of differences that makes it possible to establish the arrangement of species implies a certain number of similarities. The problem here is isomorphic with the one we have already met in relation to language[36]: for a common noun to be possible, there had to be an immediate resemblance between things that permitted the signifying elements to move along the representations, to slide across the surface of them, to cling to their similarities and thus, finally, to form collective designations. But in order to outline this rhetorical space in which nouns gradually took on their general value, there was no need to determine the status of that resemblance, or whether it was founded upon truth; it was sufficient for it to strike the imagination with sufficient force. In natural history, however, which is a well-constructed language, these analogies of the imagination cannot have the value of guarantees; and since natural history is threatened, like all language, by the radical doubt that Hume brought to bear upon the necessity for repetition in experience, it must find a way of avoiding that threat. There must be continuity in nature.

This requirement that nature should be continuous does not take exactly the same form in the systems as it does in the methods. For the system-atician, continuity consists only of the unbroken juxtaposition of the different regions that can be clearly distinguished by means of char-acters; all that is required is an uninterrupted gradation of the values that the structure selected as a character can assume in the species as a whole; starting from this principle, it will become apparent that all these values are occupied by real beings, even though they may not yet be known. 'The system indicates the plants, even those it has not mentioned; which is something that the enumeration of a catalogue can never do' [37]. And the categories will not simply be arbitrary conventions laid out over this continuity of juxtaposition; they will correspond (if they have been properly established) to areas that have a *distinct* existence on this *uninter-rupted* surface of nature; they will be areas that are larger than individuals but just as real. In this way, according to Linnaeus, the reproductive system made it possible to establish the existence of indisputably well-founded genera: 'Know that it is not the character that constitutes the genus, but the genus that constitutes the character, that the character derives from the genus, not the genus from the character' [38]. In the methods, on the other hand, since resemblances – in their massive and clearly evident form – are posited to start with, the continuity of nature will not be this purely negative postulate (no blank spaces between dis-tinct categories), but a positive requirement: all nature forms one great fabric in which beings resemble one another from one to the next, in which adjacent individuals are infinitely similar to each other; so that any dividing-line that indicates, not the minute difference of the individual, but broader categories, is always unreal. There is a continuity produced by fusion in which all generality is nominal. Our general ideas, says Buffon,

> are relative to a continuous scale of objects of which we can clearly perceive only the middle rungs and whose extremities increasingly flee from and escape our considerations . . . The more we increase the

number of divisions in the productions of nature, the closer we shall approach to the true, since nothing really exists in nature except individuals, and since genera, orders, and classes exist only in our imagination[39].

And Bonnet, meaning much the same thing, said:

There are no leaps in nature: everything in it is graduated, shaded. If there were an empty space between any two beings, what reason would there be for proceeding from the one to the other? There is thus no being above and below which there are not other beings that are united to it by some characters and separated from it by others.

It is therefore always possible to discover 'intermediate productions', such as the polyp between the animal and the vegetable, the flying squirrel between the bird and the quadruped, the monkey between the quadruped and man. Consequently, our divisions into species and classes 'are purely nominal'; they represent no more than 'means relative to our needs and to the limitations of our knowledge'[40].

In the eighteenth century, the continuity of nature is a requirement of all natural history, that is, of any effort to establish an order in nature and to discover general categories within it, whether they be real and prescribed by obvious distinctions or a matter of convenience and quite simply a pattern produced by our imagination. Only continuity can guarantee that nature repeats itself and that structure can, in consequence, become character. But this requirement immediately becomes a double one. For if it were given to experience, in its uninterrupted momentum, to traverse exactly, step by step, the great continuity comprising individuals, varieties, species, genera, and classes, there would be no need to constitute a science; descriptive designations would attain to generality quite freely, and the language of things would be constituted as scientific discourse by its own spontaneous momentum. The identities of nature would be presented to the imagination as though spelled out letter by letter, and the spontaneous shift of words within their rhetorical space would reproduce, with perfect exactitude, the identity of beings with their increasing generality. Natural history would become useless, or rather it would already have been written by man's everyday language; general grammar would at the same time be the universal *taxonomy* of beings. But if a natural history perfectly distinct from the analysis of words is indispensable, that is because experience does not reveal the continuity of nature as such, but gives it to us both broken up – since there are a great many gaps in the series of values effectively occupied by the variables (there are possible creatures whose place in the grid one can note without ever having had the opportunity to observe them) – and blurred, since the real, geographic and terrestrial space in which we find ourselves confronts us with creatures that are interwoven with one another, in an order which, in relation to the great network of *taxonomies*, is nothing more than chance, disorder, or turbulence. Linnaeus pointed out that, by associating the hydra (which is an animal) and the conferva (which is an alga), or the sponge and the coral, in the same localities, nature is not, as the order of our classifications would have it, linking together 'the most perfect plants with the animals termed very imperfect, but combining imperfect animals with imperfect plants'[41]. And Adanson remarked that nature is

> a confused mingling of beings that seem to have been brought together by chance: here, gold is mixed with another metal, with stone, with earth; there, the violet grows side by side with an oak. Among these plants, too, wander the quadruped, the reptile, and the insect; the fishes are confused, one might say, with the aqueous element in which they swim, and with the plants that grow in the depths of the waters . . . This mixture is indeed so general and so multifarious that it appears to be one of nature's laws[42].

Now, this great mixture is the result of a chronological series of events. And these events have their point of origin and their primary locus of application, not in the living species themselves, but in the space in which those species reside. They are produced in the relation of the Earth to the Sun, in climatic conditions, in the movements of the earth's crust; what they affect first are the oceans and the continents, the surface of the globe; living beings are affected only indirectly and in a secondary way: they are attracted or driven away by heat; volcanoes destroy them; they disappear with the land that crumbles away beneath them. It is possible, as Buffon, for example, supposed[43], that the earth was originally incandescent, before gradually growing colder; the animals, accustomed to living in very high temperatures, then regrouped themselves in the only region that still remains torrid, whereas the temperate or cold lands were peopled by species that had not had the opportunity to appear until that time. With the revolutions in the history of the earth, the taxonomic area (in which adjacencies are of the order of *character* and not of *modus vivendi*) was divided up into a concrete and geographical area that jumbled it all up. Moreover, it was probably broken up into fragments, and many species, adjacent to those we know or intermediary between taxonomic squares familiar to us, must have disappeared, leaving nothing behind them but traces difficult to decipher. In any case, this historical series of events is an addition to the expanse of beings: it does not properly appertain to it; its development lies in the real dimension of the world, not the analytic one of classifications; what it calls into question is the world as a locus for beings, not the beings themselves in so far as they have the property of being alive. There is a historicity, symbolized by the biblical accounts, which affects our astronomic system directly and the taxonomic grid of species indirectly; and apart from Genesis and the Flood, it is very possible that

> our globe underwent other revolutions that have not been revealed to us. It is connected to the whole astronomic system, and the links that join this globe to the other celestial bodies, in particular to the Sun and the comets, could have been the source of many revolutions that have left no traces perceptible to us, but of which the inhabitants of neighbouring worlds may perhaps have some knowledge[44].

To be able to exist as a science, natural history must, then, presuppose two groupings. One of them is constituted by the continuous network of beings; this continuity may take various spatial forms; Charles Bonnet thinks of it sometimes as a great linear scale of which one extremity is very simple, the other very complicated, with a narrow intermediary region – the only one that is visible to us – in the centre; sometimes as a central trunk from which there is a branch forking out on one side (that of the shellfish, with the crabs and crayfish as supplementary ramifications) and the series of insects on the other, branching out to include the frogs[45]; Buffon defines this same continuity 'as a wide woven strip, or rather a bundle which every so often puts out side branches that join it up with the bundles of another order'[46]; Pallas sees it as a polyhedric figure[47]; Hermann wished to constitute a three-dimensional model composed of threads all starting from a common point of origin, separating from one another, 'spreading out through a very great number of lateral branches', then coming together again[48]. The series of events, however, is quite distinct from these spatial configurations, each of which describes the taxonomic continuity in its own way; the series of events is discontinuous, and different in each of its episodes; but, as a whole, it can be drawn only as a simple line, which is that of time itself (and which can be conceived as straight, broken, or circular). In its concrete form, and in the depth that is proper to it, nature resides wholly between the fabric of the *taxinomia* and the line of revolutions. The tabulations that it forms in the eyes of men, and that it is the task of the discourse of science to traverse, are the fragments of the great surface of living species that are apparent according to the way it has been patterned, burst open, and frozen, between two temporal revolutions.

It will be seen how superficial it is to oppose, as two different opinions confronting one another in their fundamental options, a 'fixism' that is content to classify the beings of nature in a permanent tabulation, and a sort of 'evolutionism' that is supposed to believe in an immemorial history of nature and in a deep-rooted, onward urge of all beings throughout its continuity. The solidity, without gaps, of a network of species and genera, and the series of events that have blurred that network, both belong, at the same level, to the epistemological foundation that made a body of knowledge like natural history possible in the Classical age. They are not two ways of perceiving nature, radically opposed because deeply rooted in philosophical choices older and more fundamental than any science; they are two simultaneous requirements in the archaeological network that defines the knowledge of nature in the Classical age. But these two requirements are complementary, and therefore irreducible. The temporal series cannot be integrated into the gradation of beings. The eras of nature do not prescribe the internal *time* of beings and their continuity; they dictate the *intemperate* interruptions that have constantly dispersed them, destroyed them, mingled them, separated them, and interwoven them. There is not and cannot be even the suspicion of an evolutionism or a transformism in Classical thought; for time is never conceived as a principle of development for living beings in their internal organization; it is perceived only as the possible bearer of a revolution in the external space in which they live.

VI MONSTERS AND FOSSILS

It will be objected that, long before Lamarck, there already existed a whole body of thought of the evolutionist type. That its importance was considerable in the middle of the eighteenth century, and up to the sudden halt marked by the work of Cuvier. That Bonnet, Maupertuis, Diderot, Robinet, and Benoît de Maillet all very clearly articulated the idea that living forms may pass from one into another, that the present species are no doubt the result of former transformations, and that the whole of the living world is perhaps in motion towards a future point, so that one cannot guarantee of any living form that it has been definitively acquired and is now stabilized forever. In fact, such analyses are incompatible with what we understand today by evolutionary thought. They are concerned, in fact, with linking the table of identities and differences to the series of successive events. And in order to conceive of the unity of that table and that series they have only two means at their disposal.

The first consists in integrating the series of successions with the continuity of the beings and their distribution over the table. All the creatures that taxonomy has arranged in an uninterrupted simultaneity are then subjected to time. Not in the sense that the temporal series would give rise to a multiplicity of species that a horizontally oriented eye could then arrange according to the requirements of a classifying grid, but in the sense that all the points of the taxonomy are affected by a temporal index, with the result that 'evolution' is nothing more than the interdependent and general displacement of the whole scale from the first of its elements to the last. This system is that of Charles Bonnet. He implies in the first place that the chain of being, stretching up through an innumerable series of links towards the perfection of God, does not at present attain to it [49]; that the distance between God and the least defective of his creatures is still infinite; and that across this, perhaps unbridgeable, distance the whole uninterrupted fabric of beings is ceaselessly advancing towards a greater perfection. He implies further that this 'evolution' keeps intact the relation that exists between the different species: if one of them, in the process of perfecting itself, should attain the degree of complexity possessed beforehand by the species one step higher, this does not mean that the latter has thereby been overtaken, because, carried onward by the same momentum, it cannot avoid perfecting itself to an equivalent degree:

There will be a continual and more or less slow progress of all the species towards a superior perfection, with the result that all the degrees of the scale will be continually variable within a determined and constant relation . . . Man, once transported to an abode more suited to the eminence of his faculties, will leave to the monkey and the elephant that foremost place that he occupied before among the animals of our planet . . . There will be Newtons among the monkeys and Vaubans

151

among the beavers. The oysters and the polyps will stand in the same relation to the species at the top of the scale as the birds and the quadrupeds do now to man[50].

This 'evolutionism' is not a way of conceiving of the emergence of beings as a process of one giving rise to another; in reality, it is a way of generalizing the principle of continuity and the law that requires that all beings form an uninterrupted expanse. It adds, in a Leibnizian style[51], the continuity of time to the continuity of space, and the infiniteness of the progress of beings towards perfection to their infinite multiplicity. It is not a matter of progressive hierarchization, but of the constant and total force exerted by an already established hierarchy. In the end this presupposes that time, far from being a principle of *taxinomia*, is merely one of its factors, and that it is pre-established, like all the other values assumed by all the other variables. Bonnet must, therefore, be a preformationist – and as far removed as possible from what we understand, since the nineteenth century, by 'evolutionism'; he must suppose that the upheavals or catastrophes of the globe were arranged in advance as so many opportunities for the infinite chain of being to continue its progress in the direction of infinite amelioration: 'These evolutions were foreseen and inscribed in the germs of animals upon the very first day of creation. For these evolutions are linked with revolutions in the whole solar system that were arranged by God in advance.' The universe in its entirety has been a larva; now it is a chrysalis; one day it will, no doubt, become a butterfly[52]. And every species will be caught up in the same way in that great mutation. Such a system, it is clear, is not an evolutionism beginning to overthrow the old dogma of fixism; it is a *taxinomia* that includes time in addition – a generalized classification.

The other form of 'evolutionism' consists of giving time a completely opposite role to play. It is used no longer to move the classifying table as a whole along the finite or infinite line leading to perfection, but to reveal, one after the other, the squares that, when viewed together, will form the continuous network of the species. It causes the variables of the living world to assume all possible values successively: it is the immediacy of a characterization that is accomplished little by little and, as it were, element after element. The partial identities or resemblances that make a *taxinomia* possible would then be the marks, revealed in the present, of one and the same living being, persisting through all the upheavals of nature and thereby filling all the vacant possibilities offered by the taxonomic table. If birds have wings in the way that fishes have fins, Benoît de Maillet points out, it is because they were once, at the time when the original waters of the earth were ebbing, dehydrated giltheads or dolphins that passed over, once for all, into an aerial home.

The seed of these fishes, carried into swamps, may perhaps have produced the first transmigration of the species from its marine to its terrestrial home. Even though a hundred millions may have perished without having been able to grow accustomed to it, it was sufficient for two of them to arrive at that point to give rise to the species[53].

Changes in the conditions of life of living beings seem here, as in certain forms of evolutionism, to be the necessary cause of the appearance of new species. But the mode in which the air, the water, the climate, or the earth acts upon animals is not that of an environment upon a function and upon the organs in which that function takes place; here, the exterior elements intervene only in so far as they occasion the emergence of a *character*. And that emergence, though it may be chronologically determined by such and such a global event, is rendered possible *a priori* by the general table of variables that defines all the possible forms of the living world. The quasi-evolutionism of the eighteenth century seems to presage equally well the spontaneous variation of character, as it was later to be found in Darwin, and the positive action of the environment, as it was to be described by Lamarck. But this is an illusion of hindsight: for this form of thought, in fact, the sequence of time can never be anything but the line along which all the possible values of the pre-established variables succeed one another. Consequently, a principle of modification must be defined within the living being, enabling it to take on a new character when a natural revolution occurs.

We are presented, then, with another choice: either to presuppose a spontaneous aptitude in living beings to change their forms (or at least to acquire – with succeeding generations – a slightly different character from that originally given, so that it will change gradually from one to the next and finally become unrecognizable), or to attribute to them some obscure urge towards a terminal species that will possess the characters of all those that have preceded it, but in a higher degree of complexity and perfection.

The first system is that of errors to infinity – as it is to be in Maupertuis. According to this system, the table of species that it is possible for natural history to establish has been built up piecemeal by the balance, constantly present in nature, between a memory that guarantees its continuity (maintenance of the species in time and their resemblance to one another) and a tendency towards deviation that simultaneously guarantees the existence of history, differences, and dispersion. Maupertuis supposes that the particles of matter are endowed with activity and memory. When attracted to one another, the least active form mineral substances; the most active form the more complex bodies of animals. These forms, which are the result of attraction and chance, disappear if they are unable to survive. Those that do remain in existence give rise to new individuals in which the characters of the parent couple are preserved by memory. And this process continues until a deviation of the particles – a chance happening – brings into being a new species, which the stubborn force of memory maintains in existence in turn: 'By dint of repeated deviations, the infinite diversity of the animals came to pass'[54]. Thus, progressing from one to the next, living beings acquired by successive variations all the characters we now recognize in them, and, when one considers them in the dimension of time, the coherent, solid expanse they form is merely the fragmentary result of a much more tightly knit, much finer, continuity: a continuity that has been woven from an incalculable number of tiny, forgotten, or miscarried differences. The visible species that now present themselves for our analysis have been separated out from the ceaseless background of monstrosities that appear, glimmer, sink into the abyss, and occasionally survive. And this is the fundamental point: nature has a history only in so far as it is susceptible of continuity. It is because it takes on all possible characters in turn (each value of all the variables) that it is presented in the form of a succession.

The same can be said for the inverse system of the prototype and the terminal species. In this case it is necessary to suppose, with J-B. Robinet, that continuity is assured, not by memory, but by a project – the project of a complex being towards which nature makes its way from the starting-point of simple elements which it gradually combines and arranges: 'First of all, the elements combine. A small number of simple principles serves as a basis for all bodies'; these are the ones that govern exclusively the organization of minerals; then 'the magnificence of nature' continues to increase without a break 'up to the level of the beings that move upon the surface of the globe'; 'the variation of the organs in number, in size, in refinement, in internal texture, and in external form, produces species which are divided and subdivided to infinity by new arrangements'[55]. And so on, until we reach the most complex arrangement we know of.

So that the entire continuity of nature resides between an absolutely archaic prototype, buried deeper than any history, and the extreme complication of this model as it is now possible to observe it, at least on this earthly globe, in the person of the human being[56]. Between these two extremes there lie all the possible degrees of complexity and combination – like an immense series of experiments, of which some have persisted in the form of continuing species and some have sunk into oblivion. Monsters are not of a different 'nature' from the species themselves:

> We should believe that the most apparently bizarre forms . . . belong necessarily and essentially to the universal plan of being; that they are metamorphoses of the prototype just as natural as the others, even though they present us with different phenomena; that they serve as means of passing to adjacent forms; that they prepare and bring about the combinations that follow them, just as they themselves were brought about by those that preceded them; that far from disturbing the order of things, they contribute to it. It is only, perhaps, by dint of producing monstrous beings that nature succeeds in producing beings of greater regularity and with a more symmetrical structure[57].

In Robinet, as in Maupertuis, succession and history are for nature merely means of traversing the infinite fabric of variations of which it is capable. It is not, then, that time or duration ensures the continuity and specification of living beings throughout the diversity of successive environments, but that against the continuous background of all the possible variations time traces out an itinerary upon which climates and geography pick out only certain privileged regions destined to survive. Continuity is not the visible wake of a fundamental history in which one same living principle struggles with a variable environment. For continuity precedes time. It is its condition. And history can play no more than a negative role in relation to it: it either picks out an entity and allows it to survive, or ignores it and allows it to disappear.

This has two consequences. First, the necessity of introducing monsters into the scheme – forming the background noise, as it were, the endless murmur of nature. Indeed, if it is necessary for time, which is limited, to run through – or perhaps to have already run through – the whole continuity of nature, one is forced to admit that a considerable number of possible variations have been encountered and then erased; just as the geological catastrophe was necessary to enable us to work back from the taxonomic table to the continuum, through a blurred, chaotic, and frag-mented experience, so the proliferation of monsters without a future is necessary to enable us to work down again from the continuum, through a temporal series, to the table. In other words, what must be construed, as we move in one direction, as a drama of the earth and waters must be construed, in the other direction, as an obvious aberration of forms. The monster ensures in time, and for our theoretical knowledge, a continuity that, for our everyday experience, floods, volcanoes, and subsiding continents confuse in space. The other consequence is that the signs of continuity throughout such a history can no longer be of any order other than that of resemblance. Since this history is not defined by any relation of organism to environment[58], the living forms will be subjected in it to all possible metamorphoses and leave behind them no trace of the path they have followed other than the reference points represented by similitudes. How, for example, are we to recognize that nature, starting from a primitive prototype, has never ceased to work towards the provisionally terminal form that is man? By the fact that it has abandoned on the way thousands of forms that provide us with a picture of the rudimentary model. How many fossils are there, for man's ear, or skull, or sexual parts, like so many plaster statues, fashioned one day and dropped the next in favour of a more perfected form?

> The species that resembles the human heart, and for that reason is named Anthropocardite . . . is worthy of particular attention. Its sub-stance is flint inside. The form of a heart is imitated as perfectly as pos-sible. One can distinguish in it the stump of the vena cava, together with a portion of its two cross-sections. One can also see the stump of the great artery emerging from the left ventricle, together with its lower or descending branch[59].

The fossil, with its mixed animal and mineral nature, is the privileged locus of a resemblance required by the historian of the continuum, whereas the space of the *taxinomia* decomposed it with rigour.

The monster and the fossil both play a very precise role in this con-figuration. On the basis of the power of the continuum held by nature, the monster ensures the emergence of difference. This difference is still without law and without any well-defined structure; the monster is the root-stock of specification, but it is only a sub-species itself in the stub-bornly slow stream of history. The fossil is what permits resemblances to subsist throughout all the deviations traversed by nature; it functions as a distant and approximative form of identity; it marks a quasi-character in the shift of time. And this is because the monster and the fossil are merely the backward projection of those differences and those identities that provide *taxinomia* first with structure, then with character. Between table and continuum they form a shady, mobile, wavering region in which what analysis is to define as identity is still only mute analogy; and what it will define as assignable and constant difference is still only free and random variation. But, in truth, it is so impossible for *natural history* to conceive of *the history of nature*, the epistemological arrangement delineated by the table and the continuum is so fundamental, that becoming can occupy nothing but an intermediary place measured out for it solely by the requirements of the whole. This is why it occurs only in order to bring about the necessary passage from one to the other – either as a totality of destructive events alien to living beings and occurring only from outside them, or as a movement ceaselessly being outlined, then halted as soon as sketched, and perceptible only on the fringes of the table, in its unconsidered margins. Thus, against the background of the continuum, the monster provides an account, as though in caricature, of the genesis of differences, and the fossil recalls, in the uncertainty of its resemblances, the first buddings of identity.

VII   THE DISCOURSE OF NATURE

The theory of natural history cannot be dissociated from that of language. And yet it is not a question of a transference of method, from one to the other; nor of a communication of concepts; nor of the prestige of a model which, because it has 'succeeded' in one field, has been tried out in the one next to it. Nor is it a question of a more general rationality imposing identical forms upon grammatical thinking and upon *taxinomia*. Rather, it concerns a fundamental arrangement of knowledge, which orders the knowledge of beings so as to make it possible to represent them in a system of names. There were doubtless, in this region we now term life, many inquiries other than attempts at classification, many kinds of analysis other than that of identities and differences. But they all rested upon a sort of historical *a priori*, which authorized them in their dispersion and in their singular and divergent projects, and rendered equally possible all the differences of opinion of which they were the source. This *a priori* does not consist of a set of constant problems uninterruptedly presented to men's curiosity by concrete phenomena as so many enigmas; nor is it made up of a certain state of acquired knowledge laid down in the course of the preceding ages and providing a ground for the more or less irregular, more or less rapid, progress of rationality; it is doubtless not even determined by what is called the mentality or the 'framework of thought' of any given period, if we are to understand by that the historical outline of the speculative interests, beliefs, or broad theoretical options of the time. This *a priori* is what, in a given period, delimits in the totality of experience a field of knowledge, defines the mode of being of the objects that appear in that field, provides man's everyday perception with theoretical powers, and defines the conditions in which he can sustain a discourse about things that is recognized to be true. In the eighteenth century, the historical *a priori* that provided the basis for inquiry into or controversy about the existence of genera, the stability of species, and the transmission of characters from generation to generation, was the existence of a natural history: the organization of a certain visible existence as a domain of knowledge, the definition of the four variables of description, the constitution of an area of adjacencies in which any individual being whatever can find its place. Natural history in the Classical age is not merely the discovery of a new object of curiosity; it covers a series of complex operations that introduce the possibility of a constant order into a totality of representations. It constitutes a whole domain of empiricity as at the same time *describable* and *orderable*. What makes it akin to theories of language also distinguishes it from what we have understood, since the nineteenth century, by biology, and causes it to play a certain critical role in Classical thought.

Natural history is contemporaneous with language: it is on the same level as the spontaneous play that analyses representations in the memory, determines their common elements, establishes signs upon the basis of those elements, and finally imposes names. Classification and speech have their place of origin in the same space that representation opens up within itself because it is consecrated to time, to memory, to reflection, to continuity. But natural history cannot and should not exist as a language independent of all other languages unless it is a well-constructed language – and a universally valid one. In spontaneous and 'badly constructed' language, the four elements (proposition, articulation, designation, derivation) leave interstices open between them: individual experiences, needs or passions, habits, prejudices, a more or less awakened concentration, have established hundreds of different languages – languages that differ from one another not only in the form of their words, but above all in the way in which those words pattern representation. Natural history can be a well-constructed language only if the amount of play in it is enclosed: if its descriptive exactitude makes every proposition into an invariable pattern of reality (if one can always *attribute* to the representation what is *articulated* in it) and if the *designation* of each being indicates clearly the place it occupies in the general *arrangement* of the whole. In language, the function of the verb is universal and void; it merely prescribes the most general form of the proposition; and it is within the latter that the names bring their system of articulation into play; natural history regroups these two functions into the unity of the *structure*, which articulates together all the variables that can be attributed to a being. And whereas in language the designation, in its individual functioning, is exposed to the hazard of derivations, which endow the common names with their scope and extension, the *character*, as established by natural history, makes it possible both to indicate the individual and to situate it in a space of generalities that fit inside one another. So that above the ordinary, everyday words (and by means of them, since it is of course necessary to use them for the initial descriptions) there is raised the edifice of a language in the second degree in which the exact Names of things finally rule:

> The method, the soul of science, designates at first sight any body in nature in such a way that the body in question expresses the name that is proper to it, and that this name recalls all the knowledge that may, in the course of time, have been acquired about the body thus named: so that in the midst of extreme confusion there is revealed the sovereign order of nature[60].

But this essential nomination – this transition from the visible structure to the taxonomic character – leads back to a costly requirement. In order to fulfil and enclose the figure that proceeds from the monotonous function of the verb *to be* to derivation and traversal of rhetorical space, spontaneous language had no need of anything but the play of imagination: that is, of immediate resemblances. For *taxonomy* to be possible, on the other hand, nature must be truly continuous, and in all its plenitude. Where language required the similarity of impressions, classification requires the principle of the smallest possible difference between things. Now, this continuum, which appears therefore at the very basis of nomination, in the opening left between description and arrangement, is presupposed well before language, as its condition. And not only because it can provide the basis for a well-constructed language, but because it accounts for all language in general. It is without doubt the continuity of nature that gives memory the opportunity of exercising itself, as when a representation, through some confused and ill-perceived identity, recalls another and makes it possible to apply to both the arbitrary sign of a common name. What was presented in the imagination as a blind similitude was merely the blurred and unreflected trace of the great uninterrupted fabric of identities and differences. Imagination (which, by making comparison possible, justifies language) formed, without its then being known, the ambiguous locus in which the shattered but insistent continuity of nature was united with the empty but attentive continuity of consciousness. It would not have been possible to speak, there would have been no place for even the merest name, if nature, in the very depth of things, before all representation, had not been continuous. To establish the great, unflawed table of the species, genera, and classes, natural history had to employ, criticize, and finally reconstitute at new expense a language whose condition of possibility resided precisely in that continuum. Things and words are very strictly interwoven: nature is posited only through the grid of denominations, and – though without such names it would remain mute and invisible – it glimmers far off beyond them, continuously present on the far side of this grid, which nevertheless presents it to our knowledge and renders it visible only when wholly spanned by language.

This, no doubt, is why natural history, in the Classical period, cannot be established as biology. Up to the end of the eighteenth century, in fact, life does not exist: only living beings. These beings form one class, or rather several classes, in the series of all the things in the world; and if it is possible to speak of life it is only as of one character – in the taxonomic sense of that word – in the universal distribution of beings. It is usual to divide the things in nature into three classes: minerals, which are recognized as capable of growth, but not of movement or feeling; vegetables, which are capable of growth and susceptible to sensation; and animals, which are capable of spontaneous movement[61]. As for life and the threshold it establishes, these can be made to slide from one end of the scale to the other, according to the criteria one adopts. If, with Maupertuis, one defines life by the mobility and relations of affinity that draw elements towards one another and keep them together, then one must conceive of life as residing in the simplest particles of matter. But one must situate it much higher in the series if one defines it by means of a crowded and complex character, as Linnaeus did when he set up as his criteria birth (by seed or bud), nutrition (by intussusception), ageing, exterior movement, internal propulsion of fluids, diseases, death, and presence of vessels, glands, epiderms, and utricles[62]. Life does not constitute an obvious threshold beyond which entirely new forms of knowledge are required. It is a category of classification, relative, like all the other categories, to the criteria one adopts. And also, like them, subject to certain imprecisions as soon as the question of deciding its frontiers arises. Just as the zoophyte stands on the ambiguous frontier between animals and plants, so the fossils, as well as the metals, reside in that uncertain frontier region where one does not know whether one ought to speak of life or not. But the dividing-line between the living and the non-living is never a decisive problem[63]. As Linnaeus says, the naturalist – whom he calls *Historiens naturalis* – 'distinguishes the parts of natural bodies with his eyes, describes them appropriately according to their number, form, position, and proportion, and he names them'[64]. The naturalist is the man concerned with the structure of the visible world and its denomination according to characters. Not with life.

We must therefore not connect natural history, as it was manifested during the Classical period, with a philosophy of life, albeit an obscure and still faltering one. In reality, it is interwoven with a theory of words. Natural history is situated both before and after language; it decomposes the language of everyday life, but in order to recompose it and discover what has made it possible through the blind resemblances of imagination; it criticizes language, but in order to reveal its foundation. If natural history reworks language and attempts to perfect it, this is because it also delves down into the origin of language. It leaps over the everyday vocabulary that provides it with its immediate ground, and beyond that ground it searches for that which could have constituted its *raison d'être*; but, inversely, it resides in its entirety in the area of language, since it is essentially a concerted use of names and since its ultimate aim is to give things their true denomination. Between language and the theory of nature there exists therefore a relation that is of a critical type; to know nature is, in fact, to build upon the basis of language a true language, one that will reveal the conditions in which all language is possible and the limits within which it can have a domain of validity. The critical question did exist in the eighteenth century, but linked to the form of a determinate knowledge. For this reason it could not acquire either autonomy or the value of radical questioning: it prowled endlessly through a region

161

where what mattered was resemblance, the strength of the imagination, nature and human nature, and the value of general and abstract ideas – in short, the relations between the perception of similitude and the validity of the concept. In the Classical age – Locke and Linnaeus, Buffon and Hume are our evidence of this – the critical question concerned the basis for resemblance and the existence of the genus.

In the late eighteenth century, a new configuration was to appear that would definitively blur the old space of natural history for modern eyes. On the one hand, we see criticism displacing itself and detaching itself from the ground where it had first arisen. Whereas Hume made the problem of causality one case in the general interrogation of resemblances[65], Kant, by isolating causality, reverses the question; whereas before it was a question of establishing relations of identity or difference against the continuous background of similitudes, Kant brings into prominence the inverse problem of the synthesis of the diverse. This simultaneously transfers the critical question from the concept to the judgement, from the existence of the genus (obtained by the analysis of representations) to the possibility of linking representations together, from the right to name to the basis for attribution, from nominal articulation to the proposition itself, and to the verb *to be* that establishes it. Whereupon it becomes absolutely generalized. Instead of having validity solely when applied to the relations of nature and human nature, it questions the very possibility of all knowledge.

On the other hand, however, and during the same period, life assumes its autonomy in relation to the concepts of classification. It escapes from that critical relation which, in the eighteenth century, was constitutive of the knowledge of nature. It escapes – which means two things: life becomes one object of knowledge among others, and is answerable, in this respect, to all criticism in general; but it also resists this critical jurisdiction, which it takes over on its own account and brings to bear, in its own name, on all possible knowledge. So that throughout the nineteenth century, from Kant to Dilthey and to Bergson, critical forms of thought and philosophies of life find themselves in a position of reciprocal borrowing and contestation.

NOTES

[1] J. Ray published a *Historia plantarum generalis* as late as 1686.

[2] Jonston, *Historia naturalis de quadripedidus* (Amsterdam, 1657, pp. 1–11).

[3] Diderot, *Lettre sur les aveugles.* Cf. Linnaeus: 'We should reject . . . all

accidental notes that do not exist in the Plant either for the eye or for the touch' (*Philosophie botanique*, section 258).

[4] Linnaeus, *Systema naturae*, p. 214. On the limited usefulness of the microscope, cf. ibid, pp. 220–1. (We have retained throughout the author's references to the French editions of the works of Linné (Linnaeus) – translator's note.)

[5] Tournefort, *Isagoge in rem herbariam* (1719); Fr. trans. in Becker-Tournefort (Paris, 1956, p. 295). Buffon criticized the Linnaean method for relying upon characters so tenuous that it rendered the use of the microscope unavoidable. From one naturalist to another, reproof concerning the use of an optical instrument has value as a theoretical objection.

[6] Linnaeus, *Philosophie botanique*, section 299.

[7] Ibid., section 167; cf. also section 327.

[8] Tournefort, *Éléments de botanique*, p. 558.

[9] Linnaeus, *Philosophie botanique*, section 299.

[10] Linnaeus (op. cit., section 331) lists the parts of the body that can be used as archetypes, whether for dimensions or, above all, for forms: hair, nails, thumbs, palms, eyes, ears, fingers, navel, penis, vulva, breasts.

[11] Ibid., sections 328–9.

[12] Buffon, *Discours sur la manière de traiter l'histoire naturelle* (*Œuvres complètes*, t. I, p. 21).

[13] Adanson, *Familles des plantes* (Paris, 1763, t. I, préface, p. cci).

[14] Boissier de Sauvages, *Nosologie méthodique* (Fr. trans. Lyon, 1772, t. I, pp. 91–2).

[15] Linnaeus, *Philosophie botanique*, section 258.

[16] Tournefort, *Éléments de botanique*, pp. 1–2.

[17] Linnaeus, *Philosophie botanique*, section 192.

[18] Ibid., section 193.

[19] Linnaeus, *Systema naturae*, section 12.

[20] Linnaeus, *Philosophie botanique*, section 77.

[21] Linnaeus, *Systema naturae*, section 12.

[22] 'The natural character of the species is its description' (Linnaeus, *Philosophie botanique*, section 193).

[23] Tournefort, *Éléments de botanique*, p. 27.

[24] Linnaeus, *Philosophie botanique*, section 167.

[25] Linnaeus, *Système sexuel des végétaux* (Fr. trans. Paris, year VI, p. 21).

[26] Linnaeus, *Philosophie botanique*, section 212.

[27] Ibid., section 284.

[28] Ibid., section 151. These two functions, which are guaranteed by the character, correspond exactly to the functions of designation and derivation performed in language by the common noun.

[29] Adanson, *Histoire naturelle du Sénégal* (Paris, 1757).

[30] Adanson, *Cours d'histoire naturelle* (Paris, 1772; 1845 edn., p. 17).

[31] Adanson, *Familles des plantes*.

[32] Ibid., t. I, préface.

[33] Linnaeus, *Philosophie botanique*, section 105.

[34] Ibid., section 94.

[35] Cf. P. Belon, *Histoire de la nature des oiseaux*.

[36] Cf. p. 113 above.

[37] Linnaeus, *Philosophie botanique*, section 156.

[38] Ibid., section 169.

[39] Buffon, *Discours sur la manière de traiter l'histoire naturelle* (*Œuvres complètes*, t. I, pp. 36 and 39).

[40] C. Bonnet, *Contemplation de la nature*, Ière partie (*Œuvres complètes*, t. IV, pp. 35–6).

[41] Linnaeus, *Philosophie botanique*.

[42] Adanson, *Cours d'histoire naturelle*, 1845 edn., pp. 4–5.

[43] Buffon, *Histoire de la terre*.

[44] C. Bonnet, *Palingénésie philosophique* (*Œuvres complètes*, t. VII, p. 122).

[45] C. Bonnet, *Contemplation de la nature*, chap. XX, pp. 130–8.

[46] Buffon, *Histoire naturelle des oiseaux* (1770, t. I, p. 396).

[47] Pallas, *Elenchus Zoophytorum* (1786).

[48] J. Hermann, *Tabulae affinitatum animalium* (Strasbourg, 1783, p. 24).

[49] C. Bonnet, *Contemplation de la nature*, Ière partie (*Œuvres complètes*, t. IV, p. 34 *et seq.*).

[50] C. Bonnet, *Palingénésie philosophique* (*Œuvres complètes*, t. VII, pp. 149–150).

[51] C. Bonnet (*Œuvres complètes*, t. III, p. 173) quotes a letter from Leibniz to Hermann on the chain of being.

[52] C. Bonnet, *Palingénésie philosophique* (*Œuvres complètes*, t. VII, p. 193).

[53] Benoît de Maillet, *Telliamed ou les entretiens d'un philosophe chinois avec un missionnaire français* (Amsterdam, 1748, p. 142).

[54] Maupertuis, *Essai sur la formation des corps organisés* (Berlin, 1754, p. 41).

[55] J-B. Robinet, *De la nature* (3rd edn., 1766, pp. 25–8).

[56] J-B. Robinet, *Considérations philosophiques sur la gradation naturelle des formes de l'être* (Paris, 1768, pp. 4–5).

[57] Ibid., p. 198.

[58] On the non-existence of the biological notion of the 'environment' in the eighteenth century, cf. G. Canguilhem, *La Connaissance de la vie* (Paris, 2nd edn., 1965, pp. 129–54).

[59] J-B. Robinet, *Considérations philosophiques sur la gradation naturelle des formes de l'être*, p. 19.

[60] Linnaeus, *Systema naturae*, p. 13.

[61] Cf., for example, Linnaeus, *Systema naturae*, p. 215.

[62] Linnaeus, *Philosophie botanique*, section 133. Cf. also *Système sexuel des végétaux*, p. 1.

[63] Bonnet accepted a quadripartite division in nature: unstructured brute beings, inanimate structured beings (vegetables), animate structured beings (animals), animate structured and reasoning beings (men). Cf. *Contemplation de la nature*, II ième partie, chap. I.

[64] Linnaeus, *Systema naturae*, p. 215.

[65] Hume, *A treatise of human nature* (1739, book I, part III, section III, and part IV, section VI).

CHAPTER 6

Exchanging

I THE ANALYSIS OF WEALTH

There is no life in the Classical period, nor any science of life; nor any philology either. But there is natural history, and general grammar. In the same way, there is no political economy, because, in the order of knowledge, production does not exist. On the other hand, there does exist in the seventeenth and eighteenth centuries a notion that is still familiar to us today, though it has lost its essential precision for us. But 'notion' is not really the word we should apply to it, since it does not occur within an interplay of economic concepts that it might displace to some slight extent by taking over a little of their meaning or eating into their sphere of application. It is more a question of a general domain: a very coherent and very well-stratified layer that comprises and contains, like so many partial objects, the notions of value, price, trade, circulation, income, interest. This domain, the ground and object of 'economy' in the Classical age, is that of *wealth*. It is useless to apply to it questions deriving from a different type of economics – one organized around production or work, for example; useless also to analyse its various concepts (even, and above all, if their names have been perpetuated in succeeding ages with somewhat analogous meanings), without taking into account the system from which they draw their positivity. One might as well try to analyse the Linnaean genus outside the domain of natural history, or Bauzée's theory of tenses without taking into account the fact that general grammar was its historical condition of possibility.

We must therefore avoid a retrospective reading of these things that would merely endow the Classical analysis of wealth with the ulterior unity of a political economy in the tentative process of constituting itself. Yet it is in this way that historians of ideas do go about their reconstructions of the enigmatic birth of this knowledge, which, according to them, sprang up in Western thought, fully armed and already full of danger, at the time of Ricardo and J-B. Say. They presuppose that a scientific economics had for long been rendered impossible by a purely moral problematics of profit and income (theory of the fair price, justification or condemnation of interest), then by a systematic confusion between money and wealth, value and market price: and of this assimilation they take mercantilism to be one of the principle causes and the most striking manifestation. But then the eighteenth century is supposed to have provided the essential distinctions and outlined some of the great problems that positivist economics subsequently treated with tools better adapted to the task: money is supposed to have revealed in this way its conventional – though not arbitrary – character (as a consequence of the long discussion between bullionists and anti-bullionists: among the first would have to be included Child, Petty, Locke, Cantillon, Galiani; among the latter, Barbon, Boisguillebert, and, above all, Law; then, to a lesser degree, after the disaster of 1720, Montesquieu and Melon); a beginning is thought to have been made, too – in the work of Cantillon – on the task of disentangling the theory of intrinsic value from that of market value; and the great 'paradox of value' was dealt with, by opposing the useless dearness of the diamond to the cheapness of the water without which we cannot live (it is possible, in fact, to find this problem rigorously formulated in Galiani); a start is supposed to have been made, thus prefiguring the work of Jevons and Menger, at connecting value to a general theory of utility (which we find sketched out in Galiani, in Graslin, and in Turgot); an understanding of the importance of high prices to the development of trade was supposedly reached (this is the 'Becher principle', taken up in France by Boisguillebert and Quesnay); lastly – and here we meet the Physiocrats – a start was made on the analysis of the mechanics of production. And thus, in fragments here and there, political economy is thought to have been silently bringing into position its essential themes, until the moment when, taking up the analysis of production again in another direction, Adam Smith is supposed to have brought to light the process of the increasing division of labour, Ricardo the role played by capital, and J-B. Say some of the fundamental laws of the market economy. From this moment on, political economy is supposed to have begun to exist with its own proper object and its own inner coherence.

In fact, the concepts of money, price, value, circulation, and market were not regarded, in the seventeenth and eighteenth centuries, in terms of a shadowy future, but as part of a rigorous and general epistemological arrangement. It is this arrangement that sustains the 'analysis of wealth' in its overall necessity. The analysis of wealth is to political economy what general grammar is to philology and what natural history is to biology. And just as it is not possible to understand the theory of verb and noun, the analysis of the language of action, and that of roots and their development, without referring, through the study of general grammar, to the archaeological network that makes those things possible and necessary; just as one cannot understand, without exploring the domain of natural history, what Classical description, characterization, and taxonomy were, any more than the opposition between system and method, or 'fixism' and 'evolution'; so, in the same way, it would not be possible to discover the link of necessity that connects the analysis of money, prices, value, and trade if one did not first clarify this domain of wealth which is the locus of their simultaneity.

It is true that the analysis of wealth is not constituted according to the same curves or in obedience to the same rhythm as general grammar or natural history. This is because reflection upon money, trade, and exchange is linked to a practice and to institutions. And though practice and pure speculation may be placed in opposition to one another, they nevertheless rest upon one and the same fundamental ground of knowledge. A money reform, a banking custom, a trade practice can all be rationalized, can all develop, maintain themselves or disappear according to appropriate forms; they are all based upon a certain ground of knowledge: an obscure knowledge that does not manifest itself for its own sake in a discourse, but whose necessities are exactly the same as for abstract theories or speculations without apparent relation to reality. In any given culture and at any given moment, there is always only one *episteme* that defines the conditions of possibility of all knowledge, whether expressed in a theory or silently invested in a practice. The monetary reform prescribed by the States General of 1575, mercantilist measures, or Law's experiment and its liquidation, all have the same archaeological basis as the theories of Davanzatti, Bouteroue, Petty, or Cantillon. And it is these fundamental necessities of knowledge that we must give voice to.

II MONEY AND PRICES

In the sixteenth century, economic thought is restricted, or almost so, to the problem of prices and that of the best monetary substance. The question of prices concerns the absolute or relative character of the increasing dearness of commodities and the effect that successive devaluations or the influx of American metals may have had upon prices. The problem of monetary substance is that of the nature of the standard, of the price relation between the various metals employed, and of the distortion between the weights of coins and their nominal values. But these two series of problems were linked, since the metal appeared only as a sign, and as a sign for measuring wealth, in so far as it was itself wealth. It possessed the power to signify because it was itself a real mark. And just as words had the same reality as what they said, just as the marks of living beings were inscribed upon their bodies in the manner of visible and positive marks, similarly, the signs that indicated wealth and measured it were bound to carry the real mark in themselves. In order to represent prices, they themselves had to be precious. They had to be rare, useful, desirable. Moreover, all these qualities had to be stable if the mark they imprinted upon things was to be an authentic and universally legible signature. Hence the correlation between the problem of prices and the nature of money, which constitutes the privileged object of all reflection upon wealth from Copernicus to Bodin and Davanzatti.

The two functions of money, as a common measure between commodities and as a substitute in the mechanism of exchange, are based upon its material reality. A measure is stable, recognized as valid by everyone and in all places, if it has as a standard an assignable reality that can be compared to the diversity of things that one wishes to measure: as is the case, Copernicus points out, with the fathom and the bushel, whose material length and volume serve as units[1]. In consequence, money does not truly measure unless its unit is a reality that really exists, to which any commodity whatever may be referred. In this sense, the sixteenth century returns to the theory accepted during at least part of the Middle Ages, which gave either the prince or popular consent the right to fix the *valor impositus* of money, to modify its rate, to withdraw any category of coins or any particular metal. The value of money must be determined by the quantity of metal it contains; that is, it returns to what it was before, when princes had not yet stamped their effigy or seal upon pieces of metal; at that time 'neither copper, nor gold, nor silver were minted, but only valued according to their weight'[2]; arbitrary signs were not accorded the value of real marks; money was a fair measure because it signified nothing more than its power to standardize wealth on the basis of its own material reality as wealth.

169

It is upon this epistemological foundation that reforms were effected
in the sixteenth century, and that the controversies of the age assumed their
particular dimensions. There was an attempt to bring monetary signs
back to their exactitude as measures: the nominal values stamped on the
coins had to be in conformity with the quantity of metal chosen as a
standard and incorporated into each coin; money would then signify
nothing more than its measuring value. In this sense, the anonymous
author of the *Compendious* insists that all the money actually current should
cease to be so after a certain date, since the 'forcing up' of its nominal value
has long since vitiated its functions of measurement; all coinage already
minted should then be accepted only in accordance with the amount of
metal it is estimated to contain; as for new money, that will have its own
weight as its nominal value, so that henceforward only the new and the
old money will be current, each in accordance with one and the same
value, weight and denomination, so that all money will be re-established
at its former rate and regain its former goodness[3]. It is not known
whether the *Compendious*, which was not published before 1581, but was
certainly in existence and circulating in manuscript for thirty years beforehand, inspired England's monetary policy under Elizabeth. One thing
is certain: that after a series of 'forcings up' (devaluations) between 1544
and 1559, the proclamation of March 1561 'brought down' the nominal
value of money and made it equal once more to the quantity of metal
each coin contained. Similarly, in France, the States General of 1575
asked for and obtained the suppression of accounting units (which
introduced a third definition of money, a purely arithmetical one, in
addition to the definition by weight and that by nominal value: this
supplementary relation concealed the sense of monetary operations from
those who did not understand it); the edict of September 1577 established
the gold *écu* as both a real coin and an accounting unit, decreed the
subordination of all other metals to gold – in particular, silver, which retained its legality as tender but lost its legal immutability. The coinage
was thus restandardized on the basis of its metallic weight. The sign the
coins bore – the *valor impositus* – was merely the exact and transparent
mark of the measure they constituted.

But at the same time as this restandardization was being demanded,
and occasionally accomplished, a certain number of phenomena came
to light which are peculiar to the money-sign and perhaps definitively
compromised its role as a measure. First, the fact that coinage circulates
all the quicker for being less good, whereas coins with a high percentage

of metal are hoarded and do not take part in trade: this is what was called Gresham's law[4], and both Copernicus[5] and the author of the *Compendious*[6] were already aware of it. Second, and above all, there was the relation between the monetary facts and the movement of prices: it was this that revealed money as a commodity like any other – not an absolute standard for all equivalences, but a commodity whose capacity for exchange, and consequently whose value as a substitute in exchange, are modified according to its abundance or rarity: money too has its price. Malestroit[7] had pointed out that, despite appearances, there had been no increase in prices during the sixteenth century: since commodities are always what they are, and since money, in its particular nature, is a constant standard, the increased dearness of commodities can be due only to the augmentation of the nominal values borne by an unchanging metallic mass: but, for the same quantity of wheat, one still gives the same weight in silver or gold. So that 'nothing has become dearer': since the golden *écu* was worth twenty *sols tournois* in accounting money under Philippe VI, and since it is now worth fifty, it is inevitable that an ell of velvet, which formerly cost four *livres*, should now be worth ten. 'The increasing dearness of things does not come from having to deliver more but from receiving a lesser quantity of gold or fine silver than one was accustomed to before.' But once this identification has been established between the role of money and the mass of metal it causes to circulate, it becomes clearly apparent that it is subjected to the same variations as all other merchandise. And though Malestroit implicitly admitted that the quantity and marketable value of metals remained stable, Bodin, only a very few years later[8], observes that there has been an increase in the stock of metal imported from the New World, and in consequence a real increase in the price of commodities, since princes, now possessing ingots in larger quantity or receiving more from private persons, have been minting more and better-quality coins; for the same amount of a commodity one is therefore giving a larger quantity of metal. The rise in prices therefore has a 'principal cause, and that almost the only one that no one has touched upon hitherto': 'the abundance of gold and silver', 'the abundance of that which gives things estimation and price'.

The standard of equivalences is itself involved in the system of exchanges, and the buying power of money signifies nothing but the marketable value of the metal. The mark that distinguishes money, determines it, renders it certain and acceptable to all, is thus reversible, and may be construed in either direction: it refers to a quantity of metal that is a constant measure (which is the construction Malestroit puts upon it); but it also refers to certain commodities, variable in quantity and price, called metals (which is Bodin's reading of the matter). We are, then, presented with an arrangement analogous to that which characterizes the general organization of signs in the sixteenth century: signs, it will be remembered, were constituted by resemblances which, in turn, necessitated further signs in order to be recognized. Here, the monetary sign cannot define its exchange value, and can be established as a mark only on a metallic mass which in turn defines its value in the scale of other commodities. If one admits that exchange, in the system of needs, corresponds to similitude in the system of acquired knowledge, then one sees that knowledge of nature, and reflection or practices concerning money, were controlled during the Renaissance by one and the same configuration of the *episteme*.

And just as the relation of the microcosm to the macrocosm was indispensable in order to arrest the indefinite oscillation between resemblance and sign, so it was necessary to lay down a certain relation between metal and merchandise which, when it came to it, made it possible to fix the total marketable value of the precious metals, and consequently to standardize the price of all commodities in a certain and definitive fashion. This relation is the one that was established by Providence when it buried gold and silver mines under the earth, and caused them to grow, just as plants grow and animals multiply on the surface of the earth. Between all the things that man may need or desire, and the glittering, hidden veins where those metals grow in darkness, there is an absolute correspondence. As Davanzatti says:

Nature made all terrestrial things good; the sum of these, by virtue of the agreement concluded by men, is worth all the gold that is worked; all men therefore desire everything in order to acquire all things . . . In order to ascertain each day the rule and mathematical proportions that exist between things and between them and gold, we should have to be able to contemplate, from the height of heaven or some very tall observatory, all the things that exist or are done on earth, or rather their images reproduced and reflected in the sky as in a faithful mirror. We would then abandon all our calculations and we would say: there is upon earth so much gold, so many things, so many men, so many needs; and to the degree that each thing satisfies needs, its value shall be so many things, or so much gold[9].

This celestial and exhaustive calculation can be accomplished by none other than God: it corresponds to that other calculation that brings each and every element of the microcosm into relation with a corresponding element in the macrocosm – with this one difference, that the latter unites the terrestrial to the celestial, going from things, from animals, or from man, up to the stars; whereas the former links the earth to its caves and mines; it makes those things that are brought into being by the hands of men correspond with the treasures buried in the earth since the creation of the world. The marks of similitude, because they are a guide to knowledge, are addressed to the perfection of heaven; the signs of exchange, because they satisfy desire, are sustained by the dark, dangerous, and accursed glitter of metal. An equivocal glitter, for it reproduces in the depths of the earth that other glitter that sings at the far end of the night: it resides there like an inverted promise of happiness, and, because metal resembles the stars, the knowledge of all these perilous treasures is at the same time knowledge of the world. And thus reflection upon wealth has its pivot in the broadest speculation upon the cosmos, just as, inversely, profound knowledge of the order of the world must lead to the secret of metals and the possession of wealth. It becomes apparent how tightly knit is the network of necessities that, in the sixteenth century, links together all the elements of knowledge: how the cosmology of signs provides a duplication, and finally a foundation, for reflection upon prices and money; how it also authorizes theoretical and practical speculation upon metals; how it provides a communicating link between the promises of desire and those of knowledge, in the same way as the metals and the stars communicate with one another and are drawn together by secret affinities. On the confines of knowledge, in that region where it becomes all powerful and quasi-divine, three great functions meet – those of the *Basileus*, of the *Philosophos*, and of the *Metallicos*. But just as this knowledge is given only in fragments and in the attentive lightning-flash of the *divinatio*, so, in the case of the singular and partial relations of things with metal, of desire with prices, divine knowledge, or that which one might acquire from 'some very tall observatory', is not given to man. Except for brief instants, and as though at random, to those minds that know how to watch for it – in other words, to merchants. What the *soothsayers* were to the undefined interplay of resemblances and signs, the *merchants* are to the interplay, also forever open, of exchange and money.

From here below, we have difficulty in perceiving the few things that surround us, and we give a price to them according to whether we perceive them to be more or less in demand in each place and at each time. The merchants are promptly and very well advised of these things, and that is why they have an admirable knowledge of the price of things[10].

III MERCANTILISM

In order that the domain of wealth could be constituted as an object of reflection in Classical thought, the configuration established in the sixteenth century had to be dissolved. For the Renaissance 'economists', and right up to Davanzatti himself, the ability of money to measure commodities, as well as its exchangeability, rested upon its intrinsic value: they were well aware that the precious metals had little usefulness other than as coinage; but if they had been chosen as standards, if they had been employed as a means of exchange, if, in consequence, they fetched a high price, that was because they possessed, both in the natural scale of things and in themselves, an absolute and fundamental price, higher than any other, to which the value of any and every commodity could be referred[11]. Fine metal was, of itself, a mark of wealth; its buried brightness was sufficient indication that it was at the same time a hidden presence and a visible signature of all the wealth of the world. It is for this reason that it had a *price*; for this reason too that it was a *measure* of all prices; and for this reason, finally, that one could *exchange* it for anything else that had a price. It was *precious* above all other things. In the seventeenth century, these three properties are still attributed to money, but they are all three made to rest, not on the first (possession of price), but on the last (substitution for that which possesses price). Whereas the Renaissance based the two *functions* of coinage (measure and substitution) on the double nature of its intrinsic *character* (the fact that it was precious), the seventeenth century turns the analysis upside down: it is the exchanging function that serves as a foundation for the other two characters (its ability to measure and its capacity to receive a price thus appearing as *qualities* deriving from that *function*).

This reversal is the work of a complex of reflections and practices that occurred throughout the seventeenth century (from Scipion de Grammont to Nicolas Barbon) and that are grouped together under the somewhat approximate term 'mercantilism'. It is usual to characterize this rather hastily as an absolute 'monetarism', that is, a systematic (or stubborn) confusion between wealth and coinage. In fact, it is not an identity – more or less confused – that 'mercantilism' established between these two things, but a considered articulation that makes money the instrument of the representation and analysis of wealth, and makes wealth, conversely, into the content represented by money. Just as the old circular configuration of similitudes and marks had unravelled itself so that it could be redeployed to form the two correlative fabrics of representation and signs, so the circle of 'preciousness' is broken with the coming of mercantilism, and wealth becomes whatever is the object of needs and desires; it is split into elements that can be substituted for one another by the interplay of the coinage that signifies them; and the reciprocal relations of money and wealth are established in the form of circulation and exchange. If it was possible to believe that mercantilism confused wealth and money, this is probably because money for the mercantilists had the power of representing all possible wealth, because it was the universal instrument for the analysis and representation of wealth, because it covered the entire extent of its domain leaving no residuum. All wealth is *coinable*; and it is by this means that it enters into *circulation* – in the same way that any natural being was *characterizable*, and could thereby find its place in a *taxonomy*; that any individual was *nameable* and could find its place in an *articulated language*; that any representation was *signifiable* and could find its place, in order to be *known*, in a *system of identities and differences*.

But this must be examined more closely. Among all the things that exist in the world, which ones will mercantilism be able to include in the term 'wealth'? All those that, being representable, are also objects of desire – that is, moreover, those that are marked by 'necessity, or utility, or pleasure, or rarity' [12]. Now, can one say that the metals used in the manufacture of coinage (we are not concerned here with copper coinage, which is used as small change only in certain countries, but with coins that are used in foreign trade) are part of wealth? Gold and silver have very little utility – 'as far as their use in the house goes'; and, however rare they may be, their abundance still exceeds what is required by their utility. If they are sought after, if men find that they never have enough of them, if they dig mines and make war on one another in order to get hold of them, it is because the process of minting them into gold and silver coinage has given them a utility and a rarity that those metals do not possess of themselves. 'Money does not draw its value from the material of which it is composed, but rather from its form, which is the image

175

or mark of the Prince'[13]. Gold is precious because it is money – not the converse. The relation so strictly laid down in the sixteenth century is forthwith reversed: money (and even the metal of which it is made) receives its value from its pure function as sign. This entails two consequences. First, the value of things will no longer proceed from the metal itself; it establishes itself by itself, without reference to the coinage, according to the criteria of utility, pleasure, or rarity. Things take on value, then, in relation to one another; the metal merely enables this value to be represented, as a name represents an image or an idea, yet does not constitute it: 'Gold is merely the sign and the instrument commonly used to convey the value of things in practice; but the true estimation of that value has its source in human judgement and in that faculty termed the estimative'[14]. Wealth is wealth because we estimate it, just as our ideas are what they are because we represent them. Monetary or verbal signs are additional to this.

But why have gold and silver, which are scarcely wealth at all in themselves, received or taken on this signifying power? No doubt one could very well employ some other commodity to this effect 'however vile and base it might be'[15]. Copper, which in many countries is still a cheap commodity, becomes precious in others only when it is turned into coinage[16]. But in a general fashion we use gold and silver because they contain hidden within themselves 'a peculiar perfection'. A perfection that is not of the order of price, but is dependent upon their endless capacity for representation. They are hard, imperishable, uncorrodable; they can be divided into minute pieces; they can concentrate a great weight into a little volume; they can be easily transported; they are easily pierced. All these factors make gold and silver into a privileged instrument for the representation of all other kinds of wealth, and for strict comparisons between them by means of analysis. It is in this way that the relation of money to wealth has come to be defined. It is an arbitrary relation because it is not the intrinsic value of the metal that gives things their prices; any object, even one that has no price, can serve as money; but it must, nevertheless, possess peculiar properties of representation and capacities for analysis that will permit it to establish relations of equality and difference between different kinds of wealth. It is apparent, then, that the use of gold and silver for this purpose has a justifiable basis. As Bouteroue says, money 'is a portion of matter to which public authority has given a certain value and weight so that it may serve as a price and make the inequality of all things equal in trade'[17]. 'Mercantilism' freed money from the postulate of the intrinsic value of metal – the folly of those who 'say that money is a commodity like other things'[18] – and at the same time established between it and wealth a strict relation of representation and analysis. Money, says Barbon, is that by which men 'estimate the value of all other things; having regard more to the stamp and currency of the money than to the quantity of fine silver in each piece'[19].

The usual attitude towards what it has been agreed to call 'mercantilism' is doubly unjust: either it is denounced for comprising a notion it continually criticized (the intrinsic value of precious metal as the principle of wealth), or it is revealed as a series of immediate contradictions: it is accused of defining money in its pure function as a sign while insisting upon its accumulation as a commodity; of recognizing the importance of quantitative fluctuations in specie, while misunderstanding their action upon prices; of being protectionist while basing its mechanism for the increase of wealth upon exchange. In fact, these contradictions or hesitations exist only if one confronts mercantilism with a dilemma that could have no meaning for it: that of money as commodity or as sign. For Classical thought in its formative phase, money is that which permits wealth to be represented. Without such signs, wealth would remain immobile, useless, and as it were silent; in this sense, gold and silver are the creators of all that man can covet. But in order to play this role as representation, money must offer properties (physical and not economic ones) that render it adequate to its task, and in consequence precious. It is in its quality as a universal sign that it becomes a rare and unequally distributed commodity: 'The rate and value imposed upon all money is its true intrinsic goodness'[20]. Just as in the order of representations the signs that replace and analyse them must also be representations themselves, so money cannot signify wealth without itself being wealth. But it becomes wealth because it is a sign; whereas a representation must first be represented in order subsequently to become a sign.

Hence the apparent contradictions between the principles of accumulation and the rules of circulation. At any given moment of time, the number of coins in existence is determined; Colbert even thought, despite the exploitation of mines, despite the imports of metal from America, that 'the quantity of money circulating in Europe is constant'. Now it is this money that is needed to represent wealth, in other words to attract it, to make it appear by bringing it in from abroad or manufacturing it at home; it is this money, too, that is needed in order to make wealth pass from hand to hand in the process of exchange. It is necessary, there-fore, to import metal by taking it from neighbouring states: 'Trade alone, and all that depends on it, is capable of producing this great effect'[21]. The legislature must therefore take care to do two things:

> Forbid the transfer of metal abroad, or its utilization for other ends than that of coinage, and impose customs duties such that they enable the balance of trade to be always positive; encourage the importation of raw materials, prevent as far as possible that of manufactured goods, export manufactured products rather than the commodities themselves whose disappearance leads to famine and causes the rise of prices[22].

Now, the metal accumulated is not intended to sleep and grow fat; it is attracted into a state only so that it may be consumed by the process of exchange. As Becher said, everything that is expense for one of the part-ners is income for the other[23]; and Thomas Mun identified ready money with wealth[24]. This is because money becomes real wealth only to exactly the same degree to which it fulfils its representative function: when it replaces commodities, when it enables them to be moved or to wait, when it provides raw materials with the opportunity of becoming consumable, when it remunerates work. There is therefore no reason to fear that the accumulation of money in a state will cause prices to rise in it; and the principle established by Bodin that the great dearness pre-valent in the sixteenth century was caused by the influx of gold from America is not valid; though it is true that an increase in specie causes prices to rise at first, it also stimulates trade and manufacturing; the quantity of wealth grows and the number of elements among which the coinage is to be divided increases by the same amount. Rising prices are not to be feared: on the contrary, now that the number of precious objects has increased, now that the middle classes, as Scipion de Grammont puts it, can wear 'satin and velvet', the value of things, even of the rarest things, could fall only in relation to the totality of the others; similarly, each piece of metal loses some of its value with regard to the others as the mass of coinage in circulation increases[25].

The relations between wealth and money, then, are based on circulation and exchange, and no longer on the 'preciousness' of metal. When goods can circulate (and this thanks to money), they multiply, and wealth increases; when coinage becomes more plentiful, as a result of a good circulation and a favourable balance, one can attract fresh merchandise and increase both agriculture and manufacturing. As Horneck puts it, gold and silver 'are the purest part of our blood, the marrow of our strength', 'the most indispensable instruments of human activity and of our existence'[26]. We meet once more with the old metaphor of a coinage that is to society what blood is to the body[27]. But for Davanzatti, specie had no other role than that of irrigating the various parts of the nation. Now that money and wealth are both included within the area of exchange and circulation, mercantilism can adjust its analysis in terms of the model recently provided by Harvey. According to Hobbes[28], the venous circulation of money is that of duties and taxes, which levy a certain mass of bullion upon all merchandise transported, bought, or sold; the bullion levied is conveyed to the heart of Man-Leviathan – in other words, into the coffers of the state. It is there that the metal is 'made vital': the state can, in effect, melt it down or send it back into circulation. But at all events it is the state's authority alone that can give it currency; and redistributed among private persons (in the form of pensions, salaries, or renumeration for provisions bought by the state), it will stimulate, in its second, arterial circuit, exchanges of wealth, manufactures, and agriculture. Thus circulation becomes one of the fundamental categories of analysis. But the transference of this physiological metaphor was made possible only by the more profound opening up of a space common to both money and signs, to both wealth and representations. The metaphor of the city and the body, so assiduously put to work in our Western culture, derived its imaginary powers only from the much deeper foundation of archaeological necessities.

Through the mercantilist experience, the domain of wealth was constituted in the same mode as that of representations. We have seen that these latter had the power to represent themselves with themselves as the basis of that representation: to open within themselves a space in which they could analyse themselves, and to form substitutes for themselves out of their own elements, thus making it possible to establish both a system of signs and a table of identities and differences. Similarly, wealth has the power to be exchanged; to analyse itself into elements that authorize relations of equality or inequality; to signify itself by means of those completely comparable elements of wealth called precious metals. And just as the entire world of representation covers itself with representations which, at one remove, represent it, in an uninterrupted sequence, so all the kinds of wealth in the world are related one to another in so far as they are all part of a system of exchange. From one representation to another, there is no autonomous act of signification, but a simple and endless possibility of exchange. Whatever its economic determinations and consequences, mercantilism, when questioned at the level of the *episteme*, appears as the slow, long effort to bring reflection upon prices and money into alignment with the analysis of representations. It was responsible for the emergence of a domain of 'wealth' connected to that which, at about the same time, was opened up to natural history, and likewise to that which unfolded before general grammar. But whereas in these last two cases the mutation came about abruptly (a certain mode of being emerging suddenly for language in the *Grammaire de Port-Royal*, a certain mode of being for individuals in nature manifesting itself almost simultaneously with Jonston and Tournefort), the mode of being for money and wealth, on the other hand, because it was linked to an entire praxis, to a whole institutional complex, had a much higher degree of historic viscosity. Neither natural beings nor language needed the equivalent of the long mercantilist process in order to enter the domain of representation, subject themselves to its laws, and receive from it their signs and their principles of order.

IV THE PLEDGE AND THE PRICE

The Classical theory of money and prices was elaborated during a well-known series of historical experiences. First of all, there was the great crisis of monetary signs that began in Europe fairly early in the seventeenth century. Possibly we ought to construe Colbert's statement, that the quantity of bullion is stable in Europe and that imports from America can be ignored, as a first, though still marginal and allusive, sign of awareness as to what was happening. At the end of the century, at all events, the shortage of coin became an acute and direct experience: recession of trade, lowering of prices, difficulties in paying debts, rents, and duties, a fall in the value of land. Hence the great series of devaluations that took place in France during the first fifteen years of the eighteenth century in order to increase the quantity of specie; the eleven 'diminutions' (re-valuations) that were spaced out at regular intervals between 1 December 1713 and 1 September 1715, and were intended – though the attempt failed – to draw hoarded bullion back into circulation; a whole series of measures that diminished the rate of investment income and reduced nominal capital; the appearance of paper money in 1701, soon to be replaced by government bonds. Among its many other consequences, Law's experiment made possible the reappearance of metal money, price increases, the revaluation of land, and the revival of trade. The edicts of January and May 1726 established a coinage that was to remain stable throughout the eighteenth century: they decreed the minting of a *louis-d'or* worth twenty-four *livres tournois* – a value it retained right up to the Revolution.

It is usual to construe these experiences, their theoretical context, and the discussions to which they have given rise, as the confrontation of the money-as-sign faction with the upholders of money-as-commodity. In the first group we find Law, of course, together with Terrasson[29], Dutot[30], Montesquieu[31], and the Chevalier de Jaucourt[32]; on the opposing side we find Paris-Duverney[33], the Chancelier d'Aguesseau[34], Condillac, and Destutt; between the two factions, on the half-way line as it were, one would have to place Melon[35] and Graslin[36]. And it would certainly be interesting to work out a detailed account of these opinions and discover how they were distributed among the various social groups. But if we investigate the knowledge that made all those various opinions simultaneously possible, we perceive that the opposition between them is superficial; and that, though it is logically necessary, it is so on the basis of a single arrangement that simply creates, at a given point, the alternatives of an indispensable choice.

This single arrangement is that which defines money as a pledge. It is a definition we find in Locke and, slightly earlier, in Vaughan[37]; then in Melon – 'gold and silver are, by general agreement, the pledge, the equivalent, or the common measure of all that which serves for men's use'[38]; in Dutot – 'wealth of credit or opinion is only representative, as are gold, silver, bronze, and copper'[39]; in Fortbonnais – 'the important point' in conventional wealth lies 'in the confidence of the owners of money and commodities that they can exchange them when they will . . . on the footing established by custom'[40]. To say that money is a pledge is to say that it is no more than a token accepted by common consent – hence, a pure fiction; but it is also to say that it has exactly the same value as that for which it has been given, since it can in turn be exchanged for that same quantity of merchandise or the equivalent. Coinage can always bring back into the hands of its owner that which has just been exchanged for it, just as, in representation, a sign must be able to recall to thought that which it represents. Money is a material memory, a self-duplicating representation, a deferred exchange. As Le Trosne says, trade that makes use of money is an improvement in so far as it is 'an imperfect trade'[41], an act that lacks, for a time, that which recompenses it, a demi-operation that promises and expects the converse exchange whereby the pledge will be reconverted into its effective content.

But how can the monetary pledge provide this assurance? How can it escape from the dilemma of the valueless sign as opposed to the commodity analogous to all other commodities? It is here, for the Classical analysis of money, that the point of heresy occurs – the choice that divides the followers of Law from his opponents. It is conceivable, in fact, that the operation that pledges the money is guaranteed by the marketable value of the material from which it is made; or, on the other hand, by another quantity of merchandise, exterior to it, but linked to it by collective consent or the will of the prince. It is this second solution that Law chose, on account of the rarity of precious metal and the fluctuations in its market value. He thought that one could circulate paper money backed by landed property: in which case it was simply a matter of issuing 'banknotes mortgaged against lands and due to be redeemed by annual payments . . . , these notes will be exchanged, like minted coin, for the value printed on them'[42]. As we know, Law was obliged to renounce this technique in his French experiment and subsequently provided surety for his money by means of a trading company. The failure of his enterprise in no way affected the validity of the money-pledge theory that had made it possible, but that had also made possible all reflection of any kind on money, even that opposed to Law's conceptions. And when a stable metallic money was established in 1726, the pledge was required to be provided by the actual substance of the coins. What ensured the exchangeability of money, it was decided, was the market value of the metal to be found in it; and Turgot was to criticize Law for having believed that

> money is only a sign of wealth, a sign whose credit is based upon the mark of the prince. That mark is on each coin only in order to certify its weight and title . . . It is therefore as merchandise that money is, not the sign, but the common measure of all other merchandise . . . Gold derives its price from its rarity, and far from its being an evil that it should be employed at the same time as both merchandise and measure, these two uses maintain its price[43].

Law, together with his partisans, does not stand in opposition to his age as the brilliant – or imprudent – precursor of fiduciary currency. He defines money, as his opponents did, as a pledge. But he thought that it would be better guaranteed (more abundant as well as more stable) if it were based upon some merchandise exterior to monetary specie itself;

whereas his opponents thought that it would be better guaranteed (more secure and less subject to speculation) if based upon the metallic substance constituting the material reality of money. The conflict between Law and his critics concerns only the distance between the pledge and what it is pledging. In the one case, money, relieved of all marketable value, but guaranteed by a value exterior to it, is that 'by means of which' one exchanges merchandise[44]; in the other case, since money has a price in itself, it is at the same time that 'by means of which' and that 'for which' one exchanges wealth. But in both cases it is money that makes it possible to fix the price of things, thanks to a certain relation of *proportion* with various forms of wealth and a certain power to make them *circulate*.

As a pledge, money designates a certain wealth (actual or not): it establishes its price. But the relation between money and commodities, and thus the price system, is modified as soon as the quantity of money or the quantity of commodities at any moment of time is also modified. If money is in short supply with relation to goods, then it will have a high value, and prices will be low; if it increases in quantity to the point of becoming abundant in relation to wealth, then it will have a low value, and prices will be high. The power of money to represent and analyse varies with the quantity of specie on the one hand and with the quantity of wealth on the other: it would be constant only if both quantities were stable, or varied together in the same proportion.

The 'quantitative law' was not 'invented' by Locke. Bodin and Davanzatti already knew, in the sixteenth century, that an increase in the mass of metal in circulation caused the price of commodities to rise; but this mechanism seemed to them to be linked to an intrinsic devalorization of the metal itself. In the late seventeenth century, this same mechanism was defined on the basis of the representative function of money, 'the quantity of money being in proportion to the whole of trade'. More metal – and immediately any commodity existing in the world will have slightly more representative elements at its disposal; more merchandise – and each metallic unit will be slightly more heavily mortgaged. One need only take any given commodity as a stable reference point and this phenomenon of fluctuation is clearly revealed. As Locke says:

That supposing wheat a standing measure, that is, that there is constantly the same quantity of it in proportion to its vent, we shall find money to run the same variety of changes in its value, as all other commodities do . . . The reason whereof is this, that there being ten times as much

183

silver now in the world, (the discovery of the West-Indies having made the plenty) as there was then, it is $\frac{9}{10}$ less worth now than it was at that time; that is, it will exchange for $\frac{9}{10}$ less of any commodity now, which bears the same proportion to its vent as it did 200 years since[45].

The drop in the value of precious metal invoked here does not concern a certain precious quality which it is thought of as possessing in itself, but its general power of representation. Money and wealth are to be thought of as twin masses, which necessarily correspond with one another:

As the total of the one is to the total of the other, so part of the one is to part of the other . . . If there were only one commodity, divisible as gold is, then half of that commodity would correspond to half of its total on the other side[46].

Supposing that there were only one form of goods in the world, all the gold on earth would be there to represent it; and, inversely, if men possessed only one coin between them, then all the wealth produced by nature or by their own hands would have to share in its subdivisions. Given these limiting circumstances, if there is an influx of money – while commodities remain unchanged in quantity – 'the value of each division of the current specie will diminish by the same amount'; on the other hand,

if industry, the arts and the sciences introduce new objects into the circle of exchange. . . it will be necessary to apply a portion of the signs representing values to the new value of those new productions; since this portion will be taken from the whole mass of signs, it will diminish the relative quantity of that mass and increase its representative value by the same amount in order to cover the increase in values, its function being to represent them all, in the proportions appropriate to them[47].

There can therefore be no fair price: nothing in any given commodity indicates by any intrinsic character the quantity of money that should be paid for it. Cheapness is neither more nor less exact than dearness. Though there do exist rules of convention that make it possible to fix the quantity of money by means of which it is desirable to represent wealth. In the last resort, everything exchangeable should have its equivalent – 'its designation' – in specie; a state of affairs that would entail no drawbacks if the money used were of paper (which would be printed or destroyed, as Law proposed, in accordance with the needs of exchange), but that would be troublesome, or even impossible, if the money were metallic. Now, as it circulates, one and the same monetary unit acquires the power to represent several things; when it changes hands it is sometimes payment to an entrepreneur for some object, sometimes payment to a worker of his wage, sometimes payment to a merchant for some commodity, sometimes payment to a farmer for his produce, sometimes payment to a landowner of his rent. A single piece of metal can, in the course of time and according to the individuals that receive it, represent several equivalent things (an object, work, a measure of wheat, a portion of income) – just as a common noun has the power to represent several things, or a taxonomic character has the power to represent several individuals, several species, several genera, etc. But whereas the character can cover a larger generality only by becoming simpler, money can represent more kinds of wealth only by circulating faster. The extension of a character is defined by the number of species it includes (therefore by the area it occupies in the table); speed of circulation is defined by the number of hands through which money passes during the time it takes to return to its starting-point (this is why payment to agriculture for the products of its harvest is taken as a first source, because there one has absolutely reliable annual cycles to deal with). It will be seen, therefore, that the speed of monetary movement during a set time corresponds to the taxonomic extension of a character within the simultaneous space of the table.

This speed is limited in two directions: an infinitely rapid speed would imply an immediate exchange in which money would have no role to play, and an infinitely slow speed would mean that every element of wealth possesses its permanent monetary double. Between these two extremes there are variable speeds to which the quantities of money that make them possible correspond. Now, the cycles of circulation are determined by the yearly occurrence of the harvests: it is possible, therefore, given the harvests and taking into account the number of individuals making up the population of a state, to define the necessary and sufficient quantity of money there must be if it is to pass through everyone's hands and to represent at least the means of subsistence to them all. It is thus understandable how, in the eighteenth century, analyses of the circulation of money based upon agricultural revenue were linked to the problem of population growth and to calculation of the optimum quantity of coinage. A triple question that is posited in a normative form: for the problem is not to discover by what mechanisms money circulates or fails to circulate, how it is expended or accumulated (such questions are possible only in an economy that poses problems of production or capital), but what the necessary quantity of money is in a given country that will provide a sufficiently rapid circulation and pass through a sufficiently large number of hands. Thus prices will not be intrinsically 'fair', but exactly regulated: the divisions of the monetary mass will analyse wealth according to an articulation that will be neither too loosely nor too tightly knit. The 'table' will be well made.

This optimum proportion is not the same whether we consider a country in isolation or the movement of its foreign trade. If we suppose a state capable of living on itself, the quantity of money it would be necessary to put into circulation would depend upon several variables: the quantity of merchandise entering the exchange system; the portion of that merchandise which, being neither distributed nor paid for by barter, must at some moment during its journey be represented by money; the quantity of metal for which signed paper may be substituted; and, finally, the rhythm according to which payments must be made: it is not a matter of indifference, as Cantillon points out[48], whether workers are paid by the week or the day, or whether rents fall due at the end of every year rather than, as is customary, at the end of every quarter. Since the values of these four variables are determinable for any given country, the optimum quantity of coinage for that country can be likewise determined. In order to make a calculation of this kind, Cantillon begins with what is produced by the land, from which all wealth is directly or indirectly derived. This product is divided into three revenues in the hands of the farmer: the revenue paid to the landowner; that which is used for the maintenance of the farmer himself and that of his men and horses; and, lastly, 'a third which should remain in order to make his enterprise profitable'[49]. Now, only the first of these and roughly half of the third have to be paid in specie; the rest can be paid in the form of direct exchanges of goods. Taking into account the fact that one-half of the population lives in towns and must therefore expend more on upkeep than do peasants, it is apparent that the monetary mass in circulation should be almost equal to two-thirds of production – if, that is, all payments were made once a year; but, in fact, ground rent falls due every quarter; it is therefore sufficient if the quantity of coinage is equivalent to one-sixth of production. Moreover, many other payments are made daily or weekly; the quantity of coin required is therefore of the order of a ninth part of production – in other words, one-third of the landowners' revenue from ground rent[50].

But this calculation is exact only on condition that our imaginary nation is wholly isolated. Now, the majority of states maintain a trade with one another in which the only means of payment are barter, metal estimated according to its weight (and not in the form of coins with their nominal value), and, on occasion, bankers' drafts. In this case also it is possible to calculate the relative quantity of money that it is desirable to put into circulation: however, this estimate should not be arrived at with reference to the production of the land but rather with reference to a certain relation of wages and prices with those in force in foreign countries. In fact, in a country where prices are relatively low (because the quantity of money in circulation is small), foreign money is attracted by the greater buying power it acquires there: the quantity of metal increases. The state, as we say, becomes 'rich and powerful'; it is able to maintain a fleet and an army, achieve conquests, and enrich itself further. The quantity of coinage in circulation causes prices to rise, while at the same time affording private persons the resources to buy abroad, where prices are lower: little by little, the metal disappears, and the state becomes poor once again. Such is the cycle that Cantillon described and formulated into a general principle: 'The excessive abundance of money, which makes the power of states while it lasts, thrusts them imperceptibly and naturally back into indigence'[51].

It would, no doubt, be impossible to avoid these fluctuations did there not exist in the order of things a contrary tendency, which ceaselessly aggravates the poverty of nations that are already poor and, on the other hand, increases the prosperity of states that are rich. For population tends to move in the contrary direction to money. The latter moves out from the prosperous states into the regions where prices are low; whereas men are attracted towards high wages, therefore towards countries that have an abundant coinage at their disposal. The poorer countries thus have a tendency to become depopulated; their agriculture and industries deteriorate and poverty increases. In rich countries, in contrast, the influx of labour makes possible the exploitation of new wealth, the sale of which proportionately increases the amount of metal in circulation[52]. Governmental policy should therefore attempt to come to terms with these two contrary movements on the part of population and currency. The number of inhabitants must grow, gradually but uninterruptedly, so that manufacturing industries will always have an abundance of workers to draw on; then wages will not increase at a greater rate than wealth, nor prices with them; and the balance of trade will be able to remain favourable: one recognizes in all this the foundation of the populationist theses [53]. But, on the other hand, it is also necessary that the quantity of specie should be slightly but constantly on the rise: the only means of making sure that the products of the land or of industry will be well remunerated, that wages will be sufficient, and that the population will not be poverty stricken in the midst of the wealth it is creating: hence all the measures intended to encourage foreign trade and maintain a positive balance.

What ensures the equilibrium of the economy, therefore, and prevents profound fluctuations between wealth and poverty, is not a certain and definitively acquired economic constitution, but the balanced interaction – at once natural and deliberately maintained – of two tendencies. There is prosperity within a state, not when coin is plentiful and prices are high, but when the coinage has reached that stage of augmentation – which must be made to continue indefinitely – that makes it possible to maintain wages without increasing prices any further: this being so, the population grows at a steady rate, its work constantly produces more, and, since each consecutive increase in the coinage is divided up (in accordance with the law of representativity) between small quantities of wealth, prices will not increase in relation to those in force abroad. It is only between an increase in the quantity of gold and a rise in prices that an increasing quantity of gold and silver encourages industry. A nation whose coinage is in process of diminution is, at any given moment of comparison, weaker and poorer than another nation which has no greater possessions but whose coinage is in process of growth. This is the explanation of the Spanish disaster: its mining possessions had, in fact, increased the nation's coinage – and, consequently, prices – to a massive degree, without giving industry, agriculture, and population the time, between cause and effect, to develop proportionately: it was inevitable that American gold should spread throughout Europe, buy commodities there, cause manufacturing to develop, and enrich its farms, while leaving Spain more poverty stricken than it had ever been. England, on the other hand, though it attracted bullion too, did so always for the profit of labour and not merely to provide its inhabitants with luxury, that is, in order to increase the number of its workers and the quantity of its products before any increase in prices occurred [54].

Such analyses are important because they introduce the notion of progress into the order of human activity. But they are still more important in that they provide the interplay of signs and representations with a temporal index that gives progress a definition of its condition of possibility. An index not to be found in any other area of the theory of order. Money, as conceived by Classical thought, cannot, in fact, represent wealth without that power being modified, from within, by time – whether a spontaneous cycle augments, after having first diminished, its capacity for representing wealth, or whether governmental policy, by dint of concerted efforts, keeps its representativity constant. In the order of natural history, the *characters* (the groups of identities selected to represent and distinguish a number of species or a number of genera) resided within the continuous area of nature, which they divided into a taxonomic table; time intervened only from without, in order to upset the continuity of the very smallest differences and to scatter them in accordance with the fragmented localities of geography. Here, on the contrary, time belongs to the inner law of the representations and is part of it; it follows and modifies without interruption the power possessed by wealth to represent itself and so analyse itself by means of a monetary system. Where natural history revealed squares of identities separated by differences, the analysis of wealth reveals 'differentials' – tendencies towards increase and towards diminution.

It was inevitable that this function of time within wealth should become apparent as soon as money was defined (as it was at the end of the seventeenth century) as a pledge and assimilated into credit: it then became necessary that the duration of the credit, the rapidity with which repayment fell due, the number of hands through which it passed in a given time, should become characteristic variables of its representative power. But all this was merely the consequence of a form of reflection that placed the monetary sign, with relation to wealth, in a posture of *representation* in the full sense of the term. It is, therefore, the same archaeological network that supports the theory of *money-as-representation* in the analysis of wealth and the theory of *character-as-representation* in natural history. The character designates natural beings by situating them in their surroundings; monetary price designates wealth, but in the movement of its growth or diminution.

V THE CREATION OF VALUE

The theory of money and trade responds to the question: how, in the movement of exchange, can prices characterize things – how can money establish a system of signs and designation between kinds of wealth? The theory of value responds to a question that intersects this first one, a question that probes, as it were vertically and in depth, the horizontal area in which exchange is continuously taking place: why are there things that men seek to exchange; why are some of them worth more than others, why do some of them, that have no utility, have a high value, whereas others, that are indispensable, have no value at all? It is thus no longer a question of knowing in accordance with what mechanism kinds of wealth can represent each other (and represent themselves by means of that universally representative wealth constituted by precious metal), but why objects of desire and need have to be represented, how one posits the value of a thing, and why one can affirm that it is worth this or that.

To be worth, for Classical thought, is first of all to be worth something, to be substitutable for that thing in a process of exchange. Money was invented, prices were fixed and can modify themselves, only in so far as that process of exchange exists. Now, exchange is only apparently a simple process. In fact, exchange by barter is possible only if each of the two parties concerned recognizes a value in what the other possesses. In one sense, therefore, these exchangeable things, together with their particular values, should exist in advance in the hands of each party so that the double cession and double acquisition can finally take place. But, from another point of view, what each person eats and drinks, what he needs in order to live, has no value as long as he does not relinquish it; and what he does not need is equally devoid of value as long as he does not employ it to acquire something he does need. In other words, in order that one thing can represent another in an exchange, they must both exist as bearers of value; and yet value exists only within the representation (actual or possible), that is, within the exchange or the exchangeability. Hence two simultaneously possible ways of construing the matter: the one analyses value in the act of exchange itself, at the point where the given and the received intersect; the other analyses it as anterior to the exchange and as a primary condition without which that exchange could not take place. The first of these two readings corresponds to an analysis that places and encloses the whole essence of language within the proposition; the second corresponds to an analysis that reveals this same essence of language as residing in the region of primitive designations (language of action or roots); in the first case, language does, in fact, find its field of possibility in a predication provided by the verb – that is, by the element of language that is set apart from all other words, yet relates them to one another; the verb, which renders all the words of language possible on the basis of their propositional connection, corresponds to the exchange, which, as an act antedating the others, provides a basis for the value of the things exchanged and for the price for which they are relinquished; in the other form of analysis, language is rooted outside itself and, as it were, in the nature or the analogies of things; the root, the first cry that gave rise to words even before language itself was born, corresponds to the immediate formation of value prior to exchange and the reciprocal measurements of need.

For grammar, however, these two forms of analysis – based on the proposition or based on roots – are perfectly distinct, because grammar is dealing with language, that is, with a system of representation required both to designate and to judge, or again, related to both an object and a truth. In the economic sphere this distinction does not exist, since, for desire, the relation to its object and the affirmation that it is desirable are one and the same thing; to designate it is already to posit the connection. So that, whereas grammar had two separate and reciprocally adjusted theoretical segments at its disposal, forming first of all an analysis of the proposition (or the judgement), then an analysis of designation (the gesture or the root), the economy knows only a single theoretical segment, but one that is simultaneously susceptible of two readings made in contrary directions. The one analyses value in terms of the exchange of objects of need – of *useful objects*; the other in terms of the formation and origin of objects whose exchange will later define their value – in terms of nature's prolixity. Between these two possible readings we recognize a point of heresy that is by now familiar: it separates what is termed the 'psychological theory' of Condillac, Galiani, and Graslin, from that of the Physiocrats, with Quesnay and his school. The doctrines of the Physiocrats may not really possess the importance attributed to them by economists of the early nineteenth century, when the latter were seeking in them the foundation stone of political economy; but it would be equally vain to attribute the same role – as the marginalists in fact did – to the 'psychological school'. There are no differences between these two modes of analysis other than the point of origin and the direction chosen to traverse a network of necessity that remains identical in both.

In order that there may be values and wealth, say the Physiocrats, an exchange must be possible: that is, one should have at one's disposal a superfluity that the other party needs. The fruit I am hungry for, which I pick and eat, is a *commodity* presented to me by nature; there can be no *wealth* unless the fruits on my tree are sufficiently numerous to exceed my appetite. Even then, someone else must be hungry and require those fruit of me. 'The air we breathe,' says Quesnay, 'the water we draw from the stream, and all the other superabundant goods or forms of wealth common to all men, are not marketable: they are commodities, not wealth'[55]. Before exchange, there is nothing but that rare or abundant reality provided by nature; demand on the one hand and relinquishment on the other are alone capable of producing value. Now, the purpose of exchange is precisely that of distributing whatever is in excess in such a manner that it will be passed on to those who need it. It is therefore 'wealth' only provisionally, during the time when, possessed by some and needed by others, it begins and completes the trajectory that will convey it to the consumers and thus restore it to its original nature as a commodity. 'The aim of exchange,' says Mercier de La Rivière, 'is enjoyment, consumption. Trade, then, can be summarized as the exchange of everyday things in order to achieve their distribution into the hands of their consumers'[56]. Now, this constitution of value by means of trade[57] cannot be achieved without a subtraction of goods: trade, in fact, transports goods, and entails cartage, storage, processing, and selling costs[58]: in short, it costs a certain consumption of *goods* for the *goods* themselves to be converted into *wealth*. The only sort of trade that would cost nothing would be simple barter, since in that case the goods are wealth and have value only for the brief instant during which the exchange is made: 'If the exchange could be made immediately and without cost, it could be only the more advantageous to the two exchangers: it is therefore a grievous mistake to take for trade itself those intermediary operations that serve as the means of trade'[59]. The Physiocrats allow themselves to posit only the material reality of goods, which means that the formation of value in exchange becomes a process costly in itself and must be debited against existing goods. The creation of value is therefore not a means of satisfying a greater number of needs; it is the sacrifice of a certain quantity of goods in order to exchange others. Values thus form the negative of goods.

But how is it that value can be formed in this way? What is the origin of this excess that makes it possible for goods to be transformed into wealth without being effaced and finally disappearing altogether as a result of successive exchanges and continual circulation? How is it that the cost of this continuous creation of value does not exhaust the goods that men have at their disposal?

Is it that trade is able to find this necessary supplement in itself? Certainly not, since its aim is to exchange value for value in accordance with the greatest possible equality. 'In order to receive much, one must give much; and in order to give much, one must receive much. That is the whole art of trade. Trade, by its very nature, exchanges together only things of equal value'[60]. It is true that a commodity taken to a distant market can be exchanged for a price higher than that which it would command in its place of origin; but this increase corresponds to the real expense of transporting it; and the only reason it does not lose anything because of this fact is that the stationary merchandise for which it is exchanged loses those freightage charges out of its own price. One may haul one's merchandise from one end of the world to the other, but the cost of its exchange is always levied on the goods exchanged. It is not trade that has produced the superfluity of goods: the excess must already have existed in order for trade to be possible.

Nor is industry capable of compensating for the cost of the creation of value. In fact, manufactured products may be sold in accordance with two different systems. If prices are free, competition tends to lower them to the point where, apart from the cost of the raw materials, they cover no more than the work of the worker who made the product; according to Cantillon's definition, this wage corresponds to the worker's subsistence during the time he takes to do the work; and doubtless one should also add the subsistence and profits of the entrepreneur; but in any case, the increase in value due to the manufacturing process represents the consumption of those whom it remunerates; so that in order to produce wealth it has been necessary to sacrifice some goods: 'The artisan destroys as much in subsistence as he produces by his work'[61]. When prices are controlled by a monopoly, the selling price of objects can rise considerably. But this does not mean that the labour of the workers will be better remunerated: the competition existing between them tends to maintain their wages at the level that is just indispensable for their subsistence[62]; as for the profits of the entrepreneurs, it is true that monopolistic prices increase them to the degree that the value of the objects put on the market is increased; but this increase is merely the proportional drop in the exchange value of other merchandise: 'All these entrepreneurs make fortunes only because others incur expenses'[63]. Industry appears to increase values; in fact, it deducts the cost of one or several subsistences from the exchange itself. Value is created, or increased, not by production, but by consumption – whether it be that of the worker in order to subsist, that of the entrepreneur taking his profit, or that of the non-worker who buys. 'The increase in market value which is due to the sterile class is the effect of the worker's expenditure, not of his work. For the idle man who expends without working produces the same effect in this respect'[64]. Value arises only where goods have disappeared; and work functions as an expenditure: it turns the subsistence which it has itself consumed into a price.

This is even true of agricultural work. The status of the worker who ploughs is in no way different from that of the worker who weaves or carts; he is only one of 'the tools of work or cultivation'[65] – a tool that requires a subsistence, and deducts it from what the land produces. As in all the other cases, the remuneration of agricultural labour tends to regulate itself so as to provide that subsistence exactly. Yet agricultural labour does possess one privilege, not an economic one, in the system of exchanges, but a physical one, in the sphere of the production of goods: the land, when worked, provides a possible quantity of subsistence much greater than that actually needed by the labourer who works it. As re-munerated work, therefore, the agricultural worker's labour is just as negative and wasteful as that of factory workers; but, as 'physical com-merce' with nature[66], it is the source of an immense fecundity. And though it is true that this lavishness is remunerated in advance by the costs of ploughing, sowing, and animal fodder, everyone knows that where you sow a grain of wheat you reap an ear; and that herds and flocks grow fatter every day even while they rest, which cannot be said of a bale of silk or wool in storage'[67]. Agriculture is the only sphere in which the increase in value due to production is not equivalent to the main-tenance of the producer. This is because there is really an invisible pro-ducer who does not require any remuneration; it is with him that the farmer is, without knowing it, in partnership; and while the labourer consumes an amount equal to his work, that same work, by virtue of the labourer's Co-Author, produces all the goods from which the creation of values will be deducted: 'Agriculture is a manufacture of divine in-stitution in which the manufacturer has as his partner the Author of nature, the Producer of all goods and all wealth'[68].

It is understandable, therefore, why the Physiocrats accorded such theoretical and practical importance to ground rent – and not to agricul-tural labour. This is because the latter is remunerated by consumption, whereas ground rent represents, or ought to represent, the net product: the quantity of goods provided by nature over and above the subsistence it yields to the worker and the remuneration it demands for itself in order to go on producing. It is this rent that permits the transformation of goods into values or into wealth. It provides the remuneration for all other kinds of work and all the consumption corresponding to them. Hence two major concerns: to have a large quantity of specie at one's disposal, so that labour, trade, and industry can be adequately supplied with it; and to see to it that absolute protection is given to that part of the working capital that must return to the land in order to allow it to go on producing. The Physiocrats' economic and political programme must therefore include: an increase in agricultural prices, but not in the wages of those who work the land; the levying of all taxes on ground rent itself; the abolition of monopolistic prices and all trade preferences (so that industry and trade, regulated by competition, will be forced to maintain fair prices); a vast reinvestment of money in the land for the advances necessary for future production.

The whole system of exchanges, the whole costly creation of values, is referred back to the unbalanced, radical, and primitive exchange established between the advances made by the landowner and the generosity of nature. This exchange alone is absolutely profitable, and it is from within this net profit that deductions of goods can be made to cover the costs necessitated by each exchange, and thus by the appearance of each new element of wealth. It would be untrue to say that nature spontaneously produces values; but it is the inexhaustible source of the goods that exchange transforms into values, though not without expenditure and consumption. Quesnay and his disciples analyse wealth on the basis of what is given in exchange – that is, on the basis of the superfluity that exists without any value, but that becomes value by taking part in a circuit of substitutions, in which it must remunerate each of its movements, each of its transformations, with wages, food, and subsistence, in short, with a part of that surplus of which it is itself a part. The Physiocrats begin their analysis with the thing itself which is designated in value, but which exists prior to the system of wealth. The same is true of grammarians when they analyse words on the basis of their roots, of the immediate relation that unites a sound and a thing, and of the successive abstractions by means of which that root becomes a name in a language.

VI   UTILITY

The analysis of Condillac, Galiani, Graslin, and Destutt corresponds to the grammatical theory of the proposition. It selects as its point of departure, not what is given in an exchange, but what is received: the same thing, in fact, but seen from the point of view of the person who needs it, who wants it, and who agrees to give up what he possesses in order to obtain this other thing which in his estimation is more useful and to which he attaches greater value. The Physiocrats and their opponents are in fact traversing the same theoretical segment, but in opposite directions: the former are asking themselves on what condition – and at what cost – an article can become a value in a system of exchanges; the latter, on what condition a judgement of appraisal can be transformed into a price in that same system of exchanges. It is understandable, then, why the analyses of the Physiocrats and those of the utilitarians are often so close, and sometimes complementary; why Cantillon could be claimed by the former – for his theory of the three fundamental revenues and the importance he gives to land – as well as by the latter – for his analysis of circulation and the role he gives to money[69]; why Turgot was able to be faithful to Physiocrat doctrine in *Réflexions sur la formation et la distribution des richesses*, and yet very close to Galiani in *Valeur et monnaie*.

Let us imagine the most rudimentary of all exchange situations: a man who has nothing but corn or wheat confronted with another who has nothing but wine or wood. As yet, there is no fixed price, no equivalence, no common measure. Yet if these men have gone to the trouble to collect the wood, to sow and harvest the corn or the wheat, it is because they have passed a certain judgement on these things; without having to compare it with anything else, they judged that this wheat or that wood was able to satisfy one of their needs – that it would be *useful* to them: 'To say that a thing has value is to say that it is, or that we esteem it, good for some use. The value of things is thus founded on their utility, or, what amounts to the same thing, on the use we can make of them'[70]. This judgement is the foundation of what Turgot terms the 'estimative value' of things[71]. A value that is absolute, since it concerns each commodity individually and without its being compared with any other; yet it is also relative and changing, since it is modified in accordance with men's appetite, desires, and need.

However, the exchange achieved upon the basis of these primary utilities is not their simple reduction to a common denominator. It is in itself a creator of utility, since it presents for the appraisal of one party what until then had possessed only slight utility for the other. At this point, three possibilities exist. It may be that the 'surplus of each', as Condillac[72] puts it – that which he has not utilized or does not expect to utilize immediately – corresponds in quality and in quantity to the needs of the other: the whole surplus of the wheat-owner is revealed, in the exchange situation, as being useful to the wine-owner, and vice versa; in this case, what was useless becomes totally useful, through a creation of simultaneous and equal values on each side; what was estimated as null by the one becomes positive in the estimation of the other; and since the situation is symmetrical, the estimative values thus created are automatically equivalent; utility and price correspond exactly, with no residuum; the appraisal adjusting itself automatically to the estimate. Or it may be that the surplus of the one party is not sufficient for the needs of the other, and that the latter will refrain from giving all that he possesses; he will keep some part of it in order to obtain from a third party the additional quantity indispensable to his need; this deducted portion – which the second party will try to reduce to a minimum, since he needs all the first's surplus – gives rise to price: it is no longer an excess of wheat that is being exchanged for an excess of wine, but, as the result of an altercation, so many hogsheads of wine for so many bushels of wheat. Shall we say, then, that the party who gives the most is losing some of the value of what he possessed in this exchange? Not at all, for the surplus is of no use to him, or at all events, since he has agreed to exchange it, he must be according a greater value to what he receives than to what he relinquishes. Or it may be, and this is the third hypothesis, that there is nothing absolutely superfluous to either party, since each of them knows that he can use, sooner or later, the totality of what he possesses: the state of *need* is therefore general, and every item of goods owned becomes wealth. In this case, the two parties may very well exchange nothing at all; but equally, each one of them may calculate that a portion of the other's commodity would be more useful to him than a portion of his own. They both establish – but each for himself, and therefore in accordance with differing calculations – a minimum inequality: so many measures of the corn I do not have, one of them says, will be worth a little more to me than so many measures of my wood; such and such a quantity of wood, says the other, will be more valuable to me than such and such a quantity of corn. These two estimative inequalities define for each party the relative value he gives to what he possesses and to what

197

he does not possess. And the only means of reconciling these two in-equalities is to establish between them the equality of two relations: the exchange will take place when the relation of corn to wood for the one party becomes equal to the relation of wood to corn for the other. Whereas estimative value is defined solely by the interaction of a need and an object – and thus by a single interest in an isolated individual – in appreciative value, as it now appears,

> there are two men who compare and there are four interests being compared; but the two private interests of each of the two contracting parties have first been compared with one another separately, and it is the results of this comparison that are then compared in order to arrive at an average estimative value;

this equality of relation makes it possible to say, for example, that four measures of corn and five bundles of wood have an equal exchangeable value[73]. But this equality does not mean that one exchanges utility for utility in identical portions: one exchanges inequalities, which means that on both sides – and despite the fact that each element traded has an intrinsic utility – more value is acquired than was originally possessed. Instead of two immediate utilities, one has two others which are considered to satisfy larger needs.

Such analyses show how value and exchange interlock: there would be no exchange if there were no immediate values – that is, if there did not exist in things 'an attribute which is accidental to them and which is dependent solely upon man's needs, as an effect is dependent upon its cause'[74]. But the exchange creates value in its turn, and in two ways. First, it renders useful things that without it would be of slight utility or perhaps none at all: what can a diamond be worth to men who are hungry or need clothes? But it is sufficient that there exists one woman in the world with a desire to be attractive, together with the trade capable of conveying it into her hands, for that stone to become 'indirect wealth for its owner who does not need it . . . the value of that object is for him an exchange value'[75]; and he will be able to feed himself by selling something that can serve only to glitter: hence the importance of luxury goods, hence the fact that, from the point of view of wealth, there is no difference between need, comfort, and pleasure[76]. On the other hand, exchange gives rise to a new type of value, which is 'appreciative': it organizes a reciprocal relation between utilities, which parallels the re-lation to mere need; and which also, and above all, modifies it: for in the sphere of appreciation, and thus of the comparison of each value with all others, the least new creation of utility diminishes the relative value of all those already in existence. The total of wealth does not increase, despite the appearance of new objects capable of satisfying needs; all production creates only 'a new order of values relative to the mass of wealth; the first objects of need will have diminished in value so as to make room in the mass for the new value of objects of comfort or pleasure' [77]. Exchange is therefore that which increases values (by giving rise to new utilities which, at least indirectly, satisfy needs); but it is equally that which diminishes values (in relation to one another, in the appreciation made of each). By means of it, the non-useful becomes useful, and the more useful becomes less useful in exactly the same proportion. Such is the constituent role of exchange in the action of value: it gives each thing a price, and it lowers the price of each one in doing so.

It will be seen that the theoretical elements are the same in the works of the Physiocrats as in those of their opponents. The body of fundamental propositions used is common to both: all wealth springs from the land; the value of things is linked with exchange; money has value as the representation of the wealth in circulation; circulation should be as simple and as complete as possible. But these theoretical segments are arranged by the Physiocrats and by the 'utilitarians' in inverse orders; and as a result of the interplay of these differing arrangements, what plays a positive role in one theory becomes negative in the other. Condillac, Galiani, and Graslin start from the exchange of utilities as the subjective and positive foundation of all values; all that satisfies a need, has, therefore, a value, and any transformation or transference that makes it possible to satisfy a greater number of needs constitutes an increase of value: it is this increase that makes it possible to remunerate workers, by giving them an amount, deducted from this increase, which is equivalent to their subsistence. But all these positive elements which constitute value are based upon a certain state of need present in men, and therefore upon the finite character of nature's fecundity. For the Physiocrats, the same sequence must be gone through in the opposite direction: all transformation of the products of the land, and all work on them, is remunerated by the worker's subsistence; it must therefore be debited to the totality of goods as a diminution; value arises only where there is consumption. For value to be created, then, nature must be endowed with endless fecundity. All that is perceived positively and, as it were, in relief, in one of these two interpretations is perceived negatively, like a cast of the first, in the other. The 'utilitarians' base their *attribution* of a certain value to things upon the *articulation* of exchanges; the Physiocrats explain the progressive *patterning* of values by the *existence* of wealth. But in both interpretations the theory of value, like that of *structure* in natural history, links the moment of *attribution* and that of *articulation*.

Perhaps it would have been simpler to say that the Physiocrats represented the landowners and the 'utilitarians' the merchants and entrepreneurs. That the latter, in consequence, believed that the value of what the land produced was increased when it was transformed or transported; that they were preoccupied, by force of circumstance, with a market economy in which needs and desires created the laws. And that the Physiocrats, on the other hand, believed only in agricultural production, and claimed that its remuneration should be higher; that, being landowners, they attributed a natural basis to ground rent, and that, since they were claiming political power, they wanted to be the only ones subject to taxation, and thus in exclusive enjoyment of the rights taxation conferred. And there is no doubt that the broad economic choices of both sides can be perceived beyond their coherence of interests. But though membership of a social group can always explain why such and such a person chose one system of thought rather than another, the condition enabling that system to be thought never resides in the existence of the group. We must be careful to distinguish here between two forms and two levels of investigation. The first would be a study of opinions in order to discover who in the eighteenth century was a Physiocrat and who an Antiphysiocrat; what interests were at stake; what were the points and arguments of the polemic; how the struggle for power developed. The other, which takes no account of the persons involved, or their history, consists in defining the conditions on the basis of which it was possible to conceive of both 'physiocratic' and 'utilitarian' knowledge in interlocking and simultaneous forms. The first analysis would be the province of a doxology. Archaeology can recognize and practise only the second.

VII   GENERAL TABLE

The general organization of the empirical spheres can now be sketched out as a whole. (see p. 201).

The first thing we observe is that *analysis of wealth* obeys the same configuration as *natural history* and *general grammar*. The theory of value makes it possible, in fact, to explain (whether by dearth and need or by

Seventeenth and Eighteenth Centuries

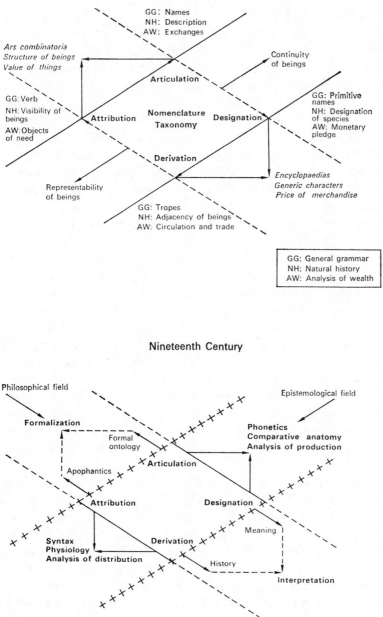

GG: Names
NH: Description
AW: Exchanges

Ars combinatoria
Structure of beings
Value of things

Continuity
of beings

Articulation

GG: Verb
NH: Visibility of beings
AW: Objects of need

Attribution   Nomenclature   Designation
               Taxonomy

GG: Primitive names
NH: Designation of species
AW: Monetary pledge

Derivation

Representability
of beings

Encyclopaedias
Generic characters
Price of merchandise

GG: Tropes
NH: Adjacency of beings
AW: Circulation and trade

GG: General grammar
NH: Natural history
AW: Analysis of wealth

Nineteenth Century

Philosophical field

Epistemological field

Formalization

Formal
ontology

Phonetics
Comparative anatomy
Analysis of production

Apophantics   Articulation

Attribution   Designation

Syntax
Physiology
Analysis of distribution

Derivation

Meaning

History

Interpretation

the superabundance of nature) how certain objects can be introduced into the system of exchanges, how, by means of the primitive process of barter, one thing can be posited as the equivalent of another, how the estimate of the first can be related to the estimate of the second in accordance with a relation of equality (A and B have the same value) or one of analogy (the value of A, possessed by my counterpart, is to my need what the value of B, which I possess, is to him). Value corresponds, then, to the attributive function which, for *general grammar*, is performed by the verb, and which, giving rise to the proposition, constitutes the initial threshold beyond which there is language. But when appreciative value becomes estimative value, that is, when it is defined and limited within the system constituted by all possible exchanges, then each value finds itself positioned and patterned by all the others: when this happens, value assumes the articulatory role recognized by *general grammar* in all the non-verbal elements of the proposition (that is, in nouns, and in all words that, whether visibly or in secret, contain a nominal function). In the system of exchanges, in the interplay that permits each portion of wealth to signify the others or to be signified by them, value is at the same time *verb* and *noun*, power to connect and principle of analysis, attribution, and pattern. *Value*, then, occupies exactly the same position in the analysis of wealth as *structure* does in natural history; like structure, it unites in one and the same operation the function that permits the attribution of one sign to another sign, of one representation to another, and the function that permits the articulation of the elements that compose the totality of representations or the signs that decompose them.

For its part, the theory of money and trade explains how any given form of matter can take on a signifying function by being related to an object and serving as a permanent sign for it; it also explains (by the interaction of trade and the increase and diminution of the quantity of specie) how this relation of sign to the thing signified can be modified without ever disappearing, how the same monetary element can signify more or less wealth, how it can shift, dilate, and shrink in relation to the values it has the task of representing. The theory of monetary prices corresponds, therefore, to what in *general grammar* appears in the form of an analysis of roots and of the language of action (the function of *designation*) and to what appears in the form of tropes and shifts of meaning (the function of *derivation*). Money, like words, has the role of designating, yet never ceases to fluctuate around that vertical axis: variations of price are to the initial establishment of the relation between metal and wealth what rhetorical displacements are to the original value of verbal signs. Moreover, by ensuring, on the basis of its own possibilities, the designation of wealth, the establishment of prices, the modification of nominal values, and the impoverishment and enrichment of nations, money functions in relation to wealth in the same way as *character* does in relation to natural beings: it makes it possible both to impose a particular mark upon it and to indicate a place for it – no doubt a provisional one – in the area actually defined by the totality of things and of the signs at one's disposal. The theory of money and prices occupies the same position in the analysis of wealth as the theory of character does in natural history. Like the latter, it unites into one and the same function the possibility of giving things a sign, of representing one thing by another, and the possibility of causing a sign to shift in relation to what it designates.

The four functions that define the verbal sign in its particular properties, and distinguish it from all other signs that representation can provide for itself, are thus to be found in the theoretical signalization of natural history and in the practical utilization of monetary signs. The order of wealth and the order of natural beings are established and revealed in so far as there are established between objects of need, and between visible individuals, systems of signs which make possible the designation of representations one by another, the derivation of signifying representations in relation to those signified, the articulation of what is represented, and the attribution of certain representations to certain others. In this sense, it can be said that, for Classical thought, systems of natural history and theories of money or trade have the same conditions of possibility as language itself. This means two things: first, that order in nature and order in the domain of wealth have the same mode of being, for the Classical experience, as the order of representations as manifested by words; second, that words form a system of signs sufficiently privileged, when it is a question of revealing the order of things, for natural history – if it is well organized – and money – if it is well regulated – to function in the same way as language. What algebra is to mathesis, signs, and words in particular, are to *taxinomia*: a constitution and evident manifestation of the order of things.

There does exist, however, a major difference that prevents classification from being the spontaneous language of nature and prices from being the natural discourse of wealth. Or rather there exist two differences: one makes it possible to distinguish the domains of verbal signs from that of wealth or that of natural beings; the other makes it possible to distinguish the theory of natural history from that of value or prices.

The four moments that define the essential functions of language (attribution, articulation, designation, derivation) are solidly linked to one another, since they require one another as soon as, with the advent of the verb, one has crossed the threshold beyond which language exists. But in the real genesis of actual languages, the process does not take place either in the same direction or with the same rigour: on the basis of primitive designations, men's imaginations (according to the climates they live in, the conditions of their existence, their feelings and their passions, their experiences) give rise to derivations which differ from people to people, and which doubtless explain, in addition to the diversity of languages, the relative instability of each of them. At any given moment of this derivation, and within any particular language, men have at their disposal a totality of words, of names which are articulated one upon another and provide the pattern of their representations; but this analysis is so imperfect, it allows so many imprecisions and overlappings to persist, that men employ various words and formulate different propositions with the same representations: their reflection is not wholly protected against error. Between designation and derivation, shifts of the imagination multiply; between articulation and attribution, errors of reflection proliferate. This is why, on the perhaps endlessly postponed horizon of language, there is projected the idea of a universal language in which the representative value of words would be sufficiently clearly fixed, sufficiently securely based, sufficiently clearly recognized for reflection to be able to come to a decision with total clarity about any proposition whatever – by means of this language 'peasants could better judge of the truth of things than philosophers now do'[78]; a perfectly distinct language would make possible an entirely clear discourse: this language would be an *Ars combinatoria* in itself. It is also why the practice of any real language should be reinforced by an Encyclopaedia which defines the progress of words, prescribes the most natural routes for them to take, traces out the legitimate shifts of knowledge, and codifies the relationships of adjacency and resemblance. The Dictionary is created as a means of controlling the play of derivations on the basis of the primary designation of words, just as the Universal Language is created in order to control the errors of reflection – when it is formulating a judgement – on the basis of a well-established articulation. The *Ars combinatoria* and the Encyclopaedia together compensate for the imperfection of real languages.

Natural history, since it must of necessity be a science, and the circulation of wealth, since it is an institution created by men and also controlled by them, are bound to escape the perils inherent in spontaneous languages. There is no error possible between articulation and attribution in the order of natural history, since the structure is given in its immediate visibility; no imaginary shifts either, no false resemblances, no incongruous juxtapositions placing a correctly designated natural being in a space not its own, since character is established either by the coherence of the system or by the exactness of the method. In natural history, structure and character ensure the theoretical closing of what remains open in language and gives rise on its frontiers to the projects of essentially uncompleted arts. Similarly, value, which automatically changes from being estimative to being appreciative, and money, which by growth or diminution of its quantity causes yet always limits fluctuations of prices, ensure in the sphere of wealth the congruity of attribution and articulation, and that of designation and derivation. Value and prices ensure the virtual closing of those segments that remain open in language. Structure enables natural history to find itself immediately in the element of a combination, and character allows it to establish an exact and definitive poetics with regard to beings and their resemblances. Value combines the forms of wealth one with another, money permits their real exchange. Where the disordered order of language implies the continuous relation to an art and its endless tasks, the orders of nature and wealth are expressed in the mere existence of structure and character, value and money.

It should be noted, however, that the natural order is formulated in a theory that has value as the correct interpretation of a real series or table: moreover, the structure of beings is both the immediate form of the visible and its articulation; similarly, character designates and localizes in one and the same movement. On the other hand, estimative value becomes appreciative only by means of a transformation; and the initial relation between metal and merchandise becomes only gradually a price subject to variations. In the first case, there is an exact superimposition of attribution and articulation, designation and derivation; in the second, a transition linked to the nature of things and to human activity. With language, the system of signs is passively accepted in its imperfection, and only an art can rectify it: the theory of language is immediately prescriptive. Natural history establishes of itself a system of signs for denoting beings, and that is why it is a theory. Wealth is a system of signs that are created, multiplied, and modified by men; the theory of wealth is linked throughout to politics.

However, the other two sides of the fundamental quadrilateral remain open. How can designation (a single, precise act) make possible an articulation of nature, wealth, and representations? How, generally speaking, can the two opposite segments (those of judgement and signification for language, of structure and character for natural history, of value and prices for the theory of wealth) relate to each other in such a way as to make possible a language, a system of nature, and the uninterrupted flow of wealth? It is here that it becomes really necessary to suppose that representations resemble one another and suggest one another in the imagination; that natural beings are in relations of adjacency and resemblance to one another; and that men's needs correspond to one another and are capable of satisfaction. The interconnection of representations, the unbroken expanse of beings, and the proliferation of nature are still required if there is to be language, if there is to be a natural history, and if it is to be possible for there to be wealth and use of wealth. The continuum of representation and being, an ontology defined negatively as an absence of nothingness, a general representability of being, and being as expressed in the presence of representation – all this is included in the total configuration of the Classical *episteme*. One can see in this principle of continuity the metaphysically strong moment of seventeenth- and eighteenth-century thought (that which enables the form of the proposition to have an effective meaning, structure to be ordered as character, and the value of things to be calculated as prices); whereas the relations between articulation and attribution, designation and derivation (that which provides a foundation for judgement on the one hand and for meaning on the other, structure and character, value and prices) define the scientifically strong moment of that thought (that which makes possible grammar, natural history, and the science of wealth). The ordering of empiricity is thus linked to the ontology that characterizes Classical thought; indeed, from the very outset, this thought exists within an ontology rendered transparent by the fact that being is offered to representation without interruption; and within a representation illuminated by the fact that it releases the continuity of being.

It is now possible, from a distance, to characterize the mutation that occurred in the entire Western *episteme* towards the end of the eighteenth century by saying that a scientifically strong moment was created in just that area where the Classical *episteme* was metaphysically strong; and that, on the other hand, a philosophical space emerged in that very area where Classicism had most firmly established its epistemological grip.

In fact, the analysis of production, as the new project of the new 'political economy', has as its essential role the analysis of the relation between value and prices; the concepts of organisms and organic structure, the methods of comparative anatomy – in short, all the themes of the new 'biology' – explain how structures observable in individuals can have validity as general characters for genera, families, sub-kingdoms; and lastly, in order to unify the formal arrangements of a language (its ability to establish propositions) and the meaning belonging to words, 'philology' would no longer study the representative functions of discourse, but a totality of morphological constants subject to a history. Philology, biology, and political economy were established, not in the places formerly occupied by *general grammar, natural history*, and the *analysis of wealth*, but in an area where those forms of knowledge did not exist, in the space they left blank, in the deep gaps that separated their broad theoretical segments and that were filled with the murmur of the ontological continuum. The object of knowledge in the nineteenth century is formed in the very place where the Classical plenitude of being has fallen silent.

Inversely, a new philosophical space was to emerge in the place where the objects of Classical knowledge dissolved. The moment of attribution (as a form of judgement) and that of articulation (as a general patterning of beings) separated, and thus created the problem of the relations between a formal apophantics and a formal ontology; the moment of primitive designation and that of derivation through time also separated, opening up a space in which there arose the question of the relations between original meaning and history. Thus the two great forms of modern philosophic reflection were established. The first questions the relations between logic and ontology; it proceeds by the paths of formalization and encounters, in a new form, the problem of *mathesis*. The second questions the relations of signification and time; it undertakes an unveiling which is not and probably never can be completed, and it brings back into prominence the themes and methods of *interpretation*. Probably the most fundamental question that can present itself to philosophy, then, concerns the relation between these two forms of reflection. It is certainly not within the province of archaeology to say whether this relation is possible, or how it could be provided with a foundation; but archaeology can designate the region in which that relation seeks to exist, in what area of the *episteme* modern philosophy attempts to find its unity, in what point of knowledge it discovers its broadest domain: in such a place the formal (in apophantics and ontology) would meet the significative as illuminated in interpretation. The essential problem of Classical thought lay in the relations between *name* and *order*: how to discover a *nomenclature* that would be a *taxonomy*, or again, how to establish a system of signs that would be transparent to the continuity of being. What modern thought is to throw fundamentally into question is the relation of meaning with the form of truth and the form of being: in the firmament of our reflection there reigns a discourse – a perhaps inaccessible discourse – which would at the same time be an ontology and a semantics. Structuralism is not a new method; it is the awakened and troubled consciousness of modern thought.

VIII DESIRE AND REPRESENTATION

The men of the seventeenth and eighteenth centuries do not think of wealth, nature, or languages in terms that had been bequeathed to them by preceding ages or in forms that presaged what was soon to be discovered; they think of them in terms of a general arrangement that not only prescribes their concepts and methods, but also, more fundamentally, defines a certain mode of being for language, natural individuals, and the objects of need and desire; this mode of being is that of representation. As a result, a whole common ground appears upon which the history of the sciences figures as a surface effect. This does not mean that it can now be left to one side; but that a reflection upon the history of a particular branch of knowledge can no longer content itself with following the development of that body of knowledge in a temporal sequence; such a body of knowledge is not, in fact, a phenomenon of heredity and tradition; and one does not explain how it came about simply by describing the state of knowledge that preceded it and what it has provided by way of – as we say – 'original contributions'. The history of knowledge can be written only on the basis of what was contemporaneous with it, and certainly not in terms of reciprocal influence, but in terms of conditions and *a prioris* established in time. It is in this sense that archaeology can give an account of the *existence* of a general grammar, a natural history, and an analysis of wealth, and thus open up a free, undivided area in which the history of the sciences, the history of ideas, and the history of opinions can, if they wish, frolic at ease.

Though the analyses of representation, language, natural orders, and wealth are perfectly coherent and homogeneous with regard to one another, there exists, nevertheless, a profound disequilibrium. For representation governs the mode of being of language, individuals, nature, and need itself. The analysis of representation therefore has a determining value for all the empirical domains. The whole Classical system of order, the whole of that great *taxinomia* that makes it possible to know things by means of the system of their identities, is unfolded within the space that is opened up inside representation when representation represents itself, that area where being and the Same reside. Language is simply the representation of words; nature is simply the representation of beings; need is simply the representation of needs. The end of Classical thought – and of the *episteme* that made general grammar, natural history, and the science of wealth possible – will coincide with the decline of representation, or rather with the emancipation of language, of the living being, and of need, with regard to representation. The obscure but stubborn spirit of a people who talk, the violence and the endless effort of life, the hidden energy of needs, were all to escape from the mode of being of representation. And representation itself was to be paralleled, limited, circumscribed, mocked perhaps, but in any case regulated from the outside, by the enormous thrust of a freedom, a desire, or a will, posited as the metaphysical converse of consciousness. Something like a will or a force was to arise in the modern experience – constituting it perhaps, but in any case indicating that the Classical age was now over, and with it the reign of representative discourse, the dynasty of a representation signifying itself and giving voice in the sequence of its words to the order that lay dormant within things.

This reversal is contemporaneous with Sade. Or rather, that inexhaustible body of work manifests the precarious balance between the law without law of desire and the meticulous ordering of discursive representation. Here, the order of discourse finds its Limit and its Law; but it is still strong enough to remain coexistensive with the very thing that governs it. Here, without doubt, is the principle of that 'libertinage' which was the last in the Western world (after it the age of sexuality begins): the libertine is he who, while yielding to all the fantasies of desire and to each of its furies, can, but also must, illumine their slightest movement with a lucid and deliberately elucidated representation. There is a strict order governing the life of the libertine: every representation must be immediately endowed with life in the living body of desire, every desire must be expressed in the pure light of a representative discourse. Hence that rigid sequence of 'scenes' (the scene, in Sade, is profligacy subjected to the order of representation) and, within the scenes, the meticulous balance between the conjugation of bodies and the concatenation of reasons. Possibly *Justine* and *Juliette* are in the same position on the threshold of modern culture as that occupied by *Don Quixote* between the Renaissance and Classicism. Cervantes's hero, construing the relations of world and language as people had done in the sixteenth century, decoding inns into castles and farm girls into ladies with no other key than the play of resemblance, was imprisoning himself without knowing it in the mode of pure representation; but since this representation had no other law but similitude, it could not fail to become visible in the absurd form of madness. Now, in the second part of the novel, Don Quixote received his truth and his law from that represented world; he had nothing more to expect from the book in which he was born, which he had not read but whose course he was bound to follow, but a fate henceforth imposed upon him by others. He had only to allow himself to live in a castle in which he himself, having penetrated by means of his madness into the world of pure representation, finally became a mere character in the artifice of a representation. Sade's characters correspond to him at the other end of the Classical age, at the moment of its decline. It is no longer the ironic triumph of representation over resemblance; it is the obscure and repeated violence of desire battering at the limits of representation. *Justine* would correspond to the second part of *Don Quixote*: she is the unattainable object of the desire of which she is the pure origin, just as Don Quixote is, despite himself, the object of the representation which he also is in the depth of his being. In Justine, desire and representation communicate only through the presence of Another who represents the heroine to himself as an object of desire, while she herself knows nothing of desire other than its diaphanous, distant, exterior, and icy form as representation. Such is her misfortune: her innocence acts as a perpetual chaperone between desire and its representation. Juliette, on the other hand, is no more than the subject of all possible desires; but those desires are carried over, without any residuum, into the representation that provides them with a reasonable foundation in *discourse* and transforms them spontaneously into *scenes*. So that the great narrative of Juliette's life reveals, throughout the desire, violence, savagery, and death, the glittering table of representation. But this table is so thin, so transparent to all the figures of desire that untiringly accumulate within it and multiply there simply by the force of their combination, that it is just as lacking in reason as that of Don Quixote, when he believed himself to be progressing, from similitude to similitude, along the commingled paths of the world and books, but was in fact getting more and more entangled in the labyrinth of his own representations. *Juliette* thins out this inspissation of the represented so that, without the slightest blemish, the slightest reticence, the slightest veil, all the possibilities of desire may rise to the surface.

With that, this story closes the Classical age upon itself, just as *Don Quixote* had opened it. And though it is true that this is the last language still contemporaneous with Rousseau and Racine, though it is the last discourse that undertakes to 'represent', to *name*, we are well enough aware that it simultaneously reduces this ceremony to the utmost precision (it calls things by their strict name, thus eliminating the space occupied by rhetoric) and extends it to infinity (by naming everything, including the slightest of possibilities, for they are all traversed in accordance with the Universal Characteristic of Desire). Sade attains the end of Classical discourse and thought. He holds sway precisely upon their frontier. After him, violence, life and death, desire, and sexuality will extend, below the level of representation, an immense expanse of shade which we are now attempting to recover, as far as we can, in our discourse, in our freedom, in our thought. But our thought is so brief, our freedom so enslaved, our discourse so repetitive, that we must face the fact that that expanse of shade below is really a bottomless sea. The prosperities of *Juliette* are still more solitary – and endless.

NOTES

[1] Copernicus, *Discours sur la frappe des monnaies* (in J-Y. Le Branchu, *Écrits notables sur la monnaie*, Paris, 1934, t. I, p. 15).

[2] Anonymous, *Compendieux ou bref examen de quelques plaintes* (in J-Y. Le Branchu, op. cit., t. II, p. 117).

[3] Ibid., p. 155.

[4] Gresham, *Avis de Sir Thomas Gresham* (in J-Y. Le Branchu, op. cit., t. II, pp. 7 and 11.

[5] Copernicus, *Discours sur la frappe des monnaies*, loc. cit., I, p. 12.

[6] *Compendieux ou bref examen de quelques plaintes*, loc. cit., II, p. 156.

[7] Malestroit, *Le Paradoxe sur le fait des monnaies* (Paris, 1566).

[8] Bodin, *La Réponse aux paradoxes de M. de Malestroit* (1568).

[9] Davanzatti, *Leçon sur la monnaie* (in Le Branchu, op. cit., t. II, pp. 230–1).

[10] Ibid., p. 231.

[11] Cf. further this proposition of Antoine de La Pierre early in the seventeenth century: 'The essential value of gold and silver coins is based upon the precious material they contain' (*De la nécessité du pèsement*).

[12] Scipion de Grammont, *Le Denier royal, traité curieux de l'or et de l'argent* (Paris, 1620, p. 48).

[13] Ibid., pp. 13–14.

[14] Ibid., pp. 46–7.

[15] Ibid., p. 14.

[16] Schroeder, *Fürstliche Schatz und Rentkammer*, p. 111. Montanari, *Della moneta*, p. 35.

[17] Bouteroue, *Recherches curieuses des monnaies de France* (Paris, 1666, p. 8).

[18] J. Gee, *Considerations on trade* (London, 1730, p. 7).

[19] N. Barbon, *A discourse concerning coining the new money lighter* (London, 1696, unpaginated).

[20] Dumoulin (quoted in Gonnard, *Histoire des théories monétaires*, I, p. 173).

[21] Clément, *Lettres, instructions et mémoires de Colbert*, t. VII, p. 239.

[22] Ibid., p. 284. Cf. also Bouteroue, *Recherches curieuses . . .*, pp. 10–11.

[23] J. Becher, *Politischer Diskurs* (1668).

[24] Thomas Mun, *England's treasure by foreign trade* (1664, chap. II).

[25] Scipion de Grammont, *Le Denier royal*, pp. 116–19.

[26] Horneck, *Oesterreich über alles, wenn es will* (1684, pp. 8 and 188).

[27] Cf. Davanzatti, *Leçon sur la monnaie* (quoted by J-Y. Le Branchu, op. cit., t. II, p. 230).

[28] T. Hobbes, *Leviathan* (1651; Cambridge, 1904 edn., pp. 179–80).

[29] Terrasson, *Trois lettres sur le nouveau système des finances* (Paris, 1720).

[30] Dutot, *Réflexions sur le commerce et les finances* (Paris, 1738).

[31] Montesquieu, *L'Esprit des lois*, livre XXII, chap. II.

[32] *Encyclopédie*, article 'Monnaie'.

[33] Paris-Duverney, *Examen des réflexions politiques sur les finances* (The Hague, 1740).

[34] D'Aguesseau, *Considérations sur la monnaie* (1718; *Œuvres*, Paris, 1777, t. X).

[35] Melon, *Essai politique sur le commerce* (Paris, 1734).

[36] Graslin, *Essai analytique sur les richesses* (London, 1767).

[37] Vaughan, *A discourse of coin and coinage* (London, 1675, p. 1). Locke, *Some considerations of the consequences of the lowering of interest* (London, 1692).

[38] Melon, *Essai politique sur le commerce* (in Daire, *Économistes et financiers du XVIIIe siècle*, p. 761).

[39] Dutot, *Réflexions sur le commerce et les finances* (ibid., pp. 905–6).

[40] Véron de Fortbonnais, *Éléments du commerce*, t. II, p. 91. Cf. also *Recherches et considérations sur les richesses de la France*, t. II, p. 582.

[41] Le Trosne, *De l'intérêt social* (in Daire, *Les Physiocrates*, p. 908).

[42] Law, *Considérations sur le numéraire* (in Daire, *Économistes et financiers du XVIIIe siècle*, p. 519).

[43] Turgot, *Seconde lettre à l'abbé de Cice* (1749, *Œuvres complétes*, ed. Schelle, t. I, pp. 146–7).

[44] Law, *Considérations sur le numéraire*, p. 472 *et seq.*

[45] Locke, *Some considerations of the consequences of the lowering of interest* (London, 1692, pp. 71–2).

[46] Montesquieu, *L'Esprit des lois*, livre XXII, chap. VII.

[47] Graslin, *Essai analytique sur les richesses*, pp. 54–5.

[48] Cantillon, *Essai sur la nature du commerce en général* (1952 edn., p. 73).

[49] Ibid., pp. 68–9.

[50] Ibid., pp. 69–73. Petty gives the analogous proportion of one-tenth (*Political anatomy of Ireland*).

[51] Cantillon, loc. cit., p. 76.

[52] Dutot, *Réflexions sur le commerce et les finances*, pp. 862 and 906.

[53] Cf. Véron de Fortbonnais, *Éléments du commerce*, t. I, p. 45, and above all Tucker, *Questions importantes sur le commerce* (Fr. trans. by Turgot, *Œuvres*, I, p. 335).

[54] Véron de Fortbonnais, in his *Éléments du commerce* (t. I, pp. 51–2), gives the eight fundamental rules of English trade.

[55] Quesnay, article 'Hommes' (in Daire, *Les Physiocrates*, p. 42).

[56] Mercier de La Rivière, *L'Ordre naturel et essentiel des sociétés politiques* (in Daire, op. cit., p. 709).

[57] 'Considered as marketable wealth, wheat, iron, vitriol, and diamonds are equally forms of wealth whose value consists only in their price' (Quesnay, article 'Hommes', loc. cit., p. 138).

[58] Dupont de Nemours, *Réponse demandée*, p. 16.

[59] Saint-Péravy, *Journal d'agriculture*, December 1765.

[60] Ibid.

[61] *Maximes de gouvernement* (in Daire, *Les Physiocrates*, p. 289).

[62] Turgot, *Réflexions sur la formation et la distribution des richesses*, section 6.

[63] *Maximes de gouvernement* (in Daire, op. cit., p. 289).

[64] Mirabeau *Philosophie rurale*, p. 56.

[65] Ibid., p. 8.

[66] Dupont de Nemours, *Journal agricole*, May 1766.

[67] Mirabeau, *Philosophie rurale*, p. 37.

[68] Ibid., p. 33.

[69] Cantillon, *Essai sur la nature du commerce en général*, pp. 68, 69, and 73.

[70] Condillac, *Le Commerce et le gouvernement* (*Œuvres*, t. IV, p. 10).

[71] Turgot, *Valeur et monnaie* (*Œuvres complètes*, ed. Schelle, t. III, pp. 91–2).

[72] Condillac, *Le Commerce et le gouvernement*, p. 28.

[73] Turgot, *Valeur et monnaie* (*Œuvres complètes*, t. III, pp. 91–3).

[74] Graslin, *Essai analytique sur les richesses*, p. 33.

[75] Ibid., p. 45.

[76] By 'need', Graslin means 'necessity, utility, taste, and pleasure' (*Essai analytique sur les richesses*, p. 24).

[77] Graslin, op. cit., p. 36.

[78] Descartes, Lettre à Mersenne, 20 November 1629 (*A.T.*, I, p. 76).

PART II

CHAPTER 7

The Limits of Representation

I THE AGE OF HISTORY

The last years of the eighteenth century are broken by a discontinuity similar to that which destroyed Renaissance thought at the beginning of the seventeenth; then, the great circular forms in which similitude was enclosed were dislocated and opened so that the table of identities could be unfolded; and that table is now about to be destroyed in turn, while knowledge takes up residence in a new space – a discontinuity as enigmatic in its principle, in its original rupture, as that which separates the Paracelsian circles from the Cartesian order. Where did this unexpected mobility of epistemological arrangement suddenly come from, or the drift of positivities in relation to one another, or, deeper still, the alteration in their mode of being? How is it that thought detaches itself from the squares it inhabited before – general grammar, natural history, wealth – and allows what less than twenty years before had been posited and affirmed in the luminous space of understanding to topple down into error, into the realm of fantasy, into non-knowledge? What event, what law do they obey, these mutations that suddenly decide that things are no longer perceived, describes, expressed, characterized, classified, and known in the same way, and that it is no longer wealth, living beings, and discourse that are presented to knowledge in the interstices of words or through their transparency, but beings radically different from them? For an archaeology of knowledge, this profound breach in the expanse of continuities, though it must be analysed, and minutely so, cannot be 'explained' or even summed up in a single word. It is a radical event that is distributed across the entire visible surface of knowledge, and whose signs, shocks, and effects it is possible to follow step by step. Only thought re-apprehending itself at the root of its own history could provide a foundation, entirely free of doubt, for what the solitary truth of this event was in itself.

Archaeology, however, must examine each event in terms of its own evident arrangement; it will recount how the configurations proper to each positivity were modified (in the case of grammar, for example, it will analyse the eclipse of the major role hitherto accorded to the name, and the new importance of systems of inflection; or, another example, the subordination of character to function in living beings); it will analyse the alteration of the empirical entities which inhabit the positivities (the substitution of languages for discourse, of production for wealth); it will study the displacement of the positivities each in relation to the others (for example, the new relation between biology, the sciences of language, and economics); lastly, and above all, it will show that the general area of knowledge is no longer that of identities and differences, that of non-quantitative orders, that of a universal characterization, of a general *taxinomia*, of a non-measurable mathesis, but an area made up of organic structures, that is, of internal relations between elements whose totality performs a function; it will show that these organic structures are discontinuous, that they do not, therefore, form a table of unbroken simultaneities, but that certain of them are on the same level whereas others form series or linear sequences. So that we see emerging, as the organizing principles of this space of empiricities, *Analogy* and *Succession*: the link between one organic structure and another can no longer, in fact, be the identity of one or several elements, but must be the identity of the relation between the elements (a relation in which visibility no longer plays a role) and of the functions they perform; moreover, if these organic structures happen to be adjacent to one another, on account of a particularly high density of analogies, it is not because they occupy proximate places within an area of classification; it is because they have both been formed at the same time, and the one immediately after the other in the emergence of the successions. Whereas in Classical thought the sequence of chronologies merely scanned the prior and more fundamental space of a table which presented all possibilities in advance, from now on, the contemporaneous and simultaneously observable resemblances in space will be simply the fixed forms of a succession which proceeds from analogy to analogy. The Classical order distributed across a permanent space the non-quantitative identities and differences that separated and united things: it was this order that held sovereign sway – though in each case in accordance with slightly differing forms and laws – over men's discourse, the table of natural beings, and the exchange of wealth. From the nineteenth century, History was to deploy, in a temporal series, the analogies that connect distinct organic structures to one another. This same History will also, progressively, impose its laws on the analysis of production, the analysis of organically structured beings, and, lastly, on the analysis of linguistic groups. History *gives place* to analogical organic structures, just as Order opened the way to *successive* identities and differences.

Obviously, History in this sense is not to be understood as the compilation of factual successions or sequences as they may have occurred; it is the fundamental mode of being of empiricities, upon the basis of which they are affirmed, posited, arranged, and distributed in the space of knowledge for the use of such disciplines or sciences as may arise. Just as Order in Classical thought was not the visible harmony of things, or their observed arrangement, regularity, or symmetry, but the particular space of their being, that which, prior to all effective knowledge, established them in the field of knowledge, so History, from the nineteenth century, defines the birthplace of the empirical, that from which, prior to all established chronology, it derives its own being. It is no doubt because of this that History becomes so soon divided, in accordance with an ambiguity that it is probably impossible to control, into an empirical science of events and that radical mode of being that prescribes their destiny to all empirical beings, to those particular beings that we are. History, as we know, is certainly the most erudite, the most aware, the most conscious, and possibly the most cluttered area of our memory; but it is equally the depths from which all beings emerge into their precarious, glittering existence. Since it is the mode of being of all that is given us in experience, History has become the unavoidable element in our thought: in this respect, it is probably not so very different from Classical Order. Classical Order, too, could be established as a framework for acquired knowledge, but it was more fundamentally the space in which every being approached man's consciousness; and the Classical metaphysic resided precisely in that gap between order and Order, between classifications and Identity, between natural beings and Nature; in short, between men's perception (or imagination) and the understanding and will of God. In the nineteenth century, philosophy was to reside in the gap between history and History, between events and the Origin, between evolution and the first rending open of the source, between oblivion and the Return. It will be Metaphysics, therefore, only in so far as it is Memory, and it will necessarily lead thought back to the question of knowing what it means for thought to have a history. This question was to bear down upon philosophy, heavily and tirelessly, from Hegel to Nietzsche and beyond. But we must not see this as the end of an autonomous philosophical reflection that came too early, and was too proud to lean, exclusively, upon what was said before it and by others; let us not use this as a pretext for disparaging a thought powerless to stand on its own feet, and always forced to find support by winding itself around a previously established body of thought. It is enough to recognize here a philosophy deprived of a certain metaphysics because it has been separated off from the space of order, yet doomed to Time, to its flux and its returns, because it is trapped in the mode of being of History.

But we must return in a little more detail to what happened at the end of the eighteenth and the beginning of the nineteenth century: to that too sketchily outlined mutation of Order into History, and to the fundamental modification of those positivities which, for nearly a century and a half, had given place to so many adjacent kinds of knowledge – analysis of representations, general grammar, natural history, reflections on wealth and trade. How were these ways of ordering empiricity – *discourse*, the *table*, *exchange* – eclipsed? In what new space, and in accordance with what forms, have words, beings, and objects of need taken their places and arranged themselves in relation to one another? What new mode of being must they have received in order to make all these changes possible, and to enable to appear, after scarcely more than a few years, those now familiar forms of knowledge that we have called, since the nineteenth century, *philology*, *biology*, and *economics*? We tend to imagine that if these new domains were defined during the last century, it was simply that a slight increase in the objectivity of knowledge, in the precision of observation, in the rigour of our reasoning, in the organization of scientific research and information – that all this, with the aid of a few fortunate discoveries, themselves helped by a little good luck or genius, enabled us to emerge from a prehistoric age in which knowledge was still stammering out the *Grammaire de Port-Royal*, the classifications of Linnaeus, and the theories of trade or agriculture. But though we may indeed talk of prehistory from the point of view of the rationality of learning, from the point of view of positivities we can speak, quite simply, of history. And it took a fundamental event – certainly one of the most radical that ever occurred in Western culture – to bring about the dissolution of the positivity of Classical knowledge, and to constitute another positivity from which, even now, we have doubtless not entirely emerged.

This event, probably because we are still caught inside it, is largely beyond our comprehension. Its scope, the depth of the strata it has affected, all the positivities it has succeeded in disintegrating and recomposing, the sovereign power that has enabled it, in only a few years, to traverse the entire space of our culture, all this could be appraised and measured only after a quasi-infinite investigation concerned with nothing more nor less than the very being of our modernity. The constitution of so many positive sciences, the appearance of literature, the folding back of philosophy upon its own development, the emergence of history as both knowledge and the mode of being of empiricity, are only so many signs of a deeper rupture. Signs scattered through the space of knowledge, since they allow themselves to be perceived in the formation, here of philology, there of economics, there again of biology. They are chronologically scattered too: true, the phenomenon as a whole can be situated between easily assignable dates (the outer limits are the years 1775 and 1825); but in each of the domains studied we can perceive two successive phases, which are articulated one upon the other more or less around the years 1795–1800. In the first of these phases, the fundamental mode of being of the positivities does not change; men's riches, the species of nature, and the words with which languages are peopled, still remain what they were in the Classical age: double representations – representations whose role is to designate representations, to analyse them, to compose and decompose them in order to bring into being within them, together with the system of their identities and differences, the general principle of an order. It is only in the second phase that words, classes, and wealth will acquire a mode of being no longer compatible with that of representation. On the other hand, what is modified very early on, beginning with the analyses of Adam Smith, A-L. de Jussieu, or Vicq d'Azyr, at the time of Jones or Anquetil-Duperron, is the configuration of positivities: the way in which, within each one, the representative elements function in relation to one another, in which they perform their double role as designation and articulation, in which they succeed, by means of the interplay of comparisons, in establishing an order. It is this first phase that will be investigated in the present chapter.

II THE MEASURE OF LABOUR

It is often asserted that Adam Smith founded modern political economy – one might say economics *tout court* – by introducing the concept of labour into a domain of reflection not previously aware of it: all the old analyses of money, trade, and exchange were relegated at a single blow to a prehistoric age of knowledge – with the one possible exception of the Physiocratic doctrine, which is accorded the merit of having at least attempted the analysis of agricultural production. It is true that from the very outset Adam Smith relates the notion of wealth to that of labour:

> The annual labour of every nation is the fund which originally supplies it with all the necessaries and conveniences of life which it annually consumes, and which consist always either in the immediate produce of that labour, or in what is purchased with that produce from other nations[1];

it is also true that Smith relates the 'value in use' of things to men's needs, and their 'value in exchange' to the quantity of labour applied to its production:

> The value of any commodity, therefore, to the person who possesses it, and who means not to use or consume it himself, but to exchange it for other commodities, is equal to the quantity of labour which it enables him to purchase or command[2].

In fact, the difference between Smith's analyses and those of Turgot or Cantillon is less than is supposed; or, rather, it does not lie where it is generally believed to lie. From the time of Cantillon, and even before him, the distinction between value in use and value in exchange was being clearly made; and again, from Cantillon, quantity of labour was being used as a measurement of the latter. But the quantity of labour inscribed in the price of things was no more than a relative and reducible tool of measurement. A man's labour was in fact equal to the value of the quantity of nourishment necessary to maintain him and his family for as long as a given task lasted[3]. So that in the last resort, need – for food, clothing, housing – defined the absolute measure of market price. All through the Classical age, it was necessity that was the measure of equivalences, and value in use that served as absolute reference for exchange values; the gauge of prices was food, which resulted in the generally recognized privilege accorded in this respect to agricultural production, wheat and land.

Adam Smith did not, therefore, invent labour as an economic concept, since it can be found in Cantillon, Quesnay, and Condillac; he does not even give it a new role to play, since he too uses it as a measure of exchange value: 'Labour, therefore, is the real measure of the exchangeable value of all commodities'[4]. But he does displace it: he maintains its function as a means of analysing exchangeable wealth; but that analysis is no longer simply a way of expressing exchange in terms of need (and trade in terms of primitive barter); it reveals an irreducible, absolute unit of measurement. At the same time, wealth no longer establishes the internal order of its equivalence by a comparison of the objects to be exchanged, or by an appraisal of the power peculiar to each represent an object of need (and, in the last resort, the most fundamental of all, food); it is broken down according to the units of labour that have in reality produced it. Wealth is always a functioning representative element: but, in the end, what it represents is no longer the object of desire; it is labour.

But two objections immediately present themselves: how can labour be a fixed measure of the natural price of things when it has itself a price – and a variable price? How can labour be an absolute unit when it changes its form, and when industrial progress is constantly making it more productive by introducing more and more divisions into it? Now, it is precisely through these objections, and through their spokesman, as it were, that it is possible to reveal the irreducibility of labour and its primary character. There are, in fact, countries in the world, and, in a particular country, times, in which labour is dear: workers are few, wages are high; elsewhere, or at other times, manpower is plentiful, it is badly remunerated, and labour is cheap. But what is modified in these alternating states is the quantity of food that can be procured with a day's work; if commodities are in short supply and there are many consumers, each unit of labour will be remunerated with only a small quantity of subsistence; but if, on the other hand, commodities are in good supply, it will be well paid. These are merely the consequences of a market situation; the labour itself, the hours spent at it, the toil and trouble, are in every case the same; and the greater the number of units required, the more costly the products will be. 'Equal quantities of labour, at all times and places, may be said to be of equal value to the labourer'[5].

And yet one could say that this unit is not a fixed one, since to produce the self-same object will require more or less labour according to the perfection of the manufacturing process (that is, according to the degree of the division of labour). But it is not really the labour itself that has changed; it is the relation of the labour to the production of which it is capable. Labour, in the sense of a day's work, toil and trouble, is a fixed numerator: only the denominator (the number of objects produced) is capable of variations. A single worker who had to perform on his own the eighteen distinct operations required in the manufacture of a pin would certainly not produce more than twenty pins in the course of a whole day. But ten workers who each had to perform only one or two of those operations could produce between them more than forty-eight thousand pins in a day; thus each of those workers, producing a tenth part of the total product, can be considered as making four thousand eight hundred pins during his working day[6]. The productive power of labour has been multiplied; within a single unit (a wage-earner's day), the objects manufactured have been increased in number; their exchange value will therefore fall, that is, each of those objects will be able to buy only a proportionately smaller amount of work in turn. Labour has not diminished in relation to the things; it is the things that have, as it were, shrunk in relation to the unit of labour.

It is true that we exchange because we have needs; without them, trade would not exist, nor labour either, nor, above all, the division that renders it more productive. Inversely, it is needs, when they are satisfied, that limit labour and its improvement: 'As it is the power of exchange that gives occasion to the division of labour, so the extent of this division must always be limited to the extent of that power, or in other words, by the extent of the market'[7]. Needs, and the exchange of products that can answer to them, are still the principle of the economy: they are its prime motive and circumscribe it; labour and the division that organizes it are merely its effects. But within exchange, in the order of equivalences, the measure that establishes equalities and differences is of a different nature from need. It is not linked solely to individual desires, modified by them, or variable like them. It is an absolute measure, if one takes that to mean that it is not dependent upon men's hearts, or upon their appetites; it is imposed upon them from outside: it is their time and their toil. In relation to that of his predecessors, Adam Smith's analysis represents an essential hiatus: it distinguishes between the reason for exchange and the measurement of that which is exchangeable, between the nature of what is exchanged and the units that enable it to be broken down. People exchange because they have needs, and they exchange precisely the objects that they need; but the order of exchanges, their hierarchy and the differences expressed in that hierarchy, are established by the units of labour that have been invested in the objects in question. As men experience things – at the level of what will soon be called psychology – what they are exchanging is what is 'indispensable, commodious or pleasurable' to them, but for the economist, what is actually circulating in the form of things is labour – not objects of need representing one another, but time and toil, transformed, concealed, forgotten.

This hiatus is of great importance. It is true that Adam Smith is still, like his predecessors, analysing the field of positivity that the eighteenth century termed 'wealth'; and by that term he too means objects of need – and thus the objects of a certain form of representation – representing themselves in the movements and methods of exchange. But within this duplication, and in order to regulate its laws – the units and measures of exchange – he formulates a principle of order that is irreducible to the analysis of representation: he unearths labour, that is, toil and time, the working-day that at once patterns and uses up man's life. The equivalence of the objects of desire is no longer established by the intermediary of other objects and other desires, but by a transition to that which is radically heterogeneous to them; if there is an order regulating the forms of wealth, if this can buy that, if gold is worth twice as much as silver, it is not because men have comparable desires; it is not because they experience the same hunger in their bodies, or because their hearts are all swayed by the same passions; it is because they are all subject to time, to toil, to weariness, and, in the last resort, to death itself. Men exchange because they experience needs and desires; but they are *able* to exchange and to *order* these exchanges because they are subjected to time and to the great exterior necessity. As for the fecundity of labour, it is not so much due to personal ability or to calculations of self-interest; it is based upon conditions that are also exterior to its representation: industrial progress, growing division of tasks, accumulation of capital, division of productive labour and non-productive labour. It is thus apparent how, with Adam Smith, reflection upon wealth begins to overflow the space assigned to it in the Classical age; then, it was lodged within 'ideology' – inside the analysis of representation; from now on, it is referred, diagonally as it were, to two domains which both escape the forms and laws of the decomposition of ideas: on the one hand, it is already pointing in the direction of an anthropology that will call into question man's very essence (his finitude, his relation with time, the imminence of death) and the object in which he invests his days of time and toil without being able to recognize in it the object of his immediate need; on the other, it indicates the still unfulfilled possibility of a political economy whose object would no longer be the exchange of wealth (and the interplay of representations which is its basis), but its real production: forms of labour and capital. It is understandable how, between these newly formed positivities – an anthropology dealing with a man rendered alien to himself and an economics dealing with mechanisms exterior to human consciousness – Ideology, or the Analysis of representations, was soon to find itself reduced to being no more than a psychology, whereas opposite, in opposition, and soon to dominate ideology from its full height, there was to emerge the dimension of a possible history. From Smith onward, the time of economics was no longer to be the cyclical time of alternating impoverishment and wealth; nor the linear increase achieved by astute policies, constantly introducing slight increases in the amount of circulating specie so that they accelerated production at a faster rate than they raised prices; it was to be the interior time of an organic structure which grows in accordance with its own necessity and develops in accordance with autochthonous laws – the time of capital and production.

III THE ORGANIC STRUCTURE OF BEINGS

In the domain of natural history, the modifications observable between the years 1775 and 1795 are of the same type. The principle of classifications is not called in question: their aim is still to determine the 'character' that groups individuals and species into more general units, that distinguishes those units one from another, and that enables them to fit together to form a table in which all individuals and all groups, known or unknown, will have their appropriate place. These characters are drawn from the total representation of the individuals concerned; they are the analysis of that representation and make it possible, by representing those representations, to constitute an order; the general principles of *taxinomia* – the same principles that had determined the systems of Tournefort and Linnaeus and the method of Adanson – preserve the same kind of validity for A-L. de Jussieu, Vicq d'Azyr, Lamarck, and Candolle. Yet the technique that makes it possible to establish the character, the relation between visible structure and criteria of identity, are modified in just the same way as Adam Smith modified the relations of need or price. Throughout the eighteenth century, classifiers had been establishing character by comparing visible structures, that is, by correlating elements that were homogeneous (since each element, according to the ordering principle selected, could be used to represent all the others): the only difference lay in the fact that for the systematicians the representative elements were fixed from the outset, whereas for the methodists they were the gradual result of a progressive confrontation. But, the transition from described structure to classifying character took place wholly at the level of the representative functions exercised by the visible with regard to itself. From Jussieu, Lamarck, and Vicq d'Azyr onward, character, or rather the transformation of structure into character, was to be based upon a principle alien to the domain of the visible – an internal principle not reducible to the reciprocal interaction of representations. This principle (which corresponds to labour in the economic sphere) is *organic structure*. And as a basis for taxonomies, organic structure appears in four different ways.

1. First, in the form of a hierarchy of characters. If one does not, in fact, arrange the species side by side in all their vast diversity, but, in order to limit the field of investigation forthwith, if one accepts the broad groupings evident at a first glance – such as the Gramineae, the Compositae, the Cruciferae, and the Leguminosae for plants; or worms, fishes, birds, and quadrupeds, for animals – it becomes apparent that certain characters are absolutely constant and occur in all the genera and all the species it is possible to distinguish: for example, the insertion of the stamens, their position in relation to the pistil, the insertion of the corolla when it bears the stamens, the number of lobes surrounding the embryo in the seed. Other characters are very frequent throughout a family, but do not attain the same degree of constancy; this is because they are formed by less essential organs (number of petals, presence or absence of the corolla, respective position of the calyx or the pistil); these are the 'secondary sub-uniform' characters. Finally, the 'tertiary semi-uniform' characters are sometimes constant and sometimes variable (unifoliate or polyfoliate calyx, number of cells in the fruit, position of flowers and leaves, nature of the stem): with these semi-uniform characters it is not possible to define families or orders – not because they are not capable, if applied to all the species, of forming general entities, but because they do not concern what is essential in a group of living beings. Each great natural family has requisites that define it, and the characters that make it recognizable are the nearest to these fundamental conditions: thus, reproduction being the major function of the plant, the embryo will be its most important part, and it becomes possible to divide the vegetable kingdom into three classes: acotyledons, monocotyledons, and dicotyledons. Against the background of these essential and 'primary' characters, the others can appear and introduce more detailed distinctions. It will be seen that character is no longer drawn directly from the visible structure, and without any criterion other than its presence or absence; it is based upon the existence

of functions essential to the living being, and upon relations of importance that are no longer merely a matter of description.

2. Characters are linked, therefore, to functions. In one sense, there has been a return to the old theory of signatures or marks, which supposed that each being bore the sign of what was most essential in it upon the most visible point of its surface. But here the relations of importance are relations of functional subordination. If the number of cotyledons is decisive in the classification of plants, that is because they play a particular role in the reproductive function, and because they are for that very reason linked to the plant's entire internal organic structure; they indicate a function that governs the individual's entire arrangement[8]. In the same way, Vicq d'Azyr showed that in the case of animals it is the alimentary functions that are without doubt the most important; it is for this reason that 'there exist constant relations between the structure of the carnivores' teeth and that of their muscles, toes, claws, tongues, stomachs, and intestines'[9]. Character is not, then, established by a relation of the visible to itself; it is nothing in itself but the visible point of a complex and hierarchized organic structure in which function plays an essential governing and determining role. It is not because a character occurs frequently in the structures observed that it is important; it is because it is functionally important that it is often encountered. As Cuvier was to point out, summing up the work of the century's last great methodists, the higher we move towards the more generalized classes,

> the more the properties that remain common are constant; and as the most constant relations are those that pertain to the most important parts, so the characters of the higher divisions will be found to be drawn from the most important parts . . . It is in this way that the method will be natural, since it takes into account the importance of the organs[10].

3. Given these conditions, it is understandable how the notion of life could become indispensable to the ordering of natural beings. It became so for two reasons: first, it was essential to be able to apprehend in the depths of the body the relations that link superficial organs to those whose existence and hidden forms perform the essential functions; thus Storr proposes classifying mammals according to the formation of their hoofs; the reason being that this is linked to methods of locomotion and to the animal's possibilities of movement; now, these methods of locomotion can be correlated in turn with the form of alimentation and the different

organs of the digestive system[11]. Furthermore, the most important characters may also be the most hidden; it had already proved possible to observe in the vegetable kingdom that it is not flowers and fruits – the most easily visible parts of the plant – that are the significant elements, but the embryonic organization and such organs as the cotyledon. This phenomenon is even more frequent in animals. Storr thought that the broader classifications ought to be defined according to the forms of circulation; and Lamarck, though he himself did not practise dissection, rejects any principle of classification for the lower animals based solely upon visible form:

> Consideration of the articulations of the bodies and limbs of the crustaceans has led all naturalists to regard them as true insects, and I myself long followed the general opinion in this regard. But since it is recognized that organic structure is of all considerations the most essential as a guide in a methodical and natural distribution of animals, as well as in determining the true relations between them, it follows that the crustaceans, which breathe solely by means of gills in the same way as molluscs, and like them have a muscular heart, ought to be placed immediately after them, before the arachnids and the insects, which do not have a like organic structure[12].

To classify, therefore, will no longer mean to refer the visible back to itself, while allotting one of its elements the task of representing the others; it will mean, in a movement that makes analysis pivot on its axis, to relate the visible to the invisible, to its deeper cause, as it were, then to rise upwards once more from that hidden architecture towards the more obvious signs displayed on the surfaces of bodies. As Pinel said, in his work as a naturalist, 'to restrict oneself to the exterior characters assigned by nomenclatures, is this not to ignore the most fertile source of information, and to refuse to open, as it were, the great book of nature which is precisely what one has set out to know?'[13] Henceforth, character resumes its former role as a visible sign directing us towards a buried depth; but what it indicates is not a secret text, a muffled word, or a resemblance too precious to be revealed; it is the coherent totality of an organic structure that weaves back into the unique fabric of its sovereignty both the visible and the invisible.

4. The parallelism between classification and nomenclature is thus, by this very fact, dissolved. As long as classification consisted of a pattern of progressively smaller areas fitted into a visible space, it was quite conceivable that the delimitation and denomination of the resultant groups

could be accomplished simultaneously. The problem of the name and the problem of the genus were isomorphic. But now that character can classify only by means of prior reference to the organic structure of individuals, 'distinction' can no longer be achieved in accordance with the same criteria, or by means of the same operations, as 'denomination'. In order to discover the fundamental groups into which natural beings can be divided, it has become necessary to explore in depth the space that lies between their superficial organs and their most concealed ones, and between these latter and the broad functions that they perform. Any good nomenclature, on the other hand, will continue to be deployed in the horizontal dimension of the table: starting from the visible characters of the individual, one must find one's way to that precise square in which is to be found the name of its genus and its species. There is a fundamental distortion between the space of organic structure and that of nomenclature: or rather, instead of being exactly superimposed, they are now perpendicular to one another; and at the point where they meet we find the manifest character, which indicates a function in the vertical plane and makes it possible to discover a name in the horizontal one. This distinction, which within a few years will render natural history and the pre-eminence of *taxinomia* obsolescent, we owe to the genius of Lamarck: in the Preliminary Discourse to *La Flore française* he set out the two tasks of botany as two radically distinct entities: 'determination', which applies the rules of analysis and makes it possible to discover the name of an individual by the simple use of a binary method (either such and such a character is present in the individual being examined, in which case one must look for its location in the right-hand part of the table; or it is not present, in which case one must look in the left-hand part; and so on until the name has finally been determined); and the discovery of the real relations of resemblance, which presupposes an examination of the entire organic structure of species[14]. Names and genera, designation and classification, language and nature, cease to be automatically interlocked. The order of words and the order of beings no longer intersect except along an arti-ficially defined line. Their old affinity, which had been the foundation of natural history in the Classical age, and which had led structure to char-acter, representation to denomination, and the visible individual to the abstract genus, all with one and the same movement, is beginning to dissolve. There is talk of things that take *place* in another space than that of words. By making such a distinction, and by making it so early on, Lamarck brought the era of natural history to a close and provided a much clearer, a much more certain and radical glimpse of the era of biology than he did twenty years later by taking up once more the already well-known theme of the single series of species and their progressive transformation.

The concept of organic structure already existed in eighteenth-century natural history – just as, in the sphere of the analysis of wealth, the notion of labour was not invented at the end of the Classical age; but it was a concept that served at that time to define a certain mode of composition of complex individuals, on the basis of more elementary materials; Linnaeus, for example, distinguished between 'juxtaposition', which causes growth in minerals, and 'intussusception', which enables the vegetable kingdom to develop by feeding itself[15]. Bonnet contrasted the 'aggregation' of 'unrefined solids' with the 'composition of organic solids', which 'weaves together an almost infinite number of parts, some fluid, others solid'[16]. Now, this concept of organic structure had never been used before the end of the century as a foundation for ordering nature, as a means of defining its space or delimiting its forms. It is through the works of Jussieu, Vicq d'Azyr, and Lamarck that it begins to function for the first time as a method of characterization: it subordinates characters one to another; it links them to functions; it arranges them in accordance with an architecture that is internal as well as external, and no less invisible than visible; it distributes them throughout a space that is other than that of names, discourse, and language. It is thus no longer content to designate one category of beings among other categories; it no longer merely indicates a dividing-line running through the taxonomic space; it defines for certain beings the internal law that enables a particular one of their structures to take on the value of a character. Organic structure intervenes between the articulating structures and the designating characters – creating between them a profound, interior, and essential space.

This important mutation further exerts its influence upon the element of natural history; it modifies the methods and the techniques of a *taxinomia*; but it does not refute its fundamental conditions of possibility; it has not yet touched the mode of being of a natural order. It does, however, entail one major consequence: the radicalization of the dividing-line between organic and inorganic. In the table of beings unfolded by natural history, the terms organized and non-organized defined merely two categories; these two categories overlapped, but did not necessarily coincide with, the antithesis of living and non-living. From the moment when organic structure becomes a basic concept of natural characterization, and makes possible the transition from visible structure to designation, it must of course cease to be no more than a character itself; it surrounds the taxonomic space in which it lay before, and in turn provides the ground for a possible classification. This being so, the opposition between organic and inorganic becomes fundamental. It is, in fact, from the period 1775–95 onward that the old articulation of the three or four kingdoms disappears; the opposition of the two kingdoms – organic and inorganic – does not replace that articulation exactly; but rather, by imposing another division, at another level and in another space, it makes the old articulation impossible. Pallas and Lamarck[17] formulate this great dichotomy – a dichotomy with which the opposition of the living and the non-living coincides. 'There are only two kingdoms in nature,' wrote Vicq d'Azyr in 1786, 'one enjoys life and the other is deprived of it'[18]. The organic becomes the living and the living is that which produces, grows, and reproduces; the inorganic is the non-living, that which neither develops nor reproduces; it lies at the frontiers of life, the inert, the unfruitful – death. And although it is intermingled with life, it is so as that element within it that destroys and kills it. 'There exist in all living beings two powerful forces, which are very distinct and always in opposition to each other, so much so that each perpetually destroys the effects that the other succeeds in producing'[19]. It can be seen how, by fragmenting in depth the great table of natural history, something resembling a biology was to become possible; and also how, in the analyses of Bichat, the fundamental opposition of life and death was able to emerge. What was to take place was not the more or less precarious triumph of a vitalism over a mechanism; vitalism and its attempt to define the specificity of life are merely the surface effects of those archaeological events.

IV WORD INFLECTION

The exact counterpart of these events is to be found in the area of language analysis. Though it is true that they take a more discreet form and obey a slower chronology than in the field of natural history. There is an easily discoverable reason for this; it is that, throughout the Classical age, language was posited and reflected upon as discourse, that is, as the spontaneous analysis of representation. Of all the forms of non-quantitative order it was the most immediate, the least deliberate, the most profoundly linked to the movement of representation itself. And to that extent it was more firmly rooted in representation and in the mode of being of representation than were the more intellectual orders – disinterested or interested – based upon the classification of beings or the exchange of wealth. Technical modifications such as those that affected the measurement of exchange values, or the methods of arriving at 'characters', were sufficient to change considerably the analysis of wealth or natural history. In order that the science of language could undergo mutations as important as these, even profounder events were necessary, events capable of changing the very being of representations in Western culture. Just as, in the seventeenth and eighteenth centuries, the theory of the name had its place as near as possible to representation and thus governed, to a certain degree, the analysis of structures and character in living beings, and that of price and value in the sphere of wealth, so in the same way, at the end of the Classical age, it was this theory that subsisted longest, breaking up only late in the day, at the moment when representation itself was modified at the deepest level of its archaeological organization.

Until the beginning of the nineteenth century, analyses of language show little change. Words are still investigated on the basis of their representative values, as virtual elements of discourse which prescribes one and the same mode of being for them all. And yet, these representative contents are no longer analysed only in the dimension that brings representation near to an absolute origin, whether mythical or not. In *general grammar*, in its purest form, all the words of a language were bearers of a more or less hidden, more or less derived, signification whose original *raison d'être* lay in an initial designation. Every language, however complex, was situated in the opening that had been created, once and for all, by archaic cries. Lateral resemblances with other languages – similar sounds applied to analogous significations – were noted and listed only in order to confirm the vertical relation of each to these deeply buried, silted over, almost mute values. In the last quarter of the eighteenth century, the horizontal comparison of languages acquires another function: it no longer makes it possible to know what each language may still preserve of its ancestral memory, what marks from before Babel have been preserved in the sounds of its words; but it should make it possible to measure the extent to which languages resemble one another, the density of their similitudes, the limits within which they are transparent to one another. Hence those great confrontations between various languages that we see appearing at the end of the century – in some cases brought about by the pressure of political motives, as with the attempts made in Russia[20] to establish an abstract of all the languages of the Empire; in

1787 there appeared in Petersburg the first volume of the *Glossarium comparativum totius orbis*; it had to include references to 279 languages: 171 in Asia, 55 in Europe, 30 in Africa, 23 in America[21]. The comparisons are still made exclusively on the basis of and in terms of representative contents: a single kernel of signification – which is used as an invariable – is related to the words by means of which the various languages are able to designate it (Adelung[22] gives 500 different versions of *Pater* in different languages and dialects); or one root is selected as a constant element running through a variety of slightly differing forms, and the full array of meanings that it can take on is progressively determined (these are the first attempts at Lexicography, such as that of Buthet de La Sarthe). All these analyses always refer back to two principles, which were already those of *general grammar*: that of an original and common language which supposedly provided the initial batch of roots; and that of a series of historical events, foreign to language, which, from outside, bend it, wear it away, refine it, make it more flexible, by multiplying or combining its forms (invasions, migrations, advances in learning, political freedom or slavery, etc.).

Now, the confrontation of languages at the end of the eighteenth century brings to light a form intermediary between the articulation of contents and the value of roots: namely, inflection. It is true that grammarians had long been familiar with inflectional phenomena (just as, in natural history, the concept of organic structure was familiar before Pallas or Lamarck; and, in economics, the concept of labour was known before Adam Smith); but inflections had been analysed only for their representative value – whether they were considered as accessory representations, or were seen as a way of linking representations together (rather like another kind of word order). But when one compares, as Coeurdoux[23] and William Jones[24] did, the different forms of the verb *to be* in Sanskrit and Latin or Greek, one discovers a relation of constancy the reverse of the one usually admitted: it is the root that is modified, and the inflections that are analogous. The Sanskrit series *asmi, asi, asti, smas, stha, santi* corresponds exactly, but by inflectional analogy, with the Latin series *sum, es, est, sumus, estis, sunt*. It is true that Coeurdoux and Anquetil-Duperron remained at the level of analysis as practised in *general grammar*, when the former saw this parallelism as evidence of the remains of an original common language, and the latter saw it as the result of the historic mixture that may have occurred between Hindus and Mediterranean peoples at the time of the Bactrian kingdom. But what was at stake in this comparison of conjugations was no longer the link between original syllable and primary meaning; it was already a more complex relation between the modifications of the radical and the functions of grammar; it was being discovered that in two different languages there was a constant relation between a determinate series of formal modifications and an equally determinate series of grammatical functions, syntactical values, or modifications of meaning.

For this very reason, *general grammar* begins to change its configuration: its various theoretical segments are no longer linked together in exactly the same way; and the network that joins them already suggests a slightly different route. At the time of Bauzée or Condillac, the relation between roots, with their great lability of form, and the meaning patterned out of representations, or again, the link between the power to designate and the power to articulate, was assured by the sovereignty of the Name. Now a new element intervenes: on the one hand, on the side of meaning or representation, it indicates only an accessory and necessarily secondary value (it is a question of the role played by the individual or thing designated as either subject or complement; it is a question of the time of the action); but on the other hand, on the side of form, it constitutes the solid, constant, almost unalterable totality whose sovereign law is so far imposed upon the representative roots as to modify even those roots themselves. Moreover, this element, secondary in its significative value, primary in its formal consistence, is not itself an isolated syllable, like a sort of constant root; it is a system of modifications of which the various segments are interdependent: the letter *s* does not signify the second person in the way that the letter *e*, according to Court de Gébelin, signified breathing, life, and existence; it is the totality of the modifications *m*, *s*, *t* that gives the verbal root the values of the first, second, and third person.

Until the end of the eighteenth century, this new analysis has its place in the search for the representative values of language. It is still a question of discourse. But already, through the inflectional system, the dimension of the purely grammatical is appearing: language no longer consists only of representations and of sounds that in turn represent the representations and are ordered among them as the links of thought require; it consists also of formal elements, grouped into a system, which impose upon the sounds, syllables, and roots an organization that is not that of representation. Thus an element has been introduced into the analysis of language that is not reducible to it (as labour was introduced into the analysis of exchange, or organic structure into that of characters). As a primary consequence of this, one may note the appearance at the end of the eighteenth century of a phonetics that is no longer an investigation of primary expressive values, but an analysis of sounds, of their relations, and of their possible transformation one into another; in 1781, we find Helwag defining the vocalic triangle[25]. One can note also the beginnings of a comparative grammar: the object selected for comparison in the various languages is no longer the couple formed by a group of letters and a meaning, but groups of modifications of a grammatical nature (conjugations, declensions, suffixes, and prefixes). Languages are no longer contrasted in accordance with what their words designate, but in accordance with the means whereby those words are linked together; from now on they will communicate, not via the intermediary of that anonymous and general thought they exist to represent, but directly from one to the other, thanks to these delicate instruments, so fragile in appearance yet so constant and so irreducible, by which words are arranged in relation to each other. As Monboddo said:

> The art of a language is less arbitrary and more determined by rule than either the sound or sense of the words, it is one of the principal things by which the connection of languages with one another is to be discovered. And, therefore, when we find that two languages practise the three great arts of language, derivation, composition, and flexion, in the same way, we may conclude that the one language is the original of the other, or that they are both dialects of the same language[26].

As long as language was defined as discourse, it could have no other history than that of its representations: if ideas, things, knowledge, or feelings happened to change, then and only then did a given language undergo modification, and in exactly the same proportion as the changes in question. But from now on there is an interior 'mechanism' in languages which determines not only each one's individuality but also its resemblances to the others: it is this mechanism, the bearer of identity and difference, the sign of adjacency, the mark of kinship, that is now to become the basis for history. By its means, historicity will be able to introduce itself into the density of the spoken word itself.

V IDEOLOGY AND CRITICISM

There took place therefore, towards the last years of the eighteenth century, in *general grammar*, in *natural history*, and in the *analysis of wealth*, an event that is of the same type in all these spheres. The signs whose representations were affected, the analysis of identities and differences that it was possible to establish at that time, the continuous, yet articulated, table that was set up in the teeming profusion of similitudes, the clearly defined order among the empirical multiplicities, none of these can henceforth be based solely upon the duplication of representation in relation to itself. From this event onward, what gives value to the objects of desire is not solely the other objects that desire can represent to itself, but an element that cannot be reduced to that representation: *labour*; what makes it possible to characterize a natural being is no longer the elements that we can analyse in the representations we make for ourselves of it and other beings, it is a certain relation within this being, which we call its *organic structure*; what makes it possible to define a language is not the way in which it represents representations, but a certain internal architecture, a certain manner of modifying the words themselves in accordance with the grammatical position they take up in relation to one another; in other words, its *inflectional system*. In all these cases, the relation of representation to itself, and the relations of order it becomes possible to determine apart from all quantitative forms of measurement, now pass through conditions exterior to the actuality of the representation itself. In order to link the representation of a meaning with that of a word, it is necessary to refer to, and to have recourse to, the purely grammatical laws of a language which, apart from all power of representing representations, is subjected to the rigorous system of its phonetic modifications and its synthetic subordinations; in the Classical age, languages had a grammar because they had the power to represent; now they represent on the basis of that grammar, which is for them a sort of historical reverse side, an interior and necessary volume whose representative values are no more than the glittering, visible exterior. In order to link together, in a defined character, a partial structure and the visible totality of a living being, it is now necessary to refer to the purely biological laws, which, apart from all descriptive signs and as it were set back from them, organize the relations between functions and organs; living beings no longer define their resemblances, their affinities, and their families on the basis of their displayed descriptability; they possess characters which language can scan and define because they have a structure that is, in a way, the dark, concave, inner side of their visibility: it is on the clear and discursive surface of this secret but sovereign mass that characters emerge, a sort of storehouse exterior to the periphery of organisms now bound in upon themselves. Finally, when it is a matter of linking the representation of some object of need to all the others that can confront it in the act of exchange, it is necessary to have recourse to the form and quantity of a piece of work, which determine its value; what creates a hierarchy among things in the continuous circulation of the market is not other objects or other needs; it is the activity that has produced them and has silently lodged itself within them; it is the days and hours required for their manufacture, extraction, or transportation that constitute their proper weight, their marketable solidity, their internal law, and thus what one can call their real price; it is on the basis of this essential nucleus that exchanges can be accomplished and that market prices, after having fluctuated, can find their point of rest.

This somewhat enigmatic event, this event rising up from below which occurred towards the end of the eighteenth century in these three domains, subjecting them at one blow to one and the same break, can now be located within the unity that forms a foundation for its diverse forms. Quite obviously, it would be superficial to seek this unity in some progress made in rationality, or in the discovery of a new cultural theme. The complex phenomena of biology, of the history of languages, or of industrial production, were not, in the last years of the eighteenth century, introduced into forms of rational analysis to which until then they had remained entirely foreign; nor was there a sudden interest – provoked by the 'influence' of a budding 'romanticism' – in the complex forms of life, history, and society; there was no detachment, under the pressure of its problems, from a rationalism subjected to the model of mechanics, to the rules of analysis and the laws of understanding. Or rather, all this did in fact happen, but as a surface movement: a modification and shifting of cultural interests, a redistribution of opinions and judgements, the appearance of new forms in scientific discourse, wrinkles traced for the first time upon the enlightened face of knowledge. In a more fundamental fashion, and at the level where acquired knowledge is rooted in its positivity, the event concerns, not the objects aimed at, analysed, and explained in knowledge, not even the manner of knowing them or rationalizing them, but the relation of representation to that which is posited in it. What came into being with Adam Smith, with the first philologists, with Jussieu, Vicq d'Azyr, or Lamarck, is a minuscule but absolutely essential displacement, which toppled the whole of Western thought: representation has lost the power to provide a foundation – with its own being, its own deployment and its power of doubling over on itself – for the links that can join its various elements together. No composition, no decomposition, no analysis into identities and differences can now justify the connection of representations one to another; order, the table in which it is spatialized, the adjacencies it defines, the successions it authorizes as so many possible routes between the points on its surface – none of these is any longer in a position to link representations or the elements of a particular representation together. The condition of these links resides henceforth outside representation, beyond its immediate visibility, in a sort of behind-the-scenes world even deeper and more dense than representation itself. In order to find a way back to the point where the visible forms of beings are joined – the structure of living beings, the value of wealth, the syntax of words – we must direct our search towards that peak, that necessary but always inaccessible point, which drives down, beyond our gaze, towards the very heart of things. Withdrawn into their own essence, taking up their place at last within the force that animates them, within the organic structure that maintains them, within the genesis that has never ceased to produce them, things, in their fundamental truth, have now escaped from the space of the table; instead of being no more than the constancy that distributes their representations always in accordance with the same forms, they turn in upon themselves, posit their own volumes, and define for themselves an *internal* space which, to our representation, is on the *exterior*. It is from the starting-point of the architecture they conceal, of the cohesion that maintains its sovereign and secret sway over each one of their parts, it is from the depths of the force that brought them into being and that remains in them, as though motionless yet still quivering, that things – in fragments, outlines, pieces, shards – offer themselves, though very partially, to representation. And from their inaccessible store, representation can draw out, piece by piece, only tenuous elements whose unity, whose point of connection, always remains hidden in that beyond. The space of order, which served as a *common place* for representation and for things, for empirical visibility and for the essential rules, which united the regularities of nature and the resemblances of imagination in the grid of identities and differences, which displayed the empirical sequence of representations in a simultaneous table, and made it possible to scan step by step, in accordance with a logical sequence, the totality of nature's elements thus rendered contemporaneous with one another – this space of order is from now on shattered: there will be things, with their own organic structures, their hidden veins, the space that articulates them, the time that produces them; and then representation, a purely temporal succession, in which those things address themselves (always partially) to a subjectivity, a consciousness, a singular effort of cognition, to the 'psychological' individual who from the depth of his own history, or on the basis of the tradition handed on to him, is trying to know. Representation is in the process of losing its power to define the mode of being common to things and to knowledge. The very being of that which is represented is now going to fall outside representation itself.

Yet that proposition is imprudent. At any rate, it anticipates an arrangement of the field of knowledge that is not yet definitively established by the end of the eighteenth century. It must not be forgotten that, though Smith, Jussieu, and W. Jones made use of the notions of labour, organic structure, and grammatical system, their aim in doing so was not to break out of the tabular space laid out by Classical thought, or to find a way around the visibility of things and to escape from the play of representation representing itself; it was simply to establish within it a form of connection that would be at the same time analysable, constant, and well founded. It was still a matter of discovering the general order of identities and differences. The great detour, the great quest, beyond representation, for the very being of what is represented has not yet been made; only the place from which that quest will become possible has so far been established. But this place still figures among the interior arrangements of representations. And there is no doubt that there exists, corresponding to this ambiguous epistemological configuration, a philosophic duality which indicates its imminent dissolution.

The coexistence of Ideology and critical philosophy at the end of the eighteenth century – of Destutt de Tracy and Kant – divides, into two forms of thought, exterior to one another, yet simultaneous, what scientific forms of reflection, on the other hand, hold together in a unity doomed to imminent dissociation. In Destutt or Gerando, Ideology posits itself both as the only rational and scientific form that philosophy can assume and as the sole philosophic foundation that can be proposed for the sciences in general and for each particular sphere of knowledge. Being a science of ideas, Ideology should be a kind of knowledge of the same type as those that take as their object the beings of nature, the words of language, or the laws of society. But precisely in so far as its object is ideas, the manner in which they are expressed in words and linked together in reasoning, it has validity as the Grammar and the Logic of all possible science. Ideology does not question the foundation, the limits, or the root of representation; it scans the domain of representations in general; it determines the necessary sequences that appear there; it defines the links that provide its connections; it expresses the laws of composition and decomposition that may rule it. It situates all knowledge in the space of representations, and by scanning that space it formulates the knowledge of the laws that provide its organization. It is in a sense the knowledge of all knowledge. But this duplication upon which it is based does not cause it to emerge from the field of representation; the aim of that duplication is to superimpose all knowledge upon a representation from whose immediacy one never escapes:

> Have you ever understood at all precisely what thinking is, what you experience when you think, anything at all? . . . You say to yourself: *I think that*, when you have an opinion, when you form a judgement. In fact, to pass a judgement, true or false, is an act of thought; this act consists in feeling that there is a connection, a relation . . . *To think*, as you see, *is always to feel*, and is nothing other than to feel[27].

We should note, however, that, in defining the thought of a relation by the sensation of that relation, or, in briefer terms, thought in general by sensation, Destutt is indeed covering, without emerging from it, the whole domain of representation; but he reaches the frontier where sensation as the primary, completely simple form of representation, as the minimum content of what can be given to thought, topples over into the domain of the physiological conditions that can provide an awareness of it. That which, when read in one sense, appears as the most tenuous generality of thought, appears, when deciphered in another direction, as the complex result of a zoological singularity: 'We have only an incomplete know-ledge of an animal if we do not know its intellectual faculties. Ideology is a part of zoology, and it is above all in man that this part is important and merits delving into'[28]. Analysis of representation, at the moment when it attains its greatest degree of extension, brushes with its very outermost edge a domain that is more or less – or rather, that will be more or less, for it does not exist as yet – that of a natural science of man.

Different as they are in form, style, and aim, the Kantian question and the question of the 'Idéologues' have the same point of application: the relation of representations to each other. But Kant does not seek this relation – what gives it its foundation and justification – on the level of representation, even attenuated in its content so far as to be nothing more, on the confines of passivity and consciousness, than mere sensation; he questions it as to what renders it possible in general. Instead of basing the connection between representations on a foundation arrived at by a sort of internal hollowing-out process, which gradually whittles it away until there is nothing left but the pure impression, he establishes it on the conditions that define its universally valid form. By directing his inquiry in this direction, Kant avoids representation itself and what is given within it, in order to address himself to that on the basis of which all representation, whatever its form, may be posited. It is therefore not representations themselves that, in accordance with their own laws, could be deployed and, in one and the same movement, decomposed (by analysis) and recomposed (by synthesis): only judgements derived from experience or empirical observations can be based upon the contents of representation. Any other connection, if it is to be universal, must have its foundation beyond all experience, in the *a priori* that renders it possible. Not that it is a question of another world, but of the conditions in accordance with which any representation of the world in general can exist.

There is thus a definite correspondence between the Kantian critique and what in the same period was posited as the first almost complete form of ideological analysis. But Ideology, by extending its reflection over the whole field of knowledge – from primary impressions to political economy, by way of logic, arithmetic, the sciences of nature, and grammar – tried to resume in the form of representation precisely what was being formed and re-formed outside representation. This resumption could be accomplished only in the quasi-mythical form of a simultaneously singular and universal genesis: an isolated, empty, and abstract consciousness must, beginning with the most tenuous form of representation, build up little by little the great table of all that is representable. In this sense, Ideology is the last of the Classical philosophies – rather as *Juliette* is the last of the Classical narratives. Sade's scenes and reasoning recapture all the fresh violence of desire in the deployment of a representation that is transparent and without flaw; the analyses of Ideology recapture in their narrative of a birth all the forms of representation, even the most complex ones. Confronting Ideology, the Kantian critique, on the other hand, marks the threshold of our modernity; it questions representation, not in accordance with the endless movement that proceeds from the simple element to all its possible combinations, but on the basis of its rightful limits. Thus it sanctions for the first time that event in European culture which coincides with the end of the eighteenth century: the withdrawal of knowledge and thought outside the space of representation. That space is brought into question in its foundation, its origin, and its limits: and by this very fact, the unlimited field of representation, which Classical thought had established, which Ideology had attempted to scan in accordance with a step-by-step, discursive, scientific method, now appears as a metaphysics. But as a metaphysics that had never stepped outside itself, that had posited itself in an uninformed dogmatism, and that had never brought out into the light the question of its right. In this sense, Criticism brings out the metaphysical dimension that eighteenth-century philosophy had attempted to reduce solely by means of the analysis of representation. But it opens up at the same time the possibility of another metaphysics; one whose purpose will be to question, apart from representation, all that is the source and origin of representation; it makes possible those philosophies of Life, of the Will, and of the Word, that the nineteenth century is to deploy in the wake of criticism.

VI OBJECTIVE SYNTHESES

From this, there springs an almost infinite series of consequences – of unlimited consequences, at least, since our thought today still belongs to the same dynasty. In the first rank, we must undoubtedly place the simultaneous emergence of a transcendental theme and new empirical fields – or, if not new, at least distributed and founded in a new way. We have seen how, in the seventeenth century, the appearance of the mathesis as a general science of order not only played a founding role in the mathematical disciplines but was correlative in the formation of various purely empirical domains, such as general grammar, natural history, and the analysis of wealth; these latter were not constructed in accordance with a 'model' supposedly prescribed for them by the mathematicization or mechanization of nature; they were constituted and arranged against the background of a general possibility: that which made it possible to establish an ordered table of identities and differences between representations. It was the dissolution of this homogeneous field of orderable representations, in the last years of the eighteenth century, that brought about the correlative appearance of two new forms of thought. The first questions the conditions of a relation between representations from the point of view of what in general makes them possible: it thus uncovers a transcendental field in which the subject, which is never given to experience (since it is not empirical), but which is finite (since there is no intellectual intuition), determines in its relation to an object $= x$ all the formal conditions of experience in general; it is the analysis of the transcendental subject that isolates the foundation of a possible synthesis between representations. Opposite this opening to the transcendental, and symmetrical to it, another form of thought questions the conditions of a relation between representations from the point of view of the being itself that is represented: what is indicated, on the horizon of all actual representations, as the foundation of their unity, is found to be those never objectifiable objects, those never entirely representable representations, those simultaneously evident and invisible visibilities, those realities that are removed from reality to the degree to which they are the foundation of what is given to us and reaches us: the force of labour, the energy of life, the power of speech. It is on the basis of these forms, which prowl around the outer boundaries of our experience, that the value of things, the organic structure of living beings, the grammatical structure and historical affinities of languages, attain our representations and urge us on to the perhaps infinite task of knowing. In this case, the conditions of possibility of experience are being sought in the conditions of possibility of the object and its existence, whereas in transcendental reflection the conditions of possibility of the objects of experience are identified with the conditions of possibility of experience itself. The new positivity of the sciences of life, language, and economics is in correspondence with the founding of a transcendental philosophy.

Labour, life, and language appear as so many 'transcendentals' which make possible the objective knowledge of living beings, of the laws of production, and of the forms of language. In their being, they are outside knowledge, but by that very fact they are conditions of knowledge; they correspond to Kant's discovery of a transcendental field and yet they differ from it in two essential points: they are situated with the object, and, in a way, beyond it; like the Idea in the transcendental Dialectic, they totalize phenomena and express the *a priori* coherence of empirical multiplicities; but they provide them with a foundation in the form of a being whose enigmatic reality constitutes, prior to all knowledge, the order and the connection of what it has to know; moreover, they concern the domain of *a posteriori* truths and the principles of their synthesis – and not the *a priori* synthesis of all possible experience. The first difference (the fact that the transcendentals are situated with the object) explains the origin of those metaphysical doctrines that, despite their post-Kantian chronology, appear as 'pre-critical': they do, in fact, avoid any analysis of the conditions of knowledge as they may be revealed at the level of transcendental subjectivity; but these metaphysics develop on the basis of transcendental objectives (the Word of God, Will, Life) which are possible only in so far as the domain of representation has been previously limited; they therefore have the same archaeological subsoil as Criticism itself. The second difference (the fact that these transcendentals concern *a posteriori* syntheses) explains the appearance of a 'positivism': there is a whole layer of phenomena given to experience whose rationality and interconnection rest upon an objective foundation which it is not possible to bring to light; it is possible to know phenomena, but not substances; laws, but not essences; regularities, but not the beings that obey them. Thus, on the basis of criticism – or rather on the basis of this displacement of being in relation to representation, of which Kantian doctrine is the first philosophical statement – a fundamental correlation is established: on the one hand there are metaphysics of the object, or, more exactly, metaphysics of that never objectifiable depth from which objects rise up towards our superficial knowledge; and, on the other hand, there are philosophies that set themselves no other task than the observation of precisely that which is given to positive knowledge. It will be seen how the two terms of this opposition lend one another support and reinforce one another; it is in the treasury of positive branches of knowledge (and above all of those that biology, economics, or philology are able to release) that the metaphysics of the 'depths' or of the objective 'transcendentals' will find their point of attack; and, inversely, it is in the division between the unknowable depths and the rationality of the knowable that the positivisms will find their justification. The criticism-positivism-metaphysics triangle of the object was constitutive of European thought from the beginning of the nineteenth century to Bergson.

Such a structure is linked, in its archaeological possibility, to the emergence of those empirical fields of which mere internal analysis of representation can now no longer provide an account. It is thus correlative with a certain number of arrangements proper to the modern *episteme*.

To begin with, a theme comes to light which until this point had remained unformulated, not to say non-existent. It may seem strange that no attempt was made during the Classical era to mathematicize the sciences of observation, or grammatical learning, or the economic experience. As though the Galilean mathematicization of nature and the founding of mechanics were enough on their own to accomplish the project of a mathesis. There is nothing paradoxical in this: the analysis of representations in accordance with their identities and differences, their ordering into permanent tables, automatically situated the sciences of the qualitative in the field of a universal mathesis. At the end of the eighteenth century, a new and fundamental division arises: now that the link between representations is no longer established in the very movement that decomposes them, the analytic disciplines are found to be epistemologically distinct from those that are bound to make use of synthesis. The result is that on the one hand we have a field of *a priori* sciences, pure formal sciences, deductive sciences based on logic and mathematics, and on the other hand we see the separate formation of a domain of *a posteriori* sciences, empirical sciences, which employ the deductive forms only in fragments and in strictly localized regions. Now, this division has as its consequence an epistemological concern to discover at some other level the unity that has been lost with the dissociation of the mathesis and the universal science of order. Hence a certain number of efforts that characterize modern reflection on the sciences: the classification of the domains of knowledge on the basis of mathematics, and the hierarchy established to provide a progression towards the more complex and the less exact; reflection on empirical methods of induction, and the effort made to provide them with both a philosophical foundation and a formal justification; the endeavour to purify, formalize, and possibly mathematicize the domains of economics, biology, and finally linguistics itself. In counterpoint to these attempts to reconstitute a unified epistemological field, we find at regular intervals the affirmation of an impossibility: this was thought to be due either to the irreducible specificity of life (which there is an attempt to isolate especially in the early nineteenth century) or to the particular character of the human sciences, which were supposedly resistant to all methodological reduction (the attempt to define and measure this resistance occurred mostly in the second half of the nineteenth century). In this double affirmation – alternating or simultaneous – of being able and not being able to formalize the empirical, perhaps we should recognize the ground-plan of that profound event which, towards the end of the eighteenth century, detached the possibility of synthesis from the space of representations. It is this event that places formalization, or mathematicization, at the very heart of any modern scientific project; it is this event, too, that explains why all hasty mathematicization or naïve formalization of the empirical seems like 'pre-critical' dogmatism and a return to the platitudes of Ideology.

We should also evoke a second characteristic of the modern *episteme*. During the Classical age, the constant, fundamental relation of knowledge, even empirical knowledge, to a universal mathesis justified the project

– constantly resumed in various forms – of a finally unified *corpus* of learning; this project assumed in turn, though without its foundation undergoing any modification, the aspect of a general science of movement, that of a universal characteristic, that of a language reflected upon and reconstituted in all its analytic values and all its syntactical possibilities, and, finally, that of an alphabetical or analytical Encyclopaedia of knowledge; it is of little importance that these endeavours did not reach fulfilment or that they did not entirely accomplish the purpose that had brought them into being: they all expressed, on the visible surface of events or texts, the profound unity that the Classical age had established by positing the analysis of identities and differences, and the universal possibility of tabulated order, as the archaeological basis of knowledge. So that Descartes, Leibniz, Diderot, and d'Alembert, even in what may be termed their failure, in their unfinished or deflected achievements, remained as close as possible to what constituted Classical thought. At the beginning of the nineteenth century, the unity of the mathesis was fractured. Doubly fractured: first, along the line dividing the pure forms of analysis from the laws of synthesis, second, along the line that separates, when it is a matter of establishing syntheses, transcendental subjectivity and the mode of being of objects. These two forms of fracture give rise to two series of endeavours which a certain striving towards universality would seem to categorize as echoes of the Cartesian or Leibnizian undertakings. But, if we look more closely, the unification of the field of knowledge does not and cannot have the same forms, the same claims, or the same foundations in the nineteenth century as in the Classical period. At the time of Descartes or Leibniz, the reciprocal transparency of knowledge and philosophy was total, to the point that the universalization of knowledge in a philosophical system of thought did not require a specific mode of reflection. From Kant onward, the problem is quite different; knowledge can no longer be deployed against the background of a unified and unifying mathesis. On the one hand, there arises the problem of the relations between the formal field and the transcendental field (and at this level all the empirical contents of knowledge are placed between parentheses and remain suspended from all validity); and, on the other hand, there arises the problem of the relations between the domain of empiricity and the transcendental foundation of knowledge (in which case the pure order of the formal is set apart as non-pertinent to any account of that region in which all experience, even that of the pure forms of thought, has its foundation). But in both these cases the philosophical thought concerned with universality is on a different level from that of the field of real knowledge; it is constituted either as pure reflection capable of *providing a foundation*, or as a resumption capable of *revealing*. The first of these forms of philosophy manifested itself initially in Fichte's undertaking to deduce genetically the totality of the transcendental domain from the pure, universal, and empty laws of thought; this opened up a field of inquiry in which an attempt is made either to reduce all transcendental reflection to the analysis of formalisms, or to discover, in transcendental subjectivity, a basis for the possibility of all formalism. The second philosophical path appeared first of all with Hegelian phenomenology, when the totality of the empirical domain was taken back into the interior of a consciousness revealing itself to itself as spirit, in other words, as an empirical and a transcendental field simultaneously.

It is thus apparent how the phenomenological task that Husserl was later to set himself is linked, in its profoundest possibilities and impossibilities, to the destiny of Western philosophy as it was established in the nineteenth century. It is trying, in effect, to anchor the rights and limitations of a formal logic in a reflection of the transcendental type, and also to link transcendental subjectivity to the implicit horizon of empirical contents, which it alone contains the possibility of constituting, maintaining, and opening up by means of infinite explicitations. But perhaps it does not escape the danger that, even before phenomenology, threatens every dialectical undertaking and causes it to topple over, willy-nilly, into an anthropology. It is probably impossible to give empirical contents transcendental value, or to displace them in the direction of a constituent subjectivity, without giving rise, at least silently, to an anthropology – that is, to a mode of thought in which the rightful limitations of acquired knowledge (and consequently of all empirical knowledge) are at the same time the concrete forms of existence, precisely as they are given in that same empirical knowledge.

The most distant consequences – and the most difficult ones for us to evade – of the fundamental event that occurred in the Western *episteme* towards the end of the eighteenth century may be summed up as follows: negatively, the domain of the pure forms of knowledge becomes isolated, attaining both autonomy and sovereignty in relation to all empirical knowledge, causing the endless birth and rebirth of a project to formalize the concrete and to constitute, in spite of everything, pure sciences; positively, the empirical domains become linked with reflections on subjectivity, the human being, and finitude, assuming the value and function of philosophy, as well as of the reduction of philosophy or counter-philosophy.

NOTES

[1] A. Smith, *The wealth of nations* (1776; University Library edition, p. 1)

[2] Ibid., p. 34.

[3] Cantillon, *Essai sur la nature du commerce en général*, pp. 17–18.

[4] Smith, op. cit., p. 34.

[5] Ibid., p. 37.

[6] Ibid., pp. 8–9.

[7] Ibid., p. 21

[8] A-L. de Jussieu, *Genera plantarum*, p. xviii.

[9] Vicq d'Azyr, *Système anatomique des quadrupèdes* (1792, Discours préliminaire, p. lxxxvii).

[10] G. Cuvier, *Tableau élémentaire de l'histoire naturelle* (Paris, year VI, pp. 20–1).

[11] Storr, *Prodromus methodi mammalium* (Tübingen, 1780, pp. 7–20).

[12] Lamarck, *Système des animaux sans vertèbres* (Paris, 1801, pp. 143–4).

[13] P. Pinel, *Nouvelle méthode de classification des quadrumanes* (*Actes de la Société d'histoire naturelle*, t. I, p. 52, quoted in Daudin, *Les Classes zoologiques*, p. 18).

[14] Lamarck, *La Flore française* (Paris, 1778; Discours préliminaire, pp. xc–cii).

[15] Linnaeus, *Système sexuel des végétaux*, p. 1.

[16] Bonnet, *Contemplation de la nature*, Ière partie (*Œuvres complètes*, t. IV, p. 40).

[17] Lamarck, *La Flore française*, pp. 1–2.

[18] Vicq d'Azyr, *Premiers discours anatomiques* (1786, pp. 17–18).

[19] Lamarck, *Mémoires de physique et d'histoire naturelle* (1797, p. 248).

[20] Bachmeister, *Idea et desideria de colligendis linguarum specimenibus* (Petersburg, 1773); Güldenstadt, *Voyage dans le Caucase*.

[21] The second edition, in four volumes, appeared in 1790–1.

[22] F. Adelung, *Mithridates* (4 vols., Berlin, 1806–17).

[23] R-P. Coeurdoux, *Mémoires de l'Académie des inscriptions*, t. XLIX, pp. 647–97.

[24] W. Jones, *Works* (13 vols., London, 1807).

[25] Helwag, *De formatione loquelae* (1781).

[26] James Burnett (Lord Monboddo), *Ancient metaphysics* (1779–99, vol. IV, p. 326).

[27] Destutt de Tracy, *Eléments d'Ideologie*, t. I, pp. 33–5.

[28] Ibid., préface, p. 1.

CHAPTER 8

Labour, Life, Language

I THE NEW EMPIRICITIES

We have now advanced a long way beyond the historical event we were concerned with situating – a long way beyond the chronological edges of the rift that divides in depth the *episteme* of the Western world, and isolates for us the beginning of a certain *modern* manner of knowing empiricities. This is because the thought that is contemporaneous with us, and with which, willy-nilly, we think, is still largely dominated by the impossibility, brought to light towards the end of the eighteenth century, of basing syntheses in the space of representation, and by the correlative obligation – simultaneous but immediately divided against itself – to open up the transcendental field of subjectivity, and to constitute inversely, beyond the object, what are for us the 'quasi-transcendentals' of Life, Labour, and Language. In order to bring about the emergence of this obligation and this impossibility in all the harshness of their historical irruption, it was necessary to let analysis run right through the thought that finds its source in such a chasm; it was necessary that verbal formulation should waste no time in traversing the destiny or slope of modern thought in order to reach at last the point where it could turn back: this clarity of our day, still pale but perhaps decisive, that enables us, if not to avoid entirely, at least to dominate by fragments, and to master to some extent what, from that thought formed on the threshold of the modern age, still reaches us, invests us, and serves as a continuous ground for our discourse. And yet the other half of the event – probably the more important, for it concerns in their very being, in their roots, the positivities by which our empirical forms of knowledge are sustained – has remained in suspense; and it is this other half that we must now analyse.

In a first phase – which extends chronologically from 1775 to 1795, and whose configuration we can indicate by means of the works of Smith,

Jussieu, and Wilkins – the concepts of labour, organism, and grammatical system had been introduced – or reintroduced with a particular status – into the analysis of representations and into the tabulated space in which that analysis had hitherto been deployed. No doubt their function was still only to provide authority for this analysis, to allow the establishment of identities and differences, and to provide the tool – a sort of qualitative yardstick – for the ordering of nature. But neither labour, nor the grammatical system, nor organic structure could be defined, or established, by the simple process whereby representation was decomposed, analysed, and recomposed, thus representing itself to itself in a pure duplication; the space of analysis could not fail, therefore, to lose its autonomy. Henceforth, the table, ceasing to be the ground of all possible orders, the matrix of all relations, the form in accordance with which all beings are distributed in their singular individuality, forms no more than a thin surface film for knowledge; the adjacencies it expresses, the elementary identities it circumscribes and whose repetition it shows, the resemblances it dissolves by displaying them, the constants it makes it possible to scan – these are nothing more than the effects of certain syntheses, or structures, or systems, which reside far beyond all the divisions that can be ordered on the basis of the visible. The visible order, with its permanent grid of distinctions, is now only a superficial glitter above an abyss.

The space of Western knowledge is now about to topple: the *taxinomia*, whose great, universal expanse extended in correlation with the possibility of a mathesis, and which constituted the down-beat of knowledge – at once its primary possibility and the end of its perfection – is now about to order itself in accordance with an obscure verticality: a verticality that is to define the law of resemblances, prescribe all adjacencies and discontinuities, provide the foundation for perceptible arrangements, and displace all the great horizontal deployments of the *taxinomia* towards the somewhat accessory region of consequences. Thus, European culture is inventing for itself a depth in which what matters is no longer identities, distinctive characters, permanent tables with all their possible paths and routes, but great hidden forces developed on the basis of their primitive and inaccessible nucleus, origin, causality, and history. From now on things will be represented only from the depths of this density withdrawn into itself, perhaps blurred and darkened by its obscurity, but bound tightly to themselves, assembled or divided, inescapably grouped by the vigour that is hidden down below, in those depths. Visible forms, their connections, the blank spaces that isolate them and surround their outlines – all these will now be presented to our gaze only in an already composed state, already articulated in that nether darkness that is fomenting them with time.

Then – and this is the second phase of the event – knowledge in its positivity changes its nature and its form. It would be false – and above all inadequate – to attribute this mutation to the discovery of hitherto unknown objects, such as the grammatical system of Sanskrit, or the relation between anatomical arrangements and organic functions in living beings, or the economic role of capital. And it would be no more accurate to imagine that general grammar became philology, natural history biology, and the analysis of wealth political economy, because all these modes of knowledge corrected their methods, came closer to their objects, rationalized their concepts, selected better models of formalization – in short, because they freed themselves from their prehistories through a sort of auto-analysis achieved by reason itself. What changed at the turn of the century, and underwent an irremediable modification, was knowledge itself as an anterior and indivisible mode of being between the knowing subject and the object of knowledge; if there were those who began to study the cost of production, and if the ideal and primitive barter situation was no longer employed as a means of analysing the creation of value, it is because, at the archaeological level, exchange had been replaced as a fundamental figure in the space of knowledge by production, bringing into view on the one hand new knowable objects (such as capital) and prescribing, on the other, new concepts and new methods (such as the analysis of forms of production). Similarly, if, after Cuvier, research was directed towards the internal organic structure of living beings, and if in order to make this possible the methods of comparative anatomy were used, it is because Life, as a fundamental form of knowledge, had also produced new objects (such as the relation of character to function) and new methods (such as the search for analogies). Finally, if Grimm and Bopp attempted to define the laws of vowel gradation or consonant mutation, it is because Discourse as a mode of knowledge had been replaced by Language, which defines objects not hitherto apparent (such as families of languages whose grammatical systems are analogous) and prescribes methods that had not previously been employed (analysis of the rules governing the modifications of consonants and vowels). Production, life, language – we must not seek to construe these as objects that imposed themselves from the outside, as though by their own weight and as a result of some autonomous pressure, upon a body of learning that had ignored them for too long; nor must we see them as concepts gradually built up, owing to new methods, through the progress of sciences advancing towards their own rationality. They are fundamental modes of knowledge which sustain in their flawless unity the secondary and derived correlation of new sciences and techniques with unprecedented objects. The constitution of these fundamental modes is doubtless buried deep down in the dense archaeological layers: one can, nevertheless, discern some signs of them in the works of Ricardo, in the case of economics, of Cuvier, in the case of biology, and of Bopp, in the case of philology.

II   RICARDO

In Adam Smith's analysis, labour owed its privileged position to the power it was recognized to possess to establish a constant measure between the values of things; it made it possible to achieve equivalence in the exchange of objects of need whose standardization would otherwise have been exposed to change, or subjected to an essential relativity. But it could assume such a role only at the price of one condition: it was necessary to suppose that the quantity of labour indispensable for the production of a thing was equal to the quantity of labour that the thing, in return, could buy in the process of exchange. Now, how could this identity be justified? On what could it be based, if not on a certain assimilation accepted as taking place in the more than illumined shadow lying between labour as productive activity and labour as a commodity that can be bought and sold? In the second sense, labour cannot be used as a constant measure, since it 'is subject to as many fluctuations as the commodities compared with it'[1]. In Adam Smith, this confusion originated in the precedence accorded to representation: all merchandise represented a certain labour, and all labour could represent a certain quantity of merchandise. Men's activity and the value of things were seen as communicating in the transparent element of representation. It is here that Ricardo's analysis finds its place and the reason for its decisive importance. It is not the first to give labour an important place in the economic process; but it explodes the unity of that notion, and singles out in a radical fashion, for the first time, the worker's energy, toil, and time that are bought and sold, and the activity that is at the origin of the value of things. On the one hand, then, we are left with the labour contributed by the workers, accepted or demanded by the entrepreneurs, and remunerated by wages;

on the other, we have the labour that extracts metals, produces commodities, manufactures objects, transports merchandise, and thus forms exchangeable values which did not exist before it and would never have arisen without it.

It is true that, for Ricardo as for Smith, labour can measure the equivalence of merchandise which takes part in the circulation of exchanges:

> In the early stages of society, the exchangeable value of these commodities, or the rule which determines how much of one should be given in exchange for another, depends almost exclusively on the comparative quantity of labour expended on each[2].

But the difference between Smith and Ricardo is this: for the first, labour, because it is analysable into days of subsistence, can be used as a unit common to all other merchandise (including even the commodities necessary to subsistence themselves); for the second, the quantity of labour makes it possible to determine the value of a thing, not only because the thing is representable in units of work, but first and foremost because labour as a producing activity is 'the source of all value'. Value can no longer be defined, as in the Classical age, on the basis of a total system of equivalences, and of the capacity that commodities have of representing one another. Value has ceased to be a sign, it has become a product. If things are worth as much as the labour devoted to them, or if their value is at least proportionate to that labour, it is not that labour is a fixed and constant value exchangeable as such in all places and all times, it is because any value, whatever it may be, has its origin in labour. And the best proof of this is that the value of things increases with the quantity of labour that must be devoted to them if we wish to produce them; but it does not change with the increase or decrease of the wages for which labour, like all other commodities, is exchanged[3]. As they circulate through the market, while they are being exchanged for one another, values still have a power of representation. But this power is drawn from elsewhere – from the labour that is more primitive and more radical than all representation, and that cannot, in consequence, be defined by exchange. Whereas in Classical thought trade and exchange serve as an indispensable basis for the analysis of wealth (and this is still true of Smith's analysis, in which the division of labour is governed by the criteria of barter), after Ricardo, the possibility of exchange is based upon labour; and henceforth the theory of production must always precede that of circulation.

Hence three consequences to be borne in mind. The first is the establishing of a causal series which is radically new in its form. The eighteenth century was not ignorant – far from it – of the play of economic determinations: it had provided explanations of how money could flow into a country or out of it, how prices rose or fell, how production grew, stagnated, or diminished; but all these movements were defined on the basis of a tabulated space in which all values were able to represent one another; prices increased when the representing elements increased faster than the elements represented; production diminished when the instruments of representation diminished in relation to the things to be represented, etc. It was always a question of a circular and surface causality, since it was never concerned with anything but the reciprocal powers of that which was analysing and that which was analysed. From Ricardo on, labour, having been displaced in its relation to representation, and installed in a region where representation has no power, is organized in accordance with a causality peculiar to itself. The quantity of labour necessary for the manufacture (or harvesting, or transporting) of a thing, and determining its value, depends upon the forms of production: production will be modified according to the degree of division of labour, the quantity and nature of the tools used, the mass of capital the entrepreneur has at his disposal, and the amount he has invested in the fitting out of his factory; in certain cases it will be costly; in others it will be less so[4]. But since this cost (wages, capital and income, profits) is in every case determined by labour already accomplished and applied to this new production, we see the emergence of a great linear, homogeneous series, which is that of production. All labour gives a result which, in one form or another, is applied to a further labour whose cost it defines; and this new labour participates in turn in the creation of a value, etc. This accumulation in series breaks for the first time with the reciprocal determinations that were the sole active factors in the Classical analysis of wealth. It introduces, by its very existence, the possibility of a continuous historical time, even if in fact, as we shall see, Ricardo conceives of the evolution ahead only as a slowing down and, at most, a total suspension of history. At the level of the conditions of possibility pertaining to thought, Ricardo, by dissociating the creation of value from its representativity, made possible the articulation of economics upon history. 'Wealth', instead of being distributed over a table and thereby constituting a system of equivalences, is organized and accumulated in a temporal sequence: all value is determined, not according to the instruments that permit its analysis, but

255

according to the conditions of production that have brought it into being; and, even prior to that, the conditions in question are determined by the quantities of labour applied in producing them. Even before economic reflection was linked to the history of events or societies in an explicit discourse, the mode of being of economics had been penetrated, and probably for a long while, by historicity. The mode of being of economics is no longer linked to a simultaneous space of differences and identities, but to the time of successive productions.

The second, no less decisive, consequence is concerned with the notion of scarcity. For Classical analysis, scarcity was defined in relation to need: it was accepted that scarcity became more pronounced, or was displaced, as needs increased or took on new forms; for those who are hungry, wheat is scarce; but for the rich who make up society, diamonds are scarce. The economists of the eighteenth century – whether Physiocrats or not – thought that land, or labour applied to the land, made it possible to overcome this scarcity, at least in part: this was because the land had the marvellous property of being able to account for far more needs than those of the men cultivating it. In Classical thought, scarcity comes about because men represent to themselves objects that they do not have; but there is wealth because the land produces, in some abundance, objects that are not immediately consumed and that can therefore represent others in the processes of exchange and the circulation of wealth. Ricardo inverts the terms of this analysis: the apparent generosity of the land is due, in fact, to its growing avarice; what is primary is not need and the representation of need in men's minds, it is merely a fundamental insufficiency.

In fact, labour – that is, economic activity – did not make its appearance in world history until men became too numerous to be able to subsist on the spontaneous fruits of the land. Some, lacking the means of subsistence, died, and many others would have died had they not begun to work the land. And as the population increased, new areas of forest had to be felled, cleared, and brought under cultivation. At every moment of its history, humanity is henceforth labouring under the threat of death: any population that cannot find new resources is doomed to extinction; and, inversely, to the degree that men multiply, so they undertake more numerous, more distant, more difficult, and less immediately fruitful labours. Since the prospect of death becomes proportionately more fearful as the necessary means of subsistence become more difficult of access, so, inversely, labour must grow in intensity and employ all possible means to make itself more prolific. What makes economics possible, and necessary, then, is a perpetual and fundamental situation of scarcity: confronted by a nature that in itself is inert and, save for one very small part, barren, man risks his life. It is no longer in the interplay of representation that economics finds its principle, but near that perilous region where life is in confrontation with death. And thus economics refers us to that order of somewhat ambiguous considerations which may be termed anthropological: it is related, in fact, to the biological properties of a human species, which, as Malthus showed in the same period as Ricardo, tends always to increase unless prevented by some remedy or constraint; it is related also to the situation of those living beings that run the risk of not finding in their natural environment enough to ensure their existence; lastly, it designates in labour, and in the very hardship of that labour, the only means of overcoming the fundamental insufficiency of nature and of triumphing for an instant over death. The positivity of economics is situated in that anthropological hollow. *Homo oeconomicus* is not the human being who represents his own needs to himself, and the objects capable of satisfying them; he is the human being who spends, wears out, and wastes his life in evading the imminence of death. He is a finite being: and just as, since Kant, the question of finitude has become more fundamental than the analysis of representations (the latter now being necessarily a derivation of the former), since Ricardo, economics has rested, in a more or less explicit fashion, upon an anthropology that attempts to assign concrete forms to finitude. Eighteenth-century economics stood in relation to a mathesis as to a general science of all possible orders; nineteenth-century economics will be referred to an anthropology as to a discourse on man's natural finitude. By this very fact, need and desire withdraw towards the subjective sphere – that sphere which, in the same period, is becoming an object of psychology. It is precisely here that in the second half of the nineteenth century the marginalists will seek the notion of utility. The belief will then arise that Condillac, or Graslin, or Fortbonnais, was 'already' a 'psychologist', since he analysed value in terms of need; similarly, it will be believed that the Physiocrats were the first ancestors of an economics which, from Ricardo onwards, analysed value in terms of production costs. What will have happened, in fact, is that the configuration that made Quesnay and Condillac simultaneously possible will have been left behind; the reign of the *episteme* that based knowledge upon the ordering of representations will have been broken; and a new epistemological arrangement will have replaced it, an arrangement that distinguishes, though not without referring them to one another, between a psychology of needs represented and an anthropology of natural finitude.

Finally, the last consequence concerns the evolution of economics. Ricardo shows that we should not interpret as a sign of nature's fruitfulness that which indicates, and in an ever more insistent manner, its essential avarice. The 'rent of land', which all economists, up to and including Adam Smith himself[5], saw as the sign of a fruitfulness proper to land, exists precisely in so far as agricultural labour becomes increasingly hard and less and less 'rentable'. As one is forced by the uninterrupted growth of the population to clear and cultivate less fertile tracts of land, so the harvesting of these new units of wheat requires more and more labour: either because the land must be ploughed more deeply, or because a greater surface must be sown, or because more fertilizer is needed; the cost of production is thus much higher for these later harvests than it was for the first ones, which were obtained originally from rich and fertile lands. Now, these commodities, though so difficult to produce, are no less indispensable than the others if one does not wish a certain portion of humanity to die of hunger. It is therefore the cost of production of wheat grown on the most barren of the available land that will determine the price of wheat in general, even though it may have been obtained with two or three times less labour. This leads to an increased profit for the easily cultivable lands, which will enable the owners of those lands to lease them out in return for considerable rents. Ground rent is the effect, not of a prolific nature, but of the avarice of the land. Now, this avarice becomes more perceptible every day: the population, in fact, increases; progressively poorer land is brought under cultivation; the costs of production increase; the prices of agricultural products increase, and ground rents with them. Under this pressure, it is very possible – indeed necessary – that the nominal wage of the labourers will also begin to rise, in order to cover the minimum costs of their subsistence; but, for the same reason, their real wage can never rise in practice above the sum that is indispensable to provide them with clothing, shelter, and food. And finally, the profit of the entrepreneurs will decrease in exactly the same proportion as ground rent increases, and as the labourers' remuneration remains fixed. It would continue to decrease indefinitely, until it disappeared altogether, were it not that there is a limit to the process: after a certain point, in fact, industrial profits will be so low that it will become impossible to provide work for new workers; for lack of additional wages, the labour force will no longer be able to grow, and the population will remain constant; it will no longer be necessary to clear and cultivate fresh tracts of land even more infertile than the previous ones; ground rent will reach a ceiling and will cease to exert its customary pressure upon industrial profits, which will then become stabilized. The tide of History will at last become slack. Man's *finitude* will have been *defined* – once and for all, that is, for an *indefinite* time.

Paradoxically, it is the historicity introduced into economics by Ricardo that makes it possible to conceive of this immobilization of History. Classical thought, of course, conceived of the economy as possessing an ever open, ever-changing future; but the type of modification in question was, in fact, spatial: the table that wealth was supposed to form as it was displayed, exchanged, and arranged in order, could very well be enlarged; in which case it remained the same table, with each element losing some of its relative surface, but entering into relations with new elements. On the other hand, it is the cumulative time of population and production, the uninterrupted history of scarcity, that makes it possible from the nineteenth century to conceive of the impoverishment of History, its progressive inertia, its petrification, and, ultimately, its stony immobility. We see what roles History and anthropology are playing in relation to one another. History exists (that is, labour, production, accumulation, and growth of real costs) only in so far as man as a natural being is finite: a finitude that is prolonged far beyond the original limits of the species and its immediate bodily needs, but that never ceases to accompany, at least in secret, the whole development of civilizations. The more man makes himself at home in the heart of the world, the further he advances in his possession of nature, the more strongly also does he feel the pressure of his finitude, and the closer he comes to his own death. History does not allow man to escape from his initial limitations – except in appearance, and if we take the word limitation in its superficial sense; but if we consider the fundamental finitude of man, we perceive that his anthropological situation never ceases its progressive dramatization of his History, never ceases to render it more perilous, and to bring it closer, as it were, to its own impossibility. The moment History reaches such boundaries, it can do nothing but stop, quiver for an instant upon its axis, and immobilize itself forever. But this can occur in two different ways: either it can move gradually, and with increasing slowness, towards a state of stability that justifies, in the indefiniteness of time, what it has always been advancing towards, what it has never really ceased to be from the start; or it may attain a point of reversal at which it becomes fixed only in so far as it suppresses what it had always and continuously been beforehand.

In the first solution (represented by Ricardo's 'pessimism'), History functions with regard to anthropological determinations as a sort of vast compensating mechanism; true, it is situated within human finitude, but its aspect is that of a positive form, appearing in relief; it enables man to overcome the scarcity to which he is doomed. As this scarcity becomes daily more constricting, so labour becomes more intense; production increases in absolute figures, but, at the same time, and driven by the same forces, the costs of production – that is, the quantities of labour necessary to produce the same object – also increase. So that there must inevitably come a time when labour is no longer supported by the commodity it produces (the latter costing no more than the food of the labourer producing it). Production can no longer make good the deficit. In which case scarcity will limit itself (by a process of demographic stabilization) and labour will adjust itself exactly to needs (by a determined distribution of wealth). From then on, finitude and production will be exactly superimposed to form a single figure. Any additional agricultural labour would be useless; any excess population would perish. Life and death will fit exactly one against the other, surface to surface, both immobilized and as it were reinforced by their reciprocal antagonism. History will have led man's finitude to that boundary-point at which it will appear at last in its pure form; it will have no more margin permitting it to escape from itself, it will have no more effort to make to provide a future for itself, and no new lands to open up for future men; subjected to the great erosion of History, man will gradually be stripped of everything that might hide him from his own eyes; he will have exhausted all the possible elements that tend to blur and disguise beneath the promises of time his anthropological nakedness; by long, but inevitable and tyrannical paths, History will have led man to the truth that brings him to a halt, face to face with himself.

In the second solution (represented by Marx), the relation of History to anthropological finitude is construed in the opposite direction. History, in this case, plays a negative role: it is History itself, in fact, that augments the pressures of need, that causes want to increase, obliging men constantly to work and to produce more and more, although they receive no more than what is indispensable to them to subsist, and sometimes a little less. So that, with time, the product of labour accumulates, while ceaselessly eluding those who accomplish that labour: these latter produce infinitely more than the share of value that returns to them in the form of wages, and thus provide capital with the possibility of buying further labour. In this way the number of those maintained by History at the limit of their conditions of existence ceaselessly grows; and because of this, those conditions become increasingly more precarious until they approach the point where existence itself will be impossible; the accumulation of capital, the growth of enterprises and of their capacities, the constant pressure on wages, the excess of production, all cause the labour market to shrink, lowering wages and increasing unemployment. Thrust back by poverty to the very brink of death, a whole class of men experience, nakedly, as it were, what need, hunger, and labour are. What others attribute to nature or to the spontaneous order of things, these men are able to recognize as the result of a history and the alienation of a finitude that does not have this form. For this reason they are able – they alone are able – to re-apprehend this truth of the human essence and so restore it. But this can be achieved only by the suppression, or at least the reversal, of History as it has developed up to the present: then alone will a time begin which will have neither the same form, nor the same laws, nor the same mode of passing.

But the alternatives offered by Ricardo's 'pessimism' and Marx's revolutionary promise are probably of little importance. Such a system of options represents nothing more than the two possible ways of examining the relations of anthropology and History as they are established by economics through the notions of scarcity and labour. For Ricardo, History fills the void produced by anthropological finitude and expressed in a perpetual scarcity, until the moment when a point of definitive stabilization is attained; according to the Marxist interpretation, History, by dispossessing man of his labour, causes the positive form of his finitude to spring into relief – his material truth is finally liberated. There is certainly no difficulty in understanding, on the level of opinion, how such real choices were distributed, and why some opted for the first type of analysis and others for the second. But these are merely derived differences which stem first and last from a doxological investigation and treatment. At the deepest level of Western knowledge, Marxism introduced no real discontinuity; it found its place without difficulty, as a full, quiet, comfortable and, goodness knows, satisfying form for a time (its own), within an epistemological arrangement that welcomed it gladly (since it was this arrangement that was in fact making room for it) and that it, in return, had no intention of disturbing and, above all, no power to modify, even one jot, since it rested entirely upon it. Marxism exists in nineteenth-century thought like a fish in water: that is, it is unable to breathe anywhere else. Though it is in opposition to the 'bourgeois' theories of economics, and though this opposition leads it to use the project of a radical reversal of History as a weapon against them, that conflict and that project nevertheless have as their condition of possibility, not the reworking of all History, but an event that any archaeology can situate with precision, and that prescribed simultaneously, and according to the same mode, both nineteenth-century bourgeois economics and nineteenth-century revolutionary economics. Their controversies may have stirred up a few waves and caused a few surface ripples; but they are no more than storms in a children's paddling pool.

What is essential is that at the beginning of the nineteenth century a new arrangement of knowledge was constituted, which accommodated simultaneously the historicity of economics (in relation to the forms of production), the finitude of human existence (in relation to scarcity and labour), and the fulfilment of an end to History – whether in the form of an indefinite deceleration or in that of a radical reversal. History, anthropology, and the suspension of development are all linked together in accordance with a figure that defines one of the major networks of nineteenth-century thought. We know, for example, the role that this arrangement played in reviving the weary good intentions of the humanisms; we know how it brought the utopias of ultimate development back to life. In Classical thought, the utopia functioned rather as a fantasy of origins: this was because the freshness of the world had to provide the ideal unfolding of a table in which everything would be present and in its proper place, with its adjacencies, its peculiar differences, and its immediate equivalences; in this primal light, representations could not yet have been separated from the living, sharp, perceptible presence of what they represent. In the nineteenth century, the utopia is concerned with the final decline of time rather than with its morning: this is because knowledge is no longer constituted in the form of a table but in that of a series, of sequential connection, and of development: when, with the promised evening, the shadow of the *dénouement* comes, the slow erosion or violent eruption of History will cause man's anthropological truth to spring forth in its stony immobility; calendar time will be able to continue; but it will be, as it were, void, for historicity will have been superimposed exactly upon the human essence. The flow of development, with all its resources of drama, oblivion, alienation, will be held within an anthropological finitude which finds in them, in turn, its own illuminated expression. *Finitude*, with its truth, is posited in *time*; and *time* is therefore *finite*. The great dream of an end to History is the utopia of causal systems of thought, just as the dream of the world's beginnings was the utopia of the classifying systems of thought.

This arrangement maintained its firm grip on thought for a long while; and Nietzsche, at the end of the nineteenth century, made it glow into brightness again for the last time by setting fire to it. He took the end of time and transformed it into the death of God and the odyssey of the last man; he took up anthropological finitude once again, but in order to use it as a basis for the prodigious leap of the superman; he took up once again the great continuous chain of History, but in order to bend it round into the infinity of the eternal return. It is in vain that the death of God, the imminence of the superman, and the promise and terror of the great year take up once more, as it were term by term, the elements that are arranged in nineteenth-century thought and form its archaeo-logical framework. The fact remains that they sent all these stable forms up in flames, that they used their charred remains to draw strange and perhaps impossible faces; and by a light that may be either – we do not yet know which – the reviving flame of the last great fire or an indication of the dawn, we see the emergence of what may perhaps be the space of contemporary thought. It was Nietzsche, in any case, who burned for us, even before we were born, the intermingled promises of the dialectic and anthropology.

III CUVIER

In his project for establishing a classification that would be as faithful as a method and as strict as a system, Jussieu had discovered the rule of the subordination of characters, just as Smith had used the constant value of labour to establish the natural price of things in the play of equivalences. And just as Ricardo freed labour from its role as a measure in order to introduce it, prior to all exchange, into the general forms of production, so Cuvier freed the subordination of characters from its taxonomic func-tion in order to introduce it, prior to any classification that might occur, into the various organic structural plans of living beings. The internal link by which structures are dependent upon one another is no longer situated solely at the level of frequency; it becomes the very foundation of all correlation. It is this displacement and this inversion that Geoffroy

Saint-Hilaire expressed when he said: 'Organic structure is becoming an abstract being . . . capable of assuming numerous forms'[6]. The space of living beings pivots around this notion, and everything that until then had been able to make itself visible through the grid of natural history (genera, species, individuals, structures, organs), everything that had been presented to view, now takes on a new mode of being.

First and foremost are those distinct groups of elements that the eye is able to articulate as it scans the bodies of individuals, and that are called *organs*. In Classical analysis, the organ was defined by both its structure and its function; it was like a double-entry system which could be read exhaustively either from the point of view of the role it played (reproduction, for example), or from that of its morphological variables (form, magnitude, arrangement, and number): the two modes of decipherment coincided exactly, but they were nevertheless independent of one another – the first expressing the *utilizable*, the second the *identifiable*. It is this arrangement that Cuvier overthrows: doing away with the postulates of both their coincidence and their independence, he gives function prominence over the organ – and to a large extent – and subjects the arrangement of the organ to the sovereignty of function. He rejects, if not the individuality of the organ, at least its independence: it is an error to believe that 'everything is important in an important organ'; our attention must be directed 'rather upon the functions themselves than upon the organs'[7]; before defining organs by their variables, we must relate them to the functions they perform. Now, these functions are relatively few in number: respiration, digestion, circulation, locomotion . . . So the visible diversity of structures no longer emerges from the background of a table of variables, but from the background of a few great functional units capable of being realized and of accomplishing their aims in various ways:

> What is common in all animals to each kind of organ considered reduces itself to very little indeed, and often organs resemble one another only in the effect they produce. This must have been especially striking as regards respiration, which operates in the different classes by means of organs so various that their structures offer no points in common[8].

When we consider the organ in relation to its function, we see, therefore, the emergence of 'resemblances' where there is no 'identical' element; a resemblance that is constituted by the transition of the function into evident invisibility. It matters little, after all, that gills and lungs may have a few variables of form, magnitude, or number in common: they resemble one another because they are two varieties of that non-existent, abstract, unreal, unassignable organ, absent from all describable species, yet present in the animal kingdom in its entirety, which serves for *respiration in general*. Thus there is a return in the analysis of living beings to Aristotelian analogies: the gills are to respiration in water what the lungs are to respiration in air. True, such relations were perfectly well known in the Classical age; but they were used only to determine functions; they were not used to establish the order of things within the space of nature. From Cuvier onward, function, defined according to its non-perceptible form as an effect to be attained, is to serve as a constant middle term and to make it possible to relate together totalities of elements without the slightest visible identity. What to Classical eyes were merely differences juxtaposed with identities must now be ordered and conceived on the basis of a functional homogeneity which is their hidden foundation. When the Same and the Other both belong to a single space, there is *natural history*; something like *biology* becomes possible when this unity of level begins to break up, and when differences stand out against the background of an identity that is deeper and, as it were, more serious than that unity.

This reference to function, and this uncoupling of the level of identities from that of differences, give rise to new relations: those of *coexistence*, of *internal hierarchy*, and of *dependence* with regard to the *level of organic structure*. *Coexistence* designates the fact that an organ or system of organs cannot be present in a living being unless another organ or another system of organs, of a particular nature and form, is also present:

> All the organs of one and the same animal form a single system of which all the parts hold together, act, and react upon each other; and there can be no modifications in any one of them that will not bring about analogous modifications in them all[9].

Within the digestive system, the form of the teeth (whether they are incisors or molars) varies with the 'length, convolutions, and dilations of the alimentary system'; or again, as an example of coexistence between different systems, the digestive organs cannot vary independently of the morphology of the limbs (and especially of the form of the nails); according to whether they will be provided with claws or hoofs – and therefore whether the animal will be able to grasp and tear up its food or not – so the alimentary canal, the 'dissolving juices', and the form of the teeth will also differ[10]. These are lateral correlations that establish relations of concomitance, based upon functional necessities, between elements on the same level: since it is *necessary* that the animal should feed itself, the nature of its prey and its mode of capture cannot remain irrelevant to the masticatory and digestive systems (and vice versa).

Nevertheless, there is a *hierarchy* of levels. We know how Classical analysis had been brought to the point of suspending the privileged position of the most important organs in order to concentrate attention on their taxonomic efficacity. Now that we are no longer dealing with independent variables, but with systems governed by one another, we are confronted once again with the problem of reciprocal importance. Thus the alimentary canal of mammals is not merely in a relation of possible covariation with the organs of locomotion and prehension; it is also determined, at least in part, by the mode of reproduction. Indeed, in its viviparous form, reproduction does not merely imply the presence of those organs immediately connected with it; it also requires the existence of organs of lactation, and the possession of lips and a fleshy tongue; on the other hand, it prescribes the existence of warm, circulating blood and the bilocularity of the heart[11]. The analysis of organisms, and the possibility of resemblances and distinctions between them, presupposes, therefore, a table, composed not of the elements, which may vary from species to species, but of the functions, which, in living beings in general, govern, complement, and order one another: not a polygon of possible modifications, but a hierarchical pyramid of importance. At first, Cuvier thought that the functions of existence preceded those of relationships ('for the animal *is* first, then it *feels* and *acts*'): he supposed, therefore, that reproduction and circulation must in the first place determine a certain number of organs to whose arrangement others would find themselves subject; the former organs would form the primary characters, and the latter the secondary ones[12]. Then he subordinated circulation to digestion, because the latter exists in all animals (the polyp's entire body is no more than a sort of digestive apparatus), whereas blood and blood vessels are found 'only in the higher animals and progressively disappear in those of the lower classes'[13]. Later still, it was the nervous system (together with the presence or absence of a spinal cord) that seemed to him the determining factor in all organic arrangements: 'It is really the whole animal: the other systems are there only to serve and maintain it'[14].

This pre-eminence of one function over the others implies that the organism, in its visible arrangements, obeys a *plan*. Such a plan ensures the control of the essential functions and brings under that control, though with a greater degree of freedom, the organs that perform less vital functions. As a hierarchical principle, this plan defines the most important functions, arranges the anatomical elements that enable it to operate, and places them in the appropriate parts of the body; thus, within the vast group of the Articulata, the class of Insects reveals the paramount importance of the locomotive functions and the organs of movement; in the other three classes, on the other hand, it is the vital functions that are most important[15]. In the regional control it exercises over the less fundamental organs, the plan of organic structure plays a less determining role; it becomes more liberal, as it were, as it moves further away from the centre, permitting of modifications, alterations, changes in the possible form or utilization. It is still there, but it has become more flexible, and more permeable to other forms of determination. This process is easily observed in the locomotive system of mammals. The four propulsive limbs belong to the plan of the organic structure, but only as a secondary character; they are therefore never eliminated, or absent or replaced, but they are 'masked sometimes as in the wings of the bat and the posterior fins of seals'; it may even happen that they are 'denatured by use as in the pectoral fins of the cetaceans . . . Nature has made a fin out of an arm. You perceive that there is always a sort of constancy in the secondary characters in accordance with their disguise'[16]. It is understandable, then, how the species can at the same time resemble one another (so as to form groups such as the genera, the classes, and what Cuvier calls the sub-kingdoms) and be distinct from one another. What draws them together is not a certain quantity of coincident elements; it is a sort of focus of identity which cannot be analysed into visible areas because it defines the reciprocal importance of the various functions; on the basis of this imperceptible centre of identities, the organs are arranged in the body, and the further they are from the centre, the more they gain in flexibility, in possibilities of variation, and in distinctive characters. Animal species differ at their peripheries, and resemble each other at their centres; they are connected by the inaccessible, and separated by the apparent. Their generality lies in that which is essential to their life; their singularity in that which is most accessory to it. The more extensive the groups one wishes to find, the deeper must one penetrate into the organism's inner darkness, towards the less and less visible, into that dimension that eludes perception; the more one wishes to isolate the individuality of the organism, the further must one go towards its surface, and allow the perceptible forms to shine in all their visibility; for multiplicity is apparent and unity is hidden. In short, living species 'escape' from the teeming profusion of individuals and species; they can be classified only because they are alive and on the basis of what they conceal.

It must now be apparent what an immense reversal all this presupposes in relation to the Classical *taxonomy*. This taxonomy was constructed entirely upon the basis of the four variables of description (forms, number, arrangement, magnitude), which could be scanned, as it were in one and the same movement, by language and by the eye; and in this deployment of the visible, life appeared as the effect of a patterning process – a mere classifying boundary. From Cuvier onward, it is life in its non-perceptible, purely functional aspect that provides the basis for the exterior possibility of a classification. The classification of living beings is no longer to be found in the great expanse of order; the possibility of classification now arises from the depths of life, from those elements most hidden from view. Before, the living being was a locality of natural classification; now, the fact of being classifiable is a property of the living being. So the project of a general *taxinomia* disappears; the possibility of deploying a great natural order which would extend continuously from the simplest and most inert of things to the most living and the most complex disappears; and the search for order as the ground and foundation of a general science of nature also disappears. 'Nature', too, disappears – it being understood that nature, throughout the Classical age, did not exist in the first place as a 'theme', as an 'idea', as an endless source of knowledge, but as a homogeneous space of orderable identities and differences.

This space has now been dissociated and as it were opened up in depth. Instead of a unitary field of visibility and order, whose elements have a distinctive value in relation to each other, we have a series of oppositions, of which the two terms are never on the same level: on the one hand, there are the secondary organs, which are visible on the surface of the body and offer themselves without intervention to immediate perception, and, on the other, the primary organs, which are essential, central, hidden, and unreachable except by dissection – that is, by materially removing the coloured envelope formed by the secondary organs. There is also, at an even deeper level, the opposition between the organs in general, which are spatial, solid, directly or indirectly visible, and the functions, which are not perceptible, but determine, as though from below, the arrangement of what we do perceive. Lastly, and at the furthest extreme, there is the opposition between identities and differences: they are no longer of the same fabric, they are no longer established in relation to each other on a homogeneous surface: the differences proliferate on the surface, but deeper down they fade, merge, and mingle, as they approach the great, mysterious, invisible focal unity, from which the multiple seems to derive, as though by ceaseless dispersion. Life is no longer that which can be distinguished in a more or less certain fashion from the mechanical; it is that in which all the possible distinctions between living beings have their basis. It is this transition from the taxonomic to the synthetic notion of life which is indicated, in the chronology of ideas and sciences, by the recrudescence, in the early nineteenth century, of vitalist themes. From the archaeological point of view, what is being established at this particular moment is the conditions of possibility of a *biology*.

In any case, this series of oppositions, dissociating the space of natural history, has had important consequences. In practice, this means the appearance of two correlated techniques which are connected and support each other. The first of these techniques is constituted by comparative anatomy: this discipline gives rise to an interior space, bounded on the one hand by the superficial stratum of teguments and shells, and on the other by the quasi-invisibility of that which is infinitely small. For comparative anatomy is not merely a deepening of the descriptive techniques employed in the Classical age; it is not content with seeking to look underneath, more precisely and more closely; it establishes a space which is neither that of visible characters nor that of microscopic elements[17]. Within that space it reveals the reciprocal arrangement of the organs, their correlation, and the way in which the principal stages of any function are broken down, spatialized, and ordered in relation to one another. And thus, in contrast with the mere gaze, which by scanning organisms in their wholeness sees unfolding before it the teeming profusion of their differences, anatomy, by really cutting up bodies into patterns, by dividing them up into distinct portions, by fragmenting them in space, discloses the great resemblances that would otherwise have remained invisible; it reconstitutes the unities that underlie the great dispersion of visible differences. The creation of the vast taxonomic unities (classes and orders) in the seventeenth and eighteenth centuries was a problem of *linguistic patterning*: a name had to be found that would be both general and justified; now, it is a matter of an *anatomic disarticulation*; the major functional system has to be isolated; it is now the real divisions of anatomy that will make it possible to form the great families of living beings.

The second technique is based on anatomy (since it is a result of it), but is in opposition to it (because it makes it possible to dispense with it);

this technique consists in establishing indicative relations between superficial, and therefore visible, elements and others that are concealed in the depths of the body. Through the law of the interdependence of the parts of an organism, we know that such and such a peripheral and accessory organ implies such and such a structure in a more essential organ; thus, it is possible 'to establish the correspondence between exterior and interior forms which are all integral parts of the animal's essence'[18]. Among insects, for example, the location of the antennae has no distinctive value because it is not in correlation with any of the main internal structures; the form of the lower jaw, on the other hand, can play a leading role in arranging them according to their resemblances and differences; for it is connected with the insect's food and digestion, and thus with its essential functions: 'the organs of mastication must be related to those of digestion, consequently to the whole mode of life, and consequently to the whole organic structure'[19]. As a matter of fact, this technique of indications does not necessarily work only from the visible periphery to the grey forms of organic interiority: it can establish necessary networks connecting any point in the body with any other: thus, in certain cases, a single element may be enough to suggest the general architecture of an organism; an entire animal may be recognized 'from a single bone, from a single facet of a bone: a method that has given such curious results when applied to fossilized animals'[20]. Whereas for eighteenth-century thought the fossil was a prefiguration of existing forms, and thus an indication of the great continuity of time, it was henceforth to be the indication of the form to which it once really belonged. Anatomy has not only shattered the tabular and homogeneous space of identities; it has broken the supposed continuity of time.

This is because, from the theoretical point of view, Cuvier's analyses entirely recompose the organization of natural continuities and discontinuities. Comparative anatomy makes it possible, in effect, to establish two quite distinct forms of continuity in the living world. The first concerns the great functions to be found in the majority of species (respiration, digestion, circulation, reproduction, locomotion . . .): it establishes in the whole living world a vast resemblance which can be arranged in a scale of decreasing complexity, from man down to the zoophyte; in the higher species all these functions are present; but as we move down the scale, so we see them disappear one after the other, until finally, in the zoophyte, there is 'no centre of circulation, no nerves, no centre of sensation; each point seems to feed itself by suction'[21]. But this mode of continuity is weak and relatively loose, forming, by means of the restricted number of essential functions, a simple table of presences and absences. The other continuity is much more closely knit: it deals with the greater or lesser perfection of the organs. But one can establish only limited series on this basis, regional continuities which are soon interrupted and which, moreover, intertwine with one another in different directions; this is because, in the various species, 'the organs do not all follow the same order of degradation: one organ is at its highest degree of perfection in one species, while another reaches that same degree of perfection in a different species'[22]. We are left, therefore, with what might be called 'micro-series', limited and partial series which relate not so much to the species themselves as to a particular organ; and, at the other extreme, with a 'macro-series', a discontinuous, loose series which relates not so much to the organisms themselves as to the great fundamental gamut of functions.

Between these two continuities, which are neither superimposed nor fitted together, we find great discontinuous masses being distributed. These masses obey different structural plans, the same functions being ordered in accordance with varying hierarchies, and realized by organs of various types. It is easy, for example, to discover in the octopus 'all the functions that occur in fishes, and yet there is no resemblance, no analogy of arrangement'[23]. Each of these groups must therefore be analysed in itself. We must consider not the narrow thread of resemblances that may attach it to another group, but the cohesive force that folds it so tightly in upon itself. We shall not seek to know whether red-blooded animals are part of the same series as white-blooded animals, with nothing more than supplementary improvements; we shall establish the fact that any animal with red blood – and it is in this that it is based on an autonomous plan – always has a bony head, a vertebral column, limbs (with the exception of snakes), arteries, veins, a liver, a pancreas, a spleen, and kidneys[24]. Vertebrates and invertebrates form absolutely isolated sub-areas, between which it is impossible to find intermediate forms providing a transition in either direction:

Whatever arrangement one attributes to animals with vertebrae and those without vertebrae, it will never prove possible to find at the end of one of these great classes, or at the head of the other, two animals that resemble one another sufficiently to serve as a link between them[25].

It is thus apparent that the theory of sub-kingdoms does not simply add a supplementary taxonomic frame to the previous traditional classifications; it is linked to the constitution of a new space of identities and differences. A space without essential continuity. A space that is posited from the very outset in the form of fragmentation. A space crossed by lines which sometimes diverge and sometimes intersect. In order to designate its general form, then, it is necessary to substitute for the image of the continuous scale which had been traditional in the eighteenth century, from Bonnet to Lamarck, that of a radiation, or rather of a group of centres from which there spreads outwards a multiplicity of beams; thus each being could be placed 'in this vast network, which constitutes organized nature . . . but ten or twenty beams would not suffice to express these innumerable relations'[26].

Whereupon it is the entire Classical experience of difference that topples and falls, and with it the relation between being and nature. In the seventeenth and eighteenth centuries, it was the function of difference to connect all the species together, and thus to fill in the hiatus between the extremities of being; difference played a 'concatenating' role: it was as restricted and as tenuous as possible; it was situated in the very tightest possible grid; it was always divisible, and could occur even below the threshold of perception. From Cuvier onward, on the other hand, it multiplies itself, adds up diverse forms, reverberates and is diffused throughout the organism, isolating it from all the others in various simultaneous ways; for it no longer resides in the interstices between beings in order to connect them together; it functions in relation to the organism itself, so that it can 'integrate' with itself and maintain itself in life; it does not fill up the interval between beings with successive tenuities; it makes it deeper by making itself deeper, in order to define in isolation the great types of compatibility. Nineteenth-century nature is discontinuous exactly in so far as it is alive.

The importance of this upheaval can be appreciated; in the Classical period, natural beings formed a continuous totality because they were beings and because there was no reason for any interruption in their deployment. It was not possible to represent what separated the being from itself; the continuity of representation (signs and characters) and the continuity of beings (the extreme proximity of structures) were thus correlative. It is this fabric, ontological and representative at the same time, that is definitively torn apart with Cuvier: living beings, because they are alive, can no longer form a tissue of progressive and graduated differences;

they must group themselves around nuclei of coherence which are totally distinct from one another, and which are like so many different plans for the maintenance of life. Classical being was without flaw; life, on the other hand, is without edges or shading. Being was spread out over an immense table; life isolates forms that are bound in upon themselves. Being was posited in the perpetually analysable space of representation; life withdraws into the enigma of a force inaccessible in its essence, apprehendable only in the efforts it makes here and there to manifest and maintain itself. In short, throughout the Classical age, life was the province of an ontology which dealt in the same way with all material beings, all of which were subject to extension, weight, and movement; and it was in this sense that all the sciences of nature, and especially that of living beings, had a profound mechanistic vocation; from Cuvier onward, living beings escape, in the first instance at least, the general laws of extensive being; biological being becomes regional and autonomous; life, on the confines of being, is what is exterior to it and also, at the same time, what manifests itself within it. And though the question of its relations with the non-living, or that of its physico-chemical determinations, does arise, it does so not along the lines of a 'mechanism' stubbornly clinging to its Classical modalities, but in an entirely new way, in order to articulate two natures one upon the other.

But since the discontinuities must be explained by the maintenance of life and its conditions, we see the emergence of an unexpected continuity – or at least a play of as yet unanalysed interactions – between the organism and that which enables it to live. If the Ruminants are distinct from the Rodents, and if that distinction rests upon a whole system of massive differences that there can be no question of attenuating, it is because they possess different kinds of dentition, different digestive systems, differently formed extremities and nails; it is because they cannot capture the same kinds of food, or deal with it in the same way; it is because they do not have to digest the same forms of nourishment. The living being must therefore no longer be understood merely as a certain combination of particles bearing definite characters; it provides the outline of an organic structure, which maintains uninterrupted relations with exterior elements that it utilizes (by breathing and eating) in order to maintain or develop its own structure. Around the living being, or rather through it and by means of the filtering action of its surface, there is effected 'a continual circulation from the outside to the inside, and from the inside to the outside, constantly maintained and yet fixed within certain limits. Thus, living bodies should be considered as kinds of furnaces into which dead substances are successively introduced in order to be combined together in various ways' [27]. The living being, by the action and sovereignty of the same force that keeps it in discontinuity with itself, finds itself subjected to a continuous relation with all that surrounds it. In order that the living being can live, there must exist several functional structures, all irreducible one to another, and also an uninterrupted movement between each one of those structures and the air it breathes, the water it drinks, the food it absorbs. Breaking the old Classical continuity of being and nature, the divided force of life will reveal forms that are scattered, yet all linked to the conditions of existence. In a few years, at the end of the eighteenth century and the beginning of the nineteenth, European culture completely changed the fundamental spatialization of the living being: for the Classical experience, the living being was a square, or a series of squares, in the universal *taxinomia* of being; if geographical localization had a role (as it did in Buffon), it was that of revealing variations that were already possible. From Cuvier onward, the living being wraps itself in its own existence, breaks off its taxonomic links of adjacency, tears itself free from the vast, tyrannical plan of continuities, and constitutes itself as a new space: a double space, in fact – since it is both the interior one of anatomical coherences and physiological compatibilities, and the exterior one of the elements in which it resides and of which it forms its own body. But both these spaces are subject to a common control: it is no longer that of the possibilities of being, it is that of the conditions of life.

The whole historical *a priori* of a science of living beings is thus overthrown and then renewed. Seen in its archaeological depth, and not at the more visible level of discoveries, discussion, theories, or philosophical options, Cuvier's work dominates from afar what was to be the future of biology. An opposition is often set up between Lamarck's 'transformist' intuitions, which seem to 'prefigure' what was to be evolutionism, and the old fixism, impregnated through and through with traditional prejudices and theological postulates, in which Cuvier stubbornly persisted. And through a whole series of amalgams, metaphors, and inadequately tested analogies, the outline emerges of a 'reactionary' system of thought which clings passionately to the immobility of things in order to preserve the precarious order of human life; this, it is claimed, is the philosophy of Cuvier, the man possessed of all the powers; opposite is depicted the difficult destiny of a progressive system of thought which believes in the energy of movement, in ceaseless renewal, in the vitality of adaptation: Lamarck, the revolutionary, is supposed to be in this camp. Thus, under pretext of writing the history of ideas in a strictly historical sense, a fine example of simple-mindedness is perpetuated. For what counts, in the historicity of knowledge, is not opinions, nor the resemblances that can be established between them from period to period (there is indeed a 'resemblance' between Lamarck and a certain kind of evolutionism, as there is between the latter and the ideas of Diderot, or Robinet, or Benoît de Maillet); what is important, what makes it possible to articulate the history of thought within itself, is its internal conditions of possibility. Now, one has only to attempt an analysis of his work to perceive immediately that Lamarck conceived of the transformations of species only upon the basis of ontological continuity, which was that of Classical natural history. He presupposed a progressive gradation, an unbroken process of improvement, an uninterrupted continuum of beings which could form themselves upon one another. What makes Lamarck's thought possible is not the distant apprehension of a future evolutionism; it is the continuity of beings as discovered and presupposed by the 'methods' of natural history. Lamarck is a contemporary of A-L. de Jussieu, not of Cuvier. For the latter introduced a radical discontinuity into the Classical scale of beings; and by that very fact he gave rise to such notions as biological incompatibility, relations with external elements, and conditions of existence; he also caused the emergence of a certain energy, necessary to maintain life, and a certain threat, which imposes upon it the sanction of death; here, we find gathered together several of the conditions that make possible something like the idea of evolution. The discontinuity of living forms made it possible to conceive of a great temporal current for which the continuity of structures and characters, despite the superficial analogies, could not provide a basis. With spatial discontinuity, the breaking up of the great table, and the fragmentation of the surface upon which all natural beings had taken their ordered places, it became possible to replace natural history with a 'history' of nature. It is true that the Classical space, as we have seen, did not exclude the possibility of development, but that development did no more than provide a means of traversing the discreetly preordained table of possible variations. The breaking up of that space made it possible to reveal a historicity proper to life itself: that of its maintenance in its conditions of existence. Cuvier's 'fixism', as the analysis of such a maintenance, was the earliest mode of reflecting upon that historicity, when it first emerged in Western knowledge.

Historicity, then, has now been introduced into nature – or rather into the realm of living beings; but it exists there as much more than a probable form of succession; it constitutes a sort of fundamental mode of being. It is no doubt true that in Cuvier's time there did not yet exist a history of living beings such as was to be described by evolutionism; but from the outset the living being is conceived of in terms of the conditions that enable it to have a history. Similarly, at the time of Ricardo, wealth was accorded a status of historicity which had not yet been formulated as economic history. The approaching stability of industrial incomes, population, and rent, as predicted by Ricardo, and the fixity of animal species, as affirmed by Cuvier, might pass, on a superficial examination, as a rejection of history; in fact, Ricardo and Cuvier were rejecting only the modalities of chronological succession as conceived in the eighteenth century; they were breaking the link between time and the hierarchical or classifying order of representations. On the other hand, the actual or future immobility they described or heralded could be conceived only on the basis of the possibility of a history; and that history was provided for them either by the conditions of existence of the living being, or by the conditions of the production of value. Paradoxically, Ricardo's pessimism and Cuvier's fixism can arise only against a historical background: they define the stability of beings, which henceforth have the right, at the level of their profound modality, to possess a history; whereas the Classical idea, that wealth could grow in a continuous process, or that species could, with time, transform themselves into one another, defined the mobility of beings, which, even before any kind of history, already obeyed a system of variables, identities, or equivalences. It took the suspension, and, as it were, the placing between parentheses, of that kind of history to give the beings of nature and the products of labour a historicity that would enable modern thought to encompass them, and subsequently to deploy the discursive science of their succession. For eighteenth-century thought, chronological sequences are merely a property and a more or less blurred expression of the order of beings; from the nineteenth century, they express, in a more or less direct fashion, and even in their interruptions, the profoundly historical mode of being of things and men.

In any case, the constitution of a living historicity has had vast consequences for European thought. Quite as vast, without any doubt, as those brought about by the formation of an economic historicity. At the superficial level of the great imaginative values, life, henceforth pledged to history, is expressed in the form of animality. The animal, whose great threat or radical strangeness had been left suspended and as it were disarmed at the end of the Middle Ages, or at least at the end of the Renaissance, discovers fantastic new powers in the nineteenth century. In the interval, Classical nature had given precedence to vegetable values – since the plant bears upon its visible form the overt mark of every possible order; with all its forms on display, from stem to seed, from root to fruit, with all its secrets generously made visible, the vegetable kingdom formed a pure and transparent object for thought as tabulation. But when characters and structures are arranged in vertical steps towards life – that sovereign vanishing-point, indefinitely distant but constituent – then it is the animal that becomes the privileged form, with its hidden structures, its buried organs, so many invisible functions, and that distant force, at the foundation of its being, which keeps it alive. If living beings are a classification, the plant is best able to express its limpid essence; but if they are a manifestation of life, the animal is better equipped to make its enigma perceptible. Rather than the calm image of characters, it shows us the incessant transition from the inorganic to the organic by means of respiration or digestion, and the inverse transformation, brought about by death, of the great functional structures into lifeless dust:

> Dead substances are borne towards living bodies in order to take up a place and exert an action within them determined by the nature of the combinations into which they have entered, and in order to escape from them again one day so as to fall once more under the laws of inanimate nature[28].

The plant held sway on the frontiers of movement and immobility, of the sentient and the non-sentient; whereas the animal maintains its existence on the frontiers of life and death. Death besieges it on all sides; furthermore, it threatens it also from within, for only the organism can die, and it is from the depth of their lives that death overtakes living beings. Hence, no doubt, the ambiguous values assumed by animality towards the end of the eighteenth century: the animal appears as the bearer of that death to which it is, at the same time, subjected; it contains a perpetual devouring of life by life. It belongs to nature only at the price of containing within itself a nucleus of anti-nature. Transferring its most secret essence from the vegetable to the animal kingdom, life has left the tabulated space of order and become wild once more. The same movement that dooms it to death reveals it as murderous. It kills because it lives. Nature can no longer be good. That life can no longer be separated from murder, nature from evil, or desires from anti-nature, Sade proclaimed to the eighteenth century, whose language he drained dry, and to the modern age, which has for so long attempted to stifle his voice. I hope the insolence (for whom?) is excusable, but *Les 120 Journées* is the velvety, marvellous obverse of the *Leçons d'anatomie comparée*. At all events, in our archaeological calendar, they are the same age.

But this imaginative status of animality burdened with disturbing and nocturnal powers refers more profoundly to the multiple and simultaneous functions of life in nineteenth-century thought. Perhaps for the first time in Western culture, life is escaping from the general laws of being as it is posited and analysed in representation. On the other side of all the things that are, even beyond those that can be, supporting them to make them visible, and ceaselessly destroying them with the violence of death, life becomes a fundamental force, and one that is opposed to being in the same way as movement to immobility, as time to space, as the secret wish to the visible expression. Life is the root of all existence, and the non-living, nature in its inert form, is merely spent life; mere being is the non-being of life. For life – and this is why it has a radical value in nineteenth-century thought – is at the same time the nucleus of being and of non-being: there is being only because there is life, and in that fundamental movement that dooms them to death, the scattered beings, stable for an instant, are formed, halt, hold life immobile – and in a sense kill it – but are then in turn destroyed by that inexhaustible force. The experience of life is thus posited as the most general law of beings, the revelation of that primitive force on the basis of which they are; it functions as an untamed ontology, one trying to express the indissociable being and non-being of all beings. But this ontology discloses not so much what gives beings their foundation as what bears them for an instant towards a precarious form and yet is already secretly sapping them from within in order to destroy them. In relation to life, beings are no more than transitory figures, and the being that they maintain, during the brief period of their existence, is no more than their presumption, their will to survive. And so, for knowledge, the being of things is an illusion, a veil that must be torn aside in order to reveal the mute and invisible violence that is devouring them in the darkness. The ontology of the annihilation of beings assumes therefore validity as a critique of knowledge: but it is not so much a question of giving the phenomenon a foundation, of expressing both its limit and its law, of relating it to the finitude that renders it possible, as of dissipating it and destroying it in the same way as life itself destroys beings: for its whole being is mere appearance.

Thus a system of thought is being formed that is opposed in almost all its terms to the system that was linked to the formation of an economic historicity. The latter, as we have seen, took as its foundation a triple theory of irreducible needs, the objectivity of labour, and the end of history. Here, on the contrary, a system of thought is being developed in which individuality, with its forms, limits, and needs, is no more than a precarious moment, doomed to destruction, forming first and last a simple obstacle that must be removed from the path of that annihilation; a system of thought in which the objectivity of things is mere appearance, a chimera of the perceptions, an illusion that must be dissipated and returned to the pure will, without phenomenon, that brought those things into being and maintained them there for an instant; lastly, a system of thought for which the recommencement of life, its incessant resumptions, and its stubbornness, preclude the possibility of imposing a limit of duration upon it, especially since time itself, with its chronological divisions and its quasi-spatial calendar, is doubtless nothing but an illusion of knowledge. Where one mode of thought predicts the end of history, the other proclaims the infinity of life; where one recognizes the real production of things by labour, the other dissipates the chimeras of consciousness; where one affirms, with the limits of the individual, the exigencies of his life, the other masks them beneath the murmuring of death. Is this opposition the sign that from the nineteenth century the field of knowledge can no longer provide the ground for a reflection that will be homogeneous and uniform at all points? Must we admit that from now on each form of positivity will have the 'philosophy' that suits it? Economics, that of a labour stamped with the sign of need, but with the eventual promise of the great reward of time? Biology, that of a life marked by the continuity that forms beings only in order to dissolve them again, and so finds itself emancipated from all the limitations of History? And the sciences of language a philosophy of cultures, of their relativity and their individual power of expression?

There is, however, one single point, the investigation of which ought to decide every doubt, and elucidate every difficulty; the structure or comparative grammar of languages furnishes as certain a key of their genealogy as the study of comparative anatomy has done to the loftiest branch of natural science[29].

Schlegel was well aware of it: the constitution of historicity in the sphere of grammar took place in accordance with the same model as in the science of living beings. And there is nothing surprising in this, in fact, since, throughout the Classical age, the words that languages were thought to be composed of, and the characters that were used in the attempt to constitute a natural order, had had the same, the identical, status: they existed only by virtue of the representative value they possessed, and the power of analysis, of duplication, of composition and arrangement that they were accorded with regard to the things represented. With Jussieu and Lamarck in the first place, and then with Cuvier, the character had lost its representative function, or rather, though it could still 'represent' and make possible the establishment of relations of adjacency or kinship, it did so not by the virtue proper to its visible structure or to the describable elements of which it was composed, but because it had been related, at first, to a total organic structure and to a function that it could perform in a direct or indirect, major or collateral, 'primary' or 'secondary' way. In the domain of language, the word undergoes, more or less at the same period, an analogous transformation: needless to say, it does not cease to have a meaning and to be able to 'represent' something in the mind that employs or understands it; but this role is no longer constitutive of the word in its very being, in its essential architecture, in what enables it to take its place within a sentence and to link itself there with other more or less different words. If the word is able to figure in a discourse in which it means something, it will no longer be by virtue of some immediate discursivity that it is thought to possess in itself, and by right of birth, but because, in its very form, in the sounds that compose it, in the changes it undergoes in accordance with the grammatical function it is performing, and finally in the modifications to which it finds itself subject in the course of time, it obeys a certain number of strict laws which regulate, in a similar way, all the other elements of the same language; so that the word is no longer attached to a representation except in so far as it is previously a part of the grammatical organization by means of which the language defines and guarantees its own coherence. For the word to be able to say what it says, it must belong to a grammatical totality which, in relation to the word, is primary, fundamental, and determining.

This displacement of the word, this backward jump, as it were, away from its representative functions, was certainly one of the important events of Western culture towards the end of the eighteenth century. And it is also one of those that have passed most unperceived. A great deal of attention is willingly paid to the beginnings of political economy, to Ricardo's analysis of ground rent and the cost of production: that event is recognized as having reached vast dimensions, since, in the course of its progress, it has not only made possible the development of a science but also brought in its wake a certain number of economic and political mutations. The new forms taken by the sciences of nature have not been neglected either; and though it is true that Lamarck, by the influence of a retrospective illusion, has been overestimated at the expense of Cuvier, though it is true that there is little awareness of the fact that 'life' reached the threshold of its positivity for the first time with the *Leçons d'anatomie comparée*, there is nevertheless at least a diffused consciousness of the fact that Western culture began, from that moment onward, to look at the world of living beings with new eyes. On the other hand, the isolation of the Indo-European languages, the constitution of a comparative grammar, the study of inflections, the formulation of the laws of vowel gradation and consonantal changes – in short, the whole body of philological work accomplished by Grimm, Schlegel, Rask, and Bopp, has remained on the fringes of our historical awareness, as though it had merely provided the basis for a somewhat lateral and esoteric discipline – as though, in fact, it was not the whole mode of being of language (and of our own language) that had been modified through it. Certainly we ought not to attempt a justification of this neglect in spite of the importance of the change, but, on the contrary, on the basis of its importance, and on that of the blind proximity that the event still preserves for our eyes, in their continuing attachment to their customary lights. The fact is that, even at the time when it occurred, this event was already enveloped, if not in secret, at least in a certain discretion. Perhaps changes in the mode of being of language are like alterations that affect pronunciation, grammar, or semantics: swift as they are, they are never clearly grasped by those who are speaking and whose language is nevertheless already spreading these mutations; they are noticed only indirectly, for brief moments;

and then the decision is finally indicated only in the negative mode – by the radical and immediately perceptible obsoleteness of the language one has been using. It is probably impossible for a culture to become aware in a thematic and positive manner that its language is ceasing to be transparent to its representations, because it is thickening and taking on a peculiar heaviness. As one is in the act of discoursing, how is one to know – unless by means of some obscure indices that can interpret only with difficulty and badly – that language (the very language one is using) is acquiring a dimension irreducible to pure discursivity? Perhaps for all of these reasons the birth of philology has remained much more hidden from Western consciousness than that of biology and that of economics – even though it was part of the same archaeological upheaval; and even though its consequences have extended much further in our culture, at least in the subterranean strata that run through it and support it.

How was this philological positivity formed? There are four theoretical segments that provide us with indications of its constitution early in the nineteenth century – at the time of Schlegel's essay on the language and philosophy of the Indians (1808), Grimm's *Deutsche Grammatik* (1818), and Bopp's book on the conjugation system of Sanskrit (1816).

1. The first of these segments concerns the manner in which a language can be characterized from within and distinguished from other languages. In the Classical period, it was possible to define the individuality of a language on the basis of several criteria: the proportions of the different sounds employed to form the words (there are languages with a majority of vowels and others with a majority of consonants), the precedence accorded certain categories of words (languages favouring concrete substantives, languages favouring abstract substantives, etc.), the manner of representing relations (by prepositions or by declensions), the preferred order of the words (whether the logical subject is placed first, as in French, or precedence is given to the most important words, as in Latin); in these ways distinctions were made between Northern languages and Mediterranean languages, languages of feeling and languages of need, languages of freedom and languages of slavery, barbarous languages and civilized languages, languages of logical reasoning and languages of rhetorical argumentation; none of these distinctions, however, was concerned with anything but the way in which languages were able to analyse representation, and subsequently to combine its elements. But beginning with Schlegel, languages are defined, at least in their most general typology, according to the way in which they link together the

properly verbal elements that compose them; among these elements there are some, needless to say, that are representative: they do, at any rate, possess a visible representative value; whereas there are others that contain no meaning, and that serve only by means of a certain composition to determine the meaning of some other element in the unity of the discourse. It is this material – made up of nouns, verbs, words in general, but also of syllables and sounds – that languages join together to form propositions and sentences. But the material unity constituted by the arrangement of sounds, syllables, and words is not governed by the mere combination of the element of representation. It has its own principles, which differ from language to language: grammatical composition has regularities which are not transparent to the signification of the discourse. Moreover, since signification can be transformed, practically unimpaired, from one language to another, it is these regularities that will make it possible to define the individuality of a language. Each one has an autonomous grammatical space; these spaces can be compared laterally, that is, from one language to another, without its being necessary to pass through the common 'middle ground' of the field of representation with all its possible subdivisions.

It is easy to distinguish right away two broad modes of combination between grammatical elements. The first consists in juxtaposing them in such a way that they determine one another; in this case, the language is made up of fragmented elements – generally very short – which can be combined in different ways, but with each of the units preserving its autonomy, and thus the possibility of breaking the transitory link it has just established with another unit inside a sentence or proposition. The language is then defined by the number of its units, and by all the possible combinations that can be established between them in discourse; so that it is a question of an 'agglomeration of atoms . . . with no internal connection beyond the purely mechanical adaptation of particles and affixes'[30]. The second mode of connection between the elements of a language is the inflectional system, which modifies the essential syllables or words – the root forms – from within. Each of these root forms carries with it a certain number of possible variations, determined in advance; and according to the other words in the sentence, according to the relations of dependence or correlation between those words, according to the adjacencies and associations that occur, so one variation or another will be used. On the surface, this mode of connection appears less rich than the first, since the number of combinative possibilities is much more restricted; but, in reality, the inflectional system never exists in its pure and most skeletal form; the internal modification of the root enables it to have other elements added to it, themselves susceptible of internal modification, so that 'each root is like a living and productive germ, every modification of circumstance or degree being produced by internal changes; freer scope is thus given to its development, and its rich productiveness is in truth almost illimitable'[31].

Corresponding to these two broad types of linguistic organization, we find, on the one hand, Chinese, in which 'all particles indicating modification of time, person, etc., are monosyllables, perfect in themselves, and independent of the root', and, on the other, Sanskrit, whose

> structure is highly organized, formed by inflection, or the change and transposition of its primary radical signs, carried through every ramification of meaning and expression, and not by the merely mechanical process of annexing words or particles to the same lifeless and unproductive root[32].

Between these major and extreme models, any language whatever can be situated; every language will necessarily possess an organization that will approximate it to one of the two, or will place it at an equal distance from both, at the centre of the field thus defined. Nearest to Chinese, we find Basque, Coptic, and the American languages; these all use separable elements as a means of connection; but those elements, instead of remaining always in a free state, like so many irreducible verbal atoms, 'are already beginning to melt into the word'; Arabic is defined by its mixture of the system of affixes and that of inflections; Celtic is almost exclusively an inflectional language, though one still finds in it 'vestiges of affixive languages'. It may perhaps be objected that this opposition was already known in the eighteenth century, and that the ability to distinguish between the combinative structure of Chinese and the declensions and conjugations of languages like Latin and Greek was by no means new. It may also be objected that the absolute distinction established by Schlegel was criticized very shortly afterwards by Bopp: where Schlegel saw two types of language that were radically inassimilable to one another, Bopp searched for a common origin; he attempts to establish[33] that inflections are not a sort of internal and spontaneous development of the primitive element, but particles that have been agglomerated to the root syllable: the *m* of the first person in Sanskrit (*bhavâmi*) or the *t* of the third person (*bhavâti*) are the effect of the adjunction to the verbal root of the pronoun *mâm* (I) or the pronoun *tâm* (he). But what is important for the constitution of philology is not so much knowing whether the elements of conjugation may, at some more or less distant period in the past, have enjoyed the benefit of an isolated existence carrying with it an autonomous value; what is essential, and what distinguishes the analyses of Schlegel and Bopp from those that may perhaps have seemed to anticipate them in the eighteenth century[34], is that the original syllables do not grow (by means of internal adjunctions or proliferations) without a certain number of modifications regulated within the root. In a language like Chinese, there are simply laws of juxtaposition; but in languages in which the roots are subjected to growth (whether they be monosyllabic, as in Sanskrit, or polysyllabic, as in Hebrew), one always finds internal variations governed by regular forms. It is therefore understandable that the new philology, since it now has these criteria of internal structure with which to characterize languages, should have abandoned the hierarchic classifications practised in the eighteenth century: at that time, it was accepted that there were some languages that were more important than others, because they were able to analyse representations more precisely or more delicately. From now on, all languages have an equal value: they simply have different internal structures. Hence that curiosity for rare, little spoken, poorly 'civilized' languages, of which Rask gave an example with his great voyage of inquiry through Scandinavia, Russia, the Caucasus, Persia, and India.

2. The study of these *internal variations* constitutes the second important theoretical segment. In its etymological investigations, general grammar did of course study transformations of words and syllables over time; but this study was limited for three reasons. It bore more upon the metamorphosis of the letters of the alphabet than upon the manner in which the sounds actually pronounced could be modified. Moreover, the transformations were considered as the effect – always possible, at any time and under any conditions – of a certain affinity between the letters themselves; it was accepted that *p* and *b*, and *m* and *n*, were sufficiently close to one another for the one to be substituted for the other; such changes were provoked or determined exclusively by this doubtful proximity and the confusion that could result in pronouncing or hearing those letters. Finally, vowels were treated as the most fluid and unstable element of language, whereas the consonants were thought of as forming its solid framework (does not Hebrew, for example, dispense with the writing of its vowels?).

With Rask, Grimm, and Bopp, language is treated for the first time (even though there is no longer any attempt to refer it back to the cries from which it originated) as a totality of phonetic elements. Whereas, for general grammar, language arose when the noise produced by the mouth or the lips had become a *letter*, it is accepted from now on that language exists when noises have been articulated and divided into a series of distinct *sounds*. The whole being of language is now one of sound. This explains the new interest, shown by Raynouard and the brothers Grimm, in non-written literature, in folk tales and spoken dialects. Language is sought in its most authentic state: in the spoken word – the word that is dried up and frozen into immobility by writing. A whole mystique is being born: that of the verb, of the pure poetic flash that disappears without trace, leaving nothing behind it but a vibration suspended in the air for one brief moment. By means of the ephemeral and profound sound it produces, the spoken word accedes to sovereignty. And its secret powers, drawing new life from the breath of the prophets, rise up in fundamental opposition (even though they do tolerate some overlapping) to the esoteric nature of writing, which, on the other hand, presupposes some secret permanently lurking at the centre of its visible labyrinths. Language is no longer to the same extent that sign – more or less distant, similar, and arbitrary – for which the *Logique de Port-Royal* proposed as an immediate and evident model the portrait of a man, or a map. It has acquired a vibratory nature which has separated it from the visible sign and made it more nearly proximate to the note in music. And it was for this very reason that Saussure had to by-pass this moment in the history of the spoken word, which was a major event for the whole of nineteenth-century philology, in order to restore, beyond its historical forms, the dimension of language in general, and to reopen, after such neglect, the old problem of the sign, which had continued to animate the whole of thought from Port-Royal to the last of the 'Idéologues'.

Thus, in the nineteenth century, there begins an analysis of language treated as a totality of sounds emancipated from the letters that may be used to transcribe them[35]. This analysis was made in three directions. First, the typology of the various sounds employed in a language: in the case of vowels, for example, the opposition between simple and double vowels (lengthened as in *ā*, *ō*; or diphthongized as in *æ*, *ai*); among simple vowels, the opposition between those that are pure (*a*, *i*, *o*, *u*) and those that are modified (*e*, *ö*, *ü*); among those that are pure, there are those that are susceptible of various pronunciations (such as *o*), and those that have only one (*a*, *i*, *u*); finally, among this last group, some are subject to change and can receive an *umlaut* (*a* and *u*); the *i*, on the other hand, always remains the same[36]. The second form of analysis bears upon the conditions that may determine a sound change; the place of the sound within the word is in itself an important factor: a syllable is less easily able to protect its permanence if it is an ending than if it is a root; root letters, Grimm tells us, are long lived; the sounds in inflectional endings are shorter lived. But there are positive determinations as well, for 'the preservation or modification' of a given sound 'is never arbitrary'[37]. This absence of arbitrariness was for Grimm the determination of a meaning (in the root of a great many German verbs *a* stands in the same opposition to *i* as the preterite does to the present). For Bopp, it is the effect of a certain number of laws. Some of these define the rules governing the changes that occur when two consonants are adjacent: 'Thus when one says in Sanskrit *at-ti* (he eats) instead of *ad-ti* (from the root *ad*, to eat), the changing of the *d* into *t* has a physical law as its cause.' Others define the mode in which a termination acts upon the sounds of the root: 'By mechanical laws, I mean principally the laws of weight and in particular the influence exerted by the weight of inflectional verb endings upon the preceding syllable'[38]. Lastly, the third form of analysis bears upon the invariability of these transformations throughout History. Grimm, for example, drew up a table of correspondences for labials, dentals, and gutturals between Greek, 'Gothic', and High German: the *p*, *b*, and *f* of the Greeks become respectively *f*, *p*, and *b* in Gothic and *b* or *v*, *f*, and *p* in High German; *t*,*d*,*th* in Greek become *th*,*t*,*d* in Gothic, and *d*,*z*,*t* in High German. The totality of these relationships determines the courses of history; and instead of languages being subject to that external yardstick, to those things in human history that should, according to Classical thought, explain the changes in them, they themselves contain a principle of evolution. Here, as elsewhere, it is 'anatomy'[39] that determines fate.

3. This definition of a law for consonantal or vocalic modifications makes it possible to establish a *new theory of the root*. In the Classical period, roots were distinguished by a double system of constants: alphabetical constants, which bore upon an arbitrary number of letters (in some cases only one), and significative constants, which grouped together under one general theme an indefinitely extensible number of adjacent meanings; at the intersection of these two constants, at the point where an identical meaning was expressed by an identical letter or an identical

syllable, a root was taken to have been isolated. The root was an expressive nucleus transformable to infinity from the starting-point of one original sound. But if vowels and consonants change only in accordance with certain laws and under certain conditions, the radical must be a stable linguistic entity (between certain limits), which can be isolated with its possible variations, and which constitutes, with its different possible forms, an element of language. In order to determine the primary and quite simple elements of a language, general grammar was obliged to work backwards towards that imaginary point of contact where the sound, as yet not verbal, was in some sort of contact with the vital energy of representation. From now on, however, the elements of a language are interior to it (even if they also belong to other languages): there exist purely linguistic means of establishing the constants according to which they can be combined and the table of their possible modifications. Etymology will therefore cease to be an endless regress towards a primitive language entirely stocked with primal, natural cries; it becomes a definite, limited method of analysis, the aim of which is to discover within any given word the radical from which it has been formed: 'The roots of words were brought to light only after the successful analysis of inflections and derivations'[40].

It thus becomes possible to establish that in certain languages, such as the Semitic ones, the roots are bisyllabic (and generally of three letters); that in others (the Indo-Germanic ones) they are regularly monosyllabic; some are constituted by a single vowel (*i* is the root of verbs meaning 'to go', *u* of those meaning 'to reverberate'); but in general, in these languages, the root comprises at least one consonant and one vowel – the consonant being either terminal or initial; in the first case, the vowel is necessarily initial; in the second, it may be followed by a second consonant which serves it as a support (as in the root *ma*, *mad*, which gives *metiri* in Latin and *messen* in German)[41]. These monosyllabic roots may also be duplicated, as *do* is duplicated in the Sanskrit *dadami* and the Greek *didomi*, or *sta* in *tishtami* and *istemi*[42]. Above all, the nature of the root and its constituent role in language are conceived in an absolutely new mode: in the eighteenth century, the root was a rudimentary name which designated, in its origin, a concrete thing, an immediate representation, an object that was given to man's sight or to any other of his senses. Language was constructed on the basis of the interaction of its nominal characterizations: derivation extended its scope; abstraction gave rise to adjectives; and then it was sufficient to add to the latter that other irreducible element, the broad monotonous function of the verb *to be*, to bring about the formation of the category of conjugable words – a sort of squeezing together in verbal form of being and epithet. Bopp too accepts that verbs are mixtures obtained by the coagulation of verb with root. But his analysis differs in several essential points from the Classical schema: there is no question of the potential, underlying, invisible addition of the attributive function, and of the propositional meaning attributed to the verb *to be*; it is a question primarily of a material junction between a radical and the forms of the verb *to be*: the Sanskrit *as* is to be found in the sigma of the Greek aorist, in the *er* of the Latin pluperfect and future perfect; the Sanskrit *bhu* is to be found in the *b* of the Latin future and imperfect. Moreover, this adjunction of the verb *to be* makes possible, essentially, the attribution of a tense and a person to the radical (the inflectional ending constituted by the radical of the verb *to be* also carrying with it that denoting the personal pronoun, as in *scrip-s-i*)[43]. As a result, it is not the adjunction of the *to be* that transforms an epithet into a verb; the radical itself contains a verbal signification, to which the derived inflectional endings of the conjugation of *to be* add merely modifications of person and tense. Originally, therefore, the roots of verbs designate not 'things', but actions, processes, desires, wills; and it is these that, when they receive certain inflectional endings proceeding from the verb *to be* and from the personal pronouns, become susceptible of conjugation, whereas, when they receive other suffixes – themselves modifiable – they become nouns susceptible of declension. Hence the 'nouns/verb to be' bipolarity that characterized classical analysis must be replaced by a more complex arrangement: roots with a verbal signification, able to receive inflectional endings of different types, and thus capable of giving rise to conjugable verbs or to substantives. Verbs (and personal pronouns) thus become the primordial element of language – the element from which it can develop. 'The verb and the personal pronouns appear to be the true levers of language'[44].

Bopp's analyses were to be of major importance, not only in breaking down the internal composition of a language, but also in defining what language may be in its essence. It is no longer a system of representations which has the power to pattern and recompose other representations; it designates in its roots the most constant of actions, states, and wishes; what it is trying to say, originally, is not so much what one sees as what one does or what one undergoes; and though it does eventually indicate things as though by pointing at them, it does so only in so far as they are

the result, or the object, or the instrument of that action; nouns do not
so much pattern the complex table of a representation as pattern and arrest
and fix the process of an action. Language is 'rooted' not in the things
perceived, but in the active subject. And perhaps, in that case, it is a
product of will and energy, rather than of the memory that duplicates
representation. We speak because we act, and not because recognition is
a means of cognition. Like action, language expresses a profound will to
something. And this has two consequences. The first is paradoxical at
first sight: it is that at the moment when philology is constituted by the
discovery of a dimension of pure grammar, there arises once more
the tendency to attribute to language profound powers of expression
(Humboldt is not merely Bopp's contemporary; he knew his work, and in
detail); whereas in the Classical period the expressive function of language
was required only at its point of origin, and in order to explain how a
sound could represent a thing, language in the nineteenth century,
throughout its development and even in its most complex forms, was to
have an irreducible expressive value; no arbitrariness, no grammatical
convention is able to obliterate that value, for, if language expresses, it
does so not in so far as it is an imitation and duplication of things, but
in so far as it manifests and translates the fundamental will of those who
speak it. The second consequence is that language is no longer linked to
civilizations by the level of learning to which they have attained (the
delicacy of their representative grid, the multiplicity of the connections
it is possible to establish between its elements), but by the mind of the
peoples who have given rise to it, animate it, and are recognizable in it.
Just as the living organism manifests, by its inner coherence, the functions
that keep it alive, so language, in the whole architecture of its grammar,
makes visible the fundamental will that keeps a whole people alive and
gives it the power to speak a language belonging solely to itself. This
means that the conditions of historicity of language are changed at once:
its mutations no longer come from above (from the learned elite, from
the small group of merchants and travellers, from victorious armies, from
an invading aristocracy), but take their being obscurely from below, for
language is neither an instrument nor a product – an *ergon*, as Humboldt
termed it – but a ceaseless activity – an *energeïa*. In any language, the
speaker, who never ceases to speak in a murmur that is not heard although
it provides all the vividness of the language, is the people. Grimm thought
that he overheard such a murmur when he listened to the *altdeutsche
Meistergesang*, and Raynouard when he transcribed the *Poésies originales*

des troubadours. Language is no longer linked to the knowing of things, but to men's freedom: 'Language is human: it owes its origin and progress to our full freedom; it is our history, our heritage' [45]. By defining the internal laws of grammar, one is simultaneously linking language and the free destiny of men in a profound kinship. Throughout the nineteenth century, philology was to have profound political reverberations.

4. The analysis of roots made possible a new definition of the *systems of kinship* between languages. And this is the fourth broad theoretical segment that characterizes the appearance of philology. In the first place, this definition presupposes that languages are divided into broad groups which are discontinuous in relation to one another. General grammar excluded comparison in so far as it accepted the presence in any language whatever of two orders of continuity: one, a vertical continuity, permitted the arrangement of the most primitive of the allotment of roots, which, at the expense of a few transformations, bound each language to its initial articulations; the other, a horizontal one, enabled languages to communicate in the universality of representation: all languages had as their task the analysis, decomposition, and recomposition of representations, which, within fairly broad limits, were the same for the entire human race. So that it was possible to compare languages only in an indirect way, and by a triangular route, as it were; it was possible to analyse the way in which a particular language had treated and modified the common allocation of primitive roots; it was also possible to compare the way in which two languages patterned and linked together the same representations. But what becomes possible after Grimm and Bopp is the direct and lateral comparison of two or more languages. Direct, because it is no longer necessary to pass through pure representations or the absolutely primitive root; it is enough to study the modifications of the radical, the system of inflections, the series of variable terminations. Lateral, because the comparison does not reach back to the elements shared by all languages or to the representative stock upon which they draw; it is therefore not possible to relate a language to the form or the principles that render all other languages possible; they must be grouped according to their formal proximity: 'This resemblance or affinity does not exist only in the numerous roots, which it has in common with both those nations, but extends also to the grammar and internal structure' [46].

Now, these grammatical structures that it is possible to compare directly with one another present two special characteristics. First, that of existing only as systems: with monosyllabic radicals, a certain number of inflections are possible; the weight of the terminations may have effects whose number and nature are determinable; the modes of affixation correspond to a few completely fixed models; whereas, in languages with polysyllabic radicals, all the modifications and combinations will obey other laws. Between two systems like these (the one being characteristic of the Indo-European languages, the other of the Semitic languages), we find no intermediate type and no transitional forms. There is a discontinuity from one family to the other. But, on the other hand, grammatical systems, since they lay down a certain number of laws of evolution and mutation, make it possible, up to a certain point, to fix the age-scale of a language; for such and such a form to be produced from a certain radical, such and such a transformation must have occurred. In the Classical age, when two languages resembled one another, it was neces-sary either to link them both to the absolutely primitive language they both sprang from, or to admit that one developed from the other (but the criterion was external, the more derived of the two languages being that which had appeared historically at the more recent date) or, again, to admit that there had been exchanges between them (due to extra-linguistic events: invasion, trade, migration). Now, when two languages present analogous systems, one must to be able to decide either that one of them is derived from the other, or that they have both issued from a third, from which they have each developed systems which are partly different and also partly analogous. It was in this way, in the case of Sanskrit and Greek, that the hypothesis of Coeurdoux, who believed in traces of the primitive language, and that of Anquetil, who posited a mixture at the time of the Bactrian kingdom, were abandoned; and Bopp was also able to refute Schlegel, for whom the Indian language was the most ancient, and the others (Latin, Greek, Germanic and Persian lan-guages) were more modern and derived from the first. He showed that there was a relation of 'fraternity' between Sanskrit, Latin, Greek, and the Germanic languages, Sanskrit being, not the mother-language of the others, but rather their elder sister, the nearest of them to a language which had apparently been the source of this entire family.

It is apparent, then, that historicity was introduced into the domain of languages in the same way as into that of living beings. For an evolution – other than one that is solely the traversal of ontological continuities – to be conceived, the smooth unbroken plan of natural history had to be broken, the discontinuity of the sub-kingdoms had to reveal the plans of organic structure in all their diversity and without any intermediary,

organisms had to be ordered in accordance with the functional arrangements they were to perform, and thus establish the relations of the living
being with what enables it to exist. In the same way, for the history of
languages to be conceived, they had to be detached from the broad
chronological continuity that had linked them without interruption as far
back as their origin; they also had to be freed from the common expanse
of representations in which they were caught; by means of this double
break, the heterogeneity of the various grammatical systems emerged
with its peculiar patternings, the laws prescribing change within each one,
and the paths fixing possible lines of development. Once the history of
the species had been suspended as a chronological sequence of all possible
forms, then, and only then, the living being was able to assume its historicity; in the same way, in the sphere of language, if there had not been
a suspension of the analysis of those endless derivations and limitless
mixtures that general grammar perpetually presupposed, then language
would never have been affected by an internal historicity. Sanskrit,
Greek, Latin, and German had to be treated in accordance with a systematic
simultaneity; breaking with all chronology, they had to be inserted into a
fraternal time-system so that their structures could become transparent
and a history of languages could become legible in them. Here, as elsewhere, the arrangements into chronological series had to be broken up,
and their elements redistributed, then a new history was constituted, one
that does not merely express the mode of succession of beings and their
connection in time, but the modality of their formation. Empiricity – and
this is equally true of natural individuals and of the words by which they
can be named – is henceforth traversed by History, through the whole
density of its being. The order of time is beginning.

There is one major difference, however, between languages and living
beings. The latter have no true history except by means of a certain
relation between their functions and the conditions of their existence.
And though their internal composition as structured individuals makes
their historicity possible, that historicity becomes real history only by
means of the external world in which they live. Thus, to enable this
history to emerge clearly, and to be described in discourse, there had to
be, in addition to Cuvier's comparative anatomy, an analysis of the
environment and conditions that act on the living being. The 'anatomy'
of language, to use Grimm's expression, functions on the other hand
within the element of History: for it is an anatomy of possible changes,
one that expresses not the real coexistence of organs, or their mutual

exclusion, but the direction in which mutations will or will not be able to occur. The new grammar is immediately diachronic. How could it have been otherwise, since its positivity could be established only by a break between language and representation? The internal structure of languages – what they sanction and what they exclude in order to function – could be re-apprehended only in the form of words; but, in itself, this form can express its own law only if it is related back to its previous states, to the changes of which it is susceptible, to the modifications that never occur. By being cut off from what it represents, language was certainly made to emerge for the first time in its own particular legality, and at the same time it was doomed to be re-apprehensible only within history. It is well known that Saussure was able to escape from this diachronic vocation of philology only by restoring the relation of language to representation, at the expense of reconstituting a 'semiology' which, like general grammar, defined the sign as the connection between two ideas. The same archaeological event was expressed therefore in a partially different fashion in the cases of natural history and language. By separating the characters of the living being or the rules of grammar from the laws of a self-analysing representation, the historicity of life and language was made possible. But, in the sphere of biology, this historicity needed a supplementary history to express the relations of the individual with the environment; in one sense the history of life is exterior to the historicity of the living being; this is why evolutionism is a biological theory, of which the condition of possibility was a biology without evolution – that of Cuvier. The historicity of language, on the contrary, reveals its history immediately, and without intermediary; they communicate with one another internally. Whereas nineteenth-century biology was to advance more and more towards the exterior of the living being, towards what lay beyond it, rendering progressively more permeable that surface of the body at which the naturalist's gaze had once halted, philology was to untie the relations that the grammarian had established between language and external history in order to define an internal history. And the latter, once secure in its objectivity, could serve as a guiding-thread, making it possible to reconstitute – for the benefit of History proper – events long since forgotten.

V LANGUAGE BECOME OBJECT

It may be observed that the four theoretical segments that have just been analysed, perhaps because they constitute the archaeological ground of philology, correspond and contrast, term by term, with those that made it possible to define general grammar[47]. Working backwards from the last of these four segments to the first, we find that the theory of the *kinship* between languages (discontinuity between the broad families, and internal analogies in the system of changes) is opposed by the theory of *derivation*, which presupposed constant factors of attrition and admixture, acting in the same way on all languages of whatever kind, as an external principle and with unlimited effects. The theory of the *radical* contrasts with that of *designation*: for the radical is an isolable linguistic individuality, inside a group of languages, and serving above all as a nucleus of verbal forms; whereas the root, encroaching upon language from the side of nature and the primitive cry, exhausted itself till it was no more than an endlessly transformable sound which had as its function a primary nominal patterning of things. The study of the *internal variations* of language is also opposed by the theory of representative *articulation*: the latter defined words and gave them an individuality that distinguished them from each other by relating them to the content they were able to signify; the articulation of language was the visible analysis of representation; now words are characterized in the first place by their morphology and by the totality of the mutations each of their sounds is capable of undergoing. Above all, the *internal analysis* of language is opposed by the primacy accorded in Classical thought to the verb *to be*: the latter held sway on the frontiers of language, both because it was the primary link between words and because it possessed the fundamental power of affirmation; it marked the threshold of language, indicated its specificity, and connected it, in an ineffaceable way, to the forms of thought. On the other hand, the independent analysis of grammatical structures, as practised from the nineteenth century, isolates language, treats it as an autonomous organic structure, and breaks its bonds with judgements, attribution, and affirmation. The ontological transition provided by the verb *to be* between speaking and thinking is removed; whereupon language acquires a being proper to itself. And it is this being that contains the laws that govern it.

The Classical order of language has now drawn to a close. It has lost its transparency and its major function in the domain of knowledge. In the seventeenth and eighteenth centuries, it was the immediate and spontaneous unfolding of representations; it was in that order in the first place that representations received their primary signs, patterned and regrouped their common features, and established their relations of identity or attribution; language was a form of knowing and knowing was automatically discourse. Thus, language occupied a fundamental situation in relation to all knowledge: it was only by the medium of language that the things of the world could be known. Not because it was a part of the world, ontologically interwoven with it (as in the Renaissance), but because it was the first sketch of an order in representations of the world; because it was the initial, inevitable way of representing representations. It was in language that all generality was formed. Classical knowledge was profoundly nominalist. From the nineteenth century, language began to fold in upon itself, to acquire its own particular density, to deploy a history, an objectivity, and laws of its own. It became one object of knowledge among others, on the same level as living beings, wealth and value, and the history of events and men. It may possess its own concepts, but the analyses that bear upon it have their roots at the same level as those that deal with other empirical forms of knowledge. The pre-eminence that enabled *general grammar* to be *logic* while at the same time intersecting with it has now been lost. To know language is no longer to come as close as possible to knowledge itself; it is merely to apply the methods of understanding in general to a particular domain of objectivity.

This demotion of language to the mere status of an object is compensated for, however, in three ways. First, by the fact that it is a necessary medium for any scientific knowledge that wishes to be expressed in discourse. It cannot itself be arranged, deployed, and analysed beneath the gaze of a science, because it always re-emerges on the side of the knowing subject - as soon as that subject expresses what he knows. Hence two constant concerns throughout the nineteenth century. The first is the wish to neutralize, and as it were polish, scientific language to the point at which, stripped of all its singularity, purified of all its accidents and alien elements - as though they did not belong to its essence - it could become the exact reflection, the perfect double, the unmisted mirror of a non-verbal knowledge. This is the positivist dream of a language keeping strictly to the level of what is known: a table-language, like the one Cuvier was probably dreaming of when he attributed to science the project of forming a 'copy' of nature; scientific discourse was to be the 'table' of things; but 'table' here has a fundamentally different meaning from the one it possessed in the eighteenth century; then, it was a matter of dividing nature up by means of a constant table of identities and differences for which language provided a primary, approximative, and rectifiable *grid*; now, language is not so much a table as a picture, in the sense that, freed from the intricacy that gives it its immediately classifying role, it stands a certain distance apart from nature in order to draw some of it into itself by means of its own passivity, and finally to become nature's faithful portrait[48]. The other concern – entirely different from the first, even though in correlation with it – was the search for a logic independent of grammars, vocabularies, synthetic forms, and words: a logic that could clarify and utilize the universal implications of thought while protecting them from the singularities of a constituted language in which they might be obscured. It was inevitable that a symbolic logic should come into being, with Boole, at precisely that period when languages were becoming philological objects: for, despite some superficial resemblances and a few technical analogies, it was not a question, as it had been in the Classical age, of constituting a universal language, but of representing the forms and connections of thought outside all language. And since language was becoming an object of science, a language had to be invented that would be a symbolism rather than a language, and would for that reason be transparent to thought in the very movement that permits it to know. One might say in one sense that *logical algebra* and the *Indo-European languages* are two products of the dissociation of *general grammar*: the Indo-European languages expressing the shift of language in the direction of the known object, logical algebra the movement that makes it swing towards the act of knowing, stripping it in the process of all its already constituted form. But it would be inadequate to express the fact in this purely negative form: at the archaeological level, the conditions of possibility of a non-verbal logic and a historical grammar are the same. The ground of their positivity is identical.

The second compensation for this demotion of language is the critical value bestowed upon its study. Having become a dense and consistent historical reality, language forms the locus of tradition, of the unspoken habits of thought, of what lies hidden in a people's mind; it accumulates an ineluctable memory which does not even know itself as memory. Expressing their thoughts in words of which they are not the masters, enclosing them in verbal forms whose historical dimensions they are unaware of, men believe that their speech is their servant and do not realize that they are submitting themselves to its demands. The grammatical arrangements of a language are the *a priori* of what can be expressed in it. The truth of discourse is caught in the trap of philology. Hence the need to work one's way back from opinions, philosophies, and perhaps even from sciences, to the words that made them possible, and, beyond that, to a thought whose essential life has not yet been caught in the network of any grammar. This is how we must understand the revival, so marked in the nineteenth century, of all the techniques of exegesis. This reappearance is due to the fact that language has resumed the enigmatic density it possessed at the time of the Renaissance. But now it is not a matter of rediscovering some primary word that has been buried in it, but of disturbing the words we speak, of denouncing the grammatical habits of our thinking, of dissipating the myths that animate our words, of rendering once more noisy and audible the element of silence that all discourse carries with it as it is spoken. The first book of *Das Kapital* is an exegesis of 'value'; all Nietzsche is an exegesis of a few Greek words; Freud, the exegesis of all those unspoken phrases that support and at the same time undermine our apparent discourse, our fantasies, our dreams, our bodies. Philology, as the analysis of what is said in the depths of discourse, has become the modern form of criticism. Where, at the end of the eighteenth century, it was a matter of fixing the frontiers of knowledge, it will now be one of seeking to destroy syntax, to shatter tyrannical modes of speech, to turn words around in order to perceive all that is being said through them and despite them. God is perhaps not so much a region beyond knowledge as something prior to the sentences we speak; and if Western man is inseparable from him, it is not because of some invincible propensity to go beyond the frontiers of experience, but because his language ceaselessly foments him in the shadow of his laws: 'I fear indeed that we shall never rid ourselves of God, since we still believe in grammar' [49]. In the sixteenth century, interpretation proceeded from the world (things and texts together) towards the divine Word that could be deciphered in it; our interpretation, or at all events that which was formed in the nineteenth century, proceeds from men, from God, from knowledge or fantasies, towards the words that make them possible; and what it reveals is not the sovereignty of a primal discourse, but the fact that we are already, before the very least of our words, governed and paralysed by language. Modern criticism has devoted itself to a strange kind of commentary, since it does not proceed from the observation that there is language towards the discovery of what that language means, but from the deployment of manifest discourse towards a revelation of language in its crude being.

Thus the methods of interpretation of modern thought are opposed by the techniques of formalization: the first claiming to make language speak as it were below itself, and as near as possible to what is being said in it, without it; the second claiming to control any language that may arise, and to impose upon it from above the law of what it is possible to say. Interpretation and formalization have become the two great forms of analysis of our time – in fact, we know no others. But do we know what the relations of exegesis and formalization are? Are we capable of controlling and mastering them? For if exegesis leads us not so much towards a primal discourse as towards the naked existence of something like a language, will it not be obliged to express only the pure forms of language even before it has taken on a meaning? And in order to formalize what we suppose to be a language, is it not necessary to have practised some minimum of exegesis, and at least interpreted all those mute forms as having the intention of meaning something? It is true that the division between interpretation and formalization presses upon us and dominates us today. But it is not rigorous enough: the fork it forms has not been driven far enough down into our culture, its two branches are too contemporaneous for us to be able to say even that it is prescribing a simple option or that it is inviting us to choose between the past, which believed in meaning, and the present (the future), which has discovered the significant. In fact, it is a matter of two correlative techniques whose common ground of possibility is formed by the being of language, as it was constituted on the threshold of the modern age. The critical elevation of language, which was a compensation for its subsidence within the object, implied that it had been brought nearer both to an act of knowing, pure of all words, and to the unconscious element in our discourse. It had to be either made transparent to the forms of knowledge, or thrust down into the contents of the unconscious. This certainly explains the nineteenth century's double advance, on the one hand towards formalism in thought and on the other towards the discovery of the unconscious – towards Russell and Freud. It also explains the tendency of one to move towards the other, and of these two directions to cross: the attempt, for example, to discover the pure forms that are imposed upon our unconscious before all content; or again, the endeavour to raise the ground of experience, the sense of being, the lived horizon of all our knowledge to the level of our discourse. It is here that structuralism and phenomenology find, together with the arrangements proper to them, the general space that defines their *common ground*.

Finally, the last of the compensations for the demotion of language, the most important, and also the most unexpected, is the appearance of literature, of literature as such – for there has of course existed in the

Western world, since Dante, since Homer, a form of language that we now call 'literature'. But the word is of recent date, as is also, in our culture, the isolation of a particular language whose peculiar mode of being is 'literary'. This is because at the beginning of the nineteenth century, at a time when language was burying itself within its own density as an object and allowing itself to be traversed, through and through, by knowledge, it was also reconstituting itself elsewhere, in an independent form, difficult of access, folded back upon the enigma of its own origin and existing wholly in reference to the pure act of writing. Literature is the contestation of philology (of which it is nevertheless the twin figure): it leads language back from grammar to the naked power of speech, and there it encounters the untamed, imperious being of words. From the Romantic revolt against a discourse frozen in its own ritual pomp, to the Mallarméan discovery of the word in its impotent power, it becomes clear what the function of literature was, in the nineteenth century, in relation to the modern mode of being of language. Against the background of this essential interaction, the rest is merely effect: literature becomes progressively more differentiated from the discourse of ideas, and encloses itself within a radical intransitivity; it becomes detached from all the values that were able to keep it in general circulation during the Classical age (taste, pleasure, naturalness, truth), and creates within its own space everything that will ensure a ludic denial of them (the scandalous, the ugly, the impossible); it breaks with the whole definition of *genres* as forms adapted to an order of representations, and becomes merely a manifestation of a language which has no other law than that of affirming – in opposition to all other forms of discourse – its own precipitous existence; and so there is nothing for it to do but to curve back in a perpetual return upon itself, as if its discourse could have no other content than the expression of its own form; it addresses itself to itself as a writing subjectivity, or seeks to re-apprehend the essence of all literature in the movement that brought it into being; and thus all its threads converge upon the finest of points – singular, instantaneous, and yet absolutely universal – upon the simple act of writing. At the moment when language, as spoken and scattered words, becomes an object of knowledge, we see it reappearing in a strictly opposite modality: a silent, cautious deposition of the word upon the whiteness of a piece of paper, where it can possess neither sound nor interlocutor, where it has nothing to say but itself, nothing to do but shine in the brightness of its being.

NOTES

[1] Ricardo, *Works* (London, 1846, p. 11).

[2] Ibid., p. 10.

[3] Ibid., p. 25.

[4] Ibid., p. 16.

[5] Cf. Adam Smith, *The wealth of nations*, book I, chap. XI, part II.

[6] Quoted by T. Cahn, *La Vie et l'œuvre d'E. Geoffroy Saint-Hilaire* (Paris, 1962, p. 138).

[7] G. Cuvier, *Leçons d'anatomie comparée*, t. I, pp. 63–4.

[8] Ibid., pp. 34–5.

[9] Cuvier, *Rapport historique sur le progrès des sciences naturelles*, p. 330.

[10] Cuvier, *Leçons d'anatomie comparée*, t. I, p. 55.

[11] Cuvier, *Second mémoire sur les animaux à sang blanc* (1795; *Magasin encyclopédique*, II, p. 441).

[12] Ibid, p. 441.

[13] Cuvier, *Leçons d'anatomie comparée*, t. III, pp. 4–5.

[14] Cuvier, *Sur un nouveau rapprochement à établir* (*Annales du Muséum*, t. XIX, p. 76).

[15] Ibid., p. 76.

[16] Cuvier, *Second mémoire sur les animaux à sang blanc*, loc. cit.

[17] On this rejection of the microscope, which is identical in Cuvier and in the anatomo-pathologists, cf. *Leçons d'anatomie comparée*, t. V, p. 180, and *Le Règne animal distribué d'après son organisation*, t. I, p. xxviii.

[18] Cuvier, *Le Règne animal distribué d'après son organisation*, t. I, p. xiv.

[19] Cuvier, *Lettre à Hartmann*, quoted by Daudin, *Les Classes zoologiques*, t. II, p. 20, n. 1.

[20] Cuvier, *Rapport historique sur le progrès des sciences naturelles*, pp. 329–30.

[21] Cuvier, *Tableau élémentaire d'histoire naturelle*, p. 6 et seq.

[22] Cuvier, *Leçons d'anatomie comparée*, t. I, p. 59.

[23] Cuvier, *Mémoire sur les céphalopodes* (1817, pp. 42–3).

[24] Cuvier, *Tableau élémentaire d'histoire naturelle*, pp. 84–5.

[25] Cuvier, *Leçons d'anatomie comparée*, t. I, p. 60.

[26] Cuvier, *Histoire des poissons* (Paris, 1828, t. I, p. 569).

[27] Cuvier, *Leçons d'anatomie comparée*, t. I, pp. 4–5.

[28] Cuvier, *Cours d'anatomie pathologique*, t. I, p. 5.

[29] F. von Schlegel, *On the language and philosophy of the Indians* (1808; *Aesthetic and miscellaneous works*, London, 1849, p. 439).

[30] Ibid., p. 449.

[31] Ibid.

[32] Ibid, pp. 445–7.

[33] Bopp, *Über das Konjugationssystem der Sanskritsprache* (1816, p. 147).

[34] J. Horne Tooke, *On the study of language* (London, 1798).

[35] Grimm has often been criticized for having confused letters and sounds (he analyses *Schrift* into eight elements because he divides the *f* into *p* and *h*). That is how difficult it was to treat language as an element composed purely of sounds.

[36] J. Grimm, *Deutsche Grammatik* (2nd edn., 1822, vol. I, p. 5). These analyses do not occur in the first edition (1818).

[37] Ibid., p. 5.

[38] Bopp, *A comparative grammar* (London, 1845, p. 1, note).

[39] J. Grimm, *L'Origine du langage* (Fr. trans. Paris, 1859, p. 7).

[40] Ibid., p. 37. Cf. also *Deutsche Grammatik*, I, p. 588.

[41] J. Grimm, *L'Origine du langage*, p. 41.

[42] Bopp, *Über das Konjugationssystem der Sanskritsprache.*

[43] Ibid., p. 147 *et seq.*

[44] J. Grimm, *L'Origine du langage*, p. 39.

[45] Ibid., p. 50.

[46] F. von Schlegel, *On the language and philosophy of the Indians*, p. 429.

[47] Cf. p. 115 above.

[48] Cf. G. Cuvier, *Rapport historique sur le progrès des sciences naturelles*, p. 4.

[49] Nietzsche, *The twilight of the idols* (First German edn. 1889; Fr. trans. 1911, p. 130).

CHAPTER 9

Man and his Doubles

I THE RETURN OF LANGUAGE

With the appearance of literature, with the return of exegesis and the concern for formalization, with the development of philology—in short, with the reappearance of language as a multiple profusion, the order of Classical thought can now be eclipsed. At this time, from any retro-spective viewpoint, it enters a region of shade. Even so, we should speak not of darkness but of a somewhat blurred light, deceptive in its apparent clarity, and hiding more than it reveals: it seems to us, in fact, that we know all there is to be known about Classical knowledge if we under-stand that it is rationalistic, that, since Galileo and Descartes, it has accorded an absolute privilege to Mechanism, that it presupposes a general ordering of nature, that it accepts the possibility of an analysis sufficiently radical to discover elements or origins, but that it already has a presenti-ment, beyond and despite all these concepts of understanding, of the movement of life, of the density of history, and of the disorder, so diffi-cult to master, in nature. But to recognize Classical thought by such signs alone is to misunderstand its fundamental arrangement; it is to neglect entirely the relation between such manifestations and what made them possible. And how, after all (if not by a slow and laborious technique), are we to discover the complex relation of representations, identities, orders, words, natural beings, desires, and interests, once that vast grid has been dismantled, once needs have organized their production for themselves, once living beings have turned in towards the essential functions of life, once words have become weighed down with their own material his-tory – in short, once the identities of representation have ceased to express the order of beings completely and openly? The entire system of grids which analysed the sequence of representations (a thin temporal series unfolding in men's minds), arresting its movement, fragmenting it, spreading it out and redistributing it in a permanent table, all these distinctions created by words and discourse, characters and classification, equivalences and exchange, have been so completely abolished that it is difficult today to rediscover how that structure was able to function. The last 'bastion' to fall – and the one whose disappearance cut us off from Classical thought forever – was precisely the first of all those grids: discourse, which ensured the initial, spontaneous, unconsidered deployment of representation in a table. When discourse ceased to exist and to function within representation as the first means of ordering it, Classical thought ceased at the same time to be directly accessible to us.

The threshold between Classicism and modernity (though the terms themselves have no importance – let us say between our prehistory and what is still contempory) had been definitively crossed when words ceased to intersect with representations and to provide a spontaneous grid for the knowledge of things. At the beginning of the nineteenth century, they rediscovered their ancient, enigmatic density; though not in order to restore the curve of the world which had harboured them during the Renaissance, nor in order to mingle with things in a circular system of signs. Once detached from representation, language has existed, right up to our own day, only in a dispersed way: for philologists, words are like so many objects formed and deposited by history; for those who wish to achieve a formalization, language must strip itself of its concrete content and leave nothing visible but those forms of discourse that are universally valid; if one's intent is to interpret, then words become a text to be broken down, so as to allow that other meaning hidden in them to emerge and become clearly visible; lastly, language may sometimes arise for its own sake in an act of writing that designates nothing other than itself. This dispersion imposes upon language, if not a privileged position, at least a destiny that seems singular when compared with that of labour or of life. When the table of natural history was dissociated, the living beings within it were not dispersed, but, on the contrary, regrouped around the central enigma of life; when the analysis of wealth had disappeared, all economic processes were regrouped around the central fact of production and all that rendered it possible; on the other hand, when the unity of general grammar – discourse – was broken up, language appeared in a multiplicity of modes of being, whose unity was probably irrecoverable. It is for this reason, perhaps, that philosophical reflection for so long held itself aloof from language. Whereas it sought tirelessly in the regions of life or labour for something that might provide it with an object, or with its conceptual models, or its real and fundamental ground, it paid relatively little attention to language; its main concern was to clear away the obstacles that might oppose it in its task; for example, words had to be freed from the silent content that rendered them alien, or language had to be made more flexible and more fluid, as it were, from within, so that once emancipated from the spatializations of the understanding it would be able to express the movement and temporality of life. Language did not return into the field of thought directly and in its own right until the end of the nineteenth century. We might even have said until the twentieth, had not Nietzsche the philologist – and even in that field he was so wise, he knew so much, he wrote such good books – been the first to connect the philosophical task with a radical reflection upon language.

And now, in this philosophical-philological space opened up for us by Nietzsche, language wells up in an enigmatic multiplicity that must be mastered. There appear, like so many projects (or chimeras, who can tell as yet?), the themes of a universal formalization of all discourse, or the themes of an integral exegesis of the world which would at the same time be its total demystification, or those of a general theory of signs; or again, the theme (historically probably the first) of a transformation without residuum, of a total reabsorption of all forms of discourse into a single word, of all books into a single page, of the whole world into one book. The great task to which Mallarmé dedicated himself, right up to his death, is the one that dominates us now; in its stammerings, it embraces all our current efforts to confine the fragmented being of language once more within a perhaps impossible unity. Mallarmé's project – that of enclosing all possible discourse within the fragile density of the word, within that slim, material black line traced by ink upon paper – is fundamentally a reply to the question imposed upon philosophy by Nietzsche. For Nietzsche, it was not a matter of knowing what good and evil were in themselves, but of who was being designated, or rather *who was speaking* when one said *Agathos* to designate oneself and *Deilos* to designate others[1]. For it is there, in the *holder* of the discourse and, more profoundly still, in the *possessor* of the word, that language is gathered together in its entirety. To the Nietzschean question: 'Who is speaking?', Mallarmé replies – and constantly reverts to that reply – by saying that what is speaking is, in its solitude, in its fragile vibration, in its nothingness, the word itself – not the meaning of the word, but its enigmatic and precarious being. Whereas Nietzsche maintained his questioning as to who

305

is speaking right up to the end, though forced, in the last resort, to irrupt into that questioning himself and to base it upon himself as the speaking and questioning subject: *Ecce homo*, Mallarmé was constantly effacing himself from his own language, to the point of not wishing to figure in it except as an executant in a pure ceremony of the Book in which the discourse would compose itself. It is quite possible that all those questions now confronting our curiosity (What is language? What is a sign? What is unspoken in the world, in our gestures, in the whole enigmatic heraldry of our behaviour, our dreams, our sicknesses – does all that speak, and if so in what language and in obedience to what grammar? Is everything significant, and, if not, what is, and for whom, and in accordance with what rules? What relation is there between language and being, and is it really to being that language is always addressed – at least, language that speaks truly? What, then, is this language that says nothing, is never silent, and is called 'literature'?) – it is quite possible that all these questions are presented today in the distance that was never crossed between Nietzsche's question and Mallarmé's reply.

We know now where these questions come from. They were made possible by the fact that, at the beginning of the nineteenth century, the law of discourse having been detached from representation, the being of language itself became, as it were, fragmented; but they became inevitable when, with Nietzsche, and Mallarmé, thought was brought back, and violently so, towards language itself, towards its unique and difficult being. The whole curiosity of our thought now resides in the question: What is language, how can we find a way round it in order to make it appear in itself, in all its plenitude? In a sense, this question takes up from those other questions that, in the nineteenth century, were concerned with life or labour. But the status of this inquiry and of all the questions into which it breaks down is not perfectly clear. Is it a sign of the approaching birth, or, even less than that, of the very first glow, low in the sky, of a day scarcely even heralded as yet, but in which we can already divine that thought – the thought that has been speaking for thousands of years without knowing what speaking is or even that it is speaking – is about to re-apprehend itself in its entirety, and to illumine itself once more in the lightning flash of being? Is that not what Nietzsche was paving the way for when, in the interior space of his language, he killed man and God both at the same time, and thereby promised with the Return the multiple and re-illumined light of the gods? Or must we quite simply admit that such a plethora of questions on the subject of language is no more than a continuance, or at most a culmination, of the event that, as archaeology has shown, came into existence and began to take effect at the end of the eighteenth century? The fragmentation of language, occurring at the same time as its transition to philological objectivity, would in that case be no more than the most recently visible (because the most secret and most fundamental) consequence of the breaking up of Classical order; by making the effort to master this schism and to make language visible in its entirety, we would bring to completion what had occurred before us, and without us, towards the end of the eighteenth century. But what, in that case, would that culmination be? In attempting to reconstitute the lost unity of language, is one carrying to its conclusion a thought which is that of the nineteenth century, or is one pursuing forms that are already incompatible with it? The dispersion of language is linked, in fact, in a fundamental way, with the archaeological event we may designate as the disappearance of Discourse. To discover the vast play of language contained once more within a single space might be just as decisive a leap towards a wholly new form of thought as to draw to a close a mode of knowing constituted during the previous century.

It is true that I do not know what to reply to such questions, or, given these alternatives, what term I should choose. I cannot even guess whether I shall ever be able to answer them, or whether the day will come when I shall have reasons enough to make any such choice. Nevertheless, I now know why I am able, like everyone else, to ask them – and I am unable not to ask them today. Only those who cannot read will be surprised that I have learned such a thing more clearly from Cuvier, Bopp, and Ricardo than from Kant or Hegel.

II THE PLACE OF THE KING

Faced with so many instances of ignorance, so many questions remaining in suspense, no doubt some decision must be made. One must say: there is where discourse ends, and perhaps labour begins again. Yet there are still a few more words to be said – words whose status it is probably difficult to justify, since it is a matter of introducing at the last moment, rather like some *deus ex machina*, a character who has not yet appeared in the great Classical interplay of representations. And let us, if we may, look for the previously existing law of that interplay in the painting of *Las Meninas*, in which representation is represented at every point: the painter, the palette, the broad dark surface of the canvas with its back to us, the paintings hanging on the wall, the spectators watching, who are framed, in turn, by those who are watching them; and lastly, in the centre, in the very heart of the representation, nearest to what is essential, the mirror, showing us what is represented, but as a reflection so distant, so deeply buried in an unreal space, so foreign to all the gazes being directed elsewhere, that it is no more than the frailest duplication of representation. All the interior lines of the painting, and above all those that come from the central reflection, point towards the very thing that is represented, but absent. At once object – since it is what the artist represented is copying onto his canvas – and subject – since what the painter had in front of his eyes, as he represented himself in the course of his work, was himself, since the gazes portrayed in the picture are all directed towards the fictitious position occupied by the royal personage, which is also the painter's real place, since the occupier of that ambiguous place in which the painter and the sovereign alternate, in a never-ending flicker, as it were, is the spectator, whose gaze transforms the painting into an object, the pure representation of that essential absence. Even so, that absence is not a lacuna, except for the discourse laboriously decomposing the painting, for it never ceases to be inhabited, and really too, as is proved by the concentration of the painter thus represented, by the respect of the characters portrayed in the picture, by the presence of the great canvas with its back to us, and by *our* gaze, for which the painting exists and for which, in the depths of time, it was arranged.

In Classical thought, the personage for whom the representation exists, and who represents himself within it, recognizing himself therein as an image or reflection, he who ties together all the interlacing threads of the 'representation in the form of a picture or table' – he is never to be found in that table himself. Before the end of the eighteenth century, *man* did not exist – any more than the potency of life, the fecundity of labour, or the historical density of language. He is a quite recent creature, which the demiurge of knowledge fabricated with its own hands less than two hundred years ago: but he has grown old so quickly that it has been only too easy to imagine that he had been waiting for thousands of years in the darkness for that moment of illumination in which he would finally be known. Of course, it is possible to object that general grammar, natural history, and the analysis of wealth were all, in a sense, ways of recognizing the existence of man – but there is a distinction to be made. There is no doubt that the natural sciences dealt with man as with a species or a genus: the controversy about the problem of races in the

eighteenth century testifies to that. Again, general grammar and economics made use of such notions as need and desire, or memory and
imagination. But there was no epistemological consciousness of man as
such. The Classical *episteme* is articulated along lines that do not isolate,
in any way, a specific domain proper to man. And if that is not sufficient,
if it is still objected that, even so, no period has accorded more attention
to human nature, has given it a more stable, more definitive status, or
one more directly presented to discourse – one can reply by saying that
the very concept of human nature, and the way in which it functioned,
excluded any possibility of a Classical science of man.

It is essential to observe that the functions of 'nature' and 'human
nature' are in opposition to one another, term by term, in the Classical
episteme: nature, through the action of a real and disordered juxtaposition,
causes difference to appear in the ordered continuity of beings; human
nature causes the identical to appear in the disordered chain of representations, and does so by the action of a display of images. The one implies the
fragmentation of a history in order to constitute actual landscapes; the
other implies the comparison of non-actual elements which destroy the
fabric of a chronological sequence. Despite this opposition, however, or
rather through it, we see the positive relation of nature to human nature
beginning to take shape. They act, in fact, upon identical elements
(the same, the continuous, the imperceptible difference, the unbroken
sequence); both reveal against the background of an uninterrupted fabric
the possibility of a general analysis which makes possible the distribution
of isolable identities and visible differences over a tabulated space and in
an ordered sequence. But they cannot succeed in doing this without each
other, and it is there that the communication between them occurs. The
chain of representations can, in effect, by means of the power it possesses
to duplicate itself (in imagination and memory, and in the multiple
attention employed in comparison), rediscover, below the disorder of
the earth, the unbroken expanse of beings; memory, random at first, and
at the mercy of representations as they capriciously present themselves
to it, is gradually immobilized in the form of a general table of all that
exists; man is then able to include the world in the sovereignty of a discourse that has the power to represent its representation. In the act of
speaking, or rather (keeping as close as possible to what is essential in the
Classical experience of language), in the act of *naming*, human nature –
like the folding of representation back upon itself – transforms the linear
sequence of thoughts into a constant table of partially different beings: the

discourse in which it duplicates its representations and expresses them is what links it to nature. Inversely, the chain of being is linked to human nature by the play of nature: for since the real world, as it presents itself to the gaze, is not merely the unwinding of the fundamental chain of being, but offers jumbled fragments of it, repeated and discontinuous, the series of representations in the mind is not obliged to follow the continuous path of imperceptible differences; extremes meet within it, the same things occur more than once; identical traits are superimposed in the memory; differences stand out. Thus the great, endless, continuous surface is printed with distinct characters, in more or less general features, in marks of identification – and, consequently, in words. The chain of being becomes discourse, thereby linking itself to human nature and to the sequence of representations.

This establishing of communication between nature and human nature, on the basis of two opposite but complementary functions – since neither can take place without the other – carries with it broad theoretical consequences. For Classical thought, man does not occupy a place in nature through the intermediary of the regional, limited, specific 'nature' that is granted to him, as to all other beings, as a birthright. If human nature is interwoven with nature, it is by the mechanisms of knowledge and by their functioning; or rather, in the general arrangement of the Classical *episteme*, nature, human nature, and their relations, are definite and predictable functional moments. And man, as a primary reality with his own density, as the difficult object and sovereign subject of all possible knowledge, has no place in it. The modern themes of an individual who lives, speaks, and works in accordance with the laws of an economics, a philology, and a biology, but who also, by a sort of internal torsion and overlapping, has acquired the right, through the interplay of those very laws, to know them and to subject them to total clarification – all these themes so familiar to us today and linked to the existence of the 'human sciences' are excluded by Classical thought: it was not possible at that time that there should arise, on the boundary of the world, the strange stature of a being whose nature (that which determines it, contains it, and has traversed it from the beginning of time) is to know nature, and itself, in consequence, as a natural being.

In return, however, at the meeting-point between representation and being, at the point where nature and human nature intersect – at the place in which we believe nowadays that we can recognize the primary, irrefutable, and enigmatic existence of man – what Classical thought reveals is the power of discourse. In other words, language in so far as it represents – language that names, patterns, combines, and connects and disconnects things as it makes them visible in the transparency of words. In this role, language transforms the sequence of perceptions into a table, and cuts up the continuum of beings into a pattern of characters. Where there is discourse, representations are laid out and juxtaposed; and things are grouped together and articulated. The profound vocation of Classical language has always been to create a table – a 'picture': whether it be in the form of natural discourse, the accumulation of truth, descriptions of things, a body of exact knowledge, or an encyclopaedic dictionary. It exists, therefore, only in order to be transparent; it has lost that secret consistency which, in the sixteenth century, inspissated it into a word to be deciphered, and interwove it with all the things of the world; it has not yet acquired the multiple existence about which we question ourselves today; in the Classical age, discourse is that translucent necessity through which representation and beings must pass – as beings are represented to the mind's eye, and as representation renders beings visible in their truth. The possibility of knowing things and their order passes, in the Classical experience, through the sovereignty of words: words are, in fact, neither marks to be deciphered (as in the Renaissance period) nor more or less faithful and masterable instruments (as in the positivist period); they form rather a colourless network on the basis of which beings manifest themselves and representations are ordered. This would account for the fact that Classical reflection upon language, even though comprised within a general arrangement of which it forms part by the same right as do the analysis of wealth and natural history, exercises, in relation to them, a regulating role.

But the essential consequence is that Classical language, as the *common discourse* of representation and things, as the place within which nature and human nature intersect, absolutely excludes anything that could be a 'science of man'. As long as that language was spoken in Western culture it was not possible for human existence to be called in question on its own account, since it contained the nexus of representation and being. The discourse that, in the seventeenth century, provided the link between the 'I think' and the 'I am' of the being undertaking it – that very discourse remained, in a visible form, the very essence of Classical language, for what was being linked together in it was representation and being. The transition from the 'I think' to the 'I am' was accomplished in the light of evidence, within a discourse whose whole domain and functioning consisted in articulating one upon the other what one represents to one-self and what is. It cannot, therefore, be objected to this transition either that being in general is not contained in thought, or that the singular being as designated by the 'I am' has not been interrogated or analysed on his own account. Or rather, these objections may well arise and command respect, but only on the basis of a discourse which is profoundly other, and which does not have for its *raison d'être* the link between representation and being; only a problematics able to by-pass representation would formulate such objections. But as long as Classical discourse lasted, no interrogation as to the mode of being implied by the *cogito* could be articulated.

III THE ANALYTIC OF FINITUDE

When natural history becomes biology, when the analysis of wealth becomes economics, when, above all, reflection upon language becomes philology, and Classical *discourse*, in which being and representation found their common locus, is eclipsed, then, in the profound upheaval of such an archaeological mutation, man appears in his ambiguous position as an object of knowledge and as a subject that knows: enslaved sovereign, observed spectator, he appears in the place belonging to the king, which was assigned to him in advance by *Las Meninas*, but from which his real presence has for so long been excluded. As if, in that vacant space towards which Velázquez's whole painting was directed, but which it was nevertheless reflecting only in the chance presence of a mirror, and as though by stealth, all the figures whose alternation, reciprocal exclusion, interweaving, and fluttering one imagined (the model, the painter, the king, the spectator) suddenly stopped their imperceptible dance, immobilized into one substantial figure, and demanded that the entire space of the representation should at last be related to one corporeal gaze.

The motive of this new presence, the modality proper to it, the particular arrangement of the *episteme* that justifies it, the new relation that is established by means of it between words, things, and their order – all this can now be clarified. Cuvier and his contemporaries had required of life that it should itself define, in the depths of its being, the conditions of possibility of the living being; in the same way, Ricardo had required labour to provide the conditions of possibility of exchange, profit, and production; the first philologists, too, had searched in the historical depths of languages for the possibility of discourse and of grammar. This meant that representation ceased, *ipso facto*, to have validity as the locus of origin of living beings, needs, and words, or as the primitive seat of their truth; henceforth, it is nothing more in relation to them than an effect, their more or less blurred counterpart in a consciousness which apprehends and reconstitutes them. The representation one makes to oneself of things no longer has to deploy, in a sovereign space, the table into which they have been ordered; it is, for that empirical individual who is man, the phenomenon – perhaps even less, the appearance – of an order that now belongs to things themselves and to their interior law. It is no longer their identity that beings manifest in representation, but the external relation they establish with the human being. The latter, with his own being, with his power to present himself with representations, arises in a space hollowed out by living beings, objects of exchange, and words, when, abandoning representation, which had been their natural site hitherto, they withdraw into the depths of things and roll up upon themselves in accordance with the laws of life, production, and language. In the middle of them all, compressed within the circle they form, man is designated – more, required – by them, since it is he who speaks, since he is seen to reside among the animals (and in a position that is not merely privileged, but a source of order for the totality they form: even though he is not conceived as the end-product of evolution, he is recognized to be one extremity of a long series), and since, lastly, the relation between his needs and the means he possesses to satisfy them is such that he is necessarily the principle and means of all production. But this imperious designation is ambiguous. In one sense, man is governed by labour, life, and language: his concrete existence finds its determinations in them; it is possible to have access to him only through his words, his organism, the objects he makes – as though it is they who possess the truth in the first place (and they alone perhaps); and he, as soon as he thinks, merely unveils himself to his own eyes in the form of a being who is already, in a necessarily subjacent density, in an irreducible anteriority, a living being, an instrument of production, a vehicle for words which exist before him. All these contents that his knowledge reveals to him as exterior to himself, and older than his own birth, anticipate him, overhang him with all their solidity, and traverse him as though he were merely an object of nature, a face doomed to be erased in the course of history. Man's finitude is heralded – and imperiously so – in the positivity of knowledge; we know that man is finite, as we know the anatomy of the brain, the mechanics of production costs, or the system of Indo-European conjugation; or rather, like a watermark running through all these solid, positive, and full forms, we perceive the finitude and limits they impose, we sense, as though on their blank reverse sides, all that they make impossible.

But this primary discovery of finitude is really an unstable one; nothing allows it to contemplate itself; and would it not be possible to suppose that it also promises that very infinity it refuses, according to the system of actuality? The evolution of the species has perhaps not reached its culmination; forms of production and labour are still being modified, and perhaps one day man will no longer find the principle of his alienation in his labour, or the constant reminder of his limitations in his needs; nor is there any proof that he will not discover symbolic systems sufficiently pure to dissolve the ancient opacity of historical languages. Heralded in positivity, man's finitude is outlined in the paradoxical form of the endless; rather than the rigour of a limitation, it indicates the monotony of a journey which, though it probably has no end, is nevertheless perhaps not without hope. And yet all these contents, with what they conceal and what they also leave pointing towards the frontiers of time, have positivity within the space of knowledge and approach the task of a possible acquisition of knowledge only because they are thoroughly imbued with finitude. For they would not be there, in the light that partly illumines them, if man, who discovers himself through them, was trapped in the mute, nocturnal, immediate and happy opening of animal life; but nor would they posit themselves in the acute angle that hides them from their own direction if man could traverse them without residuum in the lightning flash of an infinite understanding. But to man's experience a body has been given, a body which is his body – a fragment of ambiguous space, whose peculiar and irreducible spatiality is nevertheless articulated upon the space of things; to this same experience, desire is given as a primordial appetite on the basis of which all things assume value, and relative value; to this same experience, a language is given in the thread of which all the discourses of all times, all successions and all simultaneities may be given. This is to say that each of these positive forms in which man can learn that he is finite is given to him only against the background of its own finitude. Moreover, the latter is not the most completely purified essence of positivity, but that upon the basis of which it is possible for positivity to arise. The mode of being of life, and even that which determines the fact that life cannot exist without prescribing its forms for me, are given to me, fundamentally, by my body;

the mode of being of production, the weight of its determinations upon my existence, are given to me by my desire; and the mode of being of language, the whole backwash of history to which words lend their glow at the instant they are pronounced, and perhaps even in a time more imperceptible still, are given to me only along the slender chain of my speaking thought. At the foundation of all the empirical positivities, and of everything that can indicate itself as a concrete limitation of man's existence, we discover a finitude – which is in a sense the same: it is marked by the spatiality of the body, the yawning of desire, and the time of language; and yet it is radically other: in this sense, the limitation is expressed not as a determination imposed upon man from outside (because he has a nature or a history), but as a fundamental finitude which rests on nothing but its own existence as fact, and opens upon the positivity of all concrete limitation.

Thus, in the very heart of empiricity, there is indicated the obligation to work backwards – or downwards – to an analytic of finitude, in which man's being will be able to provide a foundation in their own positivity for all those forms that indicate to him that he is not infinite. And the first characteristic with which this analytic will mark man's mode of being, or rather the space in which that mode of being will be deployed in its entirety, will be that of repetition – of the identity and the difference between the positive and the fundamental: the death that anonymously gnaws at the daily existence of the living being is the same as that fundamental death on the basis of which my empirical life is given to me; the desire that links and separates men in the neutrality of the economic process is the same as that on the basis of which everything is desirable for me; the time that bears languages along upon it, that takes up its place within them and finally wears them out, is the same time that draws my discourse out, even before I have pronounced it, into a succession that no man can master. From one end of experience to the other, finitude answers itself; it is the identity and the difference of the positivities, and of their foundation, within the figure of the *Same*. It is apparent how modern reflection, as soon as the first shoot of this analytic appears, by-passes the display of representation, together with its culmination in the form of a table as ordered by Classical knowledge, and moves towards a certain thought of the Same – in which Difference is the same thing as Identity. It is within this vast but narrow space, opened up by the repetition of the positive within the fundamental, that the whole of this analytic of finitude – so closely linked to the future of modern thought – will be

315

deployed; it is there that we shall see in succession the transcendental repeat the empirical, the cogito repeat the unthought, the return of the origin repeat its retreat; it is there, from itself as starting-point, that a thought of the Same irreducible to Classical philosophy is about to affirm itself.

It may perhaps be remarked that there was no need to wait until the nineteenth century for the idea of finitude to be revealed. It is true that the nineteenth century perhaps only displaced it within the space of thought, making it play a more complex, more ambiguous, less easily by-passed role: for seventeenth- and eighteenth-century thought, it was his finitude that forced man to live an animal existence, to work by the sweat of his brow, to think with opaque words; it was this same finitude that prevented him from attaining any absolute knowledge of the mechanisms of his body, the means of satisfying his needs, the method of thinking without the perilous aid of a language woven wholly of habits and imagination. As an inadequation extending to infinity, man's limitation accounted both for the existence of the empirical contents and for the impossibility of knowing them immediately. And thus the negative relation to infinity – whether conceived of as creation, or fall, or conjunction of body and soul, or determination within the infinite being, or individual point of view of the totality, or link between representation and impression – was posited as anterior to man's empiricity and to the knowledge he may gain of it. In a single movement, but without reciprocal return or circularity, it provided the foundation for the existence of bodies, needs, and words, and for the impossibility of subjugating them within an absolute knowledge. The experience taking form at the beginning of the nineteenth century situates the discovery of finitude not within the thought of the infinite, but at the very heart of those contents that are given, by a finite act of knowing, as the concrete forms of finite existence. Hence the interminable to and fro of a double system of reference: if man's knowledge is finite, it is because he is trapped, without possibility of liberation, within the positive contents of language, labour, and life; and inversely, if life, labour, and language may be posited in their positivity, it is because knowledge has finite forms. For Classical thought, in other words, finitude (as a determination positively constituted on the basis of the infinite) provides an account of those negative forms, which are body, needs, language, and the limited knowledge it is possible to have of them; for modern thought, the positivity of life, of production and labour (which have their own existence, historicity, and laws) provides a foundation for the limited character of knowledge as their negative correlation; and, inversely, the limits of knowledge provide a positive foundation for the possibility of knowing, though in an experience that is always limited, what life, labour, and language are. As long as these empirical contents were situated within the space of representation, a metaphysics of the infinite was not only possible but necessary: it was necessary, in fact, that they should be the manifest forms of human finitude, and yet that they should be able to have their locus and their truth within representation; the idea of infinity, and the idea of its determination in finitude, made one another possible. But when these empirical contents were detached from representation and contained the principle of their existence within themselves, then the metaphysics of infinity became useless; from that point on, finitude never ceased to refer back to itself (from the positivity of the contents to the limitations of knowledge, and from the limited positivity of knowledge to the limited knowledge of the contents). Whereupon the entire field of Western thought was inverted. Where there had formerly been a correlation between a *metaphysics* of representation and of the infinite and an *analysis* of living beings, of man's desires, and of the words of his language, we find being constituted an *analytic* of finitude and human existence, and in opposition to it (though in correlative opposition) a perpetual tendency to constitute a *metaphysics* of life, labour, and language. But these are never anything more than tendencies, immediately opposed and as it were undermined from within, for there can be no question of anything but metaphysics reduced to the scale of human finitudes: the metaphysic of a life that converges upon man even if it does not stop with him; the metaphysic of a labour that frees man so that man, in turn, can free himself from it; the metaphysic of a language that man can reappropriate in the consciousness of his own culture. Modern thought, then, will contest even its own metaphysical impulses, and show that reflections upon life, labour, and language, in so far as they have value as analytics of finitude, express the end of metaphysics: the philosophy of life denounces metaphysics as a veil of illusion, that of labour denounces it as an alienated form of thought and an ideology, that of language as a cultural episode.

But the end of metaphysics is only the negative side of a much more complex event in Western thought. This event is the appearance of man. However, it must not be supposed that he suddenly appeared upon our horizon, imposing the brutal fact of his body, his labour, and his language in a manner so irruptive as to be absolutely baffling to our reflection. It is not man's lack of positivity that reduced the space of metaphysics so violently. No doubt, on the level of appearances, modernity begins when the human being begins to exist within his organism, inside the shell of his head, inside the armature of his limbs, and in the whole structure of his physiology; when he begins to exist at the centre of a labour by whose principles he is governed and whose product eludes him; when he lodges his thought in the folds of a language so much older than himself that he cannot master its significations, even though they have been called back to life by the insistence of his words. But, more fundamentally, our culture crossed the threshold beyond which we recognize our modernity when finitude was conceived in an interminable cross-reference with itself. Though it is true, at the level of the various branches of knowledge, that finitude is always designated on the basis of man as a concrete being and on the basis of the empirical forms that can be assigned to his existence, nevertheless, at the archaeological level, which reveals the general, historical *a priori* of each of those branches of knowledge, modern man – that man assignable in his corporeal, labouring, and speaking existence – is possible only as a figuration of finitude. Modern culture can conceive of man because it conceives of the finite on the basis of itself. Given these conditions, it is understandable that Classical thought, and all the forms of thought that preceded it, were able to speak of the mind and the body, of the human being, of how restricted a place he occupies in the universe, of all the limitations by which his knowledge or his freedom must be measured, but that not one of them was ever able to know man as he is posited in modern knowledge. Renaissance 'humanism' and Classical 'rationalism' were indeed able to allot human beings a privileged position in the order of the world, but they were not able to conceive of man.

IV THE EMPIRICAL AND THE TRANSCENDENTAL

Man, in the analytic of finitude, is a strange empirico-transcendental doublet, since he is a being such that knowledge will be attained in him of what renders all knowledge possible. But did not the human nature of the eighteenth-century empiricists play the same role? In fact, what was being analysed then was the properties and forms of representation which made knowledge in general possible (it was thus that Condillac defined the necessary and sufficient operations for representation to deploy itself as knowledge: reminiscence, self-consciousness, imagination, memory);

now that the site of the analysis is no longer representation but man in his finitude, it is a question of revealing the conditions of knowledge on the basis of the empirical contents given in it. It is of little importance, for the general movement of modern thought, where these contents happened to be localized: knowing whether they were sought in introspection or in other forms of analysis is not the point. For the threshold of our modernity is situated not by the attempt to apply objective methods to the study of man, but rather by the constitution of an empirico-transcendental doublet which was called *man*. Two kinds of analysis then came into being. There are those that operate within the space of the body, and – by studying perception, sensorial mechanisms, neuro-motor diagrams, and the articulation common to things and to the organism – function as a sort of transcendental aesthetic; these led to the discovery that knowledge has anatomo-physiological conditions, that it is formed gradually within the structures of the body, that it may have a privileged place within it, but that its forms cannot be dissociated from its peculiar functioning; in short, that there is a *nature* of human knowledge that determines its forms and that can at the same time be made manifest to it in its own empirical contents. There were also analyses that – by studying humanity's more or less ancient, more or less easily vanquished illusions – functioned as a sort of transcendental dialectic; by this means it was shown that knowledge had historical, social, or economic conditions, that it was formed within the relations that are woven between men, and that it was not independent of the particular form they might take here or there; in short, that there was a *history* of human knowledge which could both be given to empirical knowledge and prescribe its forms.

Now, these analyses have this in particular about them: they apparently do not need one another in any way; moreover, they can dispense with the need for an analytic (or a theory of the subject): they claim to be able to rest entirely on themselves, since it is the contents themselves that function as transcendental reflection. But in fact the search for a nature or a history of knowledge, in the movement by which the dimension proper to a critique is fitted over the contents of empirical knowledge, already presupposes the use of a certain critique – a critique that is not the exercise of pure reflection, but the result of a series of more or less obscure divisions. And, in the first place, these divisions are relatively clearly elucidated, even though they are arbitrary: the division that distinguishes rudimentary, imperfect, unequal, emergent knowledge from knowledge that may be called, if not complete, at least constituted in its stable and definitive forms (this division makes possible the study of the natural conditions of knowledge); the division that distinguishes illusion from truth, the ideological fantasy from the scientific theory (this division makes possible the study of the historical conditions of knowledge); but there is a more obscure and more fundamental division: that of truth itself; there must, in fact, exist a truth that is of the same order as the object – the truth that is gradually outlined, formed, stabilized, and expressed through the body and the rudiments of perception; the truth that appears as illusions are dissipated, and as history establishes a dis-alienated status for itself; but there must also exist a truth that is of the order of discourse – a truth that makes it possible to employ, when dealing with the nature or history of knowledge, a language that will be true. It is the status of this true discourse that remains ambiguous. These two things lead to one conclusion: either this true discourse finds its founda-tion and model in the empirical truth whose genesis in nature and in history it retraces, so that one has an analysis of the positivist type (the truth of the object determines the truth of the discourse that describes its formation); or the true discourse anticipates the truth whose nature and history it defines; it sketches it out in advance and foments it from a dis-tance, so that one has a discourse of the eschatological type (the truth of the philosophical discourse constitutes the truth in formation). In fact, it is a question not so much of an alternative as of a fluctuation inherent in all analysis, which brings out the value of the empirical at the transcen-dental level. Comte and Marx both bear out the fact that eschatology (as the objective truth proceeding from man's discourse) and positivism (as the truth of discourse defined on the basis of the truth of the object) are archaeologically indissociable: a discourse attempting to be both empirical and critical cannot but be both positivist and eschatological; man appears within it as a truth both reduced and promised. Pre-critical naïveté holds undivided rule.

This is why modern thought has been unable to avoid – and precisely from the starting-point of this naïve discourse – searching for the locus of a discourse that would be neither of the order of reduction nor of the order of promise: a discourse whose tension would keep separate the empirical and the transcendental, while being directed at both; a discourse that would make it possible to analyse man as a subject, that is, as a locus of knowledge which has been empirically acquired but referred back as closely as possible to what makes it possible, and as a pure form immediately present to those contents; a discourse, in short, which in relation to to quasi-aesthetics and quasi-dialectics would play the role of an analytic which would at the same time give them a foundation in a theory of the subject and perhaps enable them to articulate themselves in that third and intermediary term in which both the experience of the body and that of culture would be rooted. Such a complex, over-determined, and necessary role has been performed in modern thought by the analysis of actual experience. Actual experience is, in fact, both the space in which all empirical contents are given to experience and the original form that makes them possible in general and designates their primary roots; it does indeed provide a means of communication between the space of the body and the time of culture, between the determinations of nature and the weight of history, but only on condition that the body, and, through it, nature, should first be posited in the experience of an irreducible spatiality, and that culture, the carrier of history, should be experienced first of all in the immediacy of its sedimented significations. It is easy enough to understand how the analysis of actual experience has established itself, in modern reflection, as a radical contestation of positivism and eschatology; how it has tried to restore the forgotten dimension of the transcendental; how it has attempted to exorcise the naïve discourse of a truth reduced wholly to the empirical, and the prophetic discourse which with similar naïveté promises at last the eventual attainment by man of experience. Nevertheless, the analysis of actual experience is a discourse of mixed nature: it is directed to a specific yet ambiguous stratum, concrete enough for it to be possible to apply to it a meticulous and descriptive language, yet sufficiently removed from the positivity of things for it to be possible, from that starting-point, to escape from that naïveté, to contest it and seek foundations for it. This analysis seeks to articulate the possible objectivity of a knowledge of nature upon the original experience of which the body provides an outline; and to articulate the possible history of a culture upon the semantic density which is both hidden and revealed in actual experience. It is doing no more, then, than fulfilling with greater care the hasty demands laid down when the attempt was made to make the empirical, in man, stand for the transcendental. Despite appearances to the contrary, it is evident how closely knit is the network that links thoughts of the positivist or eschatological type (Marxism being in the first rank of these) and reflections inspired by phenomenology. Their recent *rapprochement* is not of the order of a tardy reconciliation: at the level of archaeological configurations they were both necessary – and

321

necessary to one another – from the moment the anthropological postulate was constituted, that is, from the moment when man appeared as an
empirico-transcendental doublet.

The true contestation of positivism and eschatology does not lie,
therefore, in a return to actual experience (which rather, in fact, provides
them with confirmation by giving them roots); but if such a contestation
could be made, it would be from the starting-point of a question which
may well seem aberrant, so opposed is it to what has rendered the whole
of our thought historically possible. This question would be: Does man
really exist? To imagine, for an instant, what the world and thought and
truth might be if man did not exist, is considered to be merely indulging
in paradox. This is because we are so blinded by the recent manifestation
of man that we can no longer remember a time – and it is not so long ago
– when the world, its order, and human beings existed, but man did not.
It is easy to see why Nietzsche's thought should have had, and still has
for us, such a disturbing power when it introduced in the form of an
imminent event, the Promise-Threat, the notion that man would soon be
no more – but would be replaced by the superman; in a philosophy of the
Return, this meant that man had long since disappeared and would continue to disappear, and that our modern thought about man, our concern
for him, our humanism, were all sleeping serenely over the threatening
rumble of his non-existence. Ought we not to remind ourselves – we
who believe ourselves bound to a finitude which belongs only to us, and
which opens up the truth of the world to us by means of our cognition –
ought we not to remind ourselves that we are bound to the back of
a tiger?

V   THE 'COGITO' AND THE UNTHOUGHT

If man is indeed, in the world, the locus of an empirico-transcendental
doublet, if he is that paradoxical figure in which the empirical contents
of knowledge necessarily release, of themselves, the conditions that have
made them possible, then man cannot posit himself in the immediate
and sovereign transparency of a *cogito*; nor, on the other hand, can he
inhabit the objective inertia of something that, by rights, does not and
never can lead to self-consciousness. Man is a mode of being which
accommodates that dimension – always open, never finally delimited, yet
constantly traversed – which extends from a part of himself not reflected in
a *cogito* to the act of thought by which he apprehends that part; and which,

in the inverse direction, extends from that pure apprehension to the empirical clutter, the chaotic accumulation of contents, the weight of experiences constantly eluding themselves, the whole silent horizon of what is posited in the sandy stretches of non-thought. Because he is an empirico-transcendental doublet, man is also the locus of misunderstanding – of misunderstanding that constantly exposes his thought to the risk of being swamped by his own being, and also enables him to recover his integrity on the basis of what eludes him. This is why transcendental reflection in its modern form does not, as in Kant, find its fundamental necessity in the existence of a science of nature (opposed by the perpetual conflicts and uncertainties of philosophers), but in the existence – mute, yet ready to speak, and secretly impregnated with a potential discourse – of that *not-known* from which man is perpetually summoned towards self-knowledge. The question is no longer: How can experience of nature give rise to necessary judgements? But rather: How can man think what he does not think, inhabit as though by a mute occupation something that eludes him, animate with a kind of frozen movement that figure of himself that takes the form of a stubborn exteriority? How can man *be* that life whose web, pulsations, and buried energy constantly exceed the experience that he is immediately given of them? How can he *be* that labour whose laws and demands are imposed upon him like some alien system? How can he be the subject of a language that for thousands of years has been formed without him, a language whose organization escapes him, whose meaning sleeps an almost invincible sleep in the words he momentarily activates by means of discourse, and within which he is obliged, from the very outset, to lodge his speech and thought, as though they were doing no more than animate, for a brief period, one segment of that web of innumerable possibilities? – There has been a fourfold displacement in relation to the Kantian position, for it is now a question not of truth, but of being; not of nature, but of man; not of the possibility of understanding, but of the possibility of a primary misunderstanding; not of the unaccountable nature of philosophical theories as opposed to science, but of the resumption in a clear philosophical awareness of that whole realm of unaccounted-for experiences in which man does not recognize himself.

Given this displacement of the question of transcendence, contemporary thought could not avoid reviving the theme of the *cogito*. Was it not also on the basis of error, illusion, dreams and madness, all the experiences of unaccounted-for thought, that Descartes discovered the impossibility of there not being thoughts – to such effect that the thought of the ill-thought, of the non-true, of the chimerical, of the purely imaginary, emerged as the possible locus and the primary, irrefutable proof of all those experiences? But the modern *cogito* is as different from Descartes' as our notion of transcendence is remote from Kantian analysis. For Descartes was concerned to reveal thought as the most general form of all those thoughts we term error or illusion, thereby rendering them harmless, so that he would be free, once that step had been taken, to return to them, to explain them, and then to provide a method of guarding against them. In the modern *cogito*, on the other hand, we are concerned to grant the highest value, the greatest dimension, to the distance that both separates and links thought-conscious-of-itself and whatever, within thought, is rooted in non-thought. The modern *cogito* (and this is why it is not so much the discovery of an evident truth as a ceaseless task constantly to be undertaken afresh) must traverse, duplicate, and reactivate in an explicit form the articulation of thought on everything within it, around it, and beneath it which is not thought, yet which is nevertheless not foreign to thought, in the sense of an irreducible, an insuperable exteriority. In this form, the *cogito* will not therefore be the sudden and illuminating discovery that all thought is thought, but the constantly renewed interrogation as to how thought can reside elsewhere than here, and yet so very close to itself; how it can *be* in the forms of non-thinking. The modern *cogito* does not reduce the whole being of things to thought without ramifying the being of thought right down to the inert network of what does not think.

This double movement proper to the modern *cogito* explains why the 'I think' does not, in its case, lead to the evident truth of the 'I am'. Indeed, as soon as the 'I think' has shown itself to be embedded in a density throughout which it is quasi-present, and which it animates, though in an equivocal semi-dormant, semi-wakeful fashion, it is no longer possible to make it lead on to the affirmation 'I am'. For can I, in fact, say that I am this language I speak, into which my thought insinuates itself to the point of finding in it the system of all its own possibilities, yet which exists only in the weight of sedimentations my thought will never be capable of actualizing altogether? Can I say that I am this labour I perform with my hands, yet which eludes me not only when I have finished it, but even before I have begun it? Can I say that I am this life I sense deep within me, but which envelops me both in the irresistible time that grows side by side with it and poses me for a moment on its crest, and in the imminent time that prescribes my death? I can say, equally well, that I am and that I am not all this; the *cogito* does not lead to an affirmation of being, but it does lead to a whole series of questions concerned with being: What must I be, I who think and who am my thought, in order to be what I do not think, in order for my thought to be what I am not? What is this being, then, that shimmers and, as it were, glitters in the opening of the *cogito*, yet is not sovereignly given in it or by it? What, then, is the connection, the difficult link, between being and thought? What is man's being, and how can it be that that being, which could so easily be characterized by the fact that 'it has thoughts' and is possibly alone in having them, has an ineradicable and fundamental relation to the unthought? A form of reflection is established far removed from both Cartesianism and Kantian analysis, a form that involves, for the first time, man's being in that dimension where thought addresses the unthought and articulates itself upon it.

This has two consequences. The first is negative, and of a purely historical order. It may seem that phenomenology has effected a union between the Cartesian theme of the *cogito* and the transcendental motif that Kant had derived from Hume's critique; according to this view, Husserl has revived the deepest vocation of the Western *ratio*, bending it back upon itself in a reflection which is a radicalization of pure philosophy and a basis for the possibility of its own history. In fact, Husserl was able to effect this union only in so far as transcendental analysis had changed its point of application (the latter has shifted from the possibility of a science of nature to the possibility for man to conceive of himself), and in so far as the *cogito* had modified its function (which is no longer to lead to an apodictic existence, starting from a thought that affirms itself wherever it thinks, but to show how thought can elude itself and thus lead to a many-sided and proliferating interrogation concerning being). Phenomenology is therefore much less the resumption of an old rational goal of the West than the sensitive and precisely formulated acknowledgment of the great hiatus that occurred in the modern *episteme* at the turn of the eighteenth and nineteenth centuries. If phenomenology has any allegiance, it is to the discovery of life, work, and language; and also to the new figure which, under the old name of man, first appeared less than two centuries ago; it is to interrogation concerning man's mode of being and his relation to the unthought. This is why phenomenology – even though it was first suggested by way of anti-psychologism, or, rather, precisely in so far as, in opposition to anti-psychologism, it revived the problem of the *a priori* and the transcendental motif – has never been able to exorcize its insidious kinship, its simultaneously promising and threatening proximity, to empirical analyses of man; it is also why, though it was inaugurated by a reduction to the *cogito*, it has always been led to questions, to *the* question of ontology. The phenomenological project continually resolves itself, before our eyes, into a description – empirical despite itself – of actual experience, and into an ontology of the unthought that automatically short-circuits the primacy of the 'I think'.

The second consequence is a positive one. It concerns the relation of man to the unthought, or, more precisely, their twin appearance in Western culture. It seems obvious enough that, from the moment when man first constituted himself as a positive figure in the field of knowledge, the old privilege of reflexive knowledge, of thought thinking itself, could not but disappear; but that it became possible, by this very fact, for an objective form of thought to investigate man in his entirety – at the risk of discovering what could never be reached by his reflection or even by his consciousness: dim mechanisms, faceless determinations, a whole landscape of shadow that has been termed, directly or indirectly, the unconscious. For is not the unconscious what necessarily yields itself up to the scientific thought man applies to himself when he ceases to conceive of himself in the form of reflection? As a matter of fact, the unconscious, and the forms of the unthought in general, have not been the reward granted to a positive knowledge of man. Man and the unthought are, at the archaeological level, contemporaries. Man has not been able to describe himself as a configuration in the *episteme* without thought at the same time discovering, both in itself and outside itself, at its borders yet also in its very warp and woof, an element of darkness, an apparently inert density in which it is embedded, an unthought which it contains entirely, yet in which it is also caught. The unthought (whatever name we give it) is not lodged in man like a shrivelled-up nature or a stratified history; it is, in relation to man, the Other: the Other that is not only a brother but a twin, born, not of man, nor in man, but beside him and at the same time, in an identical newness, in an unavoidable duality. This obscure space so readily interpreted as an abyssal region in man's nature, or as a uniquely impregnable fortress in his history, is linked to him in an entirely different way; it is both exterior to him and indispensable to him: in one sense, the shadow cast by man as he emerged in the field of knowledge; in another, the blind stain by which it is possible to know him. In any case, the unthought has accompanied man, mutely and uninterruptedly, since the nineteenth century. Since it was really never more than an insistent double, it has never been the object of reflection in an autonomous way; it has received the complementary form and the inverted name of that for which it was the Other and the shadow: in Hegelian phenomenology, it was the *An sich* as opposed to the *Für sich*; for Schopenhauer it was the *Unbewusste*; for Marx it was alienated man; in Husserl's analyses it was the implicit, the inactual, the sedimented, the non-effected – in every case, the inexhaustible double that presents itself to reflection as the blurred projection of what man is in his truth, but that also plays the role of a preliminary ground upon which man must collect himself and recall himself in order to attain his truth. For though this double may be close, it is alien, and the role, the true undertaking, of thought will be to bring it as close to itself as possible; the whole of modern thought is imbued with the necessity of thinking the unthought – of reflecting the contents of the *In-itself* in the form of the *For-itself*, of ending man's alienation by reconciling him with his own essence, of making explicit the horizon that provides experience with its background of immediate and disarmed proof, of lifting the veil of the Unconscious, of becoming absorbed in its silence, or of straining to catch its endless murmur.

In modern experience, the possibility of establishing man within knowledge and the mere emergence of this new figure in the field of the *episteme* imply an imperative that haunts thought from within; it matters little whether it be given currency in the form of ethics, politics, humanism, a duty to assume responsibility for the fate of the West, or the mere consciousness of performing, in history, a bureaucratic function. What is essential is that thought, both for itself and in the density of its workings, should be both knowledge and a modification of what it knows, reflection and a transformation of the mode of being of that on which it reflects. Whatever it touches it immediately causes to move: it cannot *motion* discover the unthought, or at least move towards it, without immediately bringing the unthought nearer to itself – or even, perhaps, without pushing it further away, and in any case without causing man's own being to undergo a change by that very fact, since it is deployed in the distance between them. There is something here profoundly bound up with our modernity: apart from its religious moralities, it is clear that the West has known only two ethical forms. The old one (in the form of Stoicism or Epicureanism) was articulated upon the order of the world, and by discovering the law of that order it could deduce from it the principle of a code of wisdom or a conception of the city; even the political thought of the eighteenth century still belongs to this general form. The modern one, on the other hand, formulates no morality, since any imperative is lodged within thought and its movement towards the apprehension of the unthought[2]; it is reflection, the act of consciousness, the elucidation of what is silent, language restored to what is mute, the illumination of the element of darkness that cuts man off from himself, the reanimation of the inert – it is all this and this alone that constituted the content and form of the ethical. Modern thought has never, in fact, been able to propose a morality. But the reason for this is not because it is pure speculation; on the contrary, modern thought, from its inception and in its very density, is a certain mode of action. Let those who urge thought to leave its retreat and to formulate its choices talk on; and let those who seek, without any pledge and in the absence of virtue, to establish a morality do as they wish. For modern thought, no morality is possible. Thought had already 'left' itself in its own being as early as the nineteenth century; it is no longer theoretical. As soon as it functions it offends or reconciles, attracts or repels, breaks, dissociates, unites or reunites; it cannot help but liberate and enslave. Even before prescribing, suggesting a future, saying what must be done, even before exhorting or merely sounding an alarm, thought, at the level of its existence, in its very dawning, is in itself an action – a perilous act. Sade, Nietzsche, Artaud, and Bataille have understood this on behalf of all those who tried to ignore it; but it is also certain that Hegel, Marx, and Freud knew it. Can we say that it is not known by those who, in their profound stupidity, assert that there is no philosophy without political choice, that all thought is either 'progressive' or 'reactionary'? Their foolishness is to believe that all thought 'expresses' the ideology of a class; their involuntary profundity is that they point directly at the modern mode of being of thought. Superficially, one might say that knowledge of man, unlike the sciences of nature, is always linked, even in its vaguest form, to ethics or politics; more fundamentally, modern thought is advancing towards that region where man's Other must become the Same as himself.

VI THE RETREAT AND RETURN OF THE ORIGIN

The last feature that characterizes both man's mode of being and the reflection addressed to him is the relation to the origin – a relation very different from that which Classical thought tried to establish in its ideal geneses. In the eighteenth century, to return to the origin was to place one-self once more as near as possible to the mere duplication of representation. Economics was conceived on the basis of barter, because in barter the two representations that each party made to himself of his property and the other's property were equivalent; since they were offering satisfaction for almost identical desires, they were, in sum, 'alike'. The order of nature was conceived, prior to any catastrophe, as a table in which beings fol-lowed one another in so tightly knit an order, and upon so continuous a fabric, that in going from one point of this succession to another one would have moved within a quasi-identity, and in going from one extremity of it to the other one would have been led by the smooth expanse of 'likeness'. The origin of language was conceived as the trans-parency between the representation of a thing and the representation of the cry, sound, or gesture (the language of action) that accompanied it. Finally, the origin of knowledge was sought within this pure sequence of representations – a sequence so perfect and so linear that the second had replaced the first without one's becoming conscious of the fact, since they were not simultaneous, since it was not possible to establish any difference between them, and since one could not experience the second as other than 'like' the first; and it was only when a sensation appeared to be more 'like' a previous one than all the others that reminiscence could come into play, that imagination could represent a representation afresh, and that knowledge could gain a foothold in this duplication. It was of little importance whether this origin was considered fictitious or real, whether it possessed the value of an explanatory hypothesis or a historical event: in fact, these distinctions exist only for us; in a system of thought for which chronological development resides within a table, upon which it constitutes no more than a line of a certain length, its starting-point is at the same time outside real time and inside it: it is the first fold that enables all historical events to take place.

In modern thought, such an origin is no longer conceivable: we have seen how labour, life, and language acquired their own historicity, in which they were embedded; they could never, therefore, truly express their origin, even though, from the inside, their whole history is, as it were, directed towards it. It is no longer origin that gives rise to his-toricity; it is historicity that, in its very fabric, makes possible the neces-sity of an origin which must be both internal and foreign to it: like the virtual tip of a cone in which all differences, all dispersions, all discon-tinuities would be knitted together so as to form no more than a single point of identity, the impalpable figure of the Same, yet possessing the power, nevertheless, to burst open upon itself and become Other.

Man was constituted at the beginning of the nineteenth century in correlation with these historicities, with all these things involuted upon themselves and indicating, through their display but by means of their own laws, the inaccessible identity of their origin. Yet man's own relation to his origin does not occur in the same way. This is because man, in fact, can be revealed only when bound to a previously existing historicity: he is never contemporaneous with that origin which is outlined through the time of things even as it eludes the gaze; when he tries to define himself as a living being, he can uncover his own beginning only against the background of a life which itself began long before him; when he attempts to re-apprehend himself as a labouring being, he cannot bring even the most rudimentary forms of such a being to light except within a human time and space which have been previously institutionalized, and previously subjugated by society; and when he attempts to define his essence as a speaking subject, prior to any effectively constituted language, all he ever finds is the previously unfolded possibility of language, and not the stumbling sound, the first word upon the basis of which all languages and even language itself became possible. It is always against a background of the already begun that man is able to reflect on what may serve for him as origin. For man, then, origin is by no means the beginning – a sort of dawn of history from which his ulterior acquisitions would have accumulated. Origin, for man, is much more the way in which man in general, any man, articulates himself upon the already-begun of labour, life, and language; it must be sought for in that fold where man in all simplicity applies his labour to a world that has been worked for thousands of years, lives in the freshness of his unique, recent, and precarious existence a life that has its roots in the first organic formations, and composes into sentences which have never before been spoken (even though generation after generation has repeated them) words that are older than all memory. In this sense, the level of the original is probably that which is closest to man: the surface he traverses so innocently, always for the first time, and upon which his scarcely opened eyes discern figures as young as his own gaze – figures that must necessarily be just as ageless as he himself, though for an opposite reason; it is not because they are always equally young, it is because they belong to a time that has neither the same standards of measurement nor the same foundations as him. But this thin surface of the original, which accompanies our entire existence and never deserts it (not even, indeed especially not, at the moment of death, when, on the contrary, it reveals itself, as it were, naked) is not the immediacy of a birth; it is populated entirely by those complex mediations formed and laid down as a sediment in their own history by labour, life, and language; so that in this simple contact, from the moment the first object is manipulated, the simplest need expressed, the most neutral word emitted, what man is reviving, without knowing it, is all the intermediaries of a time that governs him almost to infinity. Without knowing it, and yet it must be known, in a certain way, since it is by this means that men enter into communication and find themselves in the already constructed network of comprehension. Nevertheless, this knowledge is limited, diagonal, partial, since it is surrounded on all sides by an immense region of shadow in which labour, life, and language conceal their truth (and their own origin) from those very beings who speak, who exist, and who are at work.

The original, as modern thought has never ceased to describe it since *The phenomenology of mind*, is thus very different from that ideal genesis that the Classical age had attempted to reconstitute; but it is also different (though linked to it by a fundamental correlation) from the origin that is outlined, in a sort of retrospective beyond, through the historicity of beings. Far from leading back, or even merely pointing, towards a peak – whether real or virtual – of identity, far from indicating the moment of the Same at which the dispersion of the Other has not yet come into play, the original in man is that which articulates him from the very outset upon something other than himself; it is that which introduces into his experience contents and forms older than him, which he cannot master; it is that which, by binding him to multiple, intersecting, often mutually irreducible chronologies, scatters him through time and pinions him at the centre of the duration of things. Paradoxically, the original, in man, does not herald the time of his birth, or the most ancient kernel of his experience: it links him to that which does not have the same time as himself; and it sets free in him everything that is not contemporaneous with him; it indicates ceaselessly, and in an ever-renewed proliferation, that things began long before him, and that for this very reason, and since his experience is wholly constituted and limited by things, no one can ever assign him an origin. Now, this impossibility itself has two aspects: on the one hand, it signifies that the origin of things is always pushed further back, since it goes back to a calendar upon which man does not figure; but, on the other hand, it signifies that man, as opposed to the things whose glittering birth time allows to show in all its density, is the being without origin, who has 'neither country nor date', whose birth is never accessible because it never took 'place'. What is conveyed in the immediacy of the original is, therefore, that man is cut off from the origin that would make him contemporaneous with his own existence: amid all the things that are born in time and no doubt die in time, he, cut off from all origin, is already there. So that it is in him that things (those same things that hang over him) find their beginning: rather than a cut, made at some given moment in duration, he is the opening from which time in general can be reconstituted, duration can flow, and things, at the appropriate moment, can make their appearance. Though, in the empirical order, things are always set back from him, so that they are unapprehendable at their zero point, nevertheless man finds himself fundamentally set back in relation to that setting back of things, and it is by this means that they are able to weigh down upon the immediacy of the original experience with their solid anteriority.

A task is thereby set for thought: that of contesting the origin of things, but of contesting it in order to give it a foundation, by rediscovering the mode upon which the possibility of time is constituted – that origin without origin or beginning, on the basis of which everything is able to come into being. Such a task implies the calling into question of everything that pertains to time, everything that has formed within it, everything that resides within its mobile element, in such a way as to make visible that rent, devoid of chronology and history, from which time issued. Time would then be suspended within that thought, which nevertheless cannot escape from it since it is never contemporaneous with the origin; but this suspension would have the power to revolve the reciprocal relation of origin and thought; and as it pivoted upon itself, the origin, becoming what thought has yet to think, and always afresh, would be forever promised in an imminence always nearer yet never accomplished. In that case the origin is that which is returning, the repetition towards which thought is moving, the return of that which has already always begun, the proximity of a light that has been shining since the beginning of time. Thus, for the third time, the origin is visible through time; but this time it is the recession into the future, the injunction that thought receives and imposes upon itself to advance with dove-like steps towards that which has never ceased to render it possible, to keep watch in front of itself, on the ever-receding line of its horizon, for the day from which it came and from which it is coming in such profusion.

At the very moment when it became possible for it to denounce as fantasies the ideal geneses described in the eighteenth century, modern thought was establishing a problematics of the origin at once extremely complex and extremely tangled; this problematics has served as the foundation for our experience of time, and, since the nineteenth century, as the starting-point of all our attempts to re-apprehend what beginning and re-beginning, the recession and the presence of the beginning, the return and the end, could be in the human sphere. In fact, modern thought established a relation to the origin that was inverse for man and for things: in this way it sanctioned – but outwitted in advance and preserved all its power of contestation with regard to them – the positivist attempts to insert man's chronology within that of things, in such a way that the unity of time would be restored and that man's origin would be no more than a date, a fold, in the sequential series of beings (placing that origin, and with it the appearance of culture, the dawn of civilizations, within the stream of biological evolution); it sanctioned also the inverse and complementary endeavour to align the experience man has of things, the knowledge he has acquired of them, and the sciences he has thus been able to constitute, in accordance with chronology (so that though all man's beginnings have their locus within the time of things, his individual or cultural time makes it possible, in a psychological or historical genesis, to define the moment at which things meet the face of their truth for the first time); in each of these two alignments, the origin of things and the origin of man are subordinated to each other; but the mere fact that there are two possible and irreconcilable alignments indicates the fundamental asymmetry that characterizes modern thought on origin. Moreover, this thought brings into a final light and, as it were, into an essentially reticent clarity, a certain stratum of the original in which no origin was in fact present, but in which man's time (which has no beginning) made manifest, for a possible memory, the time of things (which has no memory). This leads to a double temptation: to psychologize all knowledge, of whatever kind, and to make psychology into a sort of general science of all the sciences; or, inversely, to describe this original stratum in a style that avoids all positivism in such a way as to make it possible, on this basis, to disturb the positivity of all science and to use the fundamental, insuperable character of this experience as a weapon against it. But in setting itself the task of restoring the domain of the original, modern thought immediately encounters the recession of the origin; and, paradoxically, it proposes the solution of advancing in the direction of this ever-deepening recession; it tries to make it appear on the far side of experience, as that which sustains it by its very retreat, as that which is nearest to its most visible possibility, as that which is, within thought, imminent; and if the recession of the origin is thus posited in its greatest clarity, is it not the origin itself that is set free and travels backwards until it reaches itself again, in the dynasty of its archaism? This is why modern thought is doomed, at every level, to its great preoccupation with recurrence, to its concern with recommencement, to that strange, stationary anxiety which forces upon it the duty of repeating repetition. Thus from Hegel to Marx and Spengler we find the developing theme of a thought which, by the movement in which it is accomplished - totality attained, violent recovery at the extreme point of poverty, solar decline – curves over upon itself, illuminates its own plenitude, brings its circle to completion, recognizes itself in all the strange figures of its odyssey, and accepts its disappearance into that same ocean from which it sprang; in opposition to this return, which, even though it is not happy, is perfect, we find the experience of Hölderlin, Nietzsche, and Heidegger, in which the return is posited only in the extreme recession of the origin – in that region where the gods have turned away, where the desert is increasing, where the τεχνή has established the dominion of its will; so that what we are concerned with here is neither a completion nor a curve, but rather that ceaseless rending open which frees the origin in exactly that degree to which it recedes; the extreme is therefore what is nearest. But whether this stratum of the original, revealed by modern thought in the very movement in which it invented man, is a promise of fulfilment and perfect plenitude or restores the void of the origin – the void created both by its recession and by its approach – in any case, what it prescribes as thought is something like the 'Same': through the domain of the original, which articulates human experience upon the time of nature and life, upon history, upon the sedimented past of cultures, modern thought makes it its task to return to man in his identity, in that plenitude or in that nothing which he is himself, to history and time in the repetition which they render impossible but which they force us to conceive, and to being in that which it is.

And by this means, in this infinite task of conceiving of the origin in what is nearest to it and what is furthest from it, thought reveals that man is not contemporaneous with what makes him be – or with that upon the basis of which he is; but that he is within a power that disperses him, draws him far away from his own origin, but promises it to him in an imminence that will perhaps be forever snatched from him; now, this power is not foreign to him; it does not reside outside him in the serenity of eternal and ceaselessly recommenced origins, for then the origin would be effectively posited; this power is that of his own being. Time – the time that he himself is – cuts him off not only from the dawn from which he sprang but also from that other dawn promised him as still to come. It is clear how this fundamental time – this time on the basis of which time can be given to experience – is different from that which was active in the philosophy of representation: then, time dispersed representation, since it imposed the form of a linear sequence upon it; but representation was able to reconstitute itself for itself in imagination, and thus to duplicate itself perfectly and to subjugate time; the image made it possible to re-apprehend time in its entirety, to recover what had been conceded to succession, and to construct a knowledge as true as that of an eternal understanding. In the modern experience, on the contrary, the retreat of the origin is more fundamental than all experience, since it is in it that experience shines and manifests its positivity; it is because man is not contemporaneous with his being that things are presented to him with a time that is proper to them. And here we meet once again the initial theme of finitude. But this finitude, which was expressed first of all by the weight of things upon man – by the fact that he was dominated by life, history, and language – now appears at a more fundamental level: it is the insurmountable relation of man's being with time.

Thus, by rediscovering finitude in its interrogation of the origin, modern thought closes the great quadrilateral it began to outline when the Western *episteme* broke up at the end of the eighteenth century: the connection of the positivities with finitude, the reduplication of the empirical and the transcendental, the perpetual relation of the *cogito* to the unthought, the retreat and return of the origin, define for us man's mode of being. It is in the analysis of that mode of being, and no longer in the analysis of representation, that reflection since the nineteenth century has sought a philosophical foundation for the possibility of knowledge.

VII DISCOURSE AND MAN'S BEING

It may be observed that these four theoretical segments (analysis of finitude, of empirico-transcendental repetition, of the unthought, and of origin) stand in a certain relation to the four subordinate domains which together constituted the general theory of language in the Classical age[3]. A relation which is at first glance one of resemblance and symmetry. It will be remembered that the theory of the *verb* explained how language could overflow its own boundaries and affirm being – in a movement which, in return, assured the very being of language, since the latter could establish itself and open up its space only where there already existed, at least in a hidden form, a foundation provided by the verb *to be*; the analysis of *finitude* explains in the same way how man's being finds itself determined by positivities which are exterior to it and which link it to the density of things, but how, in return, it is finite being that gives any determination the possibility of appearing in its positive truth. Whereas the theory of *articulation* showed how the patterning of words and of the things they represent could occur without a hiatus between them, the analysis of the *empirico-transcendental reduplication* shows how what is given in experience and what renders experience possible correspond to one another in an endless oscillation. The quest for the primary *designations* of language drew out from the silent and innermost heart of words, syllables, and sounds themselves, a dormant representation that formed, as it were, their forgotten soul (which it was necessary to bring back to light, to make speak and sing once more, in order to attain a greater exactitude of thought, a more miraculous power of poetry); in a similar way, for modern thought, the inert density of the *unthought* is always inhabited in a certain manner by a *cogito*, and this thought, dormant within what is not thought, must be brought to life again and stretched out in the sovereignty of the 'I think'. Lastly, there was a theory of *derivation* in Classical reflection on language: this showed how language, from the beginning of its history and perhaps in the instant of its origin, at the very point when it began to speak, shifted inside its own space, pivoted around on itself away from its primary representation, and deposited its words, even the very oldest of them, only when they had already been deployed in the figures of rhetoric; corresponding to that analysis, we now find the effort to conceive of an ever-elusive *origin*, to advance towards that place where man's being is always maintained, in relation to man himself, in a remoteness and a distance that constitute him.

But this play of correspondences must not be allowed to delude us. We must not imagine that the Classical analysis of discourse has continued without modification through the ages merely by applying itself to a new object; that the force of some historical weight has maintained it in its identity, despite so many adjacent mutations. In fact, the four theoretical segments that outlined the space of general grammar have not been preserved: but they were dissociated, they changed both their function and their level, they modified the entire domain of their validity when, at the end of the eighteenth century, the theory of representation was eclipsed. In the Classical age, the function of general grammar was to show how a language could be introduced into the sequential chain of representations, a language that, while manifesting itself in the simple and absolutely tenuous line of discourse, presupposed forms of simultaneity (affirmation of existences and coexistences; patterning of things represented and formation of generalities; original and inerasable relation between words and things; displacement of words within their rhetorical space). In contrast, the analysis of man's mode of being as it has developed since the nineteenth century does not reside within a theory of representation; its task, on the contrary, is to show how things in general can be given to representation, in what conditions, upon what ground, within what limits they can appear in a positivity more profound than the various modes of perception; and what is then revealed, in this coexistence of man and things, through the great spatial expanse opened up by representation, is man's radical finitude, the dispersion that at the same time separates him from his origin and promises it to him, and the insuperable distance of time. The analytic of man is not a resumption of the analysis of discourse as constituted elsewhere and handed down by tradition. The presence or absence of a theory of representation, or, more exactly, the primary character or derived position of that theory, modifies the equilibrium of the system from top to bottom. As long as representation goes without question as the general element of thought, the theory of discourse serves at the same time, and in one and the same movement, as the foundation of all possible grammar and as a theory of knowledge. But as soon as the primacy of representation disappears, then the theory of discourse is dissociated, and one can encounter its disincarnated and metamorphosed form on two separate levels. On the empirical level, the four constituent segments are still to be found, but the function they perform has been wholly inverted[4]: replacing the analysis of the verb's privileged position, of its power to make discourse emerge from itself and become rooted in the being of representation, we find the analysis of an internal grammatical structure which is immanent in each language and constitutes it as an autonomous being, in other words upon itself; similarly, the analysis of the articulation common to words and things has

337

been replaced by the theory of inflections and the attempt to establish laws of mutation proper to words alone; the theory of the radical has been substituted for the analysis of the representative root; finally, where before there was the search for the boundless continuity of derivation, the lateral kinship of languages has been revealed. In other words, everything that had functioned within the dimension of the relation between things (as they are represented) and words (with their representative value) has now been drawn back into language and given the task of providing it with an internal legality. At foundation level, the four segments of the theory of discourse are still to be found: as in the Classical age, they still serve in this new analytic of the human being to express the relation to things; but this time the modification is the inverse of what it was previously; it is no longer a matter of replacing them in a space interior to language, but of freeing them from the domain of representation within which they were trapped, and of bringing them into play in that dimension of exteriority in which man appears as a finite, determined being, trapped in the density of what he does not think, and subject, in his very being, to the dispersion of time.

From the moment when it was no longer in continuity with a theory of representation, the Classical analysis of discourse found itself, as it were, split in two: on the one hand, it invested itself in an empirical knowledge of grammatical forms; and, on the other, it became an analytic of finitude; but neither of these two transferences could take place without a total inversion of function. We are now in a position to understand, in all its implications, the incompatibility that reigns between the existence of Classical discourse (based upon the unquestioned evidence of representation) and the existence of man as it is presented in modern thought (and with the anthropological reflection that it sanctions): something like an analytic of man's mode of being became possible only after the analysis of representative discourse had been dissociated, transferred, and inverted. And we can also sense how man's being, thus defined and posited, is weighed down by the contemporary reappearance of language in the enigma of its unity and its being as by a threat. Is the task ahead of us to advance towards a mode of thought, unknown hitherto in our culture, that will make it possible to reflect at the same time, without discontinuity or contradiction, upon man's being and the being of language? – If that is so, we must take the very greatest precautions to avoid anything that might be a naïve return to the Classical theory of discourse (a return all the more tempting, it must be said, because we are so ill-equipped to conceive of the shining but crude being of language, whereas the old theory of representation is there, already constituted, offering us a place in which that being can be lodged and allowed to dissolve into pure function). But the right to conceive both of the being of language and of the being of man may be forever excluded; there may be, as it were, an inerasable hiatus at that point (precisely that hiatus in which we exist and talk), so that it would be necessary to dismiss as fantasy any anthropology in which there was any question of the being of language, or any conception of language or signification which attempted to connect with, manifest, and free the being proper to man. It is perhaps here that the most important philosophical choice of our period has its roots – a choice that can be made only in the test of a future reflection. For nothing can tell us in advance upon which side the through road lies. The only thing we know at the moment, in all certainty, is that in Western culture the being of man and the being of language have never, at any time, been able to coexist and to articulate themselves one upon the other. Their incompatibility has been one of the fundamental features of our thought.

However, the mutation of the analysis of Discourse into an analytic of finitude has one other consequence. The Classical theory of the sign and the word had to show how representations, which succeeded one another in a chain so narrow and so tightly knit that distinctions did not appear, with the result that they were all, in short, alike, could be spread out to form a permanent table of stable differences and limited identities; it was a matter of a genesis of Difference starting from the secretly varied monotony of the Like. The analytic of finitude has an exactly inverse role: in showing that man is determined, it is concerned with showing that the foundation of those determinations is man's very being in its radical limitations; it must also show that the contents of experience are already their own conditions, that thought, from the very beginning, haunts the unthought that eludes them, and that it is always striving to recover; it shows how that origin of which man is never the contemporary is at the same time withdrawn and given as an imminence: in short, it is always concerned with showing how the Other, the Distant, is also the Near and the Same. Thus we have moved from a reflection upon the order of Differences (with the analysis it presupposes and that ontology of continuity and that insistence upon a full, unbroken being deployed in its perfection that presuppose a metaphysics) to a thought of the Same, still to be conquered in its contradiction: which implies

339

(apart from the ethics already mentioned) a dialectic and that form of ontology which, since it has no need of continuity and has to reflect upon being only in its limited forms or in its distance, can and must do without metaphysics. Calling to one another and answering one another throughout modern thought and throughout its history, we find a dialectical interplay and an ontology without metaphysics: for modern thought is one that moves no longer towards the never-completed formation of Difference, but towards the ever-to-be-accomplished unveiling of the Same. Now, such an unveiling is not accomplished without the simultaneous appearance of the Double, and that hiatus, minuscule and yet invincible, which resides in the 'and' of retreat *and* return, of thought *and* the unthought, of the empirical *and* the transcendental, of what belongs to the order of positivity *and* what belongs to the order of foundations. Identity separated from itself by a distance which, in one sense, is interior to it, but, in another, constitutes it, and repetition which posits identity as a datum, but in the form of distance, are without doubt at the heart of that modern thought to which the discovery of time has so hastily been attributed. In fact, if we look a little more closely, we perceive that Classical thought related the possibility of spatializing things in a table to that property possessed by pure representative succession to recall itself on the basis of itself, to fold back upon itself, and to constitute a simultaneity on the basis of a continuous time: time became the foundation of space. In modern thought, what is revealed at the foundation of the history of things and of the historicity proper to man is the distance creating a vacuum within the Same, it is the hiatus that disperses and regroups it at the two ends of itself. It is this profound spatiality that makes it possible for modern thought still to conceive of time – to know it as succession, to promise it to itself as fulfilment, origin, or return.

VIII   THE ANTHROPOLOGICAL SLEEP

Anthropology as an analytic of man has certainly played a constituent role in modern thought, since to a large extent we are still not free from it. It became necessary at the moment when representation lost the power to determine, on its own and in a single movement, the interplay of its syntheses and analyses. It was necessary for empirical syntheses to be performed elsewhere than within the sovereignty of the 'I think'. They had to be required at precisely the point at which that sovereignty reached its limit, that is, in man's finitude – a finitude that is as much that of consciousness as that of the living, speaking, labouring individual. This had already been formulated by Kant in his *Logic*, when to his traditional trilogy of questions he added an ultimate one: the three critical questions (What can I know? What must I do? What am I permitted to hope?) then found themselves referred to a fourth, and inscribed, as it were, 'to its account': *Was ist der Mensch?*[5]

This question, as we have seen, runs through thought from the early nineteenth century: this is because it produces, surreptitiously and in advance, the confusion of the empirical and the transcendental, even though Kant had demonstrated the division between them. By means of this question, a form of reflection was constituted which is mixed in its levels and characteristic of modern philosophy. The concern it has for man, which it lays claim to not only in its discourse but in its pathos, the care with which it attempts to define him as a living being, an individual at work, or a speaking subject, herald the long-awaited return of a human reign only to the high-minded few; in fact, it concerns, rather more prosaically and less morally, an empirico-critical reduplication by means of which an attempt is made to make the man of nature, of exchange, or of discourse, serve as the foundation of his own finitude. In this Fold, the transcendental function is doubled over so that it covers with its dominating network the inert, grey space of empiricity; inversely, empirical contents are given life, gradually pull themselves upright, and are immediately subsumed in a discourse which carries their transcendental presumption into the distance. And so we find philosophy falling asleep once more in the hollow of this Fold; this time not the sleep of Dogmatism, but that of Anthropology. All empirical knowledge, provided it concerns man, can serve as a possible philosophical field in which the foundation of knowledge, the definition of its limits, and, in the end, the truth of all truth must be discoverable. The anthropological configuration of modern philosophy consists in doubling over dogmatism, in dividing it into two different levels each lending support to and limiting the other: the pre-critical analysis of what man is in his essence becomes the analytic of everything that can, in general, be presented to man's experience.

In order to awaken thought from such a sleep – so deep that thought experiences it paradoxically as vigilance, so wholly does it confuse the circularity of a dogmatism folded over upon itself in order to find a basis for itself within itself with the agility and anxiety of a radically philosophical thought – in order to recall it to the possibilities of its earliest dawning, there is no other way than to destroy the anthropological 'quadrilateral' in its very foundations. We know, in any case, that all efforts to think afresh are in fact directed at that obstacle: whether it is a matter of crossing the anthropological field, tearing ourselves free from it with the help of what it expresses, and rediscovering a purified ontology or a radical thought of being; or whether, rejecting not only psychologism and historicism, but all concrete forms of the anthropological prejudice, we attempt to question afresh the limits of thought, and to renew contact in this way with the project for a general critique of reason. Perhaps we should see the first attempt at this uprooting of Anthropology – to which, no doubt, contemporary thought is dedicated – in the Nietzschean experience: by means of a philological critique, by means of a certain form of biologism, Nietzsche rediscovered the point at which man and God belong to one another, at which the death of the second is synonymous with the disappearance of the first, and at which the promise of the superman signifies first and foremost the imminence of the death of man. In this, Nietzsche, offering this future to us as both promise and task, marks the threshold beyond which contemporary philosophy can begin thinking again; and he will no doubt continue for a long while to dominate its advance. If the discovery of the Return is indeed the end of philosophy, then the end of man, for its part, is the return of the beginning of philosophy. It is no longer possible to think in our day other than in the void left by man's disappearance. For this void does not create a deficiency; it does not constitute a lacuna that must be filled. It is nothing more, and nothing less, than the unfolding of a space in which it is once more possible to think.

Anthropology constitutes perhaps the fundamental arrangement that has governed and controlled the path of philosophical thought from Kant until our own day. This arrangement is essential, since it forms part of our history; but it is disintegrating before our eyes, since we are beginning to recognize and denounce in it, in a critical mode, both a forgetfulness of the opening that made it possible and a stubborn obstacle standing obstinately in the way of an imminent new form of thought. To all those who still wish to talk about man, about his reign or his liberation, to all those who still ask themselves questions about what man is in his essence, to all those who wish to take him as their starting-point in their attempts to reach the truth, to all those who, on the other hand, refer all knowledge back to the truths of man himself, to all those who refuse to formalize without anthropologizing, who refuse to mythologize without demystifying, who refuse to think without immediately thinking that it is man who is thinking, to all these warped and twisted forms of reflection we can answer only with a philosophical laugh – which means, to a certain extent, a silent one.

NOTES

[1] Nietzsche, *Genealogy of morals*, I, section 5.
[2] The Kantian moment is the link between the two: it is the discovery that the subject, in so far as he is reasonable, applies to himself his own law, which is the universal law.
[3] Cf. p. 115 above.
[4] Cf. p. 295 above.
[5] Kant, *Logik* (*Werke*, ed. Cassirer, vol. VIII, p. 343).

CHAPTER 10

The Human Sciences

I THE THREE FACES OF KNOWLEDGE

Man's mode of being as constituted in modern thought enables him to play two roles: he is at the same time at the foundation of all positivities and present, in a way that cannot even be termed privileged, in the element of empirical things. This fact – it is not a matter here of man's essence in general, but simply of that historical *a priori* which, since the nineteenth century, has served as an almost self-evident ground for our thought – this fact is no doubt decisive in the matter of the status to be accorded to the 'human sciences', to the body of knowledge (though even that word is perhaps a little too strong: let us say, to be more neutral still, to the body of discourse) that takes as its object man as an empirical entity.

The first thing to be observed is that the human sciences did not inherit a certain domain, already outlined, perhaps surveyed as a whole, but allowed to lie fallow, which it was then their task to elaborate with positive methods and with concepts that had at last become scientific; the eighteenth century did not hand down to them, in the name of man or human nature, a space, circumscribed on the outside but still empty, which it was then their role to cover and analyse. The epistemological field traversed by the human sciences was not laid down in advance: no philosophy, no political or moral option, no empirical science of any kind, no observation of the human body, no analysis of sensation, imagination, or the passions, had ever encountered, in the seventeenth or eighteenth century, anything like man; for man did not exist (any more than life, or language, or labour); and the human sciences did not appear when, as a result of some pressing rationalism, some unresolved scientific problem, some practical concern, it was decided to include man (willy-nilly, and with a greater or lesser degree of success) among the objects of

344

science – among which it has perhaps not been proved even yet that it is absolutely possible to class him; they appeared when man constituted himself in Western culture as both that which must be conceived of and that which is to be known. There can be no doubt, certainly, that the historical emergence of each one of the human sciences was occasioned by a problem, a requirement, an obstacle of a theoretical or practical order: the new norms imposed by industrial society upon individuals were certainly necessary before psychology, slowly, in the course of the nineteenth century, could constitute itself as a science; and the threats that, since the French Revolution, have weighed so heavily on the social balances, and even on the equilibrium established by the bourgeoisie, were no doubt also necessary before a reflection of the sociological type could appear. But though these references may well explain why it was in fact in such and such a determined set of circumstances and in answer to such and such a precise question that these sciences were articulated, nevertheless, their intrinsic possibility, the simple fact that man, whether in isolation or as a group, and for the first time since human beings have existed and have lived together in societies, should have become the object of science – that cannot be considered or treated as a phenomenon of opinion: it is an event in the order of knowledge.

And this event was itself produced in a general redistribution of the *episteme*: when, abandoning the space of representation, living beings took up their places in the specific depths of life, wealth in the onward thrust of new forms of production, and words in the development of languages. It was indeed necessary, given these conditions, that the knowledge of man should appear, in its scientific aims, as contemporaneous and of the same origin as biology, economics, and philology, so that it has been viewed, quite naturally, as one of the most decisive forward steps made in the history of European culture by empirical rationality. But since the general theory of representation was disappearing at the same time, and the necessity of interrogating man's being as the foundation of all positivities was imposing itself in its place, an imbalance could not fail to occur: man became that upon the basis of which all knowledge could be constituted as immediate and non-problematized evidence; he became, *a fortiori*, that which justified the calling into question of all knowledge of man. Hence that double and inevitable contestation: that which lies at the root of the perpetual controversy between the sciences of man and the sciences proper – the first laying an invincible claim to be the foundation of the second, which are ceaselessly obliged in turn to seek their own

345

foundation, the justification of their method, and the purification of their history, in the teeth of 'psychologism', 'sociologism', and 'historicism'; and that which lies at the root of the endless controversy between philosophy, which objects to the naïveté with which the human sciences try to provide their own foundation, and those same human sciences which claim as their rightful object what would formerly have constituted the domain of philosophy.

But the fact that all these observations must be made does not necessarily mean that their development occurs within the element of pure contradiction; their existence, and their untiring repetition for more than a century, do not indicate the permanence of an ever-open question; they refer back to a precise and extremely well-determined epistemological arrangement in history. In the Classical period, the field of knowledge, from the project of an analysis of representation to the theme of the *mathesis universalis*, was perfectly homogeneous: all knowledge, of whatever kind, proceeded to the ordering of its material by the establishment of differences and defined those differences by the establishment of an order; this was true for mathematics, true also for *taxonomies* (in the broad sense) and for the sciences of nature; but it was equally true for all those approximative, imperfect, and largely spontaneous kinds of knowledge which are brought into play in the construction of the least fragment of discourse or in the daily processes of exchange; and it was true, finally, for philosophical thought and for those long chains of order that the 'Idéologues', no less than Descartes or Spinoza, though in a different way, attempted to establish in order to create a path leading necessarily from the very simplest and most evident of ideas to the most composite truths. But, from the nineteenth century, the epistemological field became fragmented, or rather exploded in different directions. It is difficult to escape the pre-eminence of linear classifications and hierarchies in the manner of Comte; but to seek to align all the branches of modern knowledge on the basis of mathematics is to subject to the single point of view of objectivity in knowledge the question of the positivity of each branch of knowledge, of its mode of being, and its roots in those conditions of possibility that give it, in history, both its object and its form.

Questioned at this archaeological level, the field of the modern *episteme* is not ordered in accordance with the ideal of a perfect mathematicization, nor does it unfold, on the basis of a formal purity, a long, descending sequence of knowledge progressively more burdened with empiricity. The domain of the modern *episteme* should be represented rather as a volume of space open in three dimensions. In one of these we would situate the mathematical and physical sciences, for which order is always a deductive and linear linking together of evident or verified propositions; in a second dimension there would be the sciences (such as those of language, life, and the production and distribution of wealth) that proceed by relating discontinuous but analogous elements in such a way that they are then able to establish causal relations and structural constants between them. These first two dimensions together define a common plane: that which can appear, according to the direction in which one traverses it, as a field of application of mathematics to these empirical sciences, or as the domain of the mathematicizable in linguistics, biology, and economics. The third dimension would be that of philosophical reflection, which develops as a thought of the Same; it forms a common plane with the dimension of linguistics, biology, and economics: it is here that we may meet, and indeed have met, the various philosophies of life, of alienated man, of symbolical forms (when concepts and problems that first arose in different empirical domains are transposed into the philosophical dimension); but we have also encountered here, if we question the foundation of these empiricities from a radically philosophical point of view, those regional ontologies which attempt to define what life, labour, and language are in their own being; lastly, the philosophical dimension and that of the mathematical disciplines combine to define another common plane: that of the formalization of thought.

From this epistemological trihedron the human sciences are excluded, at least in the sense that they cannot be found along any of its dimensions or on the surface of any of the planes thus defined. But one can equally well say that they are included in it, since it is in the interstices of these branches of knowledge, or, more exactly, in the volume defined by their three dimensions, that the human sciences have their place. This situation (in one sense minor, in another sense privileged) places them in relation to all the other forms of knowledge: they have the more or less deferred, but constant, aim of giving themselves, or in any case of utilizing, at one level or another, a mathematical formalization; they proceed in accordance with models or concepts borrowed from biology, economics, and the sciences of language; and they address themselves to that mode of being of man which philosophy is attempting to conceive at the level of radical finitude, whereas their aim is to traverse all its empirical manifestations. It is perhaps this cloudy distribution within a three-dimensional space that renders the human sciences so difficult to situate, that gives their

347

localization in the epistemological domain its irreducible precariousness, that makes them appear at once perilous and in peril. Perilous, because they represent, as it were, a permanent danger to all the other branches of knowledge: true, neither the deductive sciences, nor the empirical sciences, nor philosophical reflection run any risk, if they remain within their own dimensions, of 'defecting' to the human sciences, or of being contaminated by their impurity; but we know what difficulties may be encountered, at times, in the establishing of those intermediary planes that link together the three dimensions of the epistemological space; for the slightest deviation from these rigorously defined planes sends thought tumbling over into the domain occupied by the human sciences: hence the danger of 'psychologism', of 'sociologism', – of what we might term, in a word, 'anthropologism' – which becomes a threat as soon as the relations of thought to formalization are not reflected upon correctly, for example, or as soon as the modes of being of life, labour, and language are incorrectly analysed. 'Anthropologization' is the great internal threat to knowledge in our day. We are inclined to believe that man has emancipated himself from himself since his discovery that he is not at the centre of creation, nor in the middle of space, nor even, perhaps, the summit and culmination of life; but though man is no longer sovereign in the kingdom of the world, though he no longer reigns at the centre of being, the 'human sciences' are dangerous intermediaries in the space of knowledge. The truth of the matter is, however, that this very posture dooms them to an essential instability. What explains the difficulty of the 'human sciences', their precariousness, their uncertainty as sciences, their dangerous familiarity with philosophy, their ill-defined reliance upon other domains of knowledge, their perpetually secondary and derived character, and also their claim to universality, is not, as is often stated, the extreme density of their object; it is not the metaphysical status or the inerasable transcendence of this man they speak of, but rather the complexity of the epistemological configuration in which they find themselves placed, their constant relation to the three dimensions that give them their space.

II THE FORM OF THE HUMAN SCIENCES

We must now sketch out the form of this positivity. Usually, the attempt is made to define it in terms of mathematics: either by trying to bring it as near to mathematics as possible, by drawing up an inventory of everything in the sciences of man that is mathematicizable, and supposing that everything that is not susceptible of such a formalization has not yet attained to scientific positivity; or, on the contrary, by trying to distinguish very carefully between the domain of the mathematicizable and that other domain which is regarded as irreducible to the former because it is the locus of interpretation, because the methods applied to it are above all those of comprehension, because it finds itself wound around the clinical pole of knowledge. Such analyses are wearisome not only because they are hackneyed but, above all, because they lack relevance. Certainly there can be no doubt that this form of empirical knowledge which is applicable to man (and which, in order to conform to convention, we may still term 'human sciences' even before we know in what sense and within what limits they can be called 'sciences') has a relation to mathematics: like any other domain of knowledge, these sciences may, in certain conditions, make use of mathematics as a tool; some of their procedures and a certain number of their results can be formalized. It is undoubtedly of the greatest importance to know those tools, to be able to practise those formalizations and to define the levels upon which they can be performed; it is no doubt of interest historically to know how Condorcet was able to apply the calculation of probabilities to politics, how Fechner defined the logarithmic relation between the growth of sensation and that of excitation, how contemporary psychologists make use of information theory in order to understand the phenomena of learning. But despite the specificity of the problems posed, it is unlikely that the relation to mathematics (the possibilities of mathematicization, or the resistance to all efforts at formalization) is constitutive of the human sciences in their particular positivity. And for two reasons: because, essentially, they share these problems with many other disciplines (such as biology and genetics) even if these problems are not always identical; and, above all, because archaeological analysis has not revealed, in the historical *a priori* of the human sciences, any new form of mathematics, or any sudden advance by mathematics into the domain of the human, but rather a sort of retreat of the mathesis, a dissociation of its unitary field, and the emancipation, in relation to the linear order of the smallest possible differences, of empirical organizations such as life, language, and labour. In this sense, the appearance of man and the constitution of the human sciences (even if it were only in the form of a project) would be correlated to a sort of 'de-mathematicization'. It may well be objected that this dissociation of a body of knowledge conceived

349

in its entirety as mathesis was not in fact a recession on the part of mathematics, for the very good reason that the knowledge in question had never led (except in the case of astronomy and certain areas of physics) to an effective mathematicization; rather, by disappearing, it left nature and the entire field of empiricities free for an application, limited and controlled moment by moment, of mathematics; for do not the first great advances of mathematical physics, the first massive utilizations of the calculation of probabilities, date from the time when the attempt at an immediate constitution of a general science of non-quantifiable orders was abandoned? It cannot really be denied that the renunciation of a mathesis (provisionally at least) made it possible, in certain domains of knowledge, to remove the obstacle of quality, and to apply mathematical tools where they had been unable to penetrate hitherto. But if, on the level of physics, the dissociation of the project to create a mathesis came to exactly the same thing as the discovery of new applications for mathematics, this was not so in all the domains of knowledge: biology, for example, was constituted, outside a science of qualitative orders, as an analysis of the relations between organs and functions, as a study of structures and balances, as research into their formation and development in the history of individuals or species; all of this did not prevent biology from making use of mathematics, or the latter from being much more broadly applicable to biology than it had been in the past. But it is not in its relation to mathematics that biology acquired its autonomy and defined its particular positivity. And the same was true for the human sciences: it was the retreat of the mathesis, and not the advance of mathematics, that made it possible for man to constitute himself as an object of knowledge; it was the involution of labour, life, and language upon themselves that determined the appearance of this new domain of knowledge from outside; and it was the appearance of that empirico-transcendental being, of that being whose thought is constantly interwoven with the unthought, of that being always cut off from an origin which is promised to him in the immediacy of the return – it was this appearance that gave the human sciences their particular form. Here again, as with other disciplines, it is very possible that the application of mathematics was facilitated (and is increasingly so) by all the modifications that occurred in Western knowledge at the beginning of the nineteenth century. But to imagine that the human sciences defined their most radical project and inaugurated their positive history when it was decided to apply the calculation of probabilities to the phenomena of political opinion, and to employ logarithms as a means of measuring the increase of intensity in sensations, that would be to take a superficial counter-effect for the fundamental event.

In other words, of the three dimensions that provide the human sciences with their particular space and produce the volume in which those sciences exist as a mass, that of mathematics is perhaps the least problematical; it is with mathematics, in any case, that the human sciences maintain the clearest, the most untroubled, and, as it were, the most transparent, relations: indeed, the recourse to mathematics, in one form or another, has always been the simplest way of providing positive knowledge about man with a scientific style, form, and justification. On the other hand, the most fundamental difficulties, those that make it possible to define most clearly what the human sciences are in their essence, are situated in the direction of the two other dimensions of knowledge: that in which the analytic of finitude is deployed, and that along which are distributed the empirical sciences which have as their objects language, life, and labour.

In fact, the human sciences are addressed to man in so far as he lives, speaks, and produces. It is as a living being that he grows, that he has functions and needs, that he sees opening up a space whose movable coordinates meet in him; in a general fashion, his corporeal existence interlaces him through and through with the rest of the living world; since he produces objects and tools, exchanges the things he needs, organizes a whole network of circulation along which what he is able to consume flows, and in which he himself is defined as an intermediary stage, he appears in his existence immediately interwoven with others; lastly, because he has a language, he can constitute a whole symbolic universe for himself, within which he has a relation to his past, to things, to other men, and on the basis of which he is able equally to build something like a body of knowledge (in particular, that knowledge of himself, of which the human sciences outline one of the possible forms). The site of the sciences of man may therefore be fixed in the vicinity, on the immediate frontiers, and along the whole length of those sciences that deal with life, labour, and language. Were they not formed, after all, at precisely that period when, for the first time, man offered himself to the possibility of a positive knowledge? Nevertheless, biology, economics, and philology must not be regarded as the first human sciences, or the most fundamental. This is easily recognized in the case of biology, since it is addressed to many other living beings besides man; but it is more difficult to accept in the cases of economics and philology, which have as their particular and exclusive domain activities that are specific to man. But we do not ask ourselves why human biology or physiology, why the anatomy of the cortical centres of language, cannot in any way be considered as sciences of man. This is because the object of those sciences is never posited in the mode of being of a biological function (or even in that of its particular form, and, as it were, its extension into man); it is rather its reverse, or the hollow it would leave; it begins at the point, not where the action or the effects stop, but where that function's own being stops – at that point where representations are set free, true or false, clear or obscure, perfectly conscious or rooted in some deep sleep, observable directly or indirectly, presented within what man himself expresses, or discoverable only from the outside; research into the intracortical connections between the different centres of linguistic integration (auditive, visual, motor) is not the province of the human sciences; but those sciences will find their field of action as soon as we question that space of words, that presence or that forgetfulness of their meaning, that hiatus between what one wishes to say and the articulation in which that aim is invested, whose subject may not be conscious, but which would have no assignable mode of being if that subject did not have representations.

In a more general fashion, man for the human sciences is not that living being with a very particular form (a somewhat special physiology and an almost unique autonomy); he is that living being who, from within the life to which he entirely belongs and by which he is traversed in his whole being, constitutes representations by means of which he lives, and on the basis of which he possesses that strange capacity of being able to represent to himself precisely that life. Similarly, even though man is, if not the only species in the world that works, at least the one in whom the production, distribution, and consumption of goods have taken on so great an importance and acquired so many and such differentiated forms, economics is still not a human science. It may perhaps be objected that in order to define certain laws, even though they are interior to the mechanics of production (such as the accumulation of capital or the relations between wage rates and prices), economics has recourse to human behaviour patterns and a representation that provide its foundation (interest, the search for maximum profit, the tendency to accumulate savings); but, in doing so, it is utilizing representations as the requisite of a function (which occurs, in effect, within an explicitly human activity); on the other hand, there will be no science of man unless we examine the way in which individuals or groups represent to themselves the partners with whom they produce or exchange, the mode in which they clarify or ignore or mask this function and the position they occupy in it, the manner in which they represent to themselves the society in which it takes place, the way in which they feel themselves integrated with it or isolated from it, dependent, subject, or free; the object of the human sciences is not that man who, since the dawn of the world, or the first cry of his golden age, is doomed to work; it is that being who, from within the forms of production by which his whole existence is governed, forms the representation of those needs, of the society by which, with which, or against which he satisfies them, so that upon that basis he can finally provide himself with a representation of economics itself. The same is true of language: although man is the only being in the world who speaks, inquiry into phonetic mutations, relationships between languages, and semantic shifts, does not constitute a human science; on the other hand, it will be possible to speak of human science when an attempt is made to define the way in which individuals or groups represent words to themselves, utilize their forms and their meanings, compose real discourse, reveal and conceal in it what they are thinking or saying, perhaps unknown to themselves, more or less than they wish, but in any case leave a mass of verbal traces of those thoughts, which must be deciphered and restored as far as possible to their representative vivacity. The object of the human sciences is not language (though it is spoken by men alone); it is that being which, from the interior of the language by which he is surrounded, represents to himself, by speaking, the sense of the words or propositions he utters, and finally provides himself with a representation of language itself.

The human sciences are not, then, an analysis of what man is by nature; but rather an analysis that extends from what man is in his positivity (living, speaking, labouring being) to what enables this same being to know (or seek to know) what life is, in what the essence of labour and its laws consist, and in what way he is able to speak. The human sciences thus occupy the distance that separates (though not without connecting them) biology, economics, and philology from that which gives them possibility in the very being of man. It would therefore be wrong to see the human sciences as an extension, interiorized within the human species, within its complex organism, within its behaviour and consciousness, of biological mechanisms; and it would be no less wrong to place within the human sciences the science of economics or the science of language (whose irreducibility to the human sciences is expressed in the effort to constitute a pure economics and a pure linguistics). In fact, the human sciences are no more within these sciences than they give them interiority by deflecting them towards man's subjectivity; if they take them up again in the dimension of representation, it is rather by re-apprehending them upon their outer slope, by leaving them their opacity, by accepting as things the mechanisms and functions they isolate, by questioning those functions and mechanisms not in terms of what they are but in terms of what they cease to be when the space of representation is opened up; and upon that basis they show how a representation of what they are can come into being and be deployed. Surreptitiously, they lead the sciences of life, labour, and language back to that analytic of finitude which shows how man, in his being, can be concerned with the things he knows, and know the things that, in positivity, determine his mode of being. But what the analytic requires in the interiority, or at least in the profound kinship, of a being who owes his finitude only to himself, the human sciences develop in the exteriority of knowledge. This is why what characterizes the human sciences is not that they are directed at a certain content (that singular object, the human being); it is much more a purely formal characteristic: the simple fact that, in relation to the sciences in which the human being is given as object (exclusive in the case of economics and philology, or partial in that of biology), they are in a position of duplication, and that this duplication can serve *a fortiori* for themselves.

This position is made perceptible on two levels: the human sciences do not treat man's life, labour, and language in the most transparent state in which they could be posited, but in that stratum of conduct, behaviour, attitudes, gestures already made, sentences already pronounced or written, within which they have already been given once to those who act, behave, exchange, work, and speak; at another level (it is still the same formal property, but carried to its furthest, rarest point), it is always possible to treat in the style of the human sciences (of psychology, sociology, and the history of culture, ideas, or science) the fact that for certain individuals or certain societies there is something like a speculative knowledge of life, production, and language – at most, a biology, an economics, and a philology. This is probably no more than the indication of a possibility which is rarely realized and is perhaps not capable, at the level of the empiricities, of yielding much of value; but the fact that it exists as a possible distance, as a space given to the human sciences to withdraw into, away from what they spring from, and the fact, too, that this action can be applied to themselves (it is always possible to make human sciences of human sciences – the psychology of psychology, the sociology of

354

sociology, etc.) suffice to demonstrate their peculiar configuration. In relation to biology, to economics, to the sciences of language, they are not, therefore, lacking in exactitude and rigour; they are rather like sciences of duplication, in a 'meta-epistemological' position. Though even that prefix is perhaps not very well chosen: for one can speak of meta-language only when defining the rules of interpretation of a primary language. Here, the human sciences, when they duplicate the sciences of language, labour, and life, when at their finest point they duplicate themselves, are directed not at the establishment of a formalized discourse: on the contrary, they thrust man, whom they take as their object in the area of finitude, relativity, and perspective, down into the area of the endless erosion of time. It would perhaps be better to speak in their case of an 'ana-' or 'hypo-epistemological' position; if the pejorative connotations of this last prefix were removed, it would no doubt provide a good account of the facts: it would suggest how the invincible impression of haziness, inexactitude, and imprecision left by almost all the human sciences is merely a surface effect of what makes it possible to define them in their positivity.

III   THE THREE MODELS

At first glance, one could say that the domain of the human sciences is covered by three 'sciences' – or rather by three epistemological regions, all subdivided within themselves, and all interlocking with one another; these regions are defined by the triple relation of the human sciences in general to biology, economics, and philology. Thus one could admit that the 'psychological region' has found its locus in that place where the living being, in the extension of its functions, in its neuro-motor blueprints, its physiological regulations, but also in the suspense that interrupts and limits them, opens itself to the possibility of representation; in the same way, the 'sociological region' would be situated where the labouring, producing, and consuming individual offers himself a representation of the society in which this activity occurs, of the groups and individuals among which it is divided, of the imperatives, sanctions, rites, festivities, and beliefs by which it is upheld or regulated; lastly, in that region where the laws and forms of a language hold sway, but where, nevertheless, they remain on the edge of themselves, enabling man to introduce into them the play of his representations, in that region arise the study of literature and myths, the analysis of all oral expressions and written documents, in short, the analysis of the verbal traces that a culture or an individual may leave behind them. This division, though very summary, is probably not too inexact. It does, however, leave two fundamental problems unsolved: one concerns the form of positivity proper to the human sciences (the concepts around which they are organized, the type of rationality to which they refer and by means of which they seek to constitute themselves as knowledge); the other is their relation to representation (and the paradoxical fact that even while they take place only where there is representation, it is to unconscious mechanisms, forms, and processes, or at least to the exterior boundaries of consciousness, that they address themselves).

The controversies to which the search for a specific positivity in the field of the human sciences has given rise are only too well known: Genetic or structural analysis? Explanation or comprehension? Recourse to what is 'underneath' or decipherment kept strictly to the level of reading? In fact, all these theoretical discussions did not arise and were not pursued throughout the history of the human sciences because the latter had to deal, in man, with an object so complex that it was not yet possible to find a unique mode of access towards it, or because it was necessary to use several in turn. These discussions were able to exist only in so far as the positivity of the human sciences rests simultaneously upon the transference of three distinct models. This transference is not a marginal phenomenon for the human sciences (a sort of supporting framework, a detour to include some exterior intelligibility, a confirmation derived from sciences already constituted); nor is it a limited episode in their history (a crisis of formation, at a time when they were still so young that they could not fix their concepts and their laws themselves). On the contrary, it is a matter of an ineffaceable fact, which is bound up, forever, with their particular arrangement in the epistemological space. We should, indeed, distinguish between two different sorts of model utilized by the human sciences (leaving aside models of formalization). On the one hand, there were – and often still are – concepts introduced from another domain of knowledge, which, losing all operational efficacity in the process, now play only the role of an image (organic metaphors in nineteenth-century sociology; energy metaphors in Janet; geometrical and dynamic metaphors in Lewin). But there are also constituent models, which are not just techniques of formalization for the human sciences, or simple means of devising methods of operation with less effort; they make it possible to create groups of phenomena as so many 'objects' for a possible branch of knowledge; they ensure their connection in the empirical sphere, but they offer them to experience already linked together. They play the role of 'categories' in the area of knowledge particular to the human sciences.

These constituent models are borrowed from the three domains of biology, economics, and the study of language. It is upon the projected surface of biology that man appears as a being possessing *functions* – receiving stimuli (physiological ones, but also social, interhuman, and cultural ones), reacting to them, adapting himself, evolving, submitting to the demands of an environment, coming to terms with the modifications it imposes, seeking to erase imbalances, acting in accordance with regularities, having, in short, conditions of existence and the possibility of finding average *norms* of adjustment which permit him to perform his functions. On the projected surface of economics, man appears as having needs and desires, as seeking to satisfy them, and therefore as having interests, desiring profits, entering into opposition with other men; in short, he appears in an irreducible situation of *conflict*; he evades these conflicts, he escapes from them or succeeds in dominating them, in finding a solution that will – on one level at least, and for a time – appease their contradictions; he establishes a body of *rules* which are both a limitation of the conflict and a result of it. Lastly, on the projected surface of language, man's behaviour appears as an attempt to say something; his slightest gestures, even their involuntary mechanisms and their failures, have a *meaning*; and everything he arranges around him by way of objects, rites, customs, discourse, all the traces he leaves behind him, constitute a coherent whole and a *system* of signs. Thus, these three pairs of *function* and *norm*, *conflict* and *rule*, *signification* and *system* completely cover the entire domain of what can be known about man.

It must not be supposed, however, that any of these pairs of concepts remains localized on the projected surface on which it may have appeared: function and norm are not psychological concepts exclusively; conflict and rule do not have an application limited wholly to the sociological domain; signification and system are not valid solely for phenomena more or less akin to language. All these concepts occur throughout the entire volume common to the human sciences and are valid in each of the regions included within it: hence the frequent difficulty in fixing limits, not merely between the objects, but also between the methods proper to psychology, sociology, and the analysis of literature and myth. Nevertheless, we can say in a general way that psychology is fundamentally a study of man in terms of functions and norms (functions and norms which can,

357

in a secondary fashion, be interpreted on the basis of conflicts and sig-nifications, rules and systems); sociology is fundamentally a study of man in terms of rules and conflicts (but these may be interpreted, and one is constantly led to interpret them, in a secondary way, either on the basis of functions, as though they were individuals organically connected to them-selves, or on the basis of systems of significations, as though they were written or spoken texts); lastly, the study of literature and myth is essen-tially the province of an analysis of significations and signifying systems, but we all know that this analysis may be carried out in terms of func-tional coherence or of conflicts and rules. In this way all the human sciences interlock and can always be used to interpret one another: their frontiers become blurred, intermediary and composite disciplines multi-ply endlessly, and in the end their proper object may even disappear altogether. But whatever the nature of the analysis and the domain to which it is applied, we have a formal criterion for knowing what is on the level of psychology, what on that of sociology, and what on that of language analysis: this is the choice of the fundamental model and the position of the secondary models, which make it possible to know at what point one begins to 'psychologize' or 'sociologize' in the study of literature and myth, or at what point in psychology one has moved over into the decipherment of texts or into sociological analysis. But this superimposition of several models is not a defect of method. It becomes a defect only if the models have not been precisely ordered and explicitly articulated in relation to one another. As we know, it proved possible to conduct an admirably precise study of the Indo-European mythologies by using the sociological model superimposed upon the basic analysis of significants and significations. We know also, on the other hand, to what syncretic platitudes the still mediocre undertaking of founding a so-called 'clinical' psychology has led.

Whether properly founded and controlled, or carried out in confusion, this interlocking of constituent models explains the discussions of method referred to above. They do not have their origin and justification in a sometimes contradictory complexity which we know as the character proper to man; but in the play of oppositions, which makes it possible to define each of the three models in relation to the two others. To oppose genesis to structure is to oppose function (in its development, in its pro-gressively diversified operations, in the powers of adaptation it has acquired and balanced in time) to the synchronism of conflict and rule, of signification and system; to oppose analysis by means of that which is 'underneath' to analysis on the same level as its object is to oppose conflict (a primary, archaic datum inscribed at the same time as man's fundamental needs) to function and signification as they are deployed in their particular realization; to oppose comprehension to explanation is to oppose the technique that makes it possible to decipher a meaning on the basis of a signifying system to those that make it possible to give an account of a conflict together with its consequences, or of the forms and deformations that a function and its organs may assume or undergo. But we must go further. We know that in the human sciences the point of view of discontinuity (the threshold between nature and culture, the irreducibility one to another of the balances or solutions found by each society or each individual, the absence of intermediary forms, the non-existence of a continuum existing in space or time) is in opposition to the point of view of continuity. The existence of this opposition is to be explained by the bipolar character of the models: analysis in a continuous mode relies upon the permanence of function (which is to be found in the very depths of life in an identity that authorizes and provides roots for succeeding adaptations), upon the interconnection of conflicts (they may take various forms, but they are always present in the background), upon the fabric of significations (which link up with one another and constitute, as it were, the continuous expanse of a discourse); on the contrary, the analysis of discontinuities seeks rather to draw out the internal coherence of signifying systems, the specificity of bodies of rules and the decisive character they assume in relation to what must be regulated, and the emergence of the norm above the level of functional fluctuations.

It might be possible to retrace the entire history of the human sciences, from the nineteenth century onward, on the basis of these three models. They have, in fact, covered the whole of that history, since we can follow the dynasty of their privileges for more than a century: first, the reign of the biological model (man, his psyche, his group, his society, the language he speaks – all these exist in the Romantic period as living beings and in so far as they were, in fact, alive; their mode of being is organic and is analysed in terms of function); then comes the reign of the economic model (man and his entire activity are the locus of conflicts of which they are both the more or less manifest expression and the more or less successful solution); lastly – just as Freud comes after Comte and Marx – there begins the reign of the philological (when it is a matter of interpretation and the discovery of hidden meanings) and linguistic model (when it is a matter of giving a structure to and clarifying the signifying system). Thus a vast shift has led the human sciences from a form more dense in living models to another more saturated with models borrowed from language. But this shift was paralleled by another: that which caused the first term in each of the constituent pairs (function, conflict, signification) to recede, and the second term (norm, rule, system) to emerge with a correspondingly greater intensity and importance: Goldstein, Mauss, Dumezil may be taken to represent, as near as makes no difference, the moment at which the reversal took place within each of the models. Such a reversal has two series of noteworthy consequences: as long as the functional point of view continued to carry more weight than the normative point of view (as long as it was not on the basis of the norm and the interior of the activity determining that norm that the attempt was made to understand how a function was performed), it was of course necessary, *de facto*, to share the normal functions with the non-normal; thus a pathological psychology was accepted side by side with normal psychology, but forming as it were an inverted image of it (hence the importance of the Jacksonian notion of disintegration in Ribot or Janet); in the same way, a pathology of societies (Durkheim), of irrational and quasi-morbid forms of belief (Lévy-Bruhl, Blondel) was also accepted; similarly, as long as the point of view of conflict carried more weight than that of the rule, it was supposed that certain conflicts could not be overcome, that individuals and societies ran the risk of destroying themselves by them; finally, as long as the point of view of signification carried more weight than that of system, a division was made between significant and non-significant: it was accepted that there was meaning in certain domains of human behaviour or certain regions of the social area, but not in others. So that the human sciences laid down an essential division within their own field: they always extended between a positive pole and a negative pole; they always designated an alterity (based, furthermore, on the continuity they were analysing). When, on the other hand, the analysis was conducted from the point of view of the norm, the rule, and the system, each area provided its own coherence and its own validity; it was no longer possible to speak of 'morbid consciousness' (even referring to the sick), of 'primitive mentalities' (even with reference to societies left behind by history), or of 'insignificant discourse' (even when referring to absurd stories, or to apparently incoherent legends). Everything may be thought within the order of the system, the rule, and the norm. By pluralizing itself – since systems are isolated, since rules form closed wholes, since norms are posited in their autonomy – the field of the human sciences found itself unified: suddenly, it was no longer fissured along its former dichotomy of values. And bearing in mind that Freud more than anyone else brought the knowledge of man closer to its philological and linguistic model, and that he was also the first to undertake the radical erasure of the division between positive and negative (between the normal and the pathological, the comprehensible and the incommunicable, the significant and the non-significant), it is easy to see how he prefigures the transition from an analysis in terms of functions, conflicts, and significations to an analysis in terms of norms, rules, and systems: thus all this knowledge, within which Western culture had given itself in one century a certain image of man, pivots on the work of Freud, though without, for all that, leaving its fundamental arrangement. But even so, it is not here – as we shall see later on – that the most decisive importance of psychoanalysis lies.

In any case, this transition to the point of view of the norm, the rule, and the system brings us to a problem that has been left in suspense: that of the role of representation in the human sciences. It might already appear extremely contestable to include the human sciences (as opposed to biology, economics, and philology) within the space of representation: was it not already necessary to point out that a function can be performed, a conflict can develop its consequences, a signification can impose its intelligibility, without passing through the stage of explicit consciousness? And now, is it not necessary to recognize that the peculiar property of the norm in relation to the function it determines, of the rule in relation to the conflict it regulates, of the system in relation to the signification it makes possible, is precisely that of not being given to consciousness? Are we not forced to add a third historical gradient to the two already isolated, and to say that since the nineteenth century the human sciences have never ceased to approach that region of the unconscious where the action of representation is held in suspense? In fact, representation is not consciousness, and there is nothing to prove that this bringing to light of elements or structures that are never presented to consciousness as such enables the human sciences to escape the law of representation. The role of the concept of signification is, in fact, to show how something like a language, even if it is not in the form of explicit discourse, and even if it has not been deployed for a consciousness, can in general be given to representation; the role of the complementary concept of system is to show how signification is never primary and contemporaneous with itself, but always secondary and as it were derived in relation to a system that

361

precedes it, constitutes its positive origin, and posits itself, little by little, in fragments and outlines through signification; in relation to the consciousness of a signification, the system is indeed always unconscious since it was there before the signification, since it is within it that the signification resides and on the basis of it that it becomes effective; but because the system is always promised to a future consciousness which will perhaps never add it up. In other words, the signification/system pair is what ensures both the representability of language (as text or structure analysed by philology and linguistics) and the near but withdrawn presence of the origin (as it is manifested as man's mode of being by means of the analytic of finitude). In the same way, the notion of conflict shows how need, desire, and interest, even if they are not presented to the consciousness experiencing them, can take form in representation; and the role of the inverse concept of rule is to show how the violence of conflict, the apparently untamed insistence of need, the lawless infinity of desire are in fact already organized by an unthought which not only prescribes their rules, but renders them possible upon the basis of a rule. The conflict/rule pair ensures the representability of need (of the need that economics studies as an objective process in labour and production) and the representability of the unthought that is unveiled by the analytic of finitude. Lastly, the concept of function has the role of showing how the structures of life may give rise to representation (even though they are not conscious), and the concept of norm how function provides its own conditions of possibility and the frontiers within which it is effective.

Thus it can be understood why these broad categories can structure the entire field of the human sciences: it is because they span it from end to end, because they both hold apart and link together the empirical positivities of life, labour, and language (on the basis of which man first detached himself historically as a form of possible knowledge) and the forms of finitude that characterize man's mode of being (as he constituted himself when representation ceased to define the general space of knowledge). These categories are not, therefore, mere empirical concepts of rather broad generality; they are indeed the basis on which man is able to present himself to a possible knowledge; they traverse the entire field of his possibility and articulate it boldly in accordance with the two dimensions that form its frame.

But that is not all: they also permit the dissociation, which is characteristic of all contemporary knowledge about man, of consciousness and representation. They define the manner in which the empiricities can be

THE HUMAN SCIENCES

given to representation but in a form that is not present to the consciousness (function, conflict, and signification are indeed the manner in which life, need, and language are doubled over in representation, but in a form that may be completely unconscious); on the other hand, they define the manner in which the fundamental finitude can be given to representation in a form both positive and empirical, yet not transparent to the naïve consciousness (neither norm, not rule, not system is given in daily experience: they run through it, give rise to partial consciousnesses of themselves, but can never be wholly illumined except by a reflexive form of knowledge). So the human sciences speak only within the element of the representable, but in accordance with a conscious/unconscious dimension, a dimension that becomes more and more marked as one attempts to bring the order of systems, rules, and norms to light. It is as though the dichotomy between normal and pathological were tending to be eclipsed in favour of the bipolarity of consciousness and the unconscious.

It must not be forgotten, therefore, that the increasingly marked importance of the unconscious in no way compromises the primacy of representation. This primacy does, however, raise an important problem. Now that the empirical forms of knowledge, such as those of life, labour, and language, have escaped from its law, now that the attempt to define man's mode of being is being made outside the field of representation, what is representation, if not a phenomenon of an empirical order which occurs within man, and could be analysed as such? And if representation occurs within man, what difference is there between it and consciousness? But representation is not simply an object for the human sciences; it is, as we have just seen, the very field upon which the human sciences occur, and to their fullest extent; it is the general pedestal of that form of knowledge, the basis that makes it possible. Two consequences emerge from this. One is of a historical order: it is the fact that the human sciences, unlike the empirical sciences since the nineteenth century, and unlike modern thought, have been unable to find a way around the primacy of representation; like the whole of Classical knowledge, they reside within it; but they are in no way its heirs or its continuation, for the whole configuration of knowledge has been modified and they came into being only to the degree to which there appeared, with man, a being who did not exist before in the field of the *episteme*. However, it is easy to understand why every time one tries to use the human sciences to philosophize, to pour back into the space of thought what one has been able to learn of man, one finds oneself imitating the philosophical posture of the eighteenth

363

century, in which, nevertheless, man had no place; for by extending the domain of knowledge about man beyond its limits one is similarly extending the reign of representation beyond itself, and thus taking up one's position once more in a philosophy of the Classical type. The other consequence is that the human sciences, when dealing with what is representation (in either conscious or unconscious form), find themselves treating as their object what is in fact their condition of possibility. They are always animated, therefore, by a sort of transcendental mobility. They never cease to exercise a critical examination of themselves. They proceed from that which is given to representation to that which renders representation possible, but which is still representation. So that, unlike other sciences, they seek not so much to generalize themselves or make themselves more precise as to be constantly demystifying themselves: to make the transition from an immediate and non-controlled evidence to less transparent but more fundamental forms. This quasi-transcendental process is always given in the form of an unveiling. It is always by an unveiling that they are able, as a consequence, to become sufficiently generalized or refined to conceive of individual phenomena. On the horizon of any human science, there is the project of bringing man's consciousness back to its real conditions, of restoring it to the contents and forms that brought it into being, and elude us within it; this is why the problem of the unconscious – its possibility, status, mode of existence, the means of knowing it and of bringing it to light – is not simply a problem within the human sciences which they can be thought of as encountering by chance in their steps; it is a problem that is ultimately coextensive with their very existence. A transcendental raising of level that is, on the other side, an unveiling of the non-conscious is constitutive of all the sciences of man.

We may find in this the means of isolating them in their essential property. In any case, we can see that what manifests this peculiar property of the human sciences is not that privileged and singularly blurred object which is man. For the good reason that it is not man who constitutes them and provides them with a specific domain; it is the general arrangement of the *episteme* that provides them with a site, summons them, and establishes them – thus enabling them to constitute man as their object. We shall say, therefore, that a 'human science' exists, not wherever man is in question, but wherever there is analysis – within the dimension proper to the unconscious – of norms, rules, and signifying totalities which unveil to consciousness the conditions of its forms and contents. To speak of 'sciences of man' in any other case is simply an abuse of language. We can see, then, how vain and idle are all those wearisome discussions as to whether such and such forms of knowledge may be termed truly scientific, and to what conditions they ought to be subjected in order to become so. The 'sciences of man' are part of the modern *episteme* in the same way as chemistry or medicine or any other such science; or again, in the same way as grammar and natural history were part of the Classical *episteme*. But to say that they are part of the epistemological field means simply that their positivity is rooted in it, that that is where they find their condition of existence, that they are therefore not merely illusions, pseudo-scientific fantasies motivated at the level of opinions, interests, or beliefs, that they are not what others call by the bizarre name of 'ideology'. But that does not necessarily mean that they are sciences.

Although it is true that any science, any science whatever, when it is questioned on the archaeological level and when an attempt is made to clear the ground of its positivity, always reveals the epistemological configuration that made it possible, any epistemological configuration, on the other hand, even if it is completely assignable in its positivity, may very well not be a science: it does not thereby reduce itself, *ipso facto*, to the status of an imposture. We must distinguish carefully between three things. There are themes with scientific pretensions that one may encounter at the level of opinion and that are not (or are no longer) part of a culture's epistemological network: from the seventeenth century, for example, natural magic ceased to belong to the Western *episteme*, but it persisted for a long time in the interaction of beliefs and affective valorizations. Then there are epistemological figures whose outline, position, and function can be reconstituted in their positivity by means of an analysis of the archaeological type; and these, in turn, may obey two different organizations: some present characteristics of objectivity and systematicity which make it possible to define them as sciences; others do not answer to those criteria, that is, their form of coherence and their relation to their object are determined by their positivity alone. The fact that these latter do not possess the formal criteria of a scientific form of knowledge does not prevent them from belonging, nevertheless, to the positive domain of knowledge. It would thus be as futile and unjust to analyse them as phenomena of opinion as to contrast them historically or critically with scientific formations proper; it would be more absurd still to treat them as a combination which mixes together in variable proportions 'rational elements' and other elements that are not rational. They must be replaced on the level of positivity that renders them possible and necessarily determines their form. Archaeology, then, has two tasks with regard to these figures: to determine the manner in which they are arranged in the *episteme* in which they have their roots; and to show, also, in what respect their configuration is radically different from that of the sciences in the strict sense. There is no reason to treat this peculiar configuration of theirs as a negative phenomenon: it is not the presence of an obstacle nor some internal deficiency which has left them stranded across the threshold of scientific forms. They constitute, in their own form, side by side with the sciences and on the same archaeological ground, *other* configurations of knowledge.

We have already encountered examples of such configurations in general grammar or in the Classical theory of value; they possessed the same ground of positivity as Cartesian mathematics, but they were not sciences, at least for the majority of those who were their contemporaries. Such is also the case with what we today call the human sciences; when analysed archaeologically, they provide the outlines of completely positive configurations; but as soon as these configurations and the way in which they are arranged within the modern *episteme* are determined, we understand why they cannot be sciences: what renders them possible, in fact, is a certain situation of 'vicinity' with regard to biology, economics, and philology (or linguistics); they exist only in so far as they dwell side by side with those sciences – or rather beneath them, in the space of their projections. However, they maintain a relationship with those sciences that is radically different from that which can be established between two 'related' or 'germane' sciences: this relationship presupposes, in fact, the transposition of external models within the dimension of the unconscious and consciousness, and the flowing back of critical reflection towards the very place from which those models come. It is useless, then, to say that the 'human sciences' are false sciences; they are not sciences at all; the configuration that defines their positivity and gives them their roots in the modern *episteme* at the same time makes it impossible for them to be sciences; and if it is then asked why they assumed that title, it is sufficient to recall that it pertains to the archaeological definition of their roots that they summon and receive the transference of models borrowed from the sciences. It is therefore not man's irreducibility, what is designated as his invincible transcendence, nor even his excessively great complexity, that prevents him from becoming an object of science. Western culture has constituted, under the name of man, a being who, by one and the same interplay of reasons, must be a positive domain of *knowledge* and cannot be an object of *science*.

IV HISTORY

We have spoken of the human sciences; we have spoken of those broad regions delimited more or less by psychology, sociology, and the analysis of literature and mythology. We have not yet mentioned history, though it is the first and as it were the mother of all the sciences of man, and is perhaps as old as human memory. Or rather, it is for that very reason that we have until now passed it over in silence. Perhaps history has no place, in fact, among the human sciences, or beside them: it may well be that it maintains with them all a relation that is strange, undefined, ineffaceable, and more fundamental than any relation of adjacency in a common space would be.

It is true that History existed long before the constitution of the human sciences; from the beginnings of the Ancient Greek civilization, it has per-formed a certain number of major functions in Western culture: memory, myth, transmission of the Word and of Example, vehicle of tradition, critical awareness of the present, decipherment of humanity's destiny, anticipation of the future, or promise of a return. What characterized this History – or at least what may be used to define it in its general features, as opposed to our own – was that by ordering the time of human beings upon the world's development (in a sort of great cosmic chronology such as we find in the works of the Stoics), or inversely by extending the principle and movement of a human destiny to even the smallest particles of nature (rather in the same way as Christian Providence), it was con-ceived of as a vast historical stream, uniform in each of its points, drawing with it in one and the same current, in one and the same fall or ascension, or cycle, all men, and with them things and animals, every living or inert being, even the most unmoved aspects of the earth. And it was this unity that was shattered at the beginning of the nineteenth century, in the great upheaval that occurred in the Western *episteme*: it was discovered that there existed a historicity proper to nature; forms of adaptation to the environment were defined for each broad type of living being, which would make possible a subsequent definition of its evolutionary outline; moreover, it became possible to show that activities as peculiarly human as labour or language contained within themselves a historicity that could not be placed within the great narrative common to things and to men:

367

production has its modes of development, capital its modes of accumulation, prices their laws of fluctuation and change which cannot be fitted over natural laws or reduced to the general progress of humanity; in the same way, language is not modified as much by migrations, trade, and wars, by what happens to man or what his imagination is able to invent, as by conditions that properly belong to the phonetic and grammatical forms of which it is constituted; and if it has been possible to say that the various languages are born, live, lose their energy as they age, and finally die, this biological metaphor is not intended to dissolve their history in a time which would be that of life, but rather to underline the fact that they too have internal laws of functioning, and that their chronology unfolds in accordance with a time that refers in the first place to their own particular coherence.

We are usually inclined to believe that the nineteenth century, largely for political and social reasons, paid closer attention to human history, that the idea of an order or a continuous level of time was abandoned, as well as that of an uninterrupted progress, and that the bourgeoisie, in attempting to recount its own ascension, encountered, in the calendar of its victory, the historical density of institutions, the specific gravity of habits and beliefs, the violence of struggles, the alternation of success and failure. And we suppose that, on this basis, the historicity discovered within man was extended to the objects he had made, the language he spoke, and – even further still – to life. According to this point of view, the study of economies, the history of literatures and grammars, and even the evolution of living beings are merely effects of the diffusion, over increasingly more distant areas of knowledge, of a historicity first revealed in man. In reality, it was the opposite that happened. Things first of all received a historicity proper to them, which freed them from the continuous space that imposed the same chronology upon them as upon men. So that man found himself dispossessed of what constituted the most manifest contents of his history: nature no longer speaks to him of the creation or the end of the world, of his dependency or his approaching judgement; it no longer speaks of anything but a natural time; its wealth no longer indicates to him the antiquity or the imminent return of a Golden Age; it speaks only of conditions of production being modified in the course of history; language no longer bears the marks of a time before Babel or of the first cries that rang through the jungle; it carries the weapons of its own affiliation. The human being no longer has any history: or rather, since he speaks, works, and lives, he finds himself interwoven in his own being with histories that are neither subordinate to him nor homogeneous with him. By the fragmentation of the space over which Classical knowledge extended in its continuity, by the folding over of each separated domain upon its own development, the man who appears at the beginning of the nineteenth century is 'dehistoricized'.

And the imaginative values then assumed by the past, the whole lyrical halo that surrounded the consciousness of history at that period, the lively curiosity shown for documents or for traces left behind by time – all this is a surface expression of the simple fact that man found himself emptied of history, but that he was already beginning to recover in the depths of his own being, and among all the things that were still capable of reflecting his image (the others have fallen silent and folded back upon themselves), a historicity linked essentially to man himself. But this historicity is immediately ambiguous. Since man posits himself in the field of positive knowledge only in so far as he speaks, works, and lives, can his history ever be anything but the inextricable nexus of different times, which are foreign to him and heterogeneous in respect of one another? Will the history of man ever be more than a sort of modulation common to changes in the conditions of life (climate, soil fertility, methods of agriculture, exploitation of wealth), to transformations in the economy (and consequently in society and its institutions), and to the succession of forms and usages in language? But, in that case, man is not himself historical: since time comes to him from somewhere other than himself, he constitutes himself as a subject of history only by the superimposition of the history of living beings, the history of things, and the history of words. He is subjected to the pure events those histories contain. But this relation of simple passivity is immediately reversed; for what speaks in language, what works and consumes in economics, what lives in human life, is man himself; and, this being so, he too has a right to a development quite as positive as that of beings and things, one no less autonomous – and perhaps even more fundamental: is it not a historicity proper to man, one inscribed in the very depths of his being, that enables him to adapt himself like any living being, and to evolve like any living being (though with the help of tools, techniques, and organizations belonging to no other living being), that enables him to invent forms of production, to stabilize, prolong, or abridge the validity of economic laws by means of the consciousness he attains of them and by means of the institutions he constructs upon or around them, and that enables him to exercise upon language, with every word he speaks, a sort of constant interior pressure which makes it shift imperceptibly upon itself at any given moment in time. Thus, behind the history of the positivities, there appears another, more radical, history, that of man himself – a history that now concerns man's very being, since he now realizes that he not only 'has history' all around him, but is himself, in his own historicity, that by means of which a history of human life, a history of economics, and a history of languages are given their form. In which case, at a very deep level, there exists a historicity of man which is itself its own history but also the radical dispersion that provides a foundation for all other histories. It was just this primary erosion that the nineteenth century sought in its concern to historicize everything, to write a general history of everything, to go back ceaselessly through time, and to place the most stable of things in the liberating stream of time. Here again, we should no doubt revise the way in which we traditionally write the history of History; we are accustomed to saying that the nineteenth century brought an end to the pure chronicle of events, the simple memory of a past peopled only by individuals and accidents, and that it began the search for the general laws of development. In fact, no history was ever more 'explanatory', more preoccupied with general laws and constants, than were the histories of the Classical age – when the world and man were inextricably linked in a single history. What first comes to light in the nineteenth century is a simple form of human historicity – the fact that man as such is exposed to the event. Hence the concern either to find laws for this pure form (which gives us philosophies such as that of Spengler) or to define it on the basis of the fact that man lives, works, speaks, and thinks: and this gives us interpretations of history from the standpoint of man envisaged as a living species, or from the standpoint of economic laws, or from that of cultural totalities.

In any case, this arrangement of history within the epistemological space is of great importance for its relation with the human sciences. Since historical man is living, working, and speaking man, any content of History is the province of psychology, sociology, or the sciences of language. But, inversely, since the human being has become historical, through and through, none of the contents analysed by the human sciences can remain stable in itself or escape the movement of History. And this for two reasons: because psychology, sociology, and philosophy, even when applied to objects – that is, men – which are contemporaneous with them, are never directed at anything other than synchronological patternings within a historicity that constitutes and traverses them; and because the forms successively taken by the human sciences, the choice of objects they make, and the methods they apply to them, are all provided by History, ceaselessly borne along by it, and modified at its pleasure. The more History attempts to transcend its own rootedness in historicity, and the greater the efforts it makes to attain, beyond the historical relativity of its origin and its choices, the sphere of universality, the more clearly it bears the marks of its historical birth, and the more evidently there appears through it the history of which it is itself a part (and this, again, is to be found in Spengler and all the philosophers of history); inversely, the more it accepts its relativity, and the more deeply it sinks into the movement it shares with what it is recounting, then the more it tends to the slenderness of the narrative, and all the positive content it obtained for itself through the human sciences is dissipated.

History constitutes, therefore, for the human sciences, a favourable environment which is both privileged and dangerous. To each of the sciences of man it offers a background, which establishes it and provides it with a fixed ground and, as it were, a homeland; it determines the cultural area – the chronological and geographical boundaries – in which that branch of knowledge can be recognized as having validity; but it also surrounds the sciences of man with a frontier that limits them and destroys, from the outset, their claim to validity within the element of universality. It reveals in this way that though man – even before knowing it – has always been subjected to the determinations that can be expressed by psychology, sociology, and the analysis of language, he is not therefore the intemporal object of a knowledge which, at least at the level of its rights, must itself be thought of as ageless. Even when they avoid all reference to history, the human sciences (and history may be included among them) never do anything but relate one cultural episode to another (that to which they apply themselves as their object, and that in which their existence, their mode of being, their methods, and their concepts have their roots); and though they apply themselves to their own synchronology, they relate the cultural episode from which they emerged to itself. Man, therefore, never appears in his positivity and that positivity is not immediately limited by the limitlessness of History.

Here we see being reconstituted a movement analogous to that which animated from within the entire domain of the human sciences: as analysed above, this movement perpetually referred certain positivities determining man's being to the finitude that caused those same positivities to appear; so that the sciences were themselves taken up in that great oscillation, but in such a way that they in turn took it up in the form of their own positivity by seeking to move ceaselessly backwards and forwards between the conscious and the unconscious. And now we find the beginning of a similar oscillation in the case of History; but this time it does not move between the positivity of man taken as object (and empirically manifested by labour, life, and language) and the radical limits of his being; it moves instead between the temporal limits that define the particular forms of labour, life, and language, and the historical positivity of the subject which, by means of knowledge, gains access to them. Here again, the subject and the object are bound together in a reciprocal questioning of one another; but whereas, before, this questioning took place within positive knowledge itself, and by the progressive unveiling of the unconscious by consciousness, here it takes place on the outer limits of the object and subject; it designates the erosion to which both are subjected, the dispersion that creates a hiatus between them, wrenching them loose from a calm, rooted, and definitive positivity. By unveiling the unconscious as their most fundamental object, the human sciences showed that there was always something still to be thought in what had already been thought on a manifest level; by revealing the law of time as the external boundary of the human sciences, History shows that everything that has been thought will be thought again by a thought that does not yet exist. But perhaps all we have here, in the concrete forms of the unconscious and History, is the two faces of that finitude which, by discovering that it was its own foundation, caused the figure of man to appear in the nineteenth century: a finitude without infinity is no doubt a finitude that has never finished, that is always in recession with relation to itself, that always has something still to think at the very moment when it thinks, that always has time to think again what it has thought.

In modern thought, historicism and the analytic of finitude confront one another. Historicism is a means of validating for itself the perpetual critical relation at play between History and the human sciences. But it establishes it solely at the level of the positivities: the positive knowledge of man is limited by the historical positivity of the knowing subject, so that the moment of finitude is dissolved in the play of a relativity from which it cannot escape, and which itself has value as an absolute. To be finite, then, would simply be to be trapped in the laws of a perspective which, while allowing a certain apprehension – of the type of perception or understanding – prevents it from ever being universal and definitive intellection. All knowledge is rooted in a life, a society, and a language that have a history; and it is in that very history that knowledge finds the element enabling it to communicate with other forms of life, other types of society, other significations: that is why historicism always implies a certain philosophy, or at least a certain methodology, of living comprehension (in the element of the *Lebenswelt*), of interhuman communication (against a background of social structures), and of hermeneutics (as the re-apprehension through the manifest meaning of the discourse of another meaning at once secondary and primary, that is, more hidden but also more fundamental). By this means, the different positivities formed by History and laid down in it are able to enter into contact with one another, surround one another in the form of knowledge, and free the content dormant within them; it is not, then, the limits themselves that appear, in their absolute rigour, but partial totalities, totalities that turn out to be limited by fact, totalities whose frontiers can be made to move, up to a certain point, but which will never extend into the space of a definitive analysis, and will never raise themselves to the status of absolute totality. This is why the analysis of finitude never ceases to use, as a weapon against historicism, the part of itself that historicism has neglected: its aim is to reveal, at the foundation of all the positivities and before them, the finitude that makes them possible; where historicism sought for the possibility and justification of concrete relations between limited totalities, whose mode of being was predetermined by life, or by social forms, or by the significations of language, the analytic of finitude tries to question this relation of the human being to the being which, by designating finitude, renders the positivities possible in their concrete mode of being.

V PSYCHOANALYSIS AND ETHNOLOGY

Psychoanalysis and ethnology occupy a privileged position in our knowledge – not because they have established the foundations of their positivity better than any other human science, and at last accomplished the old attempt to be truly scientific; but rather because, on the confines of all the branches of knowledge investigating man, they form an undoubted and inexhaustible treasure-hoard of experiences and concepts, and above all a perpetual principle of dissatisfaction, of calling into question, of criticism and contestation of what may seem, in other respects, to be established. Now, there is a reason for this that concerns the object they respectively give to one another, but concerns even more the position they occupy and the function they perform within the general space of the *episteme*.

Psychoanalysis stands as close as possible, in fact, to that critical function which, as we have seen, exists within all the human sciences. In setting itself the task of making the discourse of the unconscious speak through consciousness, psychoanalysis is advancing in the direction of that fundamental region in which the relations of representation and finitude come into play. Whereas all the human sciences advance towards the unconscious only with their back to it, waiting for it to unveil itself as fast as consciousness is analysed, as it were backwards, psychoanalysis, on the other hand, points directly towards it, with a deliberate purpose – not towards that which must be rendered gradually more explicit by the progressive illumination of the implicit, but towards what is there and yet is hidden, towards what exists with the mute solidity of a thing, of a text closed in upon itself, or of a blank space in a visible text, and uses that quality to defend itself. It must not be supposed that the Freudian approach is the combination of an interpretation of meaning and a dynamics of resistance or defence; by following the same path as the human sciences, but with its gaze turned the other way, psychoanalysis moves towards the moment – by definition inaccessible to any theoretical knowledge of man, to any continuous apprehension in terms of signification, conflict, or function – at which the contents of consciousness articulate themselves, or rather stand gaping, upon man's finitude. This means that, unlike the human sciences, which, even while turning back towards the unconscious, always remain within the space of the representable, psychoanalysis advances and leaps over representation, overflows it on the side of finitude, and thus reveals, where one had expected functions bearing their norms, conflicts burdened with rules, and significations forming a system, the simple fact that it is possible for there to be system (therefore signification), rule (therefore conflict), norm (therefore function). And in this region where representation remains in suspense, on the edge of itself, open, in a sense, to the closed boundary of finitude, we find outlined the three figures by means of which life, with its function and norms, attains its foundation in the mute repetition of Death, conflicts and rules their foundation in the naked opening of Desire, significations and systems their foundation in a language which is at the same time Law. We know that psychologists and philosophers have dismissed all this as Freudian mythology. It was indeed inevitable that this approach of Freud's should have appeared to them in this way; to a knowledge situated within the representable, all that frames and defines, on the out-side, the very possibility of representation can be nothing other than mythology. But when one follows the movement of psychoanalysis as it progresses, or when one traverses the epistemological space as a whole, one sees that these figures are in fact – though imaginary no doubt to the myopic gaze – the very forms of finitude, as it is analysed in modern thought. Is death not that upon the basis of which knowledge in general is possible – so much so that we can think of it as being, in the area of psychoanalysis, the figure of that empirico-transcendental *duplication* that characterizes man's mode of being within finitude? Is desire not that which remains always *unthought* at the heart of thought? And the law-language (at once word and word-system) that psychoanalysis takes such pains to make speak, is it not that in which all signification assumes an *origin* more distant than itself, but also that whose return is promised in the very act of analysis? It is indeed true that this Death, and this Desire, and this Law can never meet within the knowledge that traverses in its positivity the empirical domain of man; but the reason for this is that they designate the conditions of possibility of all knowledge about man.

And precisely when this language emerges in all its nudity, yet at the same time eludes all signification as if it were a vast and empty despotic system, when Desire reigns in the wild state, as if the rigour of its rule had levelled all opposition, when Death dominates every psychological function and stands above it as its unique and devastating norm – then we recognize madness in its present form, madness as it is posited in the modern experience, as its truth and its alterity. In this figure, which is at once empirical and yet foreign to (and in) all that we can experience, our consciousness no longer finds – as it did in the sixteenth century – the trace of another world; it no longer observes the wandering of a straying reason; it sees welling up that which is, perilously, nearest to us – as if, suddenly, the very hollowness of our existence is outlined in relief; the finitude upon the basis of which we are, and think, and know, is suddenly there before us: an existence at once real and impossible, thought that we cannot think, an object for our knowledge that always eludes it. This is why psychoanalysis finds in that madness *par excellence* – which psychia-trists term schizophrenia – its intimate, its most invincible torture: for, given in this form of madness, in an absolutely manifest and absolutely withdrawn form, are the forms of finitude towards which it usually advances unceasingly (and interminably) from the starting-point of that which is voluntarily-involuntarily offered to it in the patient's language.

So psychoanalysis 'recognizes itself' when it is confronted with those very psychoses which nevertheless (or rather, for that very reason) it has scarcely any means of reaching: as if the psychosis were displaying in a savage illumination, and offering in a mode not too distant but just too close, that towards which analysis must make its laborious way.

But this relation of psychoanalysis with what makes all knowledge in general possible in the sphere of the human sciences has yet another consequence – namely, that psychoanalysis cannot be deployed as pure speculative knowledge or as a general theory of man. It cannot span the entire field of representation, attempt to evade its frontiers, or point towards what is more fundamental, in the form of an empirical science constructed on the basis of careful observation; that breakthrough can be made only within the limits of a praxis in which it is not only the knowledge we have of man that is involved, but man himself – man together with the Death that is at work in his suffering, the Desire that has lost its object, and the language by means of which, through which, his Law is silently articulated. All analytic knowledge is thus invincibly linked with a praxis, with that strangulation produced by the relation between two individuals, one of whom is listening to the other's language, thus freeing his desire from the object it has lost (making him understand he has lost it), liberating him from the ever-repeated proximity of death (making him understand that one day he will die). This is why nothing is more alien to psychoanalysis than anything resembling a general theory of man or an anthropology.

Just as psychoanalysis situates itself in the dimension of the unconscious (of that critical animation which disturbs from within the entire domain of the sciences of man), so ethnology situates itself in the dimension of historicity (of that perpetual oscillation which is the reason why the human sciences are always being contested, from without, by their own history). It is no doubt difficult to maintain that ethnology has a fundamental relation with historicity since it is traditionally the knowledge we have of peoples without histories; in any case, it studies (both by systematic choice and because of the lack of documents) the structural invariables of cultures rather than the succession of events. It suspends the long 'chronological' discourse by means of which we try to reflect our own culture within itself, and instead it reveals synchronological correlations in other cultural forms. And yet ethnology itself is possible only on the basis of a certain situation, of an absolutely singular event which involves not only our historicity but also that of all men who can constitute the object of an ethnology (it being understood that we can perfectly well apprehend our own society's ethnology): ethnology has its roots, in fact, in a possibility that properly belongs to the history of our culture, even more to its fundamental relation with the whole of history, and enables it to link itself to other cultures in a mode of pure theory. There is a certain position of the Western *ratio* that was constituted in its history and provides a foundation for the relation it can have with all other societies, even with the society in which it historically appeared. Obviously, this does not mean that the colonizing situation is indispensable to ethnology: neither hypnosis, nor the patient's alienation within the fantasmatic character of the doctor, is constitutive of psychoanalysis; but just as the latter can be deployed only in the calm violence of a particular relationship and the transference it produces, so ethnology can assume its proper dimensions only within the historical sovereignty – always restrained, but always present – of European thought and the relation that can bring it face to face with all other cultures as well as with itself.

But this relation (in so far as ethnology does not seek to efface it, but on the contrary deepens it by establishing itself definitively within it) does not imprison it within the circular system of actions and reactions proper to historicism; rather, it places it in a position to find a way round that danger by inverting the movement that gave rise to it; in fact, instead of relating empirical contents – as revealed in psychology, sociology, or the analysis of literature and myth – to the historical positivity of the subject perceiving them, ethnology places the particular forms of each culture, the differences that contrast it with others, the limits by which it defines itself and encloses itself upon its own coherence, within the dimension in which its relations occur with each of the three great positivities (life, need and labour, and language): thus, ethnology shows how, within a given culture, there occur the normalization of the broad biological functions, the rules that render possible or obligatory all the forms of exchange, production, and consumption, and the systems that are organized around or on the model of linguistic structures. Ethnology, then, advances towards that region where the human sciences are articulated upon that biology, that economics, and that philology and linguistics which, as we have seen, dominate the human sciences from such a very great height: this is why the general problem of all ethnology is in fact that of the relations (of continuity or discontinuity) between nature and culture. But in this mode of questioning, the problem of history is found to have been reversed: for it then becomes a matter of determining, according to the symbolic systems employed, according to the prescribed rules, according to the functional norms chosen and laid down, what sort of historical development each culture is susceptible of; it is seeking to re-apprehend, in its very roots, the mode of historicity that may occur within that culture, and the reasons why its history must inevitably be cumulative or circular, progressive or subjected to regulating fluctuations, capable of spontaneous adjustments or subject to crises. And thus is revealed the foundation of that historical flow within which the different human sciences assume their validity and can be applied to a given culture and upon a given synchronological area.

Ethnology, like psychoanalysis, questions not man himself, as he appears in the human sciences, but the region that makes possible knowledge about man in general; like psychoanalysis, it spans the whole field of that knowledge in a movement that tends to reach its boundaries. But psychoanalysis makes use of the particular relation of the transference in order to reveal, on the outer confines of representation, Desire, Law, and Death, which outline, at the extremity of analytic language and practice, the concrete figures of finitude; ethnology, on the other hand, is situated within the particular relation that the Western *ratio* establishes with all other cultures; and from that starting-point it avoids the representations that men in any civilization may give themselves of themselves, of their life, of their needs, of the significations laid down in their language; and it sees emerging behind those representations the norms by which men perform the functions of life, although they reject their immediate pressure, the rules through which they experience and maintain their needs, the systems against the background of which all signification is given to them. The privilege of ethnology and psychoanalysis, the reason for their profound kinship and symmetry, must not be sought, therefore, in some common concern to pierce the profound enigma, the most secret part of human nature; in fact, what illuminates the space of their discourse is much more the historical *a priori* of all the sciences of man – those great caesuras, furrows, and dividing-lines which traced man's outline in the Western *episteme* and made him a possible area of knowledge. It was quite inevitable, then, that they should both be sciences of the unconscious: not because they reach down to what is below consciousness in man, but because they are directed towards that which, outside man, makes it possible to know, with a positive knowledge, that which is given to or eludes his consciousness.

On this basis, a certain number of decisive facts become comprehensible.

378

And the first is this: that psychoanalysis and ethnology are not so much two human sciences among others, but that they span the entire domain of those sciences, that they animate its whole surface, spread their concepts throughout it, and are able to propound their methods of decipherment and their interpretations everywhere. No human science can be sure that it is out of their debt, or entirely independent of what they may have discovered, or certain of not being beholden to them in one way or another. But their development has one particular feature, which is that, despite their quasi-universal 'bearing', they never, for all that, come near to a general concept of man: at no moment do they come near to isolating a quality in him that is specific, irreducible, and uniformly valid wherever he is given to experience. The idea of a 'psychoanalytic anthropology', and the idea of a 'human nature' reconstituted by ethnology, are no more than pious wishes. Not only are they able to do without the concept of man, they are also unable to pass through it, for they always address themselves to that which constitutes his outer limits. One may say of both of them what Lévi-Strauss said of ethnology: that they dissolve man. Not that there is any question of revealing him in a better, purer, and as it were more liberated state; but because they go back towards that which foments his positivity. In relation to the 'human sciences', psychoanalysis and ethnology are rather 'counter-sciences'; which does not mean that they are less 'rational' or 'objective' than the others, but that they flow in the opposite direction, that they lead them back to their epistemological basis, and that they ceaselessly 'unmake' that very man who is creating and re-creating his positivity in the human sciences. Lastly, we can understand why psychoanalysis and ethnology should have been constituted in confrontation, in a fundamental correlation: since *Totem and taboo*, the establishment of a common field for these two, the possibility of a discourse that could move from one to the other without discontinuity, the double articulation of the history of individuals upon the unconscious of culture, and of the historicity of those cultures upon the unconscious of individuals, has opened up, without doubt, the most general problems that can be posed with regard to man.

One can imagine what prestige and importance ethnology could possess if, instead of defining itself in the first place – as it has done until now – as the study of societies without history, it were deliberately to seek its object in the area of the unconscious processes that characterize the system of a given culture; in this way it would bring the relation of historicity, which is constitutive of all ethnology in general, into play within the dimension in which psychoanalysis has always been deployed. In so doing it would not assimilate the mechanisms and forms of a society to the pressure and repression of collective hallucinations, thus discovering – though on a larger scale – what analysis can discover at the level of the individual; it would define as a system of cultural unconsciouses the totality of formal structures which render mythical discourse significant, give their coherence and necessity to the rules that regulate needs, and provide the norms of life with a foundation other than that to be found in nature, or in pure biological functions. One can imagine the similar importance that a psychoanalysis would have if it were to share the dimension of an ethnology, not by the establishment of a 'cultural psychology', not by the sociological explanation of phenomena manifested at the level of individuals, but by the discovery that the unconscious also possesses, or rather that it *is* in itself, a certain formal structure. By this means, ethnology and psychoanalysis would succeed, not in superimposing themselves on one another, nor even perhaps in coming together, but in intersecting like two lines differently oriented: one proceeding from the apparent elision of the signified in a neurosis to the lacuna in the signifying system through which the neurosis found expression; the other proceeding from the analogy between the multiple things signified (in mythologies, for example) to the unity of a structure whose formal transformations would yield up the diversity existing in the actual stories. It would thus not be at the level of the relations between the individual and society, as has often been believed, that psychoanalysis and ethnology could be articulated one upon the other; it is not because the individual is a part of his group, it is not because a culture is reflected and expressed in a more or less deviant manner in the individual, that these two forms of knowledge are neighbours. In fact, they have only one point in common, but it is an essential and inevitable one: the one at which they intersect at right angles; for the signifying chain by which the unique experience of the individual is constituted is perpendicular to the formal system on the basis of which the significations of a culture are constituted: at any given instant, the structure proper to individual experience finds a certain number of possible choices (and of excluded possibilities) in the systems of the society; inversely, at each of their points of choice the social structures encounter a certain number of possible individuals (and others who are not) – just as the linear structure of language always produces a possible choice between several words or several phonemes at any given moment (but excludes all others).

Whereupon there is formed the theme of a pure theory of language which would provide the ethnology and the psychoanalysis thus conceived with their formal model. There would thus be a discipline that could cover in a single movement both the dimension of ethnology that relates the human sciences to the positivities in which they are framed and the dimension of psychoanalysis that relates the knowledge of man to the finitude that gives it its foundation. In linguistics, one would have a science perfectly founded in the order of positivities exterior to man (since it is a question of pure language), which, after traversing the whole space of the human sciences, would encounter the question of finitude (since it is through language, and within it, that thought is able to think: so that it is in itself a positivity with the value of a fundamental). Above ethnology and psychoanalysis, or, more exactly, interwoven with them, a third 'counter-science' would appear to traverse, animate, and disturb the whole constituted field of the human sciences; and by overflowing it both on the side of positivities and on that of finitude, it would form the most general contestation of that field. Like the two other counter-sciences, it would make visible, in a discursive mode, the frontier-forms of the human sciences; like them, it would situate its experience in those enlightened and dangerous regions where the knowledge of man acts out, in the form of the unconscious and of historicity, its relation with what renders them possible. In 'exposing' it, these three counter-sciences threaten the very thing that made it possible for man to be known. Thus we see the destiny of man being spun before our very eyes, but being spun backwards; it is being led back, by those strange bobbins, to the forms of its birth, to the homeland that made it possible. And is that not one way of bringing about its end? For linguistics no more speak of man himself than do psychoanalysis and ethnology.

It may be said that, in playing this role, linguistics is doing no more than resuming the functions that had once been those of biology or of economics, when, in the nineteenth and early twentieth centuries, an attempt was made to unify the human sciences under concepts borrowed from biology or economics. But linguistics may have a much more fundamental role. And for several reasons. First, because it permits – or in any case strives to render possible – the structuration of contents themselves; it is therefore not a theoretical reworking of knowledge acquired elsewhere, the interpretation of an already accomplished reading of phenomena; it does not offer a 'linguistic version' of the facts observed in the human sciences, it is rather the principle of a primary decipherment:

to a gaze forearmed by linguistics, things attain to existence only in so far as they are able to form the elements of a signifying system. Linguistic analysis is more a perception than an explanation: that is, it is constitutive of its very object. Moreover, we find that by means of this emergence of structure (as an invariable relation within a totality of elements) the relation of the human sciences to mathematics has been opened up once more, and in a wholly new dimension; it is no longer a matter of knowing whether one can quantify results, or whether human behaviour is susceptible of being introduced into the field of a measurable probability; the question that arises is that of knowing whether it is possible without a play on words to employ the notion of structure, or at least whether it is the same structure that is referred to in mathematics and in the human sciences: a question that is central if one wishes to know the possibilities and rights, the conditions and limitations, of a justified formalization; it will be seen that the relation of the sciences of man to the axis of the formal and *a priori* disciplines – a relation that had not been essential till then, and as long as the attempt was made to identify it with the right to measure – returns to life and perhaps becomes fundamental now that within the space of the human sciences there emerges their relation both to the empirical positivity of language and to the analytic of finitude; the three axes which define the volume proper to the sciences of man thus become visible, and almost simultaneously so, in the questions they pose. Lastly, as a result of the importance of linguistics and of its application to the knowledge of man, the question of the being of language, which, as we have seen, is so intimately linked with the fundamental problems of our culture, reappears in all its enigmatic insistence. With the continually extended use of linguistic categories, it is a question of growing importance, since we must henceforth ask ourselves what language must be in order to structure in this way what is nevertheless not in itself either word or discourse, and in order to articulate itself on the pure forms of knowledge. By a much longer and much more unexpected path, we are led back to the place that Nietzsche and Mallarmé signposted when the first asked: Who speaks?, and the second saw his glittering answer in the Word itself. The question as to what language is in its being is once more of the greatest urgency.

At this point, where the question of language arises again with such heavy over-determination, and where it seems to lay siege on every side to the figure of man (that figure which had once taken the place of Classical Discourse), contemporary culture is struggling to create an important part of its present, and perhaps of its future. On the one hand, suddenly very near to all these empirical domains, questions arise which before had seemed very distant from them: these questions concern a general formalization of thought and knowledge; and at a time when they were still thought to be dedicated solely to the relation between logic and mathematics, they suddenly open up the possibility, and the task, of purifying the old empirical reason by constituting formal languages, and of applying a second critique of pure reason on the basis of new forms of the mathematical *a priori*. However, at the other extremity of our culture, the question of language is entrusted to that form of speech which has no doubt never ceased to pose it, but which is now, for the first time, posing it to itself. That literature in our day is fascinated by the being of language is neither the sign of an imminent end nor proof of a radicalization: it is a phenomenon whose necessity has its roots in a vast configuration in which the whole structure of our thought and our knowledge is traced. But if the question of formal languages gives prominence to the possibility or impossibility of structuring positive contents, a literature dedicated to language gives prominence, in all their empirical vivacity, to the fundamental forms of finitude. From within language experienced and traversed as language, in the play of its possibilities extended to their furthest point, what emerges is that man has 'come to an end', and that, by reaching the summit of all possible speech, he arrives not at the very heart of himself but at the brink of that which limits him; in that region where death prowls, where thought is extinguished, where the promise of the origin interminably recedes. It was inevitable that this new mode of being of literature should have been revealed in works like those of Artaud or Roussel – and by men like them; in Artaud's work, language, having been rejected as discourse and re-apprehended in the plastic violence of the shock, is referred back to the cry, to the tortured body, to the materiality of thought, to the flesh; in Roussel's work, language, having been reduced to powder by a systematically fabricated chance, recounts interminably the repetition of death and the enigma of divided origins. And as if this experiencing of the forms of finitude in language were insupportable, or inadequate (perhaps its very inadequacy was insupportable), it is within madness that it manifested itself – the figure of finitude thus positing itself in language (as that which unveils itself within it), but also before it, preceding it, as that formless, mute, unsignifying region where language can find its freedom. And it is indeed in this space thus revealed that literature, first with surrealism (though still in a very much disguised form), then, more and more purely, with Kafka, Bataille, and Blanchot, posited itself as experience: as experience of death (and in the element of death), of unthinkable thought (and in its inaccessible presence), of repetition (of original innocence, always there at the nearest and yet always the most distant limit of language); as experience of finitude (trapped in the opening and the tyranny of that finitude).

It is clear that this 'return' of language is not a sudden interruption in our culture; it is not the irruptive discovery of some long-buried evidence; it does not indicate a folding back of thought upon itself, in the movement by which it emancipates itself from all content, or a narcissism occurring within a literature freeing itself at last from what it has to say in order to speak henceforth only about the fact that it is language stripped naked. It is, in fact, the strict unfolding of Western culture in accordance with the necessity it imposed upon itself at the beginning of the nineteenth century. It would be false to see in this general indication of our experience, which may be termed 'formalism', the sign of a drying up, of a rarefaction of thought losing its capacity for re-apprehending the plenitude of contents; it would be no less false to place it from the outset upon the horizon of some new thought or new knowledge. It is within the very tight-knit, very coherent outlines of the modern *episteme* that this contemporary experience found its possibility; it is even that *episteme* which, by its logic, gave rise to such an experience, constituted it through and through, and made it impossible for it not to exist. What occurred at the time of Ricardo, Cuvier, and Bopp, the form of knowledge that was established with the appearance of economics, biology, and philology, the thought of finitude laid down by the Kantian critique as philosophy's task – all that still forms the immediate space of our reflection. We think in that area.

And yet the impression of fulfilment and of end, the muffled feeling that carries and animates our thought, and perhaps lulls it to sleep with the facility of its promises, and makes us believe that something new is about to begin, something we glimpse only as a thin line of light low on the horizon – that feeling and that impression are perhaps not ill founded. It will be said that they exist, that they have never ceased to be formulated over and over again since the early nineteenth century; it will be said that Hölderlin, Hegel, Feuerbach, and Marx all felt this certainty that in them a thought and perhaps a culture were coming to a close, and that from the depths of a distance, which was perhaps not invincible, another was approaching – in the dim light of dawn, in the brilliance of noon, or in the dissension of the falling day. But this close, this perilous imminence whose promise we fear today, whose danger we welcome, is probably not of the same order. Then, the task enjoined upon thought by that annunciation was to establish for man a stable sojourn upon this earth from which the gods had turned away or vanished. In our day, and once again Nietzsche indicated the turning-point from a long way off, it is not so much the absence or the death of God that is affirmed as the end of man (that narrow, imperceptible displacement, that recession in the form of identity, which are the reason why man's finitude has become his end); it becomes apparent, then, that the death of God and the last man are engaged in a contest with more than one round: is it not the last man who announces that he has killed God, thus situating his language, his thought, his laughter in the space of that already dead God, yet positing himself also as he who has killed God and whose existence includes the freedom and the decision of that murder? Thus, the last man is at the same time older and yet younger than the death of God; since he has killed God, it is he himself who must answer for his own finitude; but since it is in the death of God that he speaks, thinks, and exists, his murder itself is doomed to die; new gods, the same gods, are already swelling the future Ocean; man will disappear. Rather than the death of God – or, rather, in the wake of that death and in a profound correlation with it – what Nietzsche's thought heralds is the end of his murderer; it is the explosion of man's face in laughter, and the return of masks; it is the scattering of the profound stream of time by which he felt himself carried along and whose pressure he suspected in the very being of things; it is the identity of the Return of the Same with the absolute dispersion of man. Throughout the nineteenth century, the end of philosophy and the promise of an approaching culture were no doubt one and the same thing as the thought of finitude and the appearance of man in the field of knowledge; in our day, the fact that philosophy is still – and again – in the process of coming to an end, and the fact that in it perhaps, though even more outside and against it, in literature as well as in formal reflection, the question of language is being posed, prove no doubt that man is in the process of disappearing.

For the entire modern *episteme* – that which was formed towards the end of the eighteenth century and still serves as the positive ground of our knowledge, that which constituted man's particular mode of being and the possibility of knowing him empirically – that entire *episteme* was bound up with the disappearance of Discourse and its featureless reign, with the shift of language towards objectivity, and with its reappearance in multiple form. If this same language is now emerging with greater and greater insistence in a unity that we ought to think but cannot as yet do so, is this not the sign that the whole of this configuration is now about to topple, and that man is in the process of perishing as the being of language continues to shine ever brighter upon our horizon? Since man was constituted at a time when language was doomed to dispersion, will he not be dispersed when language regains its unity? And if that were true, would it not be an error – a profound error, since it could hide from us what should now be thought – to interpret our actual experience as an application of the forms of language to the human order? Ought we not rather to give up thinking of man, or, to be more strict, to think of this disappearance of man – and the ground of possibility of all the sciences of man – as closely as possible in correlation with our concern with language? Ought we not to admit that, since language is here once more, man will return to that serene non-existence in which he was formerly maintained by the imperious unity of Discourse? Man had been a figure occurring between two modes of language; or, rather, he was constituted only when language, having been situated within representation and, as it were, dissolved in it, freed itself from that situation at the cost of its own fragmentation: man composed his own figure in the interstices of that fragmented language. Of course, these are not affirmations; they are at most questions to which it is not possible to reply; they must be left in suspense, where they pose themselves, only with the knowledge that the possibility of posing them may well open the way to a future thought.

VI   IN CONCLUSION

One thing in any case is certain: man is neither the oldest nor the most constant problem that has been posed for human knowledge. Taking a relatively short chronological sample within a restricted geographical area – European culture since the sixteenth century – one can be certain that man is a recent invention within it. It is not around him and his secrets that knowledge prowled for so long in the darkness. In fact, among all the mutations that have affected the knowledge of things and their order, the knowledge of identities, differences, characters, equivalences, words – in short, in the midst of all the episodes of that profound history of the *Same* – only one, that which began a century and a half ago and is now perhaps drawing to a close, has made it possible for the figure of man to appear.

And that appearance was not the liberation of an old anxiety, the transition into luminous consciousness of an age-old concern, the entry into objectivity of something that had long remained trapped within beliefs and philosophies: it was the effect of a change in the fundamental arrangements of knowledge. As the archaeology of our thought easily shows, man is an invention of recent date. And one perhaps nearing its end.

If those arrangements were to disappear as they appeared, if some event of which we can at the moment do no more than sense the possibility – without knowing either what its form will be or what it promises – were to cause them to crumble, as the ground of Classical thought did, at the end of the eighteenth century, then one can certainly wager that man would be erased, like a face drawn in sand at the edge of the sea.